UNDERSTANDING EXPOSITORY TEXT

A Theoretical and
Practical Handbook
for Analyzing
Explanatory Text

PSYCHOLOGY OF READING AND READING INSTRUCTION

A series of volumes edited by **Rand Spiro**

UNDERSTANDING EXPOSITORY TEXT

A Theoretical and Practical Handbook for Analyzing Explanatory Text

Edited by
BRUCE K. BRITTON
University of Georgia
and
JOHN B. BLACK
Yale University

LEA LAWRENCE ERLBAUM ASSOCIATES, PUBLISHERS
1985   Hillsdale, New Jersey   London

Lawrence Erlbaum Associates, Inc., Publishers
365 Broadway
Hillsdale, New Jersey 07642

Library of Congress Cataloging in Publication Data
Main entry under title:

Understanding expository text.

Includes bibliographies and indexes.
1. Discourse analysis—Psychological aspects.
2. Comprehension. 3. Knowledge, Theory of. I. Britton,
Bruce K. II. Black, John B. (John Benjamin), 1947–
P302.U5 **1985**   401.41   84-13807
ISBN 0-89859-412-X

Printed in the United States of America
10 9 8 7 6 5 4 3 2 1

Dedicated to

Our Parents

Hugh and Christine Britton   *Bessie and Wilbur Black*

and

Our Mentors

Rudolph W. Schulz   *Gordon H. Bower*

Contents

THEORIES OF TEXT ANALYSIS

1 Understanding Expository Text: From Structure to Process and World Knowledge

Bruce K. Britton
University of Georgia

John B. Black
Yale University

Text is an ancient technology of information transfer. It must be almost as old as recorded history, for the record of history is preserved for the most part in the medium of text. The earliest texts whose meaning we understand describe what were apparently some objects of business and sacred transactions in Mycenaean Greece (circa 1400 B.C.; Chadwick, 1967; Ventris & Chadwick. 1956). Most of these texts (Chadwick, 1967) are of the expository form considered as "lists" by Meyer (in her chapter later in this volume), e.g.:

> One footstool inlaid with a man and a horse and an octopus and a griffin in ivory.
> One footstool inlaid with ivory lions' heads and grooves.
> One footstool inlaid with ivory nuts.

or

> Kobalos repaid the following quantity of olive oil to Eumedes: 648 liters of oil.
> From Ipsewas, thirty-eight stirrup jars.

Some of them are quite evocative:

> To all the gods, one amphora of honey.
> To the Mistress of the Labyrinth, one amphora of honey. (p. 160)

The study of discourse structure seems to have begun in the Western world before 600 B.C. The systematic investigation of discourse structure was the major topic of the Greek teachers of rhetoric, and it was they who prepared the ground for the philosophers who laid the foundation for Western civilization. In contrast, the study of discourse structure in the Eastern world seems to be less ancient in origin. The focus of ancient language studies in the South Asian tradition was instead on the phonetic aspects of speech. The accurate transmission across the centuries of the spoken forms of the sacred documents—the most ancient is the *Rigveda*—seems to have been the objective of the early Indian linguists, who believed that the sounds of the sacred texts had significance in and of themselves. It is interesting to note that the discourse structure of the *Rigveda* itself is extremely complex (Klein, 1978, 1980) showing that the development of a technology of text does not depend on an explicit formal understanding of discourse structure. But such an understanding may nevertheless be very helpful in improving the technology. Many technologies that were originally developed without formal understanding have been greatly improved by it.

The importance of written text in the psychosocial evolution of the human race is difficult to exaggerate. As an extension of spoken language across historical time, it has permitted the binding together of mental events taking place at widely separated places and times, allowing ideas to be transmitted across generations, across cultures, and from beyond the grave, allowing each generation to stand on the shoulders of its predecessors.

The rate of information growth has increased exponentially throughout human history, and the rate of increase is now so rapid that no one can make good on Francis Bacon's boast, "I have taken all knowledge to be my province." Perhaps this information overload, and the stress on persons and society that it produces, is one reason why the study of text has expanded so rapidly over the past score of years. Most human knowledge is embodied in text, and most information transfer is through the medium of text. The information overload is primarily an overload of text. It is perhaps natural that the medium in which the overload is embodied should be due for some study on its own.

During most of the history of psychology, text was a background phenomenon: It was taken for granted in the sense that all scholarly discourse was expressed in the medium of text, but psychologists did not consider text a psychological phenomenon worthy of study in itself. Ebbinghaus (1885) used text in some of his experiments, but he was entirely concerned with developing a theory of memory, not with exploring the complexities of text itself, for which he had a healthy respect, noting that in

> poetry or prose, the content is now narrative in style, now descriptive, or now reflective; it contains now a phrase that is pathetic, now one that is humorous; its metaphors are sometimes beautiful, sometimes harsh; its rhythm is sometimes smooth and sometimes rough. There is thus brought into play a multiplicity of influences which change without regularity and are therefore disturbing. Such are associations which dart here and there, different degrees of interest, lines of verse recalled because of their striking quality or their beauty, and the like. (23)

Bartlett (1932) also used text, but, like Ebbinghaus, he was not concerned with the text but with a theory of memory. Their successors in the verbal learning tradition wisely chose, in laying the foundation for the psychology of memory and thought, to simplify their materials as much as they could. They followed Ebbinghaus in his preference for meaningless materials like nonsense syllables, as a way of avoiding the complexities of text, which are

> avoided with our syllables. Among many thousand combinations there occur scarcely a few dozen that have a meaning and among these there are again only a few whose meaning was realized while they were being memorized . . . More indubitable are the advantages of our material in two other respects. In the first place it permits an inexhaustible amount of new combinations of quite homogeneous character, while different poems, different prose pieces always have something incomparable. It also makes possible quantitative variation which is adequate and certain; whereas to break off before the end or to begin in the middle of the verse or the sentence leads to new complications because of various and unavoidable disturbances of the meaning. (pp. 23–24)

There followed three quarters of a century of working upward from nonsense syllables, digits and letters to lists of unrelated words as materials, arriving at isolated sentences only during the psycholinguistic revolution begun by Chomsky (1957). The results of those decades of careful work in the verbal learning tradition underly current developments in the understanding of text.

Meanwhile the linguists were proceeding with their analyses of text structure, although largely in isolation from the psychologists. The original impetus for modern linguistic studies of text structure had a religious basis. Translations of the Christian Bible into all the languages of the world was regarded by some denominations as a fundamental precondition for the eventual establishment of the kingdom of God on Earth. This was a formidable task from the beginning of the Christian era, and became even more formidable as more languages were discovered. Each language had to be learned by a translator, and this usually involved the preparation of a comprehensive dictionary and grammar; these are still the major source of our knowledge of many languages. But these early linguistic workers soon realized that a language was more than just words and sentences, for the structures of stories in different languages differ in striking ways. The Bible, which is mostly made up of a series of narratives, stories and parables, cannot be meaningfully translated just word for word and sentence for sentence, for the nature of a story itself differs in different languages (Fuller, 1959; Grimes, 1975; Longacre, 1968, 1972; Pike, 1954; Taber, 1966). It was the linguists' analyses of narrative structures that provided the input for some of the early psychological investigations of text structure. Another linguistic current of fundamental importance has been the study of the linguistic relations between sentences (e.g., Halliday & Hasan, 1976).

In the decade of the 1970s the stage was set for the emergence of text as a major theme of psychological research. The verbal learning tradition had thoroughly worked out the major variables influencing verbal units in isolation and in unrelated groups, the psycholinguistic tradition was well advanced with the psychological analysis of the isolated sentence, and the linguists had developed text structure analyses. Also in the 1970s another major force emerged that emphasized the importance of research on text. This force is the new field of artificial intelligence (AI).

AI is the study of how to program computers so that they will exhibit intelligence. Athough AI had started in the 1950s (Feigenbaum & Feldman, 1963), it was not until the 1970s that language understanding became a major topic in the field (Schank, 1975; Schank & Colby, 1973; Winograd, 1983). Although language study in AI originally focused on words and sentences, the focus soon changed to full-fledged texts and discourses (Joshi, Webber, & Sag, 1981; Schank & Abelson, 1977). However, AI not only provided more impetus for the study of text understanding, but also indicated that the study of text structure alone was not sufficient for a complete explanation of text understanding.

In particular, merely knowing about text structure is not sufficient for the design of a computer program that will understand text; two other aspects are necessary. These aspects are (a) the processes used in understanding the text and retrieving the text information from memory later, and (b) the knowledge necessary to make the inferences that are needed to link the information in the text into a coherent mental representation of the text. Further, many of the inferences required not only knowledge about texts, but also general knowledge about the world and specialized knowledge about the domain being discussed. This knowledge is of several different kinds varying from lower-level word meanings to higher-level thematic patterns (Reiser, Black, & Lehnert, in press). The need for these different levels was highlighted by early attempts to generate inferences using only word meanings. These attempts found that inferences generated and constrained only by lower-level knowledge quickly get out of hand, so higher-level knowledge structures are necessary to channel the inferencing in appropriate directions.

For example, Rieger (1975) estimated that a single simple utterance would, if all the possible inferences were considered, generate an average of 750 inferences. This seems like a rather large number. It is instructive to consider first a much smaller set of inferences, say of size 20, not, it would seem, a very large number. But in a story of 100 utterances, with 20 possible inferences per utterance, there are 20^{100} ($= 10^{130}$) possible paths. Do readers consider all of these? To see how large this number really is, we can consider some other numbers. The number of elementary particles in the universe is 10^{79}; the number of seconds since the big bang is 10^{19}; the shortest known time for a physical event is 10^{-24} second, which is the time it takes for light to cross an atomic nucleus. Together these numbers give us a not implausible estimate of the total number of events in the universe until now of about 10^{122}. 10^{122} is less than 10^{130}. So the universe has not had enough actual states to even represent all these possible story paths. That is, understanding this simple story could not have been finished by today if the universe were a dedicated computer devoted to this story since the beginning of time (example adapted and paraphrased from Wimsatt, 1980). This illustrates the magintude of savings due to using higher-level knowledge structures and text structures to constrain the inferences made during text understanding.

Higher-level structures constrain the possible inferences because they represent information about what can follow what in texts (higher-level text structures) and the world in general (world knowledge structures). For example, one well-studied world knowledge structure is the *script* (Abbott, Black, & Smith, in press; Bower, Black, & Turner, 1979; Graesser, 1981; Schank & Abelson, 1977). Scripts represent people's knowledge about what happens in conventional, stereotyped situations like eating in a restaurant or visiting a doctor's office. Such a knowledge structure constrains inferences because it provides the actions conventionally connecting other actions in the situation. For instance, if a description of a restaurant visit stated "John sat down at the table and gave his order," then the restaurant script provides the inferences that he also probably read a menu and selected his order from the dishes listed there. The reader does not have to consider all the inferences possible when sitting at a table or giving orders, but merely the possibilities typical for that situation. Thus the world knowledge embodied in scripts provides constraints on the inferences that readers make when reading texts that evoke scripts.

A complete account of text understanding also requires specifying the processes that utilize these text and world knowledge structures to comprehend texts and build memories that represent the information in the texts in a form that facilitates later retrieval. For example, the various processes that need to be specified include those that connect meaning units in working memory (Kintsch & van Dijk, 1978), those that determine how mental resources will be allocated during reading (Britton, Glynn, Meyer, & Penland, 1982; Britton & Tesser, 1982; Graesser, Hoffman & Clark, 1980), those that evoke knowledge structures and use the structures to filter and sort the information in the text (Black, Galambos, & Read, in press), and those that organize the information for efficient retrieval (Reiser & Black, 1982). The processing aspect of text understanding has received less attention at this point than the structural and world knowledge aspects, so it is a particularly important topic for research in the near future.

Thus AI has added the study of processes and world knowledge to the traditional study of text structure. The various papers in Part 1 of this book represent these different aspects of studying expository text. In particular, Meyer (1975) was one of the first psychological studies of text structure and Meyer's chapter in this volume gives the current state of that long-standing line of research. Mayer's chapter also takes a structural approach that is compatible with Meyer's, but differs in that while Meyer focuses on predicting what readers can later recall from text, Mayer focuses on whether the reader can use the information contained in the text to perform a task. This new usability measure provides an interesting new perspective on text understanding. The chapter by Britton, Glynn and Smith and the one by Kieras take processing approaches to expository text understanding. In particular, Britton, Glynn and Smith focus on how text processing is managed in a limited working memory, while Kieras explores the processes readers use to uncover thematic statements in expository text. Finally, the chapters by Voss and Bisanz, Graesser and Goodman, and Miller investigate the world knowledge required to make the inferences needed to understand expository text. In particular, Voss and Bisanz examine the effects on text understanding of having much knowledge or only a little knowledge about a specialized domain covered in the text (e.g., baseball); Graesser and Goodman describe how one can use carefully designed questions to expose the inferences needed to form a coherent mental representation of a text and Miller describes how world knowledge is used to make the inferences necessary to construct a mental representation of the text during reading.

Miller's chapter is the latest phase in the line of text understanding research begun by Kintsch (1974). The history of this research enterprise is instructive because it illustrates all three of our aspects of text understanding. Specifically, in its early stages, the research project focused on the structure of text—namely, on the network of propositions linked by common references that comprise the "coherence graph" of the text. Next, the emphasis focused on the processes that constructed such text structures (Kintsch & van Dijk, 1978; and Miller & Kintsch, 1980). Now in the latest phase represented by Miller's chapter (and Miller & Kintsch, 1981) the emphasis is on the world knowledge needed to understand texts and how that knowledge is used to process the texts.

Thus the various chapters in this volume give examples of research on all three aspects of text understanding—namely, structure, world knowledge and process. More than this, however, the research described represents a shift in emphasis from studying stories to studying expository text. Although much early work on text understanding concerned expository text (see Reder, 1980 for a review), the investigation of story understanding came to dominate the field in the latter half of the 1970s. Thus most recent work has been on story understanding and many of the ideas now being applied to expository text were developed first with stories (see Black, in press, for a recent review). This focus on stories was probably due to the essential first step in any science of examining the simplest materials possible. For text understanding, simple children's stories seemed to fulfill this requirement (e.g., Mandler & Johnson, 1977; Rumelhart, 1975; Thorndyke, 1977). However, we thought that the time was now ripe to shift the research focus from stories to expository text and this volume is our attempt to provide this transition.

One major reason we were convinced that the time had come for a collection of papers about expository text was that research progress in any science is greatly aided by an understanding of the input objects of interest to that science.

In particular, research progress in any area of psychology is closely related to understanding the input to the information processing system—in this case, the text stimulus and the world knowledge. We thought that research progress in the understanding of expository text would be aided by the availability of example texts and the application of analysis methods to those texts. It therefore seemed desirable to encourage the use of these analysis methods by collecting the major ones between the covers of a single volume. But it was evident from early work that the published analyses were sometimes daunting in their detail and complexity. Actually, we knew that this first impression was somewhat misleading, for training in even the most complex of the analysis techniques could be accomplished for naive college students in the course of a few hours. We felt that for the use of these analysis methods to become widespread, researchers would have to learn how to use them, and this could be most effectively encouraged by providing some training aids. Part 2 of this book provides these training aids, which include some explanatory material on the technique (to supplement that provided in the corresponding chapter in Part 1), clear directions on the sequence of steps to take in performing the analysis and in many cases worked examples of analyzed texts, and of scored recall protocols. The Part 2 chapters by Meyer, Mayer, Bovair and Kieras, and Graesser and Goodman provide explanations of how to analyze the structure of expository text, while the Part 2 chapters of Voss and Bisanz, and Graesser and Goodman provide explanations of how to determine the world knowledge needed to understand expository texts.

REFERENCES

Abbott, V., Black, J. B., & Smith, E. E. The representation of scripts in memory. *Journal of Verbal Learning and Verbal Behavior,* in press.

Bartlett, F. C. *Remembering: A study in experimental and social psychology.* Cambridge, England: Cambridge University Press, 1932.

Black, J. B. Understanding and remembering stories. In J. R. Anderson & S. M. Kosslyn (Eds.), *Essays on learning and memory.* San Francisco: Freeman, in press.

Black, J. B., Galambos, J. A., & Read, S. J. Comprehending stories and social situations. In R. Wyer & T. Srull (Eds.), *Handbook of social cognition* (Vol.3). Hillsdale, N.J.: Lawrence Erlbaum Associates, in press.

Britton, B. K., Glynn, S. M., Meyer, B. J. F., & Penland, M. J. Effects of text structure on use of cognitive capacity during reading. *Journal of Educational Psychology,* 1982, *74,* 51–61.

Britton, B. K., & Tesser, A. Effects of prior knowledge on use of cognitive capacity in three complex cognitive tasks. *Journal of Verbal Learning and Verbal Behavior,* 1982, *21,* 421–436.

Bower, G. H., Black, J. B. & Turner, T. J. Scripts in memory for text. *Cognitive Psychology,* 1979, *11,* 177–220.

Chadwick, J. *The decipherment of linear B.* Cambridge, England: Cambridge University Press, 1967.

Chomsky, N. *Syntactic structures.* The Hague: Mouton, 1957.

Ebbinghaus, E. *Memory: A contribution to experimental psychology.* (Trans. by H. A. Ruger & C. M. Bussenius.) New York: Teachers College Press, 1913. (Originally published in 1885.)

Feigenbaum, E., & Feldman, J. (Eds.). *Computers and thought.* New York: McGraw-Hill, 1963.
Fuller, D. P. *The inductive method of Bible study.* Pasadena, Calif.: Fuller Theological Seminary, 1959.
Graesser, A. C. *Prose comprehension beyond the word.* New York: Springer-Verlag, 1981.
Graesser, A. C., Hoffman, N. L., & Clark, L. F. Structural components of reading time. *Journal of Verbal Learning and Verbal Behavior,* 1980, *19,* 131–151.
Grimes, J. E. *The thread of discourse.* The Hague: Mouton, 1975.
Halliday, M., & Hasan, R. *Cohesion in English.* London: Longman, 1976.
Joshi, A., Webber, B., & Sag, I. *Elements of discourse understanding.* Cambridge, England: Cambridge University Press, 1981.
Kintsch, W. *The representation of meaning in memory.* Hillsdale, N.J.: Lawrence Erlbaum Associates, 1974.
Kintsch, W., & van Dijk, T. A. Toward a model of text comprehension and production. *Psychological Review,* 1978, *85,* 363–394.
Klein, J. *The particle U in the Rigveda.* Gottingen: Vandenhoeck & Ruprecht, 1978.
Klein, J. Atha, Adha, and a typology of Rigveda conjunctions. *Indo-Iranian Journal,* 1980, *22,* 195–219.
Longacre, R. E. *Discourse, paragraph and sentence structure in selected Phillipine languages* (Vol. 1). Santa Anna, Calif.: Summer Institute of Linguistics, 1968.
Longacre, R. E. *Hierarchy and universality of discourse constituents in New Guinea languages.* Washington, D.C.: Georgetown University Press, 1972.
Mandler, J. M., & Johnson, N. S. Remembrance of things parsed: Story structure and recall. *Cognitive Psychology,* 1977, *9,* 111–151.
Meyer, B. J. F. *The organization of prose and its effect on recall.* Amsterdam: North-Holland, 1975.
Miller, J. R., & Kintsch, W. Readability and recall of short prose pasages: A theoretical analysis. *Journal of Experimental Psychology: Human Learning and Memory,* 1980, *6,* 335–354.
Miller, J. R., & Kintsch, W. Knowledge-based aspects of prose comprehension and readability. *Text,* 1981, *3,* 215–232.
Pike, K. L. *Language in relation to a unified theory of the structure of human behavior.* The Hague: Mouton, 1954.
Reder, L. M. The role of elaborations in the comprehension and retention of prose: A critical review. *Review of Educational Research,* 1980, *50,* 5–53.
Reiser, B. J., & Black, J. B. Processing and structural models of story understanding. *Text,* 1982, *2,* 225–252.
Reiser, B. J., Black, J. B., & Lehnert, W. G. Thematic knowledge structures in the understanding and generation of narratives. *Discourse Processes,* in press.
Rieger, C. Conceptual memory. In R. C. Schank (Ed.), *Conceptual information processing.* Amsterdam: North-Holland, 1975.
Rumelhart, D. E. Notes on a schema for stories. In D. G. Bobrow & A. H. Collins (Eds.), *Representation and understanding: Studies in cognitive science.* New York: Academic Press, 1975.
Schank, R. C. (Ed.) *Conceptual information processing.* Amsterdam: North-Holland, 1975.
Schank, R. C., & Abelson, R. P. *Scripts, plans, goals, and understanding.* Hillsdale, N.J.: Lawrence Erlbaum Associates, 1977.
Schank, R. C., & Colby, K. (Eds.) *Computer models of thought and language.* San Francisco: Freeman, 1973.
Taber, C. R. *The structure of Sango narrative.* Hartford, Conn.: Hartford Seminary Foundation, 1966.
Thorndyke, P. W. Cognitive structures in comprehension and memory of narrative discourse. *Cognitive Psychology,* 1977, *9,* 77–110.

Ventris, M., & Chadwick, J. *Documents in Mycenaean Greek.* Cambridge, England: Cambridge University Press, 1956.

Wimsatt, W. C. Reductionistic research strategies and their biases in the units of selection controversy. In T. Nickles (Ed.), *Scientific discovery: Case studies.* Dordrecht: D. Reidel, 1980.

Winograd, T. *Language as a cognitive process.* Reading, Mass.: Addison-Wesley, 1983.

2 Prose Analysis: Purposes, Procedures, and Problems[1]

Bonnie J. F. Meyer

Arizona State University

OVERVIEW OF THE CHAPTER

First, a brief preview is presented of the contents of this chapter. My chapter in the second half of this book, dealing with methods of prose analysis, fills in the details of the analysis approach outlined within this chapter.

Specification of the structure of text has three methodological uses in reading research: (1) identification of the content and organization of the text for use in a scoring system, (2) generation of models of text memory and examination of similarities and differences between the models and the performance of readers, (3) identification of significant dimensions on which to characterize text selections to aid in appropriately generalizing research results. Reasons for the appearance of different approaches to identifying prose structure are explained in terms of multiplicity of disciplines, varying purposes, and to the inherent complexity of text, the writing process, and the reading process. Meyer's approach to prose analysis is described: Three levels of expository text are identified; five basic logical relations in exposition are presented (*collection, causation, response, comparison,* and *description*); and procedures for building the analysis structure for a text are specified. A general comparison is made between this approach and other procedures.

A detailed comparison is made of the analysis procedure and scoring systems used by Kintsch and Meyer. Both approaches yield a hierarchical text structure; the hierarchy is built by repetition of concepts in the Kintsch approach, whereas

[1]Paper presented as part of an invited symposium on *Expository Text: Comprehension and Structure* at the American Educational Research Association Convention in Los Angeles, April 1981.

it is based on the semantic and logical relations in the text in the Meyer approach. Fewer discrepancies are found when the superordinate node selected for both approaches is similar. Repeated words in a text are characteristic of the highest levels in the Kintsch hierarchy, while logical relationships and the ideas they bind are characteristic of the highest levels in the Meyer hierarchy. Large variations in the two hierarchies result when different superordinate nodes are selected for the top of the hierarchy. The Meyer approach defines the superordinate node as the content bound by the top-level structure, the superordinate relation that can encompass the remaining ideas of the text. However, selection of the superordinate node in the Kintsch approach is based on intuition. The Kintsch approach appears to require less analysis time. For the text and small sample of data examined, the approach based on logical relations predicted recall better than that based on word repetition.

With regard to scoring, differences result from the different treatment of relationships in the two systems. They are scored separately in the Meyer approach, whereas they are combined with content in the Kintsch approach. Thus, it is possible to show partial recall and recall of the relationships with inaccurate or omitted content in the Meyer approach. The Kintsch scoring system is more efficient for scoring immediate free recall protocols with close correspondence to text content. The Meyer approach is more time consuming, but more effective with less accurate recall protocols. When studying delayed recall, recall of older adults, children, or less proficient learners, it would be advantageous for identifying types of differences to utilize the Meyer approach. In addition, the underlying logic processed by learners from expository text is better studied with the latter approach; differences in overall organization of the text and recall protocol have been reliably studied with this approach.

The first sections of the chapter show that the extant prose analysis systems satisfy most requirements of the first two methodological uses for prose structure (scoring and comparing variations in text model and protocol). However, progress in the clarifying discourse types has only begun. Some data collected by Meyer and Rice are presented that relate to a distinction between the time series thrust of narration and the logical thrust of exposition. Differences in type of information recalled and organization of protocols are found when a passage on railroads is processed with narrative schema (history: a collection of events on a time line) or with an expository schema (comparison and related logic). Other dimensions on which to characterize text, such as number of levels and types of detail, are also discussed in this chapter.

NECESSITY FOR IDENTIFYING TEXT STRUCTURE

The structure of discourse is the organization that binds it together, and gives it an overall organization. This structure shows how some ideas are of central importance to the author's message, which is bound by this overall organization, while other ideas are shown to be peripheral. In expository text, the text structure specifies the logical connections among ideas as well as subordination of some ideas to others. It is this structure of text that primarily differentiates text from simple lists of words or sentences.

Since text structure is an essential characteristic of text, educators and psychologists interested in reading comprehension have sought to describe and classify it. This description is necessary in order to examine how readers identify and utilize text structure in the comprehension process. For example, the theory of reading proposed by Just and Carpenter (1980) attributes processing time and capacity in reading comprehension to figuring out the relationships within sentences and among sentences and paragraphs.

A method for identifying text structure is a necessary procedure for examining the reading comprehension process. In order to examine what information a reader has processed from a text, the researcher needs to know just what information was presented in the text. Thus, the procedures for analyzing text structure and content have been put to use as scoring templates to access a reader's recall of text. For example, if a passage's structure is analyzed so that the information it contains is divided into units of topic content and relations, then this analysis can be employed to assist in scoring just which of the content and relation units were remembered by a reader.

Moreover, researchers hypothesize that the representation of the text in memory is parallel to their analysis of the text structure. Comparisons of structures identified from the text and those identified from readers' recall protocols assist investigators in attempts to validate their models of the representation of text in memory. Models of memory representations based on prose analysis procedures are usually posited for certain types of learners (i.e., skilled readers with relatively low prior knowledge on the text topic) under certain types of task conditions (i.e., reading for optimal comprehension and recall of text information with adequate time and immediate recall). Investigators examine variations between the text structure and analyses of recall protocols when the types of learners and task conditions are varied systematically.

Another reason for specifying text structure deals with the problem of generalizing research findings with a particular passage to other texts. Text structure is a significant dimension along which text selections can be evaluated as to their similarities and differences. Investigators of reading comprehension have made some progress in characterizing certain discourse types, such as simple stories (Mandler & Johnson, 1977; Rumelhart, 1977), scientific reports (Kintsch & van Dijk, 1978), and exposition (Meyer, 1977; Meyer & Freedle, 1984). However, discourse types have been examined more by rhetoricians (D'Angelo, 1976) and linguists (Longacre, 1970). Recently, Brewer (1980) has identified three underlying structures of discourse: description, narration, and exposition; and four purposes: to inform, to persuade, to entertain, and literary aesthetic; exposition was classified only under the first two purposes. We are beginning to make progress in determining which aspects of text structure are important to consider in differentiating among text selections.

REASONS FOR DIFFERENT APPROACHES FOR IDENTIFYING PROSE STRUCTURE

Given the usefulness in reading research for specifying the structure of text, it might be expected that researchers would by now have converged on a simple, universally accepted method. There are at least three reasons for the lack of such a method. First, interest in specifying text structure has historically come from a variety of disciplines, including rhetorics, folklore, linguistics, education, psychology, and artificial intelligence (cf. Meyer & Rice, 1984). These disciplines have had different approaches and goals for analyzing text structure. The multiplicity of disciplines involved serves to diversify the text structures proposed as well as enrich our understanding of text structure.

A second reason for the variety of text analysis systems currently used to study reading comprehension results from the purposes for which they were developed. For example, if the research goal is to ascertain recall of the gist of passages, the analysis structure may be quite different than if the goal is memory storage of inferences.

The most difficult obstacles are those that are inherent in the complexity of text, the writing process, and the reading process (see Fig. 2.1). Part of the problem arises from the complexity of the reading process (Meyer & Rice, 1984). Since the text and reader interact in this process, it is hard to isolate entirely textual variables. The structure of the information read from a text may appear differently to readers with different prior knowledge and purposes. A reasonable escape from this problem is to analyze text from the point of view of the author. However, there are some problems with this approach. If a poorly written exposition is selected that fails to logically interrelate ideas either explicitly or implicitly (i.e., Flower's, 1979, writer-based lists, rather than reader-based conceptual hierarchies), the text analyst may want to identify the potential conceptual structure underlying the topic in order to better score recall of more astute readers. Even with well-written text, the underlying structure may be implicit rather than explicitly signaled. In these cases, it is necessary for the text analyst to make inferences about the organization in the text. Individual differences among analysts in making such inferences can produce variability in the analyses produced.

As depicted in Fig. 2.1, a text is a result of the cognition (induction, comparison, etc.) of the author and his/her skill in putting this logic and message in written form. Brewer (1980) noted that the underlying mental processes involved in his three discourse types differed. For descriptive text, he explained that the underlying cognitive representation was visual-spatial. For narrative text, he

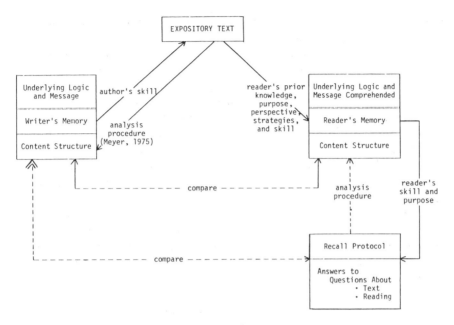

FIG. 2.1.   Complexity of prose learning paradigm.

stated that the central mental representation was a series of temporally occurring events, a time line (Litteral, 1972). Expository text was said to reflect the underlying mental processes involving logical and quasi-logical thinking.

As shown in Fig. 2.1, the match between the logic and message intended by the author and that identified in the analysis of text structure varies with the author's skills, the prose analysis procedure, and the skill of the analyst using the procedure. In most prose learning experiments, the analysis of the text structure is then compared to what the reader recalled from the text. The similarity between the analysis of the text structure and what the reader writes about what she or he remembers from the text depends on the prior knowledge, purpose, perspective, strategy, and skill level of the reader (Meyer, 1981). If the reader's purpose was to understand the topic from the author's perspective, then the correspondence between the analysis of the text structure and the recall protocol will increase with reader skill, exposure time, and recency of presentation.

MEYER'S APPROACH TO PROSE ANALYSIS

The paradigm diagrammed in Fig. 2.1 depicts the approaches that I use to study reading comprehension from expository text. The content structure represents the underlying logic and message of the text from the perspective of the author. A skilled reader, with the prior knowledge assumed by the author, and a desire to understand the author's logic, will form a representation of the text in memory parallel to that of the content structure. The comprehension process will follow a structure strategy (Meyer, Brandt, & Bluth, 1980) and involve an active effort to discover the superordinate structure of relationships and the information it binds (the gist) (for example, see Fig. 2.2 for supertanker passage).

As shown in Fig. 2.1, the content structure can serve as a scoring template to examine the amount and type of information remembered by a reader. Also, the recall protocol of the subject can be analyzed with the same prose analysis procedures to detect differences in the organization and type of information recalled. In this way, content, relationships, and superordinate organizational structures that did not occur in the original text can be identified and classified (see scoring system in Part 2). For example, Meyer, Brandt, and Bluth (1980) found that poorer comprehenders at the ninth-grade level organize their recall protocols with a list format, a collection of non-related descriptions about a topic, while good comprehenders organize recall of expository text with its inherent logic relationships. That is, the text structure as a model of text information in memory is a better representation of text memory for good comprehenders than poor comprehenders.

The method I employ to get from the text to its underlying structure and from the protocol to its underlying structure is a procedure based on the work in linguistics of Grimes (1975) and Fillmore (1968). The correspondence is considered high between the content structure analysis and the logic and message in the mind of the author and the reader. The relationships that form the logic in the content structure have been discussed as ways or schemata for thinking about ideas at least since Aristotle (trans., 1960). The content-based relationships (verb type relationships) also appear to be schemata used in cognition (Rumelhart & Ortony, 1977). The levels in the content structure are dictated by the major logical relations; the hierarchy is hypothesized to relate to allocation of processing time and access to retrieval when reading in tasks for prose learning experiments and many similar school tasks (Meyer, Brandt, & Bluth, 1980).

Three primary levels of expository text are identified in this approach to prose analysis (Meyer, 1981; van Dijk, 1979). The first is the sentence or microproposition level, which is concerned with the way ideas are organized within sentences, and the way sentences cohere and are organized within a text. The second is the macropropositional level, which pertains to the issues of logical organization and argumentation. The third is that of the top-level structure or overall organization of the text as a whole. Figure 2.2 depicts these three levels from a text on supertankers.

Micropropositions

The subordinate micropropositions are indicated by $\bigwedge$ in Fig. 2.2, but are diagrammed in the content structure which can be found with the text in Part 2 of this book. The structure of simple sentences is diagrammed with case grammar (after Fillmore, 1968, and Grimes, 1975). Most text analysis systems use case grammar at this level of analysis.

A salient property of texts is that they cohere or "hang together." A text coheres when the interpretation of one element depends upon or presupposes another (Halliday & Hasan, 1976). Halliday and Hasan (1976) have identified mechanisms (reference, substitution, ellipsis, conjunction, and lexical cohesion) by which authors tie phrases and sentences together at this microproposition level. The Meyer system provides a classification system for mechanisms of conjunction (e.g., collection, comparison, causation).

Macropropositions

The term macroproposition refers to the level of prose analysis at which gist of portions of the text is central. Whereas at the microproposition level, the relationships within and between individual sentences were at issue, at the macroproposition level the issue is with the relationships among ideas represented in complexes of propositions or paragraphs. The relationships at this level tend to be logical or rhetorical. A number of classifications of the types of logical relations that operate in text have been proposed (Beaugrande, 1980; Frederiksen, 1975; Graesser, 1981; Grimes, 1975; Halliday & Hasan, 1976; Meyer, 1975).

Five basic groups of relationships can be identified (collapsing the relationships of Grimes, 1975; Meyer, 1975, 1981) as follows:

1. *collection:* relation that shows how ideas or events are related together into a group on the basis of some commonality;
2. *causation:* relation that shows a causal relationship between ideas where one idea is the *antecedent* or cause and the other is the *consequent* or effect;
3. *response:* or problem and solution (also remark and replay, question and answer formats) is similar to the causal in that the problem is an antecedent for the solution. However, in addition, there must be some overlap in topic content between the problem and solution; that is, at least part of the solution must match an aspect of the problem;
4. *comparison:* points out differences and similarities between two or more topics;
5. *description:* gives more information about a topic by presenting attributes, specifics, manners, or settings.

In the texts that my students and I have examined, the gist or macropropositions have been explicitly stated. For example, in the supertanker passage (see

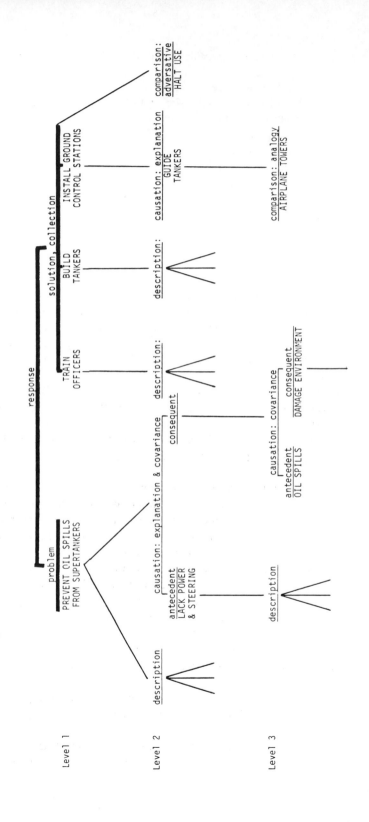

Level 1

Level 2

Level 3

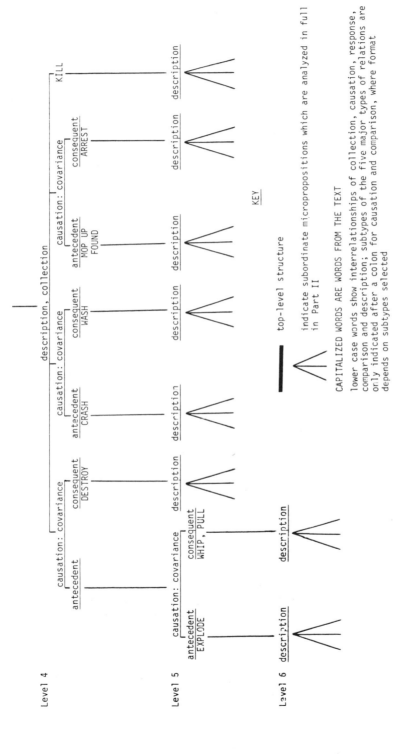

FIG. 2.2. Content structure for the Supertanker text.

19

Fig. 2.2 and Part 2), the gist is "oil spills from supertankers damage the environment; this problem results from lack of power and steering equipment in emergencies. The solution involves better training of officers, building tankers with extra power and steering equipment, and installing ground control stations." This gist statement can be written by following the superordinate structure in the top third of the content structure. In passages without explicit gist statements, macropropositions can be generated using van Dijk's (1977) macrorules. For example, the supertanker passage could have been written without the more general statement that oil spills damage the environment; instead, the four examples of oil spills (lowest three levels in Fig. 2.2) could have been presented alone. Then, the text analyst and reader would need to generate the macroproposition, oil spills from supertanker cause damage to the environment.

Top-level Structure

The top-level structure of the text corresponds to its overall organizing principle. For example, the rhetorical relationships described above can serve to organize the text as a whole. The response: problem/solution is the top-level structure that subsumes all the content and relationships in the supertanker passage (see Fig. 2.2).

The five rhetorical relationships of collection, causation, response, comparison, and description represent ways of thinking about topics (abstract schemata). The first three types of relations appear to line up on a continuum of constraints as shown in Fig. 2.3. The arguments or information to be related by the collection relation have to meet fewer constraints than do those for the response relation (for a more detailed discussion of discourse types see Meyer & Freedle, 1984). The comprison relation, like the response relation, has interlinking, subordinate arguments, but time and causality are not factors. Different types of argumentative text may differ on the extent with which their subordinate arguments overlap. For description relation the arguments are grouped on a topic but in a hierarchical manner; one argument is superordinate and the other modifies this superordinate argument. Examples of these relationships can be seen in Fig. 2.2 and Part 2. Since some of these rhetorical relations require more links among their arguments than others, a network model of memory (Anderson, 1976) might predict different memory performance with text processed and retrieved with these different structures. There is evidence (Meyer, 1977, 1984b; Meyer & Freedle, 1984; Meyer & Rice, 1983a) for inferior memory of text with top-level structures in the form of a collection of descriptions, where the descriptions are grouped on the basis of dealing with the same topic, but are not interrelated (lowest level on the continuum in Fig. 2.3).

My colleagues and I have examined exposition with this type of top-level structure, but have primarily examined text with response: problem/solution, comparative, and causative (assertion and its explanation) top-level structures.

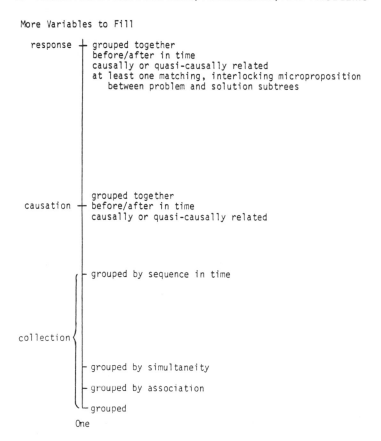

FIG. 2.3.   Continuum of argument constraints on which collection, causation, and response relations range.

The five rhetorical relations listed above can be combined in a wide variety of ways to provide a number of possibilities for the superordinate relational structures of exposition. However, the problem/solution expository texts that we have examined appear to require at least the components shown in Fig. 2.4. Most of the work pertaining to the more specific top-level structures has been done with story structures (Mandler & Johnson, 1977; Rumelhart, 1977; Stein, 1979).

Building the Content Structure

In Meyer (1975), I presented the three distinct sets of relationships identified by Halliday (1968) and Grimes (1975) as content, cohesion, and staging. I have come to realize that the content structure resulting from the prose analysis procedure embodies all three sets of relations, not just content.

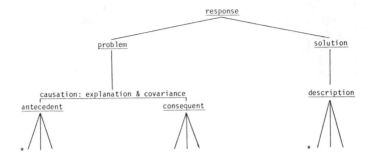

*match must exist between at least one component of the cause of the problem and one component of the proposed solution.

FIG. 2.4.   Schematic diagram of required grammatic categories of expository text organized with problem/solution top-level structure.

The content structure is best formed by following a top-down procedure. The passage is first examined for its top-level structure. This skill has been readily taught children and disabled populations (Bartlett, 1978; Bartlett, Turner, & Mathams, 1981; Jessen, in preparation). Using the five rhetorical relationships described above (rather than the more minute classification in Meyer, 1975), one of these relations can be selected as the top-level structure of a text. The top-level structure will be the relationship that can subsume the greatest amount of text (see response in the supertanker passage). If we had only the first paragraph of the supertanker passage, then the top-level structure would be description: a description with subordinate, embedded causal relationships.

The hierarchical levels of the content structure are formed by the analysis format of the rhetorical relations and the analysis format used for the case gramar analysis. The formats for the rhetorical relations are as follows (numbers 1 and 2 represent arguments that are interrelated):

collection   — equal level in the content structure

collection	
1	2

causation   — (a) equal level in the content structure

causation	
antecedent	consequent
1	2

(b) unequal level for explanation (explanations are antecedent conditions or principles, they are subordinate in staging to event or idea explained)

response — equal level in the content structure

response
─────────────
problem   solution
───────   ────────
1   2

comparison — (a) alternative, equal level; equally weighted views or options

alternative
─────────────────
1   2

(b) adversative, unequal level; unequally weighted; one is favored

For a more aesthetically pleasing top-level structure, it can be put in the following format:

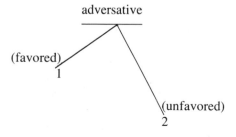

(c) analogy, unequal level; analogy is subordinate

1

analogy
___

2

description — unequal level; descriptive argument is subordinate (includes manner, attribution, specific, evidence, equivalent, settings, identifications in Meyer, 1975)

1

description
___

2

In the case of selecting adversative rather than alternative, staging or *signaling* (Meyer, 1975), such as ''the best option is,'' assist the analyst in deciding the format of the content structure. However, the signaling words themselves do not appear in the content structure, but their input is represented in its organization. The content structure is formed by unpeeling layers of rhetorical relationships in a top-down fashion. Once the top-level structure is identified, then the next most inclusive relations are identified until the case grammar level of analysis is reached.

For example, in Fig. 2.2 *response: problem/solution* interrelates all of the propositions in the text. The solution is organized with collection and comparison relationships; a collection of three favored solutions is contrasted (comparison: adversative) to an unfavored solution. Further unpeeling of the relationships in the solution requires examining each of the three posited solutions. The first solution (TRAIN OFFICERS) and the second (BUILD TANKERS) are described by giving more specific information about them. In Fig. 2.2, only the general type of relationship, *description,* is given. For some investigators interested in utilizing this analysis procedure, differentiation among the five basic groups may be sufficient. Others may want to make distinctions among different types of descriptive information, such as settings, specifics, attributes, and so forth. In contrast to Fig. 2.2, other content structures in my sections of this book make distinctions among the subtypes of the five basic relationships. These distinctions are explained in the second portion of this book.

Returning to the third solution shown in Fig. 2.2, the rationale (antecedent reasoning) for this solution is given; within this rationale or explanation for the solution is an analogy, a similarly operating and successful plan for guiding airplanes. This causative relation gives the explanation for the solution, which is staged at a more superordinate level in this text.

The problem is composed of a description of the attributes of supertankers, which can contribute to a reader's understanding of the magnitude of the ships and oil involved in the problem. The major portion of the problem is devoted to an explanation of why we have the problem of preventing oil from supertankers. Antecedent conditions that led to recognition of this problem are presented in a subordinate role to the problem itself (see *causation: explanation* under problem in Fig. 2.2). In the explanation are embedded causation: covariance relationships. LACK OF POWER AND STEERING EQUIPMENT IN EMERGENCY SITUATIONS causes two causally related events, OIL SPILLS and DAMAGE TO THE ENVIRONMENT. I have struggled with the best way to format embedded causal relationships. At this point, I suggest (1) moving down one node in the content structure when an embedded causal relation is identified (see Fig. 2.2), (2) labeling the time sequence that is a part of a causal relationship (see Fig. 2.3), and (3) using two relationship labels in the scoring structure rather than three for causation: covariance (*covariance: antecedent* and *covariance: consequent* rather than *covariance, antecedent,* and *consequent,* since you never have an antecedent without a consequent, whereas you can have a problem without a solution for the response relation where three relational labels are scored—see the scoring section of this volume). Thus, in Fig. 2.2, the LACK OF POWER AND STEERING results in the causally related OIL SPILLS and DAMAGED ENVIRONMENT which appear one level lower in the content structure than the primary antecedent or cause. The remainder of text associated with the problem can be related to the consequent DAMAGE ENVIRONMENT by a collection of descriptions (specific examples) of environmental damage with their own causative and descriptive propositions.

The format for the case grammar analysis is as follows:

VERB AND ADJUNCTS

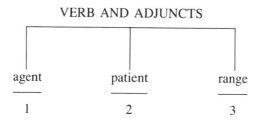

The verb (lexical predicate) is one level above the equally weighted role or case-related arguments. The role label and the content (indicated here by numbers) are at the same level in the structure.

When relating a superordinate idea to a description comprised of one or more lexical propositions that can be analyzed with case grammar, a format rule is used to avoid excessive repetition in the content structure. The idea being described is placed at the higher level in the content structure and it and its case relation are deleted in the subordinate proposition. For example, see idea units 9–26 of the content structure analysis in Part 2. In the supertanker passage, there is the sentence "Oil spills also kill microscopic plant life which provide food for sea life and produce 70 percent of the world's oxygen supply." As seen in Fig. 2.2 "Kill microscopic plant life" is one of the consequences of oil spills. The remainder of that sentence describes microscopic plant life (see idea units 159 to 171 in Part 2). As can be seen below, the agent and microscopic plant life are deleted in the subordinate propositions by this format rule.

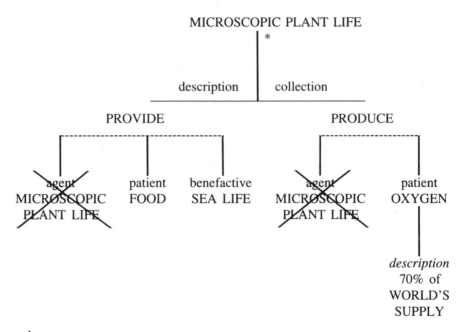

* | only these darked lines indicate movement to one level lower in the content structure.

This example also brings up the problem of how far to analyze arguments. It depends on your purpose. For teachers using the approach to teach top-level structure, they may want to stop with the top-level structure. In studying the logic of exposition in reading and writing instruction, an analysis similar to that in Fig. 2.2 may be useful. For prose learning studies, it depends on the research questions and your resources; the more minute the analysis, the longer the scoring time. For example, microscopic plant life could be analyzed as follows:

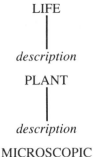

If you are interested in these distinctions in recall, then you should analyze the text at this level. If you do not analyze it completely, then you have to make scoring rules to identify crucial components (see Part 2 for sample scoring rules). Even if you do analyze to the level of each content word in the text, you still may not be at the end point of the referent indicated and activated in the mind of the author or reader. Thus, you will always need to make generous rules for scoring substantive recall.

This system of prose analysis is applicable to all types of expository prose and has also been applied to story materials (here a time line for collection: sequence is required, Meyer, Haring, Brandt, & Walker, 1980). The minimal unit of analysis is the idea unit, which includes both actual content named in the text and relational terms inferred from the text. The analysis produces a single, hierarchically organized representation of a passage's structure. It is a propositional structure with the relationships (predicates) at the microproposition level held primarily by verbs from the text, whereas at the macroproposition level, they are held by the rhetorical relations. The arguments are individual content units from the text or content units that are parts of other propositions.

Meyer (1975; Meyer, Brandt, & Bluth, 1980) has manipulated signaling independent of the content structure. The way the content structure is organized shows how the content has been staged in importance and how it has been logically organized by an author. However, explicit words of signaling (Meyer, 1975) can be added or deleted in a text. For example, the signaling words listed in the right column in the content structure of the supertanker passage (see Part 2) could be deleted from the text. Then, the readers would have to infer these relations; however, the content structure would remain the same for the signaled and non-signaled text.

Using Text Organization in the Reading Process

The structure strategy is the dominant reading strategy hypothesized for skilled comprehenders in a prose learning task. These readers search out and follow the text's superordinate relational structure (i.e., see Fig. 2.2) and focus on the text's message and how it relates to supporting major details. We have found that skilled readers approach text with knowledge about how texts are conventionally organized and a strategy to seek and use the top-level structure in a particular text as an organizational framework to facilitate encoding and retrieval (i.e., Bartlett, 1978; Meyer, 1981; Meyer, 1984a; Meyer, Brandt, & Bluth, 1980; Meyer & Freedle, 1984). Organization in text as well as other verbal tasks has been shown to be a crucial variable in learning and memory (cf. Kintsch, 1977, Chapter 5).

Processing activities hypothesized for the structure strategy are somewhat similar to explanations given for the levels effect by Anderson (1976) and Kintsch and van Dijk (1978), only primary emphasis is placed on a search for interrelationships among chunks of complex propositions in text. Anderson (1976) explained that high-level propositions, central propositions in the network of this computer simulation model, are more frequently called up to help interpret the more peripheral low-level propositions. This constitutes extra rehearsal of high-level propositions and results in increasing the probability of their recall. Similarly, Kintsch and van Dijk (1978) explained that high-level propositions are processed differently from low-level propositions. High-level propositions are hypothesized to be more frequently retrieved from long-term memory and kept in the short-term memory buffer as old propositions to be related to incoming new propositions in the reading process. In the Kintsch and van Dijk (1978) model, high-level propositions are identified by repetition of arguments or concepts. The model does not specify how the extreme superordinate proposition is identified; this proposition is crucial since repetition of its arguments dictates moving down in the hierarchy and building the text structure. At present, the superordinate proposition is selected on an intuitive basis with the expectation that further work with their macroprocesses component will help to explicate this choice.

The superordinate rhetorical relationships in text along with readers' prior knowledge of them appear to play a crucial role in comprehension and must be integrated more fully into the macroprocesses component of the Kintsch and van Dijk model. High-level propositions need not be identified solely on argument repetition, but they can be identified as the arguments of the major rhetorical relationship or top-level text structure. The extreme superordinate proposition is then identified as the content bound by the top-level structure. For example, in the first paragraph of the passage reproduced in Part 2, the extreme superordinate proposition is oil spills. It is explicitly signaled as the problem in the first sentence of this passage, which is written with a problem/solution top-level structure commonly found in scientific articles. Thus, a focus on relationships and top-level structures can be used to specify the superordinate proposition in a structural analysis.

Processing activities for the structure strategy focus on a search for major text-based relationships among propositions. That is, there is a search for relationships that can subsume all or large chunks of this information and tie it into a summarized, comprehensible whole. Readers employing the structure strategy are hypothesized to approach text looking for patterns that will tie all the propositions together and the author's primary thesis, which will provide the content to be bound by these patterns or schemata. Then, they search for relationships among this primary thesis and supporting details. For example, when reading the supertanker text they recognize in the first sentence that the propositions may fit their problem schema. Each new proposition is related back to the problem; thus, the problem of oil spills from supertankers is frequently related to incoming propositions in the short-term memory buffer. Previous knowledge about problems keeps the readers searching for causal relationships among descriptive information about the problem, such as why it is a problem and what caused it. Also, prior experience with problems leads readers to anticipate and search for solutions, solutions that must satisfy most of the previously stated causes of the problem. Thus, the problem and its causes are retrieved continually from long-term storage to the short-term memory buffer for relating to the subsequent propositions in the passage. That is, use of the problem/solution schema leads to the selection of this content for frequent binding to other propositions. The problems and solutions for supertankers are highest in the hierarchical structure due to their instantiation in the problem/solution schema selected for processing the text, and this content also has the greatest number of ideas subordinate and related to it. Both factors, height in the structure and number of propositions beneath in the structure (elaborations), increase the likelihood of recall of this information (Meyer & McConkie, 1973).

The top-level structure and major interrelationships are also employed to guide retrieval and production of the recall protocol; it is hypothesized to be primarily a top-down retrieval search guided by the structure of relationships. Readers are assumed to construct memory representations of text propositions which are similar in terms of both hierarchical relationships and content to the content structure of the writer depicted in Fig. 2.2 and in Part 2. When recalling the text, they begin their retrieval search with the top-level structure and systematically work from the superordinate relationships and content downward. Thus, propositions higher in the structure are more likely to be accessed and recalled. High-level propositions also have the advantage in recall of having greater numbers of propositions beneath them in the structure; this results in more paths for retrieval to access these high-level propositions.

Readers process text line by line in a linear fashion; they do not wait until after they have read the entire text to find the top-level structure and other superordinate relations that subsume large chunks of text. Words in the text, such as "problem," "need to prevent," "in contrast," "others disagree," "others believe," "as a result," other signaling words and content words, help readers to make educated guesses about which relational pattern or schemata to assign to the text. If later sentences are not compatible with an initial assignment, then reassignment can be made and the reader probably will reread the text segments involved.

Since explicit signaling of top-level structure and superordinate relations should make this assignment easier, we have conducted a number of studies on the effects of signaling these relationships (cf. Meyer, 1984b, in press; Meyer, Brandt, & Bluth, 1980). The presence or absence of signaling in well-organized text appears to have minimal effects on good comprehenders who employ the structure strategy. For most passages studied, it does not influence the way they organize their recall protocols, the amount of information recalled, nor the type of information recalled (cf. Meyer, 1975, 1984b; Meyer, Brandt, & Bluth, 1980). Although it does not affect reading speed, it does appear to affect cognitive capacity as measured by reaction time to a secondary task (reactions to random clicks while reading text with and without signaling, Britton, Glynn, Meyer, & Penland, 1982). Ninth graders with high reading comprehension test scores (Meyer, Brandt, & Bluth, 1980) and most students attending undergraduate and graduate colleges (cf. Meyer, 1981, 1984b) follow the structure strategy regardless of the presence of signaling. For these skilled readers, the structure strategy is extremely well learned; words like "need to prevent" are sufficient to trigger the assignment of a problem/solution schema. However, for poorer comprehenders (Meyer, Brandt, & Bluth, 1980), explicit signaling, such as "the problem is," was necessary before these readers could apply the structure strategy. The structure strategy appears to require more conscious effort for these comprehenders than proficient readers.

The exact processes involved in assigning schemata (top-level structures, superordinate relations, and more concrete content schemata) to text have not been explicated. The final section of this chapter deals with the manipulations of signaling and specificity of details that led to the assignment of different top-level structures for a text on railroads. These maniuplations in this particular text caused readers to vary in assigning either a comparison or a collection top-level structure for comprehension and recall of the text.

GENERAL COMPARISON OF MEYER'S APPROACH TO OTHERS

The Kintsch (1974) system also produces a hierarchical representation, but follows the surface structure more closely. The minimal unit of analysis is the proposition, which is defined as a relationship, and its arguments (e.g., Jennifer loves Zona is [Loves, Jennifer, Zona]). Analysis of a passage with this system produces a text base (a list of propositions), and a hierarchical ordering of these propositions. Argument repetition is the basis for forming the hierarchy. The system is applicable to expository prose in which a hierarchy of logical relations is not particularly important, though it has been applied to all varieties of prose.

It is particularly appropriate where the concern is with content items rather than their interrelationships. Since the hierarchy is built on the basis of repetition of content, rather than identification of logical relationships as in the Meyer (1975) system, it may be a simpler system to learn and to apply. However, Miller and Kintsch (1980) state that the parsing of the text into a list of propositions (the text base) "is difficult, and at times cannot help but be arbitrary." Bieger and Dunn (1980) have found Meyer's model of text structure more sensitive to developmental differences in recall than Kintsch's model; the significant difference being that Meyer's approach explicitly represents and scores both inferred and explicit relationships in text, while Kintsch's approach does not.

The text base and its hierarchical structure are the facts of the text that correspond to the microproposition level. They consist of propositions arranged in a hierarchy through argument repetition (repetition of content). In making the hierarchy, other forms of cohesion are not considered. Selection of the most superordinate proposition is done on the basis of intuition. Different hierarchies can be formed if different propositions are selected for this superordinate position.

Many of the expository texts used by Kintsch (1974) do not have summary or preview statements (signaling, Meyer, 1975), whereas Meyer's texts (frequently *Scientific American* articles) do. Thus, the macropropositions of Meyer's system are the gist or summary. The top third of the propositions in Kintsch's text base are the most important facts of the text, as indicated by the repetition of their concepts in the rest of the text. However, they do not provide a summary of the passage's gist.

Thus, Kintsch and van Dijk's model (1978) of text comprehension has the reader operating on the text to construct the macrostructure, equivalent to Meyer's macropropositions. The macrostructure results from the operation of the macro-operators, which are a set of abstraction, or summarization, rules (van Dijk, 1977).

For Kintsch and van Dijk (1978), the top-level structure is an independent organization overlaying the propositional analysis, rather than an emergent structure as in the Meyer system. This is because only highly conventionalized top-level structures have been studied, e.g., stories or scientific articles.

The Kintsch system was developed originally to aid in determining what information in a passage was available to the learner so that recall could be more easily scored (the usual comparison seen in Fig. 2.1). In more recent years, it appears as a key element in a model of text comprehension which is being developed by Kintsch, van Dijk and colleagues (Kintsch & van Dijk, 1978; Kintsch & Vipond, 1979; Miller & Kintsch, 1980). This model ingeniously and mechanically relates the levels and paths in the text hierarchy to the capacity limitations of short-term memory.

Frederiksen's (1975, 1977, 1979) system also applies to various types of expository prose. The minimal unit of analysis is the concept, which may be a single word or word group, depending on the specificity desired, and the relation. Analysis does not produce a hierarchical structure, but rather "structure graphs" which have more of the quality of networks. The Frederiksen system is particularly appropriate in situations where investigators require a method for scoring inferences made by readers.

At the microproposition level, Frederiksen describes an elaborate set of relations that hold among concepts. The system at this level is very similar to the micropropositional level of Meyer's system; however, Frederiksen's system makes more distinctions within types of relationships.

The analysis system does not provide natural segmentation into hierarchical levels. However, some logical relations defined at the micropropositional level could be adapted for use at a macroproposition level. There are no provisions for the top-level structure.

The Frederiksen system was developed to handle issues in learning and recalling of logical relations and makes finer distinctions among relationships than the other two approaches. The system was also formulated to study inferences (Frederiksen, 1975). Also, Frederiksen (1975) has defined types of information in recall protocols more descriptively: veridical recall, overgeneralization, pseudo-discriminations, text-implied inferences, and elaborations (inferences from prior knowledge). The first four are scored as present in a protocol in Meyer's system but distinctions among them are not made.

The Frederiksen system was designed to exemplify a model of text knowledge in the mind apart from the organization of the original text with its emphasis of some ideas and subordination of others. Thus, in contrast to the approach depicted in Fig. 2.1, Frederiksen attempted to move right from the text to the reader's memory. He did not look systematically at prior knowledge frames or schemata and their contribution to the text comprehended in the reader's mind as have later investigators (Beaugrande, 1980; Graesser, 1981; van Dijk, 1977). For example, van Dijk (1977) suggested identifying content-related frames or schemata to understand the reader's processing to text, such as a war schema to understand a text about a particular war. The asset to applying this sort of content analysis in the classroom is that it can help identify the background information that students will need to understand a given text. The disadvantage is that it is not possible to specify in advance a bounded set of relations to be used in the analysis, as is possible for both Meyer and Frederiksen. Graesser (1981) has independent groups of subjects recall text and generate inferences (about 15 inferences per text statement), which become part of the representational system prior to examining the recall data. However, the relationships between these inferences and prior knowledge schemata are unspecified, and the activation of all these inferences during comprehension appears questionable.

A recent approach by Beaugrande (1980) produces elaborate networks of content with relations, both syntactic and conceptual, clearly marked. This analysis of the text is called the text-world model. An important attribute of Beaugrande's approach, as well as Graesser's, is that it applies the same type of relationships to the text as to prior knowledge of readers and attempts to mesh the two. For example, Beaugrande investigates the prior knowledge schemata that subjects bring to the topic of rockets, such as the flight schema. He also produces a network of facts readers would be likely to know before encountering the text (i.e., rockets take-off), called the world-knowledge correlate. A comparison is made between the text-world model and a similar analysis of reader's recall protocol. In addition, the analyses of potential schemata and the world-knowledge correlate are compared with the analysis of the reader's recall protocol. The system is complex and does not appear to result in dimensions that could be readily used for classifying text.

In summary, the prose analysis system of Meyer, Kintsch, and Frederiksen differ in their strengths and suitability for different types of passages and research questions (see Table 2.1). Meyer's and Frederiksen's systems are better suited to examining logical relationships and comprehension of these relationships explicitly or implicitly stated in text. The logical relationships in Meyer's model closely follow those suggested by the text, while the superordinate level in Frederiksen's are drawn not from the text but from semantic knowledge (see Meyer, 1975). Thus, Meyer's system would probably be more effective for studying writing; it closely parallels work in rhetorics. In Meyer's and Frederiksen's systems protocols can be scored for recall of relationships independent from correct recall of content; this is not the case in Kintsch's system where propositions are the units for scoring rather than their component relation and arguments. Both Meyer's and Kintsch's systems provide clearly specified hierarchies, while this is not the case for Frederiksen's approach. Kintsch's system is probably the easiest to apply. However, Meyer's approach gives a more articulated structure (Cofer, Scott, & Watkins, 1978).

TABLE 2.1
Comparison of Strengths (+) for the Major Discourse Analysis
Systems Used in Educational Research Which Have Applicability to
Most Types of Classroom Learning Materials

Analysis Systems	Overall Structure: Articulation & Classification	Hierarchical Structure: Reflection of Subordination & Text Based Importance	Logical Relations: Examine & Score	Finer Distinctions: Semantic & Causal Relations; Substantive Recall	Learning Time: Simplicity	Speed in Scoring
Frederiksen			+	+		
Kintsch		+			+	+
Meyer	+	+	+			

DETAILED COMPARISON OF KINTSCH AND MEYER
APPROACHES

A more detailed examination of the approaches of Kintsch (1974) and Meyer (1975) is given here. Both approaches recognize the need for integration with knowledge frames of the reader, and so on, but this is a comparison of the systems as they currently stand. The text used for comparison of the analysis and scoring procedures is the one selected by Miller and Kintsch (1980) entitled the "Saint." The text is as follows:

> In the request to canonize the "frontier priest," John Neumann, bishop of Philadelphia in the 19th century, two miracles were attributed to him in this century. In 1923, Eva Benassi, dying from peritonitis, dramatically recovered after her nurse prayed to the bishop. In 1949, Kent Lenahan, hospitalized with two skull fractures, smashed bones and a pierced lung after a traffic accident, rose from his deathbed and resumed a normal life after his mother had prayed ardently to Neumann. (p. 341)

The text is much shorter than passages usually analyzed with the Meyer approach. The context of the text would be important to better articulate a top-level structure. However, in isolation it would be classified as a descriptive text; two examples or instances of an idea (miracles) are given in a particular setting (the request to canonize Neumann).

In order to fully understand this text, a good deal of prior knowledge is required about canonization and Saint John Nepomucene Neumann. For example, in having my students examine this passage prior to their attempts to analyze it, a number of the students suggested a causation relationship in the first sentence. That is, the occurrence of two miracles attributed to Neumann was thought to be the antecedent for initiating the request for the canonization. In considering their suggestion, I did some reading about the canonization of Saint Neumann (*New Yorker,* June 27, 1977). After living a righteous life, Neumann died in 1860; local people began praying for his intercession and claiming answered prayer at that point; a month after his death, his tomb became a shrine after his unembalmed body was examined and found intact; in 1886 Archbishop Ryan began the canonization process. Thus, the miracles in the Saint text in 1923 and 1949 were not the antecedents for requesting canonization. Conversely, attribution of the miracles to Neumann was not the consequent of trying to get him canonized since numerous miracles throughout the last 200 years were attributed to him independent of any motive to canonize him. Even though a causation top-level structure for this passage is not accurate based on world knowledge nor is it suggested by the text, it is possible that readers might utilize this structure. It is an organized approach to encoding the text and would probably yield good total recall; different intrusions over time might be expected from subjects encoding it

with a causal versus a descriptive top-level structure. Both the Kintsch and
Meyer approaches need to more fully deal with this interaction between the text
and the knowledge of the reader.

The 20 short texts in the Miller and Kintsch (1980) study were utilized so that
they could test the generality of their model on a large number of texts. However,
the generality of their texts is questionable. The emphasis on word repetition in
their model may well be overemphasized for more ecologically valid text.

At this point I have been unable to identify which *Reader's Digest* article
reported the Saint paragraph (Miller & Kintsch, 1980), but I found the same
information and additional information about the canonization of Neumann in an
issue of the 1977 *New Yorker* (entitled "Saint," June 27, 1977; 53:24–26).
Figure 2.5 presents a plausible top-level structure under which the Saint paragraph would fit.

Analysis of the Saint Text

Figure 2.6 lists the text base for the "Saint" given by Miller and Kintsch (1980).
There are 29 propositions; each can be scored. Figure 2.7 presents the content
structure of the Saint text from the Meyer approach; there are 90 idea units that
can be scored. The Meyer analysis allows each content unit and each relationship
to be scored separately. In the Kintsch analysis, only two lexical relations,

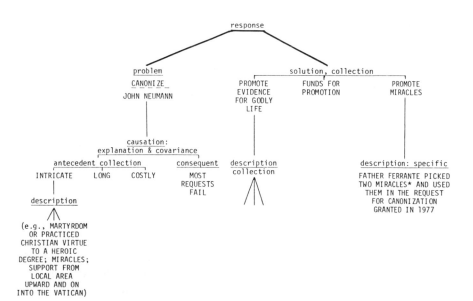

FIG. 2.5.   Possible top-level structure for the canonization of Neumann and the
Saint text's * role in that superordinate structure.

Recall Data of Miller & Kintsch (1980)	I13	I7	D7	I5	D5	D41	O1	Text Base
101	1	1	1	1	0	1	0	(P 1 (REQUEST P2 P8))
102	1	1	1	1	1	1	0	(P 2 (CANONIZE P3))
90	1	1	1	0	0	0	0	(P 3 (ISA JOHN-NEWMANN FRONTIER-PRIEST))
93	1	1	1	0	0	0	1	(P 4 (ISA JOHN-NEWMANN BISHOP))
86	1	1	1	0	0	0	0	(P 5 (LOC: IN P4 PHILADELPHIA))
60	0	1	0	0	0	0	0	(P 6 (TIME: IN P4 19TH-CENTURY))
110	1	1	0	0	0	0	0	(P 7 (TWO MIRACLES))
104[1]	1	1	0	0	0	0	0	(P 8 (ATTRIBUTED P7 JOHN-NEWMANN))
___	0	0	0	0	0	0	0	(P 9 (TIME: IN P8 THIS CENTURY))
								SENTENCE
82	0	1	0	0	0	0	0	(P10 (TIME: IN P11 1923))
69	1	1	0	0	0	0	0	(P11 (DYING EVA-BENASSI PERITONITIS))
	0	0	0	0	0	0	0	(P12 (DRAMATICALLY P13))
114	1	1	0	0	0	0	0	(P13 (RECOVERED EVA-BENASSI))
111	1	1	0	0	0	1	1	(P14 (AFTER P15 P13))
83	1	1	0	0	0	0	0	(P15 (PRAYED NURSE BISHOP))
								SENTENCE
77	1	1	0	0	0	0	0	(P16 (TIME: IN P17 1949))
	1	0	0	0	0	0	0	(P17 (HOSPITALIZED KENT-LENAHAN P18 P20 P21))
93	0	1	0	0	0	0	0	(P18 (FRACTURES SKULL KENT-LENAHAN))
63	0	1	0	0	0	0	0	(P19 (TWO P18))
74	0	1	0	0	0	0	0	(P20 (SMASHED BONES KENT-LENAHAN))
86	1	0	0	0	0	0	0	(P21 (PIERCED LUNG KENT-LENAHAN))
80	1	0	0	0	0	0	0	(P22 (AFTER P17 ACCIDENT))
56	1	0	0	0	0	0	0	(P23 (TRAFFIC ACCIDENT))
59	1	1	0	0	0	0	0	(P24 (ROSE KENT-LENAHAN DEATHBED))
98	1	1	0	0	0	0	0	(P25 (RESUMED KENT-LENAHAN P26))
97	1	1	0	0	0	0	0	(P26 (NORMAL LIFE))
104	1	1	0	0	0	1	1	(P27 (AFTER P25 P28))
84	1	1	0	0	0	0	0	(P28 (PRAYED MOTHER JOHN-NEWMANN))
___	0	1	0	0	0	0	0	(P29 (ARDENTLY P28))
								SENTENCE
	22	23	5	2	1	4	3	Total Recall

[1]Excluded by Miller & Kintsch.

FIG. 2.6. Kintsch analysis of "Saint" text used by Miller and Kintsch (1980) and scoring of sample protocols.

REQUEST (P 1) and CANONIZE (P 2), and two causal rhetorical relations, AFTER (P 14) and AFTER (P 27), can be scored regardless of whether or not readers correctly remember their arguments.

Figure 2.8 depicts the coherence graphs for the Saint text as indicated in Miller and Kintsch (1980). They indicated that at the end of processing the text, there were two separate subgraphs in memory. Since sentence 2 connects with sentence 1 by overlap of the word BISHOP, these two graphs are interrelated as shown in Fig. 2.8. For sentence 1 REQUEST was selected as the superordinate proposition on the basis of intuition. P 2, P 8, P 9 are placed at Level 2 because they share arguments with P 1. I merely used the text base (see Fig. 2.6) from Miller and Kintsch (1980) and did not arrive at the propositions in the text base myself; training would also be involved in parsing the text into a list of propositions for use in the Kintsch approach.

Figure 2.9 presents the superordinate structure of relations for the Saint text as identified by the Meyer (1975) approach. WERE ATTRIBUTED was selected for the superordinate level for the following reasons. The three sentences were searched for a rhetorical relation that would subsume all the content; none was found. However, a *description* relation interrelates MIRACLES to the two examples of miracles. The lexical proposition with the lexical relation (predicate) or verb WERE ATTRIBUTED interrelates the arguments in the first sentence, and one of its arguments MIRACLE can be related by the description relation to the propositions in the remaining two sentences. Thus, WERE ATTRIBUTED binds the information contained in the first sentence and *description, collection* binds the first sentence through MIRACLES to the examples of miracles in the next two sentences. WERE ATTRIBUTED was selected for the superordinate level rather than REQUEST because WERE ATTRIBUTED is the verb or lexical predicate binding the ideas in the first sentence, not REQUEST. REQUEST is a lexical predicate, but is not the binding relationship or verb in the first sentence. As can be seen under the first column in Fig. 2.6, which gives the recall data from the Miller and Kintsch (1980) experiment, ATTRIBUTED (104) and RE-QUEST (101) are both well recalled.

For the first sentence of the Saint text, the relative placement of ideas in the hierarchies of the two analysis systems are about the same (see Fig. 2.10). The REQUEST and ATTRIBUTED are near the top and PHILADELPHIA and 19th CENTURY are at the bottom. However, miracles is higher in the Meyer analysis (Level 2 out of 5) than in the Kintsch analysis (Level 3 out of 4); the recall of miracles is very high (110).

Larger differences between the two approaches are evident for the second sentence and its integration with the propositions of the first sentence (see Fig. 2.11). The major difference focuses around the causal relationship involved in EVA RECOVERED AFTER THE NURSE PRAYED TO THE BISHOP. For the Kintsch approach, sentences 1 and 2 are hooked together by the repetition of the word BISHOP, which is in P 15 (PRAYED NURSE BISHOP). Thus, P 15 is the highest proposition in the memory structure from sentence 2. The other propositions are ordered in the structure on the basis of repetition of arguments. This repetition rule places P 13 (RECOVERED EVA BENASSI) two levels lower than the antecedent, P 15 (PRAYED NURSE BISHOP). In contrast, from the Meyer approach RECOVERED (25) and PRAYED (37) and their arguments are found at the same level in the structure. Also, note from Fig. 2.11 that the number of levels identified in the two approaches varies at this point.

The least agreement of the two approaches to text analysis is found regarding the final sentence. For the Meyer approach, the propositions in sentence 3 are integrated into the one content structure as another example of MIRACLE. Connected memory structures for both writer and reader would be expected similar to those in Figs. 2.7 and 2.9. However, sentence 3 forms a separate subgraph in the Miller and Kintsch approach and the proposition labeled as superordinate is assigned to Level 1 in the hierarchy (see Figs. 2.8 and 2.12). For Miller and Kintsch, the superordinate level proposition (P 18 FRACTURES SKULL KENT LENAHAN) is selected by intuition. Then the connecting of the other propositions to the superordinate is done on the basis of argument overlap. More specifically, ''all propositions that share arguments with the superordinate or are embedded in the superordinate are placed at Level 2 of the graph and

	Subjects							Content Structure
I13	I7	D7	I5	D5	D41	O1		
1	1	0	0	0	1	1	1	WERE_ATTRIBUTED
1	1	0	0	0	1	0	2	description: setting location
1	1	1	1	0	1	0	3	REQUEST
1	1	1	1	0	1	0	4	patient
1	1	1	1	1	1	0	5	CANONIZE
1	1	1	1	1	1	0	6	patient
1	1	1	1	1	0	0	7	JOHN NEUMANN
1	1	1	0	0	0	0	8	description: equivalent
1	1	1	0	0	0	0	9	FRONTIER PRIEST
1	1	0	0	0	1	1	10	benefactive
1	1	1	0	0	0	1	11	JOHN NEUMANN
1	1	1	0	0	0	1	12	description: attribution
1	1	1	0	0	1	1	13	BISHOP
1	1	1	0	0	1	0	14	description: setting location
1	1	1	0	0	0	0	15	PHILADELPHIA
0	1	0	0	0	0	0	16	description: setting time
1	1	0	0	0	0	0	17	19th CENTURY
1	0	0	0	0	0	0	18	description: setting time
0	0	0	0	0	0	0	19	THIS CENTURY
1	1	0	0	0	1	1	20	patient
1	1	0	0	0	1	1	21	MIRACLES
1	1	0	0	0	1	1	22	description: specific
1	1	0	0	0	1	1	23	collection (TWO)
1	1	0	1	0	0	1	24	covariance, consequent (24, 36)
1	1	0	0	0	0	1	25	RECOVERED
1	1	0	0	0	0	0	26	description: setting time
1	1	0	0	0	0	0	27	1923
1	1	0	0	0	0	1	28	patient
1	1	0	1	1	0	0	29	EVA BENASSI
1	1	0	0	0	0	1	30	description: attribution
1	0	0	0	0	0	1	31	DYING
1	0	0	0	0	0	0	32	force
1	1	0	0	0	0	0	33	PERITONITIS
0	0	0	0	0	0	0	34	description: manner
0	0	0	0	0	0	0	35	DRAMATICALLY
1	1	0	1	0	0	1	36	causation: covariance, antecedent (24, 36)
1	1	0	1	0	0	1	37	PRAYED
1	1	0	1	0	0	1	38	agent, former
1	1	0	0	0	0	0	39	NURSE
1	1	0	0	0	0	0	40	description: specific
1	1	0	0	0	0	0	41	HER (EVA BENASSI'S NURSE)
1	1	0	1	0	0	1	42	range, latter
1	1	0	0	0	1	1	43	BISHOP (JOHN NEUMANN)
1	1	0	0	0	1	1	44	causation: covariance, consequent (44, 81)
1	1	0	0	0	0	0	45	collection
1	1	1	0	0	0	0	46	ROSE
1	1	0	0	0	0	0	47	description: setting time
1	1	0	0	0	0	0	48	1949
1	1	1	0	0	0	0	49	patient
1	1	0	0	0	0	0	50	KENT LENAHAN

FIG. 2.7. Meyer analysis of "Saint" text by Miller and Kintsch (1980) and scoring of sample protocols.

		Subjects						Content Structure
I13	I7	D7	I5	D5	D41	O1		
1	1	0	0	0	0	0	51	⌐description: attribution
1	1	0	0	0	0	0	52	⊢causation: covariance, consequent
								(68,52)
1	0	1	0	0	0	0	53	⊢HOSPITALIZED
1	0	1	0	0	0	0	54	⌐patient
1	1	0	0	0	0	0	55	⌐KENT LENAHAN
1	1	0	0	0	0	0	56	⌐description: attribution
1	1	0	1	0	0	0	57	⊢collection
1	1	0	1	0	0	0	58	⌐FRACTURES
1	1	0	1	0	0	0	59	⌐description: specific
0	1	0	0	0	0	0	60	⊢TWO
0	1	0	1	0	0	0	61	⌐SKULL
0	1	0	0	0	0	0	62	⌐SMASHED
0	1	0	0	0	0	0	63	⌐patient
0	1	0	0	0	0	0	64	⌐BONES
1	0	0	0	0	0	0	65	⌐PIERCED
1	0	0	0	0	0	0	66	⌐patient
1	0	0	1	0	0	0	67	⌐LUNG
1	1	0	0	0	0	0	68	⊢causation: covariance, antecedent
								(52, 68)
1	1	0	0	0	0	0	69	⌐ACCIDENT
1	0	0	0	0	0	0	70	⌐description: specific
1	0	0	0	0	0	0	71	⌐TRAFFIC
1	1	1	0	0	0	0	72	⊢range
1	1	1	0	0	0	1	73	⌐DEATHBED
1	1	0	0	0	1	1	74	⌐RESUMED
1	1	0	0	0	1	1	75	⌐agent
1	1	0	0	0	0	0	76	⌐KENT LENAHAN
1	1	0	0	0	1	1	77	⊢patient
1	1	0	0	0	1	1	78	⌐LIFE
1	1	0	0	0	0	0	79	⌐description: specific
1	1	0	0	0	0	0	80	⌐NORMAL
1	1	0	0	0	1	1	81	⊢causation: covariance, antecedent (44, 81)
1	1	0	0	0	1	1	82	⌐PRAYED
1	1	0	0	0	1	1	83	⌐agent, former
1	1	0	0	0	0	0	84	⌐MOTHER
1	1	0	0	0	0	0	85	⌐description: specific
1	1	0	0	0	0	0	86	⌐HIS (KENT LENAHAN'S)
0	1	0	0	0	0	1	87	⊢description: manner
0	1	0	0	0	0	0	88	⌐ardently
1	1	0	0	0	0	1	89	⊢range, latter
1	1	0	0	0	0	1	90	⌐NEUMANN
79	77	18	16	4	22	31	Total Recall	

connected by the superordinate. The propositions from this input chunk as yet unassigned to the graph are then compared to the propositions now at Level 2, and any that share arguments or are referenced by the Level 2 propositions are so connected and placed at Level 3 (Miller & Kintsch, 1980, p. 339)." P 17, P 20, P 1, P 24, and P 25 are placed at Level 2 because they all share the argument KENT LENAHAN: P 19 (TWO P 18) is also at Level 2 because P 18, the superordinate, is one of its arguments. Once intuition is applied to select the superordinate, the construction of the subgraph is built in this mechanical and objective manner. The logic of the exposition does not guide the construction of

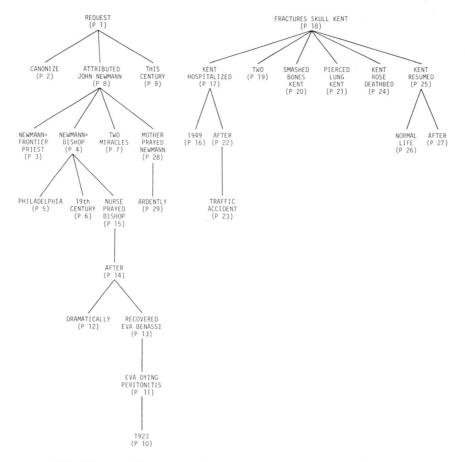

FIG. 2.8. Actual level analysis for long-term memory structure hypothesized by
Miller and Kintsch (1980) for the Saint text (Miller, personal communication).

this text structure; instead the structure is built on intuition for the main idea or
superordinate and then repetition of arguments. However, look at the high recall
of the logic in this text from the Miller and Kintsch study (see Fig. 2.6 rhetorical
relations: P 14, P 22, P 27 and lexical relations: P 1, P 2, P 8). The rhetorical
relations (AFTER) are not particularly high in the Kintsch subgraphs.

A strength of the Miller and Kintsch approach is that they relate their model to
what we know about limitations in cognitive processing (e.g., Kintsch & van
Dijk, 1978). However, the setting of the input size and buffer memory capacity
for sentence 3 results in an illogical construction of the memory structure from
the Saint text. As can be seen in Fig. 2.12, the last part of sentence 3 (HIS
MOTHER HAD PRAYED ARDENTLY TO NEUMANN) is not found in the
independent memory structure for sentence 3. Miller explained that this occurs

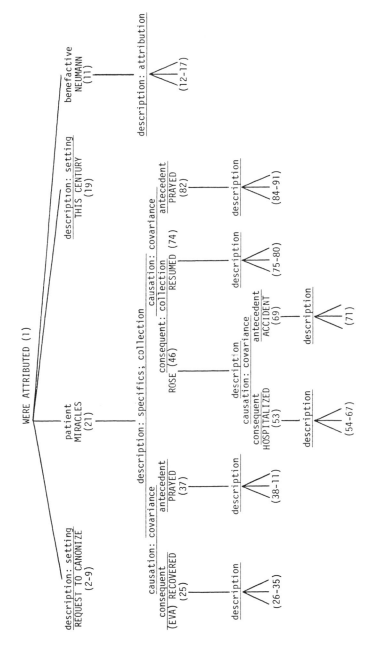

FIG. 2.9. Superordinate structure of relationships of "Saint" text (Miller & Kintsch, 1980) from Meyer approach (numbers correspond to content and relationships in Fig. 2.7).

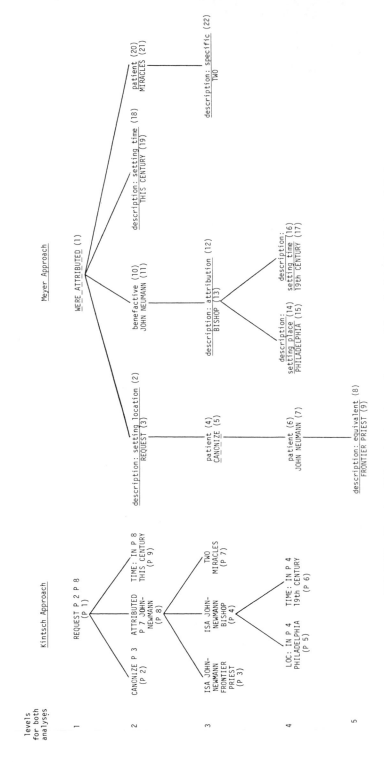

FIG. 2.10. Kintsch and Meyer level analyses of sentence 1 from the Saint text. Sentence 1: In the request to canonize the ''frontier priest,'' John Neumann, bishop of Philadelphia in the 19th century, two miracles were attributed to him in this century.

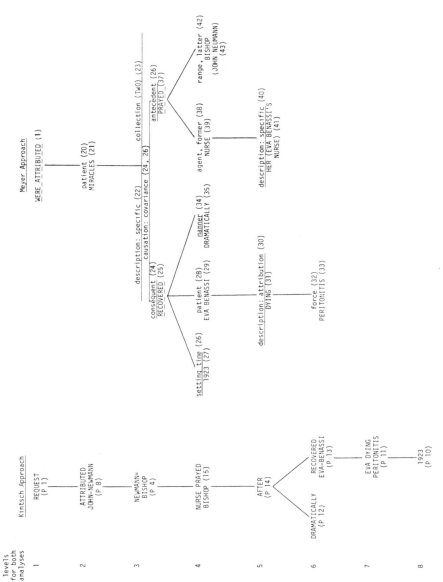

FIG. 2.11. Kintsch and Meyer level analyses of sentence 2 from the Saint text and its integration with the structure from sentence 1. Sentence 2: In 1923, Eva Benassi, dying from peritonitis, dramatically recovered after her nurse prayed to the bishop.

43

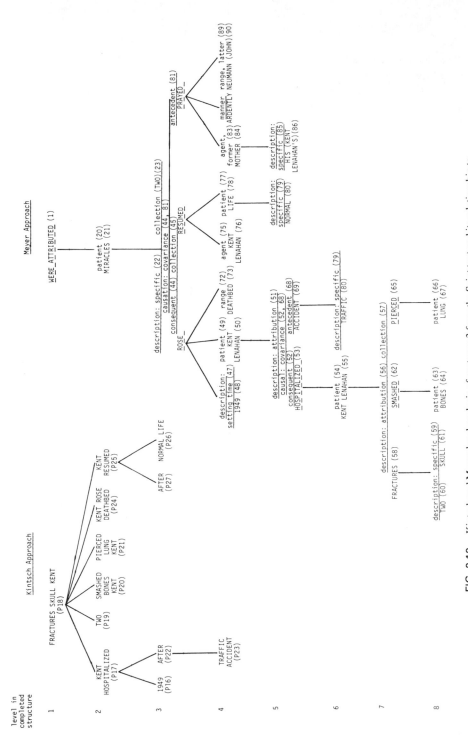

FIG. 2.12. Kintsch and Meyer level analysis of sentence 3 from the Saint text and its relationship to the preceding propositions from the text. Sentence 3: In 1949, Kent Lenahan, hospitalized with two skull fractures, smashed bones and a pierced lung after a traffic accident, rose from his deathbed and resumed a normal life after his mother had prayed ardently to Neumann.

44

due to the fact that buffer memory is too full and the remainder of the sentence is processed on a new processing cycle. The propositions in the first part of sentence 3 have no overlap with the propositions encoded from sentences 1 and 2; thus the propositions up to HIS MOTHER in sentence 3 form a separate memory representation. However, on the new processing cycle for the end of sentence 3 overlap occurs in both subgraphs; that is, the remaining propositions (P 28 and P 29) could be hooked to P 27 (AFTER P 25 P 28) or P 8 (ATTRIBUTED P 7 JOHN-NEUMANN). As seen in Fig. 2.8, they are linked to P 8 rather than P 27. I do not know the reason for this decision; it may be due to level: P 8 is at Level 2, while P 27 is at Level 3. However, P 27 is also more recent; both hierarchical level and recency are factors in the "leading edge strategy" proposed by Kintsch and van Dijk (1978) to predict contents and duration of propositions in buffer memory and subsequent recall. (The Miller and Kintsch, 1980, article indicates that P 28 is at Level 4 and linked upward to P 27, but the final long-term memory graph that Miller provided me links it as seen in Fig. 2.8).

The component of processing cycles, designed to capture aspects of memory limitations, yields an illogical final structure (see Fig. 2.8). Sentences 2 and 3 are very similar in type, essence and structure, but are diagrammed in completely different manners. To be consistent with sentence 2, the entire list of propositions from sentence 3 should be linked by P 28 (MOTHER PRAYED NEUMANN) as is found for P 15 (NURSE PRAYED BISHOP) in sentence 2. The notion that readers cannot link up most of the third sentence with their memory representation appears naive. It is merely a result of grinding the text through the microprocesses component of the Kintsch and van Dijk model. For example, the microprocesses model cannot identify the propositions in sentence 2 nor 3 as examples of miracles since it only operates on word repetition and the word miracle does not appear in these sentences. Kintsch and colleagues (e.g., Miller & Kintsch, 1981) recognize the limitations of their microprocesses component. A macroprocesses component must include prior world knowledge as well as knowledge of text structure. For example, the fact that two miracles were mentioned would lead readers to expect a second miracle after reading sentences 1 and 2. The facts about Kent's miserable physical condition in the first portion of sentence 3 should have fit nicely with expectations generated from the schema suggested by two miracles (a collection of descriptions) and partially instantiated by the causal relationship of PRAYED/RECOVERED in sentence 2.

In contrast, the Meyer approach builds the structure from the logical relationships in the text. As seen in Figs. 2.9 and 2.12, sentence 3 is connected to the rest of the text by *description, collection*. Then the sentence is examined for the superordinate relationship that can subsume all of its content. This relationship is the causal relation that links what happened to KENT LENAHAN with what his mother did—PRAYED. Thus, as shown in Figs. 2.9 and 2.12, the first step in the analysis of sentence 3 is the division of the ideas into *antecedent* and *consequent* propositions. The *antecedent* is simply analyzed with case grammar and a *descriptive* (manner) relation as shown in idea units 81–90 in the content structure (see Fig. 2.7). The *consequence* of the prayer was a *collection* of actions; KENT ROSE and RESUMED (see Figs. 2.9 and 2.12). The *description* of KENT LENAHAN when he ROSE FROM HIS DEATHBED contains another causal relation. KENT had been HOSPITALIZED with a *collection* of injuries (units 57–67 in the content structure) AFTER A TRAFFIC ACCIDENT. As shown in Figs. 2.9 and 2.12, the ACCIDENT is the *antecedent* and the *consequent* is *HOSPITALIZED* with the *collection* of injuries.

The two analysis approaches are quite different for sentence 3 due to the fact that intuition led Miller and Kintsch to select FRACTURES SKULL KENTLENAHAN as the superordinate proposition. Following the structure of rhetorical and lexical (verbs) relations (this procedure requires educated inferences) led Meyer to place this same information (idea units 55, 58, and 61 in Fig. 2.7) at the lowest levels of the hierarchy, Levels 6, 7, and 8. According to Miller and Kintsch's recall data, recall of this information was high (93), but not as high as predicted by their text structure analysis and subsequent model (102). This content FRACTURED SKULL, SMASHED BONES, PIERCED LUNG is very vivid and image evoking; this does increase recall of details.

In comparing the two approaches on scoring, I examined recall protocols from seven subjects who were exposed to the Saint text. The subjects ranged in age and verbal ability and the tasks varied in order to show various scoring problems. Thus, these data are not ideally suited for examining the relation between recall performance and the different structures derived from the two text analysis procedures. In addition, the Meyer hierarchy was not designed to predict recall of only three sentences, but larger text segments. However, the hierarchy derived from the microstructure component of the Miller and Kintsch approach should relate to recall of the Saint text since this text along with 19 similar paragraphs were selected to test the microstructure component of their model. In fact, they (Miller & Kintsch, 1980) state "Kintsch and van Dijk hypothesized that the processing of short texts might be mostly attributable to microprocesses, so it could be that, for these texts (Saint text included), the macroprocessing component would not be necessary."

The correlation between the level of each proposition in the hierarchy (see Figs. 2.6 and 2.8; Level 1 = highest) and the recall data from the Miller and Kintsch experiment is .10. The correlation between the level of the propositions in this hierarchy and the recall performance of the seven subjects described in the next section is −.16. In contrast, in the Meyer analysis the correlation for the recall of these same subjects and height in the content structure is −.50. The levels effect is most frequently examined by dividing the scorable units into groups on the basis of their level in the hierarchy; thus, the number of scorable units from each approach was divided into approximate thirds falling high, middle, or low in the hierarchical structures. Table 2.2 shows the relationship between these levels and the recall data. Both analyses show that the hierarchy

TABLE 2.2[a]
Average Number of Subjects Recalling Propositions High, Middle,
and Low in the Hierarchical Structures Derived from the Prose
Analysis Approaches of Kintsch and Meyer

Analysis Approach	Level	Number of Units	Mean Recall
Kintsch	High (1–2)	11	2.00
	Middle (3)	8	2.50
	Low (4–8)	10	1.70
Meyer	High (1–3)	25	3.71
	Middle (4)	32	2.84
	Low (5–8)	33	1.82

[a]This analysis was volunteered by Joel R. Levin.

formed with the Meyer approach is a better predictor of the data. The Meyer approach is built upon knowledge of logical relationships and discourse organizations; these components are not found in the microprocesses component of the Kintsch and van Dijk model, where coherence is only examined in terms of word repetition. Even with single paragraphs the model that emphasizes learner's knowledge of text organization (e.g., easily comprehending that the Eva Benassi and Kent Lenahan incidents are examples of miracles attributed to Neumann) matches recall better than one that focuses on word repetition. This pattern would be expected to be stronger with longer passages where there are a greater number of logical relations among propositions.

In evaluating the two analysis systems, several strengths and limitations for each approach can be seen. The Kintsch approach is simpler and probably would require less analysis time. Once the text is parsed into a text base and the superordinate proposition is selected, subgraphs can be formed simply by finding repetition of words. Problems for this approach involve selecting the superordinate proposition and linking the text's content into one coherent graph with aspects of coherence other than argument repetition. Miller and Kintsch (1980) recognize the problem inherent in their selection of the main idea based on intuition. They hope to solve this problem by yet unspecified macrocomponents for their model. Reading educators have been interested in Meyer's approach to prose analysis because it can specify how to find the main idea, the content bound by the top-level structure or superordinate relationships (Meyer, 1984b). Attention to the logical relationships in the text may assist in the formation of the needed macrocomponents of the Kintsch and van Dijk (1978) model.

In addition, the Kintsch approach is not well suited to the study of rhetorical or logical coherence in exposition. Text relationships do not give form to the text structure and are not scored separately.

The Meyer approach requires considerable training in identifying these rhetorical relationships in text. Typical signals or explicit cues for these relations can be learned; when the relations are implicit these cues can be inserted to assist in the inference process. I have taught a number of students to analyze prose; our agreement is above 90%. It is higher if we decide before beginning the procedure to analyze the text to the level of its most specific text referents, as done for the Saint text. It takes practice to master the technique and each analysis is quite time consuming. It takes about a day of work to analyze a short passage. Differences in content structures made by different text analysts can occur when the text is vague or confusing. Judgments are involved just as they are with scoring substantive recall or analyzing a sentence with case grammar; training and practice eliminate most problems.

Scoring the Saint Text

In this section a number of recall protocols written by different types of subjects under different conditions are examined using the scoring systems of Kintsch and Meyer. Three of the recall protocols were written in a delayed, unintentional learning condition. Advanced graduate students in a prose learning class had read the Saint text as part of a class activity 1 month prior to being requested to recall the text. The class activity involved using portions of the Saint text to explain the use of case grammar. The students did not anticipate recalling the text. At the time of recall, they were asked to write down all they could remember from the Miller and Kintsch (1980) text. Three of the recall protocols were also written by the advanced graduate students immediately after listening to the passages. These subjects had participated earlier in the delayed, unintentional learning condition. The instructions followed our usual procedures (see Meyer, 1975, pp. 97 and 98). The students were told that after they completed listening to the passage they would need to write down *all* they could remember from the passage. The final recall protocol to be examined with the two scoring approaches was written by an old adult with a high school education. She was instructed to read the text as she would normally read a magazine article of interest to her; also before reading the text she was told that she would need to tell the experimenter in words from the text or her own words everything she could remember from the passage. These different types of learners and learning tasks were selected to point out strengths and limitations of the two scoring systems for various learner and task conditions.

The first recall protocol, I 13, was written by a graduate student immediately after listening to the Saint text.

Recall Protocol of Subject I 13

In a request to canonize John Newman, the frontier priest, two miracles were attributed to him in the *19th century*. In 1923, Eva Benassi was dying from peritonitis, but recovered after her nurse prayed to Newman (for her) (recovery). In 1949 Kent Lanahan was hospitalized after a car accident; he had a pierced lung and *multiple fractures*. He rose from his deathbed and resumed a normal life after his mother prayed to Newman (for him). Newman was the bishop of Philadelphia.

The scoring of this protocol for the Kintsch and Meyer structures can be seen in the columns labeled I 13 in Figs. 2.6 and 2.7. A 1 in the space across from a scorable unit means that the unit was recalled, while 0 means it was not recalled. The recall protocol for subject I 13 shows extremely high recall of the text content with few prior knowledge intrusions. The circles on the protocol indicate the addition of implied patients (person prayed for) in the lexical propositions with the lexical relation PRAYED. This could be noted in either system but not scored with the structures. The italicized segments are the only points where differences in scoring between the two systems occur. The reader confused 19th CENTURY with THIS CENTURY; this confusion cannot be credited with any points in the Kintsch system; P 9 cannot be scored because THIS CENTURY was not recalled; P 6 cannot be scored because 19th CENTURY was not linked to PHILADELPHIA. However, in the Meyer approach content and relations are scored separately so some credit would be given. Accurate recall would have resulted in 4 points (units 16, 17, 18, 19); this confusion in subject I 13's recall receives 2 points (units 18 and 17) and the confusion is noted (see scoring rules in Part 2). Similar differences between the two systems can be noted for MULTIPLE FRACTURES by comparing Figs. 2.6 and 2.7.

The next protocol, I 7, is from a similar type of student under the same immediate recall conditions.

Recall Protocol of Subject I 7

In the request to canonize the frontier priest, John Neuman, bishop of Philadelphia in the 19th century, two miracles were attributed to him. In 1923, Eva Benassi, *who had peritonitis*, was cured when her nurse prayed to the priest. In 1949 Kent Lanahan, *who was in an accident* and suffered 2 skull fractures and smashed bones rose from his deathbed and resumed a normal life after his mother prayed ardently to Neuman.

Again recall is high and accurate; the differences between the two systems are identified with italics in the protocol. Credit cannot be given in the Kintsch system for WHO (KENT LENAHAN) WAS IN AN ACCIDENT because for P 22 HOSPITALIZED (P 17) is missing and for P 23 TRAFFIC is missing.

However, some credit is given for recall of this information on the Meyer structure (content structure unit 69—also 52, 69 as it relates to the rest of the sentence). For WHO (EVA BENASSI) HAD PERITONITIS I generously scored P 11 (DYING EVA-BENASSI PERITONITIS); in the Meyer system fewer points can be given to discriminate among people who know EVA HAD PERITONITIS and those who know EVA WAS DYING FROM PERITONITIS (see scoring of I 7 content structure units 29, 30, 33).

Total recall scores for the two protocols are 22 (76%) for I 13 and 23 (79%) for I 7 with the Kintsch method and 79 (88%) for I 13 and 77 (86%) for I 7 with Meyer method. The total recall scores are extremely high. For scoring recalls of this type from graduate students with high recall in an immediate recall task, Kintsch's approach is faster and effective for most purposes.

The next recall protocol, D 7, also was written by subject 7. However, it was written prior to protocol I 7 and listening to the passage. The subject was exposed to the passage as part of instruction in a class; she did not know that she would ever need to recall it.

Recall Protocol D 7

In the effort to canonize Neumann, the frontier, bishop of Philadelphia; *somebody was in the hospital* and *rose from his bed*.

For this protocol, the differences in scoring systems only come for the last sentence where recall is less accurate. Since KENT LENAHAN was not recalled, P 17 and P 24 cannot be scored in Fig. 2.6, while the correct content and relations can be scored in Fig. 2.7 (units 53, 54, 46, 49).

The recall protocol I 5 was written by a graduate student in the same experimental group as the other students immediately after listening to the passage.

Recall Protocol I 5

In an effort to canonize *Neuman,*
Eva Benassi prayed to *the saint* to help *him recover skull fractures, lung*.

In this protocol recall is low and inaccurate. Only two points (7%) of the Kintsch structure can be credited (P 1 and P 2); due to partial recall of other propositions in the Kintsch list, the italicized ideas in the protocol cannot be credited. In the Meyer analysis, the correct content and relations can be scored in isolation and credited. The recall score from the Meyer approach is 16 (18%). The following is this same subject's recall in the delayed, unintentional condition.

Recall Protocol D 5

In order to canonize *Neuman—Eva B.*

For this protocol the Kintsch approach would assign one point (3%), while the Meyer approach would assign four points (4%). For subject 5, greater differentiation between the immediate and delayed recall performance can be made with the Meyer approach than the Kintsch system (i.e., Kintsch: 2 immediate vs. 1 delay; Meyer: 16 immediate vs. 4 delay).

The next protocol D 41 was given by a graduate student in the same experimental situation for the unintentional, delayed condition.

Recall Protocol D 41

Father *somebody prayed for* a (young boy) and he *was healed.* The people from the local community (in U.S.A. = Midwest) also noticed that this had happened for others he prayed for. (Therefore), a bishop wrote a resolution to nominate him for Sainthood to the Vatican. The Pope then authorized his sainthood.

Four points (14%) for this protocol were given in the Kintsch structure; those four points correspond to the only four relations in isolation (REQUEST, CANONIZE, AFTER, AFTER). Twenty-two points (24%) were given in the Meyer structure. Neither system can do more than circle and record the prior knowledge intrusions (see scoring system in Part 2). This subject has brought in a prior knowledge frame or schema about procedures to acquire saint status in the Roman Catholic Church. An approach like Beaugrande's (1980) would be more appropriate in this situation. The protocol was written by a bright adult attempting to give coherence to fragments of knowledge about the Saint text by using a prior knowledge frame. Protocols of this type are rare in prose learning experiments with well-organized text, college subjects, and immediate free recall conditions, but extremely interesting in showing the learner's contribution to learning and memory.

The final protocol was written by a 70-year-old female with a high school education and average verbal ability immediately after reading the Saint text.

Recall Protocol 0 1

They put their (faith) in prayer. In *all* (three) *instances* they *were on their deathbed* and after they prayed they attributed *getting well* to (faith) and incessant prayer to Bishop Newmann.
If you pray (faithfully), put (faith) in it, your prayers are answered. I don't remember exactly *each instance,* but in *each instance* they were really sick and the only answer to their (hope) was prayer.

Three points (10%) were scored on the Kintsch structure in Fig. 2.6, while 31 points (34%) were given in Fig. 2.7. In the Meyer system, the correct relationships can be credited even though there are few accurate specifics.

In summary, the Kintsch scoring system is more efficient for scoring immediate free recall protocols with close correspondence to text content. The Meyer approach is more time consuming, but more effective with less accurate recall protocols. (The correlation on total recall scores was .96 between the two scoring systems for all of the subjects that I had recall the Saint text [n = 9].) When studying delayed recall, recall of older adults, children, and less proficient learners, it would be advantageous to use the Meyer approach. Bieger and Dunn (1980) found this in their study of children; the Meyer approach could identify developmental differences in children that could not be detected with the less sensitive procedure. Also, for studying recall of older adults, particularly those with lower education and verbal levels, the Meyer approach would be more satisfactory. As seen from protocol 0 1, the Kintsch approach would record little information about recall of this type of older adult. In addition, the underlying logic processed by learners from expository text is better studied with the Meyer system. Also, the organization (top-level structure) in the text and in the recall protocol has been studied reliably with the Meyer approach (see scoring in Part 2).

PURPOSES AND PROBLEMS

In the beginning of this chapter, it was explained that identification of the structure of text is a necessary methodological tool for (1) scoring recall from text, (2) generating models of text memory and examining variations between the models and the structure and content contained in reader's recall protocols, and (3) identifying significant dimensions on which texts differ to clarify limits in generalizing experimental results. Two prose analysis procedures have been examined in depth on the issue of scoring; both provide reliable and useful scoring methods. Selection of a procedure depends on the type of subjects studied and the research questions asked. The Meyer approach, with the scoring of top-level structure in text and protocol and discrete scoring of relations and content, can better examine variations between the text and the reader's memory of it. Both approaches have a need to account for prior knowledge schemata and their interaction with the text.

Progress has only begun on the problem of identifying significant dimensions on which texts differ. The work on different discourse types has been discussed previously. Meyer and Rice (1982, 1983b) have recently collected some interesting data related to the distinction between the time series thrust of narration and the logical thrust of exposition.

Meyer and Rice had 300 young, middle, and old adults read and immediately free recall the supertanker passage and a passage of comparable length, levels, number of idea units, and number of details on the topic of railroads; copies of the passages can be found in Part 2. The railroad passage explained that businessmen favored the early development of the railroad and took steps to promote its development. Then, a brief history of railroad development was given. Finally, a brief description was given about different groups of people who opposed railroad development. Five versions of each passage were written (see Table 2.3). Two versions signaled the superordinate logical structure of the text (i.e., included all the signaling words listed in the content structure of supertanker text shown in Part 2); one version contained 22 specific names, dates, and numbers at the lowest level in the content structure and the other did not. For the version without specific details general terms were substituted (i.e., THOUSANDS for 200,000 and YEARS AGO for 1975). The other three versions did not signal the logical structure of the texts; one non-signaled version contained the details, one did not, and the third contained both details and signaling that emphasized these details (i.e., disastrous year of 1967).

Figure 2.13 (taken from Meyer, 1984a) models the selection of a superordinate schema for encoding a text into memory. This model results in different predictions for the supertanker and railroad texts as shown in Figs. 2.14 and 2.15. Some support for the models was obtained by examining expectations for the various versions of the two texts generated by subjects who read and commented on a version in a sentence-by-sentence manner (Meyer & Rice, 1982).

The recall data also support the model. For the supertanker passage, signaling increases recall of the superordinate logical relations and facilitates high usage of the problem/solution structure by subjects to organize their recall protocols. The levels effect is present for all versions of the passage for all age groups of adults. As seen in Table 2.3, without signaling, the information at the highest level, which includes these signaled or non-signaled relationships, becomes equivalent in recall to the next highest structural level; both the high and medium high levels surpass recall of the next two levels. Evidently, having to make inferences to identify the logic of the text reduces the probability of its recall which, in turn, reduces the recall of Levels 1–4 in the content structure. The detail manipulation appears to have little effect on the levels effect or organization of recall protocols for the supertanker passage.

In contrast both the signaling manipulation and the detail manipulation have large effects on these dependent variables for the railroad passage. As seen in Table 2.3, only one version shows the expected levels effect and high use of the comparison top-level structure in recall protocols; this is the version with signaled logical relations and no specific details. Moderate use of the comparison top-level structure and some levels effects occur for the conditions that change either one of these conditions, that is, signaling of the logic and specific details or no signaling and no details. No levels effects and relatively low use of structure for adults (Meyer, 1984a) result in the two conditions without signaling of the logical relations and addition of details. In fact, for these two versions, the lowest level (7–9) of structural information is recalled better than Levels 1–6.

The reason for the differential effect of these manipulations for the two passages appears to lie in differences among discourse types (e.g., D'Angelo,

TABLE 2.3

Changes in Levels Effect and Organization of Recall Protocols with Variations in Signaling the Text's Logical Structure and Emphasis and Addition of Details

Signal Logical Relations	Add Specific Dates & Details	Comparison, History of Railroads Text		Problem/Solution Supertanker Text	
		Levels Effect	Use of Comparison Top-Level Structure in Subjects Recall Protocols	Levels Effect	Use of Problem/Solution Top-Level Structure in Subjects Recall Protocols
Signal	Details	Some Levels Effect $\left(\begin{array}{l}\text{Y:}^b\ \text{H} > \text{L}\ \ > \text{MH} > \text{ML} \\ \text{M: L} > \text{H}\ \ = \text{MH} > \text{ML} \\ \text{O: H} > \text{ML} = \text{L}\ \ = \text{MH}\end{array}\right)$	Moderate Use (72%)	Levels Effect (H^a> MH > ML > L)	Very High Use (93%)
Signal	No Detail	Levels Effect (H > MH > ML> L)	High Use (80%)	Levels Effect (H > MH > ML > L)	Very High Use (92%)
No Signal	Signal Details	No Levels Effect (L > H = MH = ML)	Low Use (60%)	Some Levels Effect (H = MH > ML L)	Moderate Use (78%)
No Signal	Details	No Levels Effect (L > H = ML = MH)	Low Use (68%)	Some Levels Effect (H = MH > ML > L)	High Use (85%)
No Signal	No Details	Some Levels Effect $\left(\begin{array}{l}\text{Y: H = MH = ML} > \text{L} \\ \text{M: H} > \text{ML} = \text{MH} > \text{L} \\ \text{O: H} > \text{MH} > \text{ML} > \text{L}\end{array}\right)$	Moderate Use (78%)	Some Levels Effect (H = MH > ML > L)	High Use (88%)

[a] H = Highest Levels in Content Structure, Levels 1–4
MH = Medium High, Level 5
ML = Medium Low, Level 6
L = Low, Levels 7–9

[b] Y = young adults 18–32
M = middle adults 40–54
O = old adults 65–up

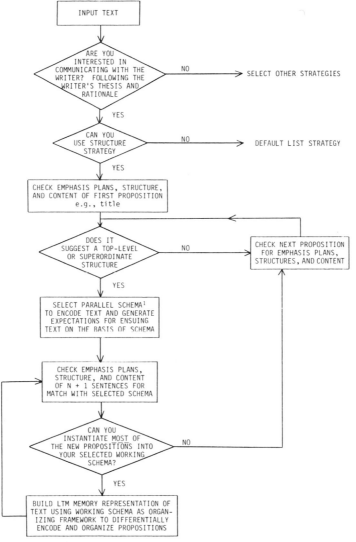

INPUT TEXT

ARE YOU INTERESTED IN COMMUNICATING WITH THE WRITER? FOLLOWING THE WRITER'S THESIS AND RATIONALE

NO → SELECT OTHER STRATEGIES

YES

CAN YOU USE STRUCTURE STRATEGY

NO → DEFAULT LIST STRATEGY

YES

CHECK EMPHASIS PLANS, STRUCTURE, AND CONTENT OF FIRST PROPOSITION e.g., title

DOES IT SUGGEST A TOP-LEVEL OR SUPERORDINATE STRUCTURE

NO → CHECK NEXT PROPOSITION FOR EMPHASIS PLANS, STRUCTURES, AND CONTENT

YES

SELECT PARALLEL SCHEMA[1] TO ENCODE TEXT AND GENERATE EXPECTATIONS FOR ENSUING TEXT ON THE BASIS OF SCHEMA

CHECK EMPHASIS PLANS, STRUCTURE, AND CONTENT OF N + 1 SENTENCES FOR MATCH WITH SELECTED SCHEMA

CAN YOU INSTANTIATE MOST OF THE NEW PROPOSITIONS INTO YOUR SELECTED WORKING SCHEMA?

NO

YES

BUILD LTM MEMORY REPRESENTATION OF TEXT USING WORKING SCHEMA AS ORGANIZING FRAMEWORK TO DIFFERENTIALLY ENCODE AND ORGANIZE PROPOSITIONS

[1]Type of schema selected here influences processes of selection and buffer rehearsal.

FIG. 2.13. Model for getting text information into organized schemata in memory.

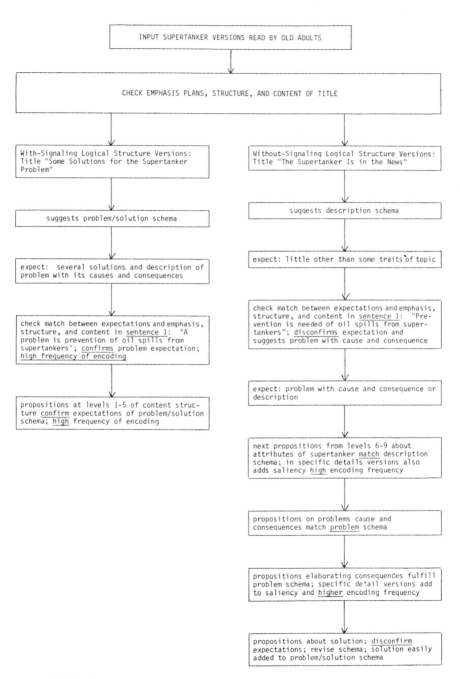

FIG. 2.14. Interaction of supertanker texts which vary in emphasis plans with structure strategy model for identification of memory schemata to organize text propositions.

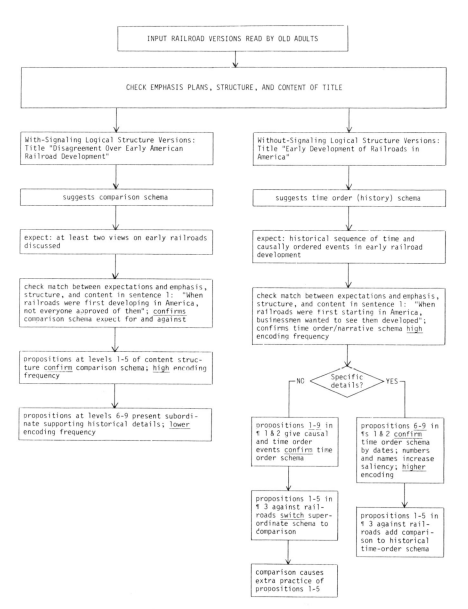

FIG. 2.15. Interaction of railroad texts which vary in emphasis plans with structure strategy model for identification of memory schemata to organize text propositions.

1976; Longacre, 1968). The supertaker text is a typical expository text; it presents logic to inform and persuade. However, the railroad text is a history with superordinate causal and descriptive relations and a comparison top-level structure. The original version of this text came from a ninth-grade social studies book (Bartlett, 1978). Histories fall under narrative discourse type. By signaling the logical relations in the railroad text, we emphasize the logic and may force a narrative (top-level structure of collection with a time line) into an expository format. By taking away the signals and leaving the details, the subjects may now process the text with their narrative schema, a collection of events on a time line. Signaling the logical structure and taking away the specific dates that tie down the time line allows subjects to process the text as an exposition; that is, they search for the logical structure to organize the text rather than utilize the narrative schema. Thus, the conditions in Table 2.3 without signaling of the text's logic and with details reorder the entire content structure.

Figures 2.16 and 2.17 show the different top-level structures for the railroad content when it is processed as a comparative expository text (Fig. 2.16) and when it is processed as narrative text (Fig. 2.17). Note the location of the dates in the two figures. For the comparative, expository processing schema (Fig. 2.16), the dates are the lowest level of the text; this is the schema thought to be utilized by the readers in the second condition listed in Table 2.3, signal logic, remove specific details. Here the levels effect is found. For the narrative processing schema (collection of descriptions on a time line, see Fig. 2.17), the dates are high in the structure; this is the schema considered to be in operation for the third and fourth conditions listed in Table 2.3, no signaling of logic, addition of specific dates and details. Figure 2.18 (from Meyer, 1984a) shows how the original content structure (Fig. 2.16) for the signaled versions is changed when the narrative processing schema becomes predominant.

Characterizing texts on the basis of discourse type, emphasis of logical structure, and amount and kind of details appear to be important steps in differentiating among text selections. An example of generalization problems for interpreting the research literature comes from an aging study with Meyer's (1975) passage entitled PARAKEETS: IDEAL PETS. Zelinski, Gilewski, and Thompson (1980) shortened the text by deleting the lowest levels (9–17) in the content structure; they found no age differences for the highest levels, but reported age-related deficits for recall of the details. Meyer and Rice (1981) used the entire text to study age differences; they also found no age deficits in recall of the highest levels in the structure, but found older adults recalled more specific details (levels 9–17) than young adults. The older adults recalled fewer major details that supported the logic of the text (levels 6–8). A review (Hartley, Harker, & Walsh, 1980) explained that one study (Zelinski et al., 1980) found deficits in old adults' recall of details, while another study (Meyer & Rice, 1981) reported superiority in recall of details by older adults. Analysis of the types of details used in the two studies revealed agreement of findings rather than disagreement. This resolution was possible since

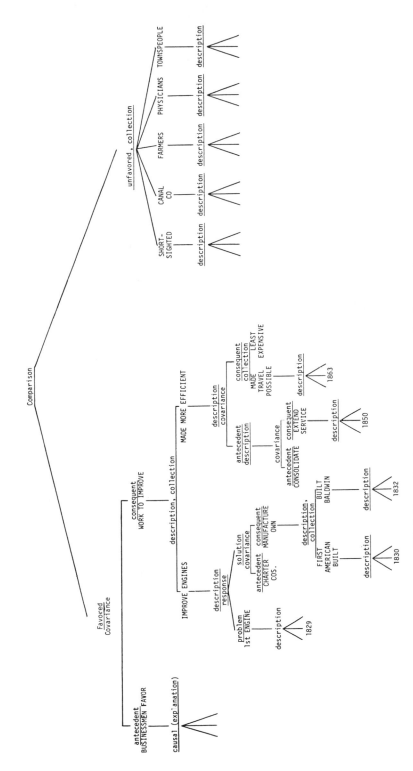

FIG. 2.16. Railroad superordinate structure analyzed as expository text.

59

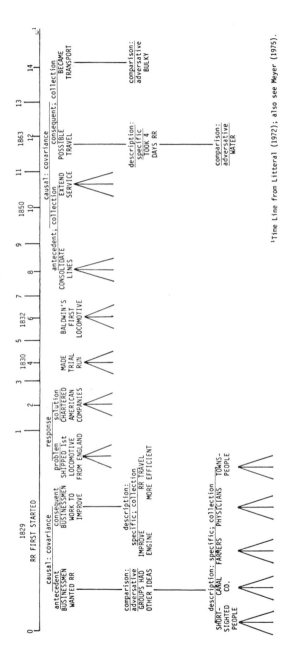

FIG. 2.17. Narrative schema applied to the railroad text.

[1]Time Line from Litteral (1972); also see Meyer (1975).

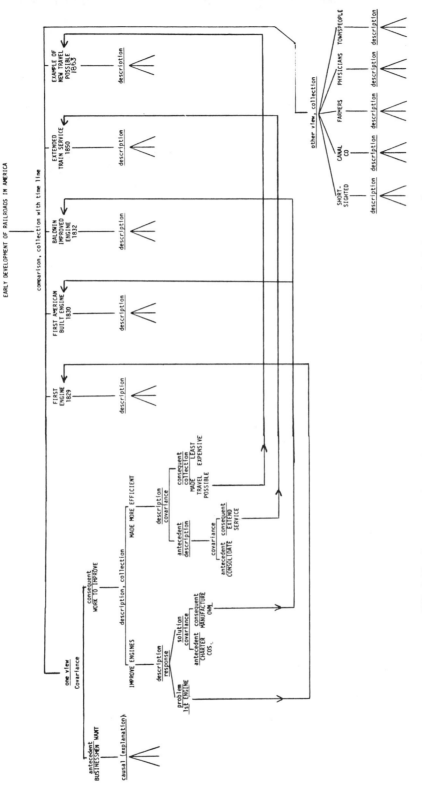

FIG. 2.18. Expectations for cognitive structure built for without-signaling logical superordinate structure + specific (± emphasized) details versions of the railroad text.

61

versions of the same passage were used; the problem would not be as easily resolved with different texts.

In conclusion, important steps have been made in the area of prose analysis. Methods for identifying text structure have resulted in an explosion of research in the area of prose learning. This research has increased our understanding of processes involved in reading and writing. There are still a number of unresolved problems. However, the potential appears great for this research area to continue in its contribution to our understanding of learning and memory.

ACKNOWLEDGMENTS

Some of the research reported in this paper was supported, in part, by Grant MH 31520 from the National Institute of Mental Health. I am grateful to G. Elizabeth Rice and Joel R. Levin for input that improved the quality of this chapter.

REFERENCES

Anderson, J. P. *Language, memory, and thought.* Hillsdale, N.J.: Lawrence Erlbaum Associates, 1976.

Aristotle. [*The rhetoric of Aristotle*] (L. Cooper, trans.). New York: Appleton-Century-Crofts, 1960.

Bartlett, B. J. *Top-level structure as an organizational strategy for recall of classroom text.* Unpublished doctoral dissertation, Arizona State University, 1978.

Bartlett, B. J., Turner, A., & Mathams, P. *Top-level structure: A significant relation for what fifth graders remember from classroom reading.* Paper presented at the annual meeting of the American Educational Research Association, Los Angeles, April 1981.

Beaugrande, R. *Text, discourse, and process.* Norwood, N.J.: Ablex, 1980.

Bieger, G. R., & Dunn, B. R. *Sensitivity to developmental differences in recall of prose: A comparison of two prose grammars.* Paper presented at the annual meeting of the American Educational Research Association, Boston, April 1980.

Brewer, W. F. Literary theory, rhetoric, and stylistics: Implications for psychology. In R. J. Spiro, B. C. Bruce, & W. F. Brewer (Eds.), *Theoretical issues in reading comprehension.* Hillsdale, N.J.: Lawrence Erlbaum Associates, 1980.

Britton, B. K., Glynn, S., Meyer, B. J. F., & Penland, M. Use of cognitive capacity in reading text: Effects of variations in surface features of text with underlying meaning held constant. *Journal of Educational Psychology,* 1982, *74,* 51–61.

Cofer, C. N., Scott, C., & Watkins, K. *Scoring systems for the analysis of passage content.* Paper presented at the annual meeting of the American Psychological Association, Toronto, August 1978.

D'Angelo, F. J. The search for intelligible structure in the teaching of composition. *College Composition and Communication,* 1976, *27,* 142–147.

Fillmore, C. The case for case. In E. Bach & R. Harms (Eds.), *Universals in linguistic theory.* New York: Holt, Rinehart & Winston, 1968.

Flower, L. Writer-based prose: A cognitive basis for problems in writing. *College English,* 1979, *41,* 19–37.

Frederiksen, C. H. Acquisition of semantic information from discourse: Effects of repeated exposures. *Journal of Verbal Learning and Verbal Behavior,* 1975, *14,* 158–169.

Frederiksen, C. H. Semantic processing units in understanding text. In R. O. Freedle (Ed.), *Discourse processes; Advances in research and theory.* Norwood, N.J.: Ablex, 1977.

Frederiksen, C. H. Discourse comprehension and early reading. In L. B. Resnick & P. A. Weaver (Eds.), *Theory and practice of early reading* (Vol. 1). Hillsdale, N.J.: Lawrence Erlbaum Associates, 1979.

Graesser, A. C. *Prose comprehension beyond the word.* New York: Springer-Verlag, 1981.

Grimes, J. E. *The thread of discourse.* The Hague: Mouton, 1975.

Halliday, M. A. K. Notes on transitivity and theme in English. *Journal of Linguistics,* 1968, *3,* 179–215.

Halliday, M. A. K., & Hasan, R. *Cohesion in English.* London: Longman, 1976.

Hartley, J. T., Harker, J. O., Walsh, D. A. Contemporary issues and new directions in adult development of learning and memory. In L. W. Poon (Ed.), *Aging in the 1980s.* Washington, D.C.: American Psychological Association, 1980.

Jessen, J. *Effects on reading comprehension of training delinquent adolescents how to identify the top-level structure in text.* Arizona State University master's thesis, in preparation.

Just, M. A., & Carpenter, P. A. A theory of reading: From eye fixations to comprehension. *Psychological Review,* 1980, *87,* 329–354.

Kintsch, W. *The representation of meaning in memory.* Hillsdale, N.J.: Lawrence Erlbaum Associates, 1974.

Kintsch, W. *Memory and cognition.* New York: Wiley, 1977.

Kintsch, W., & van Dijk, T. A. Toward a model of text comprehension and production. *Psychological Review,* 1978, *85,* 363–394.

Kintsch, W., & Vipond, D. Reading comprehension and readability in educational practice and psychological theory. In L. G. Nilsson (Ed.), *Perspectives on memory research.* Hillsdale, N.J.: Lawrence Erlbaum Associates, 1979.

Litteral, R. Rhetorical predicates and time topology in Anggor. *Foundations of Language,* 1972, *8,* 391–410.

Longacre, R. E. *Discourse, paragraph, and sentence structure in selected Philippine languages* (Vol. 1). Santa Ana: Summer Institute of Linguistics, 1968.

Mandler, J. M., & Johnson, J. S. Remembrance of things parsed: Story structure and recall. *Cognitive Psychology,* 1977, *9,* 111–151.

Meyer, B. J. F. *The organization of prose and its effects on memory.* Amsterdam: North-Holland, 1975.

Meyer, B. J. F. The structure of prose: Effects on learning and memory and implications for educational practice. In R. C. Anderson, R. Spiro, & W. Montague (Eds.), *Schooling and the acquisition of knowledge.* Hillsdale, N.J.: Lawrence Erlbaum Associates, 1977.

Meyer, B. J. F. Basic research on prose comprehension: A critical review. In D. F. Fisher & C. W. Peters (Eds.), *Comprehension and the competent reader: Inter-specialty perspectives.* New York: Praeger, 1981.

Meyer, B. J. F. Text dimensions and cognitive processing. In H. Mandl, N. Stein, & T. Trabasso (Eds.), *Learning from texts.* Hillsdale, N.J.: Lawrence Erlbaum Associates, 1984. (a)

Meyer, B. J. F. Organizational aspects of text: Effects on reading comprehension and applications for the classroom. In J. Flood (Ed.), *Reading comprehension.* Newark, DE: International Reading Association, 1984. (b)

Meyer, B. J. F. Signaling the structure of text. In D. H. Jonassen (Ed.), *The technology of text* (Vol. 2). Englewood Cliffs, N.J.: Educational Technology Publications, in press.

Meyer, B. J. F., Brandt, D. M., & Bluth, G. J. Use of the top-level structure in text: Key for reading comprehension of ninth-grade students. *Reading Research Quarterly,* 1980, *16,* 72–103.

Meyer, B. J. F., & Freedle, R. O. The effects of different discourse types of recall. *American Educational Research Journal,* 1984, *21,* 121–143.

Meyer, B. J. F., Haring, M. J., Brandt, D. M., & Walker, C. H. Comprehension of stories and expository text. *Poetics: International review for the theory of literature,* 1980, *9,* 203–211.

Meyer, B. J. F., & McConkie, G. W. What is recalled after hearing a passage? *Journal of Educational Psychology,* 1973, *65,* 109–117.

Meyer, B. J. F., & Rice, G. E. Information recalled from prose by young, middle, and old adults. *Experimental Aging Research,* 1981, *7,* 253–268.

Meyer, B. J. F., & Rice, G. E. The interaction of reader strategies and the organization of text. *Text,* 1982, *2,* 155–192.

Meyer, B. J. F., & Rice, G. E. *Effects of discourse type on recall by young, middle, and old adults with high and average vocabulary scores.* Paper presented at the National Reading Conference, Austin, Texas, December 1983. (a)

Meyer, B. J. F., & Rice, G. E. *Interaction of text variables and processing strategies for young, middle-aged, and old expert readers.* Paper presented at the American Educational Research Association Convention in Montreal, Quebec, Canada, April, 1983. (b)

Meyer, B. J. F., & Rice, G. E. The structure of text. In P. D. Pearson & M. Kamil (Eds.), *Handbook of research in reading.* New York: Longman, 1984.

Miller, J. R., & Kintsch, W. Readability and recall of short prose passages: A theoretical analysis. *Journal of Experimental Psychology: Human Learning and Memory,* 1980, *6,* 335–354.

Miller, J. R., & Kintsch, W. *Recall and readability of short prose passages.* Paper presented at the annual meeting of the American Educational Research Association, Boston, April 1980.

Miller, J. R., & Kintsch, W. Knowledge based aspects of prose comprehension and readability. *Text,* 1981, *1,* 215–232.

Rumelhart, D. E. Understanding and summarizing brief stories. In D. LaBerge & S. J. Samuels (Eds.), *Basic processes in reading: Perception and comprehension.* Hillsdale, N.J.: Lawrence Erlbaum Associates, 1977.

Rumelhart, D., & Ortony, A. The representation of knowledge in memory. In R. C. Anderson, R. Spiro, & W. Montague (Eds.), *Schooling and the acquisition of knowledge.* Hillsdale, N.J.: Lawrence Erlbaum Associates, 1977.

Stein, N. L. How children understand stories: A developmental analysis. In L. G. Katz (Ed.), *Current topics in early childhood education* (Vol. 2). Norwood, N.J.: Ablex, 1979.

van Dijk, T. A. Macrostructures and cognition. In P. Carpenter & M. Just (Eds.), *Cognitive processes in comprehension.* Hillsdale, N.J.: Lawrence Erlbaum Associates, 1977.

van Dijk, T. A. Relevance assignment in discourse comprehension. *Discourse Processes,* 1979, *2,* 113–126.

Zelinski, E. M., Gilewski, M. J., & Thompson, L. W. Do laboratory memory tests relate to everyday remembering and forgetting? In L. W. Poon, J. L. Fozard, L. S. Cermak, D. Arenberg, & L. W. Thompson (Eds.), *New directions in memory and aging: Proceedings of the George Talland Memorial Conference.* Hillsdale, N.J.: Lawrence Erlbaum Associates, 1980.

3

Structural Analysis of Science Prose: Can We Increase Problem-Solving Performance?

Richard E. Mayer

University of California, Santa Barbara

This chapter explores techniques for analyzing the structure and improving the understandability of science prose. Structure refers to a distinction between idea units that explain the mechanisms underlying a rule (explanative information) and idea units that do not (non-explanative information). Understandability is measured by tests of creative problem solving based on information in the passage. Science prose refers to a passage that contains a functional rule among two or more variables and an explanation of the underlying mechanisms. Three techniques are described for distinguishing explanative and non-explanative information: structural method, logical method, and empirical method. Then, research is provided concerning techniques that increase the subject's recall of explanative information, and thus the subject's problem-solving performance. These techniques include manipulating the reading strategy, such as by encouraging reflective or elaborative processing, and manipulating the text design, such as by organizing the text around key ideas or including a concrete model. Finally, some recommendations are suggested for improving science textbooks, with hopes that such recommendations will stimulate further research.

INTRODUCTION

Suppose we asked a student to read a scientific or technical passage—such as an explanation of how radar works, the process of photosynthesis, the concept of Ohm's law, or how to write simple computer programs. Further, suppose that the student has the reading skill to correctly "read every word." If we then gave that student a problem-solving test based on information in the passage, which factors would influence the student's performance? In short, which characteristics of the passage and of the learner are related to creative problem-solving performance? This question could be called the "creative reading problem," and is the focus of this chapter. Thus, this chapter is concerned with techniques for increasing students' understanding of scientific prose, where understanding is measured by tests of creative problem solving in the domain of the passage.

The present paper differs from other studies in several ways:

passages—the present paper focuses only on certain types of scientific passages (that we call "explanative") rather than on narratives or collections of facts.

independent and dependent variables—the present paper focuses on how reading strategy or text design manipulations influence problem-solving performance, rather than on how structural characteristics of idea units influence recall or retention score.

Each of these points is discussed in turn, below.

Passages

The text materials used in our project are somewhat restricted in comparison to some others in this symposium. Table 3.1 provides a taxonomy for classifying prose passages. The vertical dimension lists three kinds of information:

episodic: refers to passages that tell a story, including characters, events, states, and so forth, with units such as "John thanked Sue, and quietly left the room."

semantic: refers to factual information about the world, such as "There are three kinds of information: episodic, semantic, procedural."

procedural: refers to instructions about "how to do" something, such as "First add all of the scores for group 1 and for group 2."

These three types of information in passages correspond to the "traditional" distinctions among episodic, semantic, and procedural knowledge in memory.

The horizontal dimension of Table 3.1 provides an orthogonal division between two kinds of underlying structures for a text:

descriptive: refers to a text in which the key components or events are described but not explained, such as a list of facts, a series of events in a story, or a set of steps in an algorithm.

explanative: refers to a passage that expresses a functional relationship among two or more variables, and provides an explanation for the functional rule by referring to underlying mechanisms, such as explaining the t-test in terms of a sampling distribution, or explaining Ohm's Law in terms of electron flow.

This distinction is elaborated in the next section of this chapter, and is described in more detail elsewhere (Bromage & Mayer, 1981).

TABLE 3.1
Six Types of Passages

	Descriptive	*Explanative*
Episodic	A Saint	B Lion
Semantic	C Wagon	D Radar, Supertanker
Procedural	E	F Camera

The example passages provided for this symposium can be classified as follows: The "Saint" passage from Miller (1981) fits into slot A since it is a narrative in which there is no logical relation among the key events; the "lion" passage from Voss and Bisanz (1981) fits into slot B because it is a narrative in which the "motives" of animals are related to the key events. The "wagon" passage (Miller, 1981) fits into slot C because it provides a list of facts that seem to be unrelated; the "supertanker" passage (Meyer, 1981) fits into slot D because it provides facts that are supported by a set of explanative mechanisms such as "supertankers having only one boiler and one propeller," and so on. It should be noted that "supertankers" also has some narrative portions concerning histories of previous oil spills. Finally, our own work has focused mainly in slots D and F, with the radar passage falling into the D slot and a passage on how to use a camera (Bromage & Mayer, 1981) falling into slot F. In this paper, we limit our discussion to passages in slots A, C, and F, and in particular to the radar, supertankers, and lion passages. These are listed in chapter 11 of this volume, in Appendices A, B and C, respectively.

Independent and Dependent Variables

The second major distinguishing characteristic of the present project is our focus on problem solving as the dependent variable of interest, and strategy or text design modifications as the independent variable of interest. Table 3.2 provides a summary of the differences between two major research goals:

goal 1—to predict recall and retention performance, with typical independent variables of levels in a hierarchy or prior knowledge of the learner and typical dependent variables of recall or retention score.

goal 2—to predict creative problem-solving performance, with typical independent variables of advance organizers or adjunct questions and typical dependent variables of creative problem solving.

As can be seen in Table 3.2, a typical construct used in predicting recall is a structural schema—a generalized outline into which the specific content can be placed. However, the construct used in predicting problem solving is a functional schema or an "explanative representation"—this involves an integrated struc-

TABLE 3.2
Two Kinds of Research Goals

Typical Independent Variables	Typical Constructs	Typical Dependent Variables
GOAL 1: TO PREDICT RECALL OR RETENTION PERFORMANCE		

Passage Characteristics
  Level in text base
  Level in outline structure
  Level in story grammar
	Schema	Recall or
		Retention Performance

Learner Characteristics
  Perspective of reader
  Prior knowledge of reader
  Prior experience of reader		

GOAL 2: TO PREDICT PROBLEM SOLVING PERFORMANCE		

Passage Characteristics
  Headings for each section
  Advance organizer
  Signals for key ideas
	Explanative
	Representation
		Problem Solving Performance

Learner Characteristics
  Elaborative or reflective
    processing
  Question answering
  Note taking
  Prior knowledge of reader		

ture consisting of the key mechanisms and the causal relations among them. Thus, creative problem solving depends on the presence of certain "explanative" information in memory. A more complete definition and examples are provided in the next section of this chapter.

Framework for Research on Learning from Prose

Table 3.3 provides a general framework for discussing research on learning from prose. As can be seen, some typical independent variables in prose processing studies are passage characteristics, such as hierarchical structure of each idea unit or level of imagery of the words or use of headings; and learner characteristics, such as prior experience or reading strategy. Some typical dependent variables are recall, such as which ideas are remembered in a free recall test; retention, such as which answers are given on a forced-choice test covering the basic content; and problem solving, such as whether students are able to generate creative answers for transfer problems.

In order to provide a theory for relating passage and learner characteristics to test performance, a number of intervening constructs are helpful: encoding process, learning outcome, retrieval process. The encoding process refers to the process by which information in the passage is selected and integrated with knowledge in memory. Thus, encoding involves (1) various ways of selecting information from the passage, and (2) various ways of combining that information with existing knowledge. For purposes of the present paper, we make a distinction between two kinds of encoding processes:

addition encoding—in which subjects select factual details, and can relate them only in arbitrary ways, and

assimilation encoding—in which subjects select explanative information, and integrate this information.

Table 3.4 provides an example of the difference between addition and assimilative encoding for the radar passage. As can be seen, addition encoding involves selecting isolated facts and not integrating them; assimilation encoding involves selecting the explanations concerning transmitters, receivers, displays, and so on, and relating them to one another.

The learning outcome refers to the content and structure of acquired knowledge. The learning outcome for addition encoding will be an arbitrary set of facts or other idea units. For example, the learning outcome for radar may consist of unrelated ideas, such as "radar travels in straight lines," "the display seems like a second hand on a clock," "dropping a pebble in a lake causes ripples," and so forth. The learning outcome for assimilation encoding will be an integrated explanative representation that consists of all the key components and the causal relations among them. For the radar passage, the components are transmitter, pulse, object, receiver, display; and the relations involve how a pulse bounces off an object and how the time to travel is a measure of distance.

The retrieval process refers to the procedure for searching for information in memory and generating an answer for a question. The present paper focuses mainly on encoding processes.

Different learning outcomes may result in different kinds of test performance; a goal of this research project is to shed some light on this relation as well. In particular, integrated versus arbitrary learning outcomes may produce different patterns of performance on recall, retention, and problem solving tests. For recall

TABLE 3.3
General Framework for Research on Learning from Prose

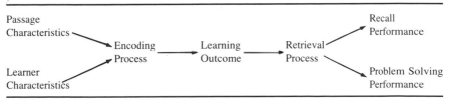

TABLE 3.4
Examples of Addition Encoding and Assimilation
Encoding for Radar Passage

	Selection of Details	Arbitrary, Isolated Relationships
Addition Encoding	travels in straight lines uses radio waves like dropping a pebble into a pond display has sweeping second hand earliest models in 1930	
	Selection of Explanations	Integrated, Unified Relationship
Assimilation Encoing	Transmitter sends out a pulse object reflects back some energy picked up by antenna makes bright spot on screen	

tests, subjects who have integrated learning outcomes should perform better on recall of the explanative information, but subjects who have arbitrary learning outcomes should perform better on recall of basic details and facts. For problem-solving tests, subjects who have integrated learning outcome should perform better on creative problem solving, while those who have arbitrary learning outcomes should excel on solving problems that are nearly identical to those given in the passage.

The remainder of this chapter consists of three parts: (1) *structural analysis of scientific prose* provides techniques for distinguishing between explanative and non-explanative information in a passage, (2) *improvement of problem-solving performance* provides summaries of research on whether techniques that enhance students' learning of explanative information also improve their problem-solving performance, and (3) *implications for text design and reading strategies* give some concrete examples of how to improve the radar, supertanker and lion passages.

STRUCTURAL ANALYSIS OF SCIENTIFIC PROSE

Unit of Analysis

The first step in analyzing scientific prose[1] is to determine a procedure for segmenting the passage into parts. In our studies we have generally used the

---

[1]The term "scientific prose" or "science passage" refers to cell D or F in Table 3.1. Thus, science passage means a passage that contains an explanation for a functional relationship. Certainly, not all passages in science textbooks fit this description; thus, this paper uses the term in a more restricted sense than is generally used.

"idea unit" as our unit of analysis. An idea unit expresses one action or event or state, and generally corresponds to a single verb clause. For some analyses, separate idea units are established for locations, times, organizational signals (such as "The next idea is . . ." or "The result of this . . .") and comments (such as "You should try to remember that . . ."). Thus, each idea unit consists of a predicate—either a verb or a location or a time marker—and one or more arguments. Unlike propositional analysis (Kintsch, 1974; Turner & Greene, 1977), our units do not give separate status to modifiers, conjunctions. connectives and the like. For example, consider the sentence:

It creates concentric circles of small waves that continue to grow outward

According to our segmentation procedure, the two main verbs are located: "creates" and "grow." Thus. this sentence is divided into two idea units:

1. It *creates* concentric *circles* of small waves
2. that continue to *grow* outward.

For purposes of scoring, the main predicate is underlined as well as any key subjects, objects, and so on. For the first idea unit "creates" and its object "circles" are underlined. For the second idea unit, only "grow" is underlined. To score a recall protocol, the information must first be divided into idea units as described above. Then, each idea unit from the passage is compared to each idea unit from the original passage. If an idea unit from the protocol contains the same keyword (e.g., "creates" and "circle") and expresses the same meaning as an idea unit from the original passage, that idea unit is scored as present.

As examples of the segmentation procedure, Appendices A, B and C (of chapter 11), respectively show how the radar, supertanker, and lion passage can be broken down into lists of idea units. The main predicate for each idea unit is underlined as well as any key arguments; information in parenthesis refers to signals or comments.

The next step is to distinguish between idea units that provide explanations of the mechanisms underlying the information (*explanative information*) and idea units that do not provide explanations of mechanisms (*non-explanative information*). For example, in an analysis of textbook lessons on Ohm's Law, White & Mayer (1980) found relatively few instances of explanative information, such as "Resistance is caused by collisions of electrons with atoms in the wire." For Ohm's Law, explanations involved the "flow of electrons," although several textbooks presented the formula without ever referring to the underlying mechanism.

Thus, explanative prose contains a functional rule that expresses a relationship among two or more variables. For example, in the radar passage, one rule is that the time for a pulse to return to the source is proportional to the distance of the remote object. In addition, explanative prose contains an explanation of the mechanisms that underlie this functional rule. For example, the explanative information in the radar passage concerns the nature of the bouncing radar pulse, as follows:

transmission—the transmitter sends out a pulse.

reflection—the pulse bounces off a remote object.

reception—the returning pulse is picked up by a receiver.

measurement—the direction of the pulse and the time for the pulse to return are measured.

conversion—these are displayed as location and distance.

These idea units refer to the major components in the radar passage—transmitter, pulse, object, receiver, display—and the relations among them. In Appendix A of chapter 11, an E indicates that the corresponding idea unit is part of the explanation.

For the supertanker passage, the key relation is "supertankers cause environmental damage" and the main explanative chain is as follows:

1. Supertankers are very large, thus difficult to maneuver.
2. Supertankers have only one boiler to provide power and one propeller to provide control.
3. In an emergency, difficulty of maneuvering increases and vulnerability of boiler and propeller increases.
4. If boiler or propeller malfunction, the ship loses power or control.
5. If the ship loses maneuverability, power or control, it can wreck onto sharp rocks.
6. When a supertanker wrecks, a storage area can be ripped open and oil will spill out.
7. When there is an oil spill, environmental damage results.

The main components are the propeller, the boiler, the size of the ship, the emergency, the storage area, the oil, the rocks. These idea units give the causal relations among the components. Note that not all the links are present in the passage. In Appendix B of chapter 11, an E indicates that the idea unit corresponds to one of the seven causal links given above.

For the lion passage, those idea units that describe motives provide a partial explanation for the events in the story. While a complete explanation is not possible, those idea units labeled with E in Appendix C of chapter 11 provide a partial explanation of the story. For example, the story makes more sense if the reader is aware that the tiger "wants to be leader of the animals."

The foregoing examples highlight the idea that the crucial link in explanative analysis is to have a procedure (1) for distinguishing explanative passages, and (2) for dividing an explanative passage into explanative idea units and non-explanative idea units. Unfortunately, the procedures are not yet well algorithmized. Clearly, the procedures for propositional analysis (Kieras, 1980;

Kintsch, 1974; Turner & Greene, 1977) are better specified. However, we have been able to provide explanative analyses of approximately 12 passages for research in our lab during the past several years. Thus, although the explanative analysis procedures need to be formalized, we have found them to be useable in our own research. In particular, we have used the following three methods for determining which idea units in a passage explain underlying mechanisms and which do not: structural method, logical method, and empirical method. These are described in the next three subsections.

Structural Method

The first step in structural analysis of a scientific passage is to locate the main functional relationship, or what White & Mayer (1980) call the "rule." A rule is an idea unit that expresses a functional relationship among two or more variables, events, and/or components. Three common kinds of rules are as follows:

Formal quantitative functions are formulas that specify a direct or inverse mathematical relationship among two or more variables. An example is the rule for Ohm's Law, "R = V/I," where R stands for resistance, V stands for potential difference, and I stands for current. Another example is "D = M/V" where D stands for density, M for mass, V for volume.

Informal quantitative functions are statements that describe a direct or inverse quantitative relationship among two or more variables, but do not specify the relation as a formula. An example is radar passage's statement that the time for receiving a reflected pulse is related to the distance of the remote object. A formula rule could be stated, such as $d = (t_r - t_t)/2s$, where d is distance of the object, t_r is the time of reception, t_t is the time of transmission, and s is the speed of the pulse. Another example, from a passage on how to use a 35mm camera (Bromage & Mayer, 1981), is the assertion that brightness of a picture depends on how wide open the shutter is.

Informal non-quantitative functions are statements in which a clear functional (or causal) relation is expressed, but which do not imply a direct or inverse quantitative relationship. For example, the supertanker passage asserts that environmental damage is caused by supertanker travel. Another example is contained in Stevens & Collins' (1977) tutor for teaching the causes of rainfall in the various geographic regions.

In all cases the rule is the most general statement of the observed relationship among variables; the rule does not explain the phenomenon but merely describes the functional relationship observed in the world. Thus, rules are like general behavioral laws in Skinner's (1953) approach to S-R psychology. For example, in the supertankers passage, the main rule gives a relation between the ultimate predicted variable, "environmental damage," and the original predictor variable, "supertanker travel." Other, intervening variables such as "oil spill," "storm," "large size," "single boiler" are not a direct part of the rule—although in another passage they *could* be part of the rule.

Once the rule has been located, the next step is to determine the mechanisms that explain the rule, or what White & Mayer (1980) call the "explanation." The explanation gives the underlying components, shows how they relate to one another, and how they can account for the rule. Thus, the explanation is like a cognitive theory for behavioral S-R laws. Each underlying component and the system uniting them must be identified: a component is an event or object that is part of the causal chain underlying the elements in the rule. For example, in the Ohm's Law example, one set of components consists of a battery that generates a potential difference between positive (+) and negative (−) poles, electrons that flow from the positive to the negative pole, a wire that carries them, a bulb that offers resistance by placing many atoms in the way of the flowing electrons, and so on. The system for uniting all these components is the circuit. The components in the radar passage consist of the transmitter for sending out pulses, the object for reflecting back some of the pulse, the receiver for picking up the pulse, a display for converting time to distance and representing it on a screen. The system for uniting all these components is the radio wave system. The components in the supertankers passage are features of the ship and the environment such as the propeller, boiler, and size of the supertanker. As can be seen, some judgment is required for locating the underlying components—electrons flowing in circuits for Ohm's Law, pulses bouncing around space for radar, and factors that limit a ship's maneuverability in storms for supertanker.

Third, the causal chain among the components must be spelled out. The causal chain is the functional relationship between the "predicted variable" and the "predictor variable" in the rule, with intervening functional relations included. For example, the rule "there is less current when resistance is increased" can be explained in a causal chain as "increasing the resistance provides more atoms for the electrons to collide into, more collisions slow down the flow of electrons and thus the current is less." Radar's rule that "the further away the object is, the further away will be the bright spot on the screen from the center" can be explained by the causal chain, "when an object is far away, it takes more time for the pulse to reach it and return, longer time is converted into longer distance on the screen, so that the bright spot will be further away from the center of the screen." For the supertanker rule, "environmental damage is caused by supertankers," an explanation includes the seven statements listed previously. Thus, the explanation involves adding intervening links in the functional relationship between variables in the rule.

The explanative idea units consist of all idea units that describe the components or the relationship with the variables in the rule. In addition, passages may contain analogies such as "echoes" in the radar passage or "water flowing in pipes" in the Ohm's Law passages. Statements about analogies or concrete examples are also explanative idea units if they refer to underlying mechanisms.

As can be seen, the structural method is based on a distinction between "description of functional rules" and "explanation of functional rules." This distinction has been of some interest to historians and philosophers of science (Bronowski, 1978; Cohen, 1960; Kearney, 1971; Westfall, 1977) and its relation to research on learning from science prose has been described elsewhere (Bromage & Mayer, 1981). To the extent that this distinction can be operationalized, it may be useful in research on prose processing. In addition, it must be noted that a large amount of prose currently in curricular materials cannot be subjected to this analysis because it does not describe a functional rule or an explanation of the rule.

Logical Method

The logical method involves determining the major transfer problem that the subject should be able to solve. Then, using a task analysis approach, the next step is to list all of the pieces of information in the passage that are needed in order to solve the problem. Thus, the analysis involves listing all idea units that serve as premises for solving the problem. Solving the problem should involve making inferences from the list of premise idea units. These premise idea units constitute the "explanative information" in the passage.

For example, in the radar problem a creative transfer question is, "How you increase the area under surveillance for a single radar station?" In order to answer this question, what must a learner know about radar? Some of the crucial idea units are the transmitter sends out a pulse, the pulse travels in straight lines so the earth's curvature interferes with long-range transmission, the pulse can bounce off an object, the reflected pulse can be picked up by a receiver, time and direction can be converted to measures of distance and location. Some possible answers are, "Use satellites to bounce the pulse on its way and from the remote object," or "Use relay stations on the ground to bounce the pulse." These answers are possible from making logical inferences from the given information.

For the supertankers passage, a possible transfer question is, "List all of the ways to prevent damage to the environment from oil spills." Answers based solely on the three suggestions given in the passage—better training, back-up boilers and propellers, and ground control stations—are not creative answers. Other answers that rely on the links in the causal chain are, "Don't travel in poor weather," or "Always travel in pairs," or "Use lots of tow boats."

Empirical Method

A third technique, which may be used as a validation technique for the foregoing two methods, is the empirical method. This method involves asking subjects to read a science passage, and then testing the subjects for which idea units are remembered and for creative problem solving.

Based on their performance on the test of creative problem solving, subjects can be ranked or partitioned into groups of good versus poor problem solvers. For each subject, there is a record of which idea units were recalled and of rating on the problem-solving test. The recall of the "good" problem solvers is then compared to the recall of the "poor" problem solvers. In particular, the goal is to determine which idea units the good problem solvers remember that the poor problem solvers do not seem to learn from the text. For example, in a passage on how to use a 35mm camera, subjects were asked to recall parts of the passage and to solve transfer problems such as how to set the camera for a pole-vaulter going over the bar on a cloudy day (Bromage & Mayer, 1981). The good and poor problem solvers did not differ in recall of the facts (such as what ASA stands for) or the rules (such as "to increase brightness of the picture, increase shutter size"), but they did differ in recall of the underlying explanations (such as "turning the focus knob moves the film away from the lens"). Thus, good problem solvers tended to differ from poor problem solvers mainly in recall of explanative material.

Another variation of this method is to use regression analysis, with the independent variables being recall of each type of information and the dependent variable being score on the problem-solving test. In the camera study (Bromage & Mayer, 1981), creative problem solving correlated well with recall of explanations but not with recall of other information. Thus, the explanative information is defined as the idea units that are related to good problem solving but not related to poor problem solving.

IMPROVEMENT OF PROBLEM-SOLVING PERFORMANCE

Predictions

The assimilation framework outlined in Table 3.3 suggests some basic predictions concerning the relation between recall of explanative information and problem-solving performance. In particular, students who are able to focus on the explanative information in science prose should be more likely to build integrated learning outcomes and hence to excel on tests of creative transfer. Two kinds of predictions may be offered:

prediction 1—subjects who recall the explanative idea units are more likely to excel on problem solving, while subjects who do not recall explanative idea units are less likely to excel on problem solving. The previously cited camera study (Bromage & Mayer, 1981) provides support for this prediction.

prediction 2—techniques or factors that increase recall of explanative information should also increase performance on problem-solving tests.

The goal of the present section is to explore techniques for increasing recall of explanative material and problem solving, i.e., to investigate the above prediction.

Although experimenters (or teachers) may be able to distinguish between the explanative and non-explanative information in a passage, there is no guarantee that a reader will be sensitive to this distinction. In fact, a reader may be presented with an explanative passage—one that contains underlying explanations of mechanisms—and may read it as a descriptive passage. Since most early reading exercises involve descriptive narratives or descriptive-semantic passages, subjects may develop expectations that are inefficient for science prose. It seems likely that many readers lack skills for dealing with science prose, i.e., for selecting explanative information. Thus, research on techniques for influencing how students read science is particularly needed.

Performance Measures

This section explores techniques that influence students' ability to use text information for creative problem solving. In particular, the focus of this section is on how to improve the students' problem-solving performance for tests based on prose information. The target behavior is transfer—the ability to use the information from the text in novel ways, going beyond what was presented in the passage. Examples of transfer questions were given in the subsection on "logical methods."

For example, a transfer question for the radar passage might be, "What can you do to increase the area under surveillance by a radar station?" Some possible answers are to bounce the radar pulse off of satellites, to bounce the radar pulse off of ground stations that circle the source, by using multiple radar stations and integrating the information by computer, and so forth. In order to answer these kinds of questions, a student needs to know the basic explanative information concerning transmission, reflection, reception, measurement and conversion. In addition, the learner must be able to put this information together in a new way. Thus, learning of the explanative information is a necessary but not a sufficient condition for creative problem solving.

The traditional measures of performance are score on a retention or recognition test, or number of idea units recalled. However, in the present studies, the measures used in this study include score of a test of creative transfer, and recall of explanative information.

In particular, the following subsections explore two basic kinds of techniques for influencing students' understanding of prose: (1) *processing strategies*—providing instruction or training in how to find the main explanative information in the passage, and (2) *text design*—organizing the text in a way that emphasizes or signals the main explanative information. These techniques are based on the idea that "what is learned" from the passage is related to creative problem-solving performance; specifically, when students are able to focus on the explanative information they should be better able to perform well on tests of creative problem solving.

Processing Strategy

"What is learned" from prose depends both on the passage itself and on how the learner processes the passage. In our lab we have been examining the effects of processing strategy on "what is learned" and on the ability to solve problems.

One set of studies (Mayer & Cook, 1981) compared a verbatim strategy to a reflective strategy for processing the radar passage (see Appendix A in Chapter 11). Subjects listened to a tape recording of the radar passage that was presented at a moderately slow rate of 70 words per minute. The passage contained pauses at natural boundaries, occurring at about every 4 to 7 words. Some subjects (verbatim processing group) were asked to shadow the passage; that is, during each pause, they were asked to repeat the words they had just heard. Other subjects (reflective processing group) were asked to listen to the passage and try to understand it; since the passage was presented at a slow rate, subjects had time to mentally connect segments of the passage during each pause.

In one experiment, all subjects took a verbatim recognition test, a retention test, and a transfer test. The retention test consisted of true-false questions covering the basic content of the passage, and revealed no differences between the two groups. Thus, if we had used only a standard measure of retention we would have concluded that processing strategy had no effect on "what is learned" in this study. However, as previously stated, a reflective processing strategy should encourage subjects to focus on the underlying theme, i.e., the explanative information, and result in superior transfer performance. Transfer was measured by asking subjects to answer essay questions that required using the presented information in a new way, such as the example question above. Similarly, a verbatim processing strategy should encourage subjects to focus on the details within each segment of the passage. Recognition tests asked subjects to choose which of a pair of sentences actually came verbatim from the passage, with the distractor having a synonym that replaced one of the original words. As predicted, there was a significant interaction in which the verbatim processing group performed better on recognition, but the reflective processing group performed better on transfer. One implication is that when the goal of instruction is creative problem solving, reflective strategies are better than "learning every word."

The foregoing differences in problem-solving performance were attributed to differences in what verbatim and reflective subjects learned from the passage. In order to test this idea more directly, an additional study was conducted. As in the previous study, one group engaged in verbatim processing and one in reflective processing of the radar tape. However, the test was to write down all that could be remembered from the passage. If we examine overall recall, we find that there is little difference between the two groups, and might conclude that "what is learned" is the same for the two processing groups. However, the problem-solving results suggest that the reflective processing group will recall more of the explanative information while the verbatim group will recall more minor details. To score the recall protocols, the passage was broken down into idea units (as shown in Appendix A of Chapter 11). As can be seen in Appendix A, some idea units were labeled as "explanative" and all others were not. Examination of the recall protocols revealed that the reflective group recalled much more of the explanative information than the verbatim group, but the groups did not differ on recall of other content information. Finally, a propositional analysis of the passage was performed based on Kintsch's system (Kintsch, 1974; Turner & Greene, 1977). Each idea unit was classified as either major (i.e., those with verbs, locations, times, causes, etc.) or minor (i.e. those giving modifiers, conjunctions, etc.). As predicted, the verbatim group performed better on recall of minor propositions than the reflective group, while the reflective group recalled more of the major propositions than the verbatim group. Thus, there is consistent evidence that the reflective group is able to focus on the explanative information and thus perform better on creative problem solving, while the verbatim group focuses on details within each word sequence and thus performs well mainly on verbatim recognition. This result is consistent with Morris, Bransford and Franks' (1977) theory of transfer appropriate processing, in which different encoding strategies support performance on different kinds of memory tests. In addition, however, the present studies extend the notion of transfer appropriate processing to tests of problem solving, and specifically focus on processing strategies that distinguish good problem-solving performance from poor performance.

In another set of experiments (Mayer, 1980) subjects read an eight-page booklet that described a simple computer programming language. Some subjects (elaboration processing group) were asked to answer questions after each page of the booklet; the questions required subjects to compare information in one part of the booklet to another or to describe information from the booklet in the context of a familiar situation. Other subjects (normal processing group) were asked to read the booklet as they normally read any textbook and to be prepared for a test.

To test problem-solving performance, subjects were asked to write and interpret programs that either were very similar to those in the booklet (near transfer problems) or required putting several statements together in a new way to form a loop (far transfer). If we looked at overall performance, combining near and far transfer, there would be no strong evidence of differences between the two processing groups. However, if elaborative processing leads to focusing on the explanative information, then the elaborative group should excel only on far transfer. The results revealed an interaction in which the elaborative processing group excelled on far transfer while the normal processing group excelled on near transfer or performed at the same level on near transfer as the elaborative processing group. Thus, there is replicatory evidence that processing strategies that encourage active integration of the information result in superior performance on tests of creative problem solving but not on tests of retention of specific content.

An implication of the foregoing result is that the elaborative processing encourages the learner to focus on explanative information, such as descriptions of the internal changes in the computer, whereas normal processing encourages the learners to focus more on surface details and symbols, such as the format for specific computer commands. In a separate series of experiments, subjects read the booklet under either elaborative processing or normal processing conditions, and then were asked to recall all they could about several portions of the booklet. In order to analyze the recall protocols, the text was broken into idea units with some being labeled as "explanative"—namely, those dealing with changes in the computer's memory, program list, output, or input stack. When overall recall was examined there was no clear superiority for the elaborative processing group, and hence no support for the idea that there were differences in "what is learned" between the two treatment groups. However, a closer investigation revealed an interesting pattern in which elaborative subjects excelled in recall of "explanative" information while the normal group excelled in recall of technical details. Thus, again, there is evidence that elaborative processing leads to subjects' learning more of the explanative information and hence to superior problem solving.

In another set of studies (Peper, 1979; Peper & Mayer, 1978), subjects viewed videotaped lectures on topics such as statistics, computer programming, or how a car engine works. Some subjects were asked to take notes on the key ideas in the lecture (notes group) while others only watched the lecture (no notes). Results indicated no overall differences in retention tests or recall tests for the two groups, and hence would have led one to conclude that there were no differences in "what is learned." However, a closer examination revealed a pattern in which note takers, especially low-ability subjects, tended to excel on tests of creative problem solving and recall of explanative information while non-note takers excelled on near transfer tests and recall of technical details. Thus, as in the foregoing studies, when subjects are asked to engage in an activity that encourages active integration of the incoming information, they are more likely to remember the explanative information and perform well on creative transfer tests.

Another set of studies investigated the effects of repetition on learning from a scientific passage. For example, when a technical or scientific passage does not make much sense, a typical approach is to read it again. What happens to the learning outcome when a passage is read over several times? In particular, does repetition have mainly a quantitative effect—in which the learner acquires more and more information—or does it also involve a qualitative effect—in which different kinds of information are acquired and the structure of the learning outcome changes?

In our lab, Bromage (1981) has conducted a study in which a passage on how to use an exposure meter was presented one, two, or three times. Recall of all kinds of information, including explanative information, increased with repetition. There was also a pattern in which the first exposure encouraged the subjects to focus on the first sentence in each paragraph, technical symbols and numbers (as in learning a list of nonsense syllables); while, by the third exposure subjects seemed to focus on other material related to the explanation. In addition, when an advance organizer was provided, the repetition effects were drastically reduced. Apparently, when the reader already knows what to look for, repetition is not as useful.

In addition, a similar set of follow-up studies was recently conducted in our lab. Subjects listened to a passage either on Ohm's Law or radar for one, two, or three presentations. The recall protocols after the first presentation emphasized symbols, numbers, and statements of definitions. Recall after the third presentation emphasized explanative information. Thus, there is some evidence that reading strategy changes with repeated exposure to a scientific passage. However, far more analysis is required before a change in processing strategy can be confirmed.

Another way to influence reading strategy may be through the use of behavioral objectives and adjunct questions. For example, objectives or adjunct questions that focus on explanative information should result in the student's ability to perform well on creative problem solving, while objectives and questions that focus on non-explanative information such as rote facts should restrict problem-solving performance. In a typical study (Mayer, 1975a) subjects read eight short lessons on set theory. After each of the first six lessons, subjects received questions that focused on non-explanative information such as formal definitions in verbatim form or questions that focused on explanative information such as a concrete model for representing the rules. An example of a concrete model is to describe combinatorial analysis in terms of R people sitting at N places at a table. On passages 7 and 8 all subjects received all kinds of problems. Subjects who expected non-explanative questions performed well on questions involving recall of details and simple retention of the formula. Subjects who expected explanative questions performed well on all kinds of problems including the transfer problems. The same effects were noted when the questions were given before each passage as an "instructional objective." Thus, there is consistent evidence that adjunct questions can serve to guide the learner's attention toward or away from explanative information in the passage.

Finally, Linda Cook and I are currently studying the idea that subjects with prerequisite knowledge are able to process scientific knowledge differently than those without such knowledge. In particular, subjects were asked to read a three-page passage concerning the concept of density, including the formula, density = mass/volume. Some subjects were given a brief introduction to the concepts of mass and volume prior to reading the passage (prior knowledge group) while other subjects were not given any prior knowledge (no prior knowledge group), and all subjects had little or no background in science. When subjects without prior knowledge were asked to recall the passage, they emphasized the formula in symbol format and produced many symbols in their protocols. When asked to solve creative problems based on the passage, subjects with no prior knowledge performed poorly. Subjects with prior knowledge tended to recall the formula in English rather than symbols and retained more of the explanative information in the passage; in problem solving, there was a trend in which subjects with prior knowledge performed better on certain questions but the differences have not yet been thoroughly tested. Apparently, when subjects read the density passage without an understanding of the concepts of mass and volume, they use a reading strategy that focuses on symbols, equations, and computing a numerical answer; however, when subjects who understand mass and volume read the density passage they tend to focus on the explanative prose rather than the symbols. Apparently, subjects are not always aware that their reading strategy is not efficient for problem solving, since many of the no prior knowledge subjects complained, "But I read every word."

Text Design

Another way to influence "what is learned" from a scientific passage is to design the passage in a way that focuses attention on the explanative information and that encourages the reader to integrate the information. The major idea explored in this section is that certain text organizations are more likely to lead to subjects' learning the explanative information and thus to creative problem solving.

The major research effort on text design carried out in our lab has involved the study of how advance organizers influence learning from scientific prose. In particular, we have used advance organizers that provide a visual or concrete model of the main components in the text—i.e. the components used in providing an explanation. For example, in the radar passage a concrete model would present a picture of the transmitter, object, receiver, display and pulse as shown in the bottom right corner of Table 3.4. For Ohm's Law an advance organizer might show an electric circuit with electrons colliding into atoms in the high resistance portion of the circuit. In our research on teaching various computer programming languages, we used an advance organizer that showed the functional units of the computer—memory scoreboard, input window, output pad, and program list. A summary of over a dozen advance organizer studies has been reported elsewhere (Mayer, 1979). In general, results are consistent with predictions cited above: There is clear evidence that advance organizers increase recall of explanative idea units (but not non-explanative idea units) and increase performance on creative problem solving (but not on simple retention).

In an earlier series of studies carried out in Jim Greeno's lab at the University of Michigan, we compared two ways of organizing mathematical prose. For example, in teaching the concept of binomial probability, a passage may begin with the formula and then tie general information to the formula later in the passage (formula-to-concrete organization) or the passage may begin with a discussion of concrete examples such as batting averages and probabilities of rainy days before moving on to the formula (concrete-to-formula). The results of a long series of over a dozen experiments on this issue have been reported elsewhere (Mayer, 1975b). However, the main results are consistent with the predictions cited above: for the formula-to-concrete organization, recall focused on symbols and formulas and creative problem solving was not present; for concrete-to-formula organization, recall focused on general explanative concepts and subjects excelled on creative problem solving.

In a recent study (Bromage & Mayer, 1981) we organized a passage on how to use a 35mm camera in two ways: One version organized the text around the major rules such as "to make the picture brighter, open the shutter" (rule organization), while the other version organized the text around the underlying components (explanation organization) such as "the particles on the film are influenced by how much light strikes them." In a previously cited study, subjects who excelled on problem solving tended to also recall more explanative information. Thus, a logical extension is to design a text that is organized so that it emphasizes the explanative information—i.e., the explanative organization version. As expected, subjects who read the explanation organization text recalled more of the explanative information and performed better on the tests of creative problem solving than the subjects who read the rule organization text. Apparently, text can be organized so that it signals the reader's attention to explanative information.

IMPLICATIONS FOR INSTRUCTION

The present paper has provided techniques for distinguishing explanative information from other types of information in science prose and has suggested techniques for improving how readers understand science prose. In this section, we offer some speculations concerning how to improve text design and text processing.

There have been numerous popular publications professing to teach authors how to write and students how to read. Most of the recommendations involve how to read or write narratives or reports, with little attention paid specifically to a focus of this chapter—scientific writing. Furthermore, most recommendations are at the level of sentence structure, grammar, punctuation, paragraph structure and the like, with little attention paid to a focus of this chapter—higher-level organization that leads to problem-solving skill. Finally, most recommendations are based on the traditional rules of English composition or on modeling the writings of "good authors," with little attention paid to a goal of this chapter—basing recommendations on empirical research. Thus, the present recommendations represent a supplement to the existing popular literature, because the present recommendations are focused primarily on science prose, on fostering problem solving, and being compatible with research.

Within the past few years, research on prose processing has allowed several researchers to offer suggestions for how to design prose. For example, Wetmore (1980, p. 4) listed seven principles for improving the "comprehensibility of text": "(1) Write unimportant ideas as briefly as possible, avoiding the use of vivid examples. (2) Tighten the relationship between examples and important concepts. (3) Turn negative statements of important principles into positive ones. (4) Enumerate important points. (5) Attach semantic labels to important concepts. (6) Underline technical terms. (7) Indicate straw men." In order to test these principles, Wetmore rewrote a passage on "biological taxonomies" so that it contained the same basic meaning as the original but was based on the seven recommendations. Results indicated that rewriting the passage increased recall of "important" idea units but not "unimportant" idea units, as compared to the original version.

Meyer (1975) has shown how "signaling" can improve recall of structurally important information. For example, use of the signals like "First . . . second . . . third . . ." or "The problem is . . . the solution is . . ." or "An example is . . ." can be used to improve recall of signaled information. In another study, Kieras (1978) found that paragraphs beginning with a topic sentence were easier to read than paragraphs that violated the "topic sentence first" convention.

Below are added some suggestions for how to increase the understandability of science text. These are offered as "good guesses" based on a general interpretation of our research, which should be subjected to additional testing. The suggestions are limited to improving understandability (as measured by tests of creative problem solving) for science prose (i.e., prose containing explanations of functional rules). The suggestions all are based on the idea that we should encourage the reader to select the explanative information in the passage and actively integrate that information with existing knowledge.

1. Early in the passage, present a concrete model that includes the major explanative components underlying the rule. (For example, in the radar passage, provide a diagram that shows the transmitter sending a pulse, an object that reflects that pulse, a receiver that picks up that pulse, and a display that converts time to a measure of distance.)

2. Signal the major explanative ideas in the text such as using numbers. (For example, "First, a pulse is sent out. Second, it strikes a remote object. Third, some of the energy returns. . . .")

3. Label the major explanative ideas. (For example, "The five steps of radar are transmission, reflection, reception, measurement, conversion."

4. Use headings and indentations to indicate the major ideas. (For example, each idea is present on its own line.)

5. Use high imagery, familiar examples and analogies for the explanative ideas. (For example, radar is like an echo.)

6. Show the mapping between examples (or analogies) and the major explanative ideas. (For example, "shouting is like transmission of a pulse".)

7. Organize the text around major ideas, and signal the organization through headings and introductory comments. (For example, the sections of the radar passage can be labeled: "Definition," "Devices," "Early Display Systems," "Modern Display Systems."

8. Shorten sentences about unimportant information, and avoid concrete examples or analogies for unimportant information. (For example, the "pebble in the pond" analogy may serve to distract from the overall theme.)

9. Provide definitions and examples of any prerequisite information. (For example, the reader should understand the concepts of a radio wave.)

10. To encourage active processing, include questions in the text that focus attention on explanative information. (For example, after each section questions could be inserted.)

11. To direct the reader's attention, include objectives that state creative problem solving as the goal of instruction. (For example, before the passage some creative transfer questions may be given as examples.)

12. Provide summaries that emphasize the key ideas so that the reader can compare his notes with the author's.

13. Underline technical terms and provide a glossary for all technical terms, so that unfamiliar words will not make smooth reading impossible.

14. Include repetition of important ideas in various wordings; build redundancy into the passage so that the reader has several opportunities to get exposed to the main points.

In general, these recommendations allow the author to tell the reader which ideas are the explanative ones. An example of a rewritten version of the radar passage is given in Appendix D of Chapter 11. Although it does not include all the recommendations, many are incorporated into the revision. It seems unlikely that any one of these recommendations is always "right"; however, the attempt to study them and revise them may provide the basis for a theory of science prose learning.

In conclusion, this chapter has shown (1) that it is possible to locate "explanative" information in a science passage, (2) that there are techniques for influencing whether readers build learning outcomes that are based on this explanative information, and (3) that techniques that encourage explanative processing also tend to increase problem-solving performance for material in the passage.

Thus, in response to the question, "Can we increase problem-solving performance?" this paper offers some reason to suppose the answer is yes. It is hoped that this summary of our preliminary ideas, and findings, and even our speculative recommendations, will foster additional research on how to improve the understandability of science textbooks.

ACKNOWLEDGMENTS

Preparation of this paper was supported by Grant SED-80-14950 from the National Science Program, Program in Research in Science Education. This paper was presented at the "Symposium on Expository Text: Comprehension and Structure" held on April 14, 1981 in Los Angeles at the annual meetings of the American Educational Research Association.

REFERENCES

Bromage, B. K. *Effects of repetition on technical learning.* Santa Barbara, CA: University of California at Santa Barbara, Ph.D. Thesis, 1981.

Bromage, B. K., & Mayer, R. E. Relationship between what is remembered and creative problem solving performance in science learning. *Journal of Educational Psychology,* 1981, *73,* 451–461.

Bronowski, J. *The common sense of science.* Cambridge, Mass.: Harvard University Press, 1978.

Cohen, I. B. *The birth of new physics.* Garden City, N.Y.: Doubleday Anchor, 1960.

Kearney, H. *Science and change.* New York: McGraw-Hill, 1971.

Kieras, D. E. *Abstracting main ideas from technical prose: A preliminary study of six passages.* Tucson: University of Arizona, Department of Psychology, Technical Report No. 5, 1980.

Kieras, D. E. Good and bad structure in simple paragraphs: Effects on apparent theme, reading time, and recall. *Journal of Verbal Learning and Verbal Behavior,* 1978, *17,* 13–28.

Kintsch, W. *The representation of meaning in memory.* Hillsdale, N.J.: Lawrence Erlbaum Associates, 1974.

Mayer, R. E. Forward transfer of different reading strategies evoked by test-like events in mathematics text. *Journal of Educational Psychology,* 1975, *67,* 105–109. (a)

Mayer, R. E. Information processing variables in learning to solve problems. *Review of Educational Research,* 1975, *45,* 525–541. (b)

Mayer, R. E. Can advance organizers influence meaningful learning? *Review of Educational Research,* 1979, *49,* 371–383.

Mayer, R. E. Elaboration techniques that increase the meaningfulness of technical text: An experimental test of the learning strategy hypothesis. *Journal of Educational Psychology,* 1980, *72,* 770–784.

Mayer, R. E., & Cook, L. K. Effects of shadowing on prose comprehension and problem solving. *Memory & Cognition,* 1981, *9,* 101–109.

Meyer, B. J. F. *The organization of prose and its effects on memory.* Amsterdam: North-Holland, 1975.

Meyer, B. J. F. *Strengths, weaknesses, and uses of various prose analysis techniques.* Paper presented at Symposium on Expository Text, American Educational Research Association, Los Angeles, April 14, 1981.

Miller, J. *A knowledge-based model of prose comprehension: Application to expository text.* Paper presented at Symposium on Expository Text, American Educational Research Association, Los Angeles, April 14, 1981.

Morris, C. D., Bransford, J. D., & Franks, J. J. Levels of processing versus transfer appropriate processing. *Journal of Verbal Learning and Verbal Behavior,* 1977, *16,* 519–533.

Peper, R. J. *The effects of elaborative activities on cognitive structure: Note taking, summary note taking, and meaningful adjunct questions.* Santa Barbara, Calif.: University of California at Santa Barbara, Department of Psychology, Ph.D. Thesis, 1979.

Peper, R. J., & Mayer, R. E. Note taking as a generative activity. *Journal of Educational Psychology,* 1978, *70,* 514–522.

Skinner, B. F. *Science and human behavior.* New York: Macmillan, 1953.

Stevens, A. L., & Collins, A. *The goal structure of a socratic tutor.* Cambridge, Mass.: Bolt, Beranek & Newman, Report No. 3518, March 1977.

Turner, A., & Greene, E. *The construction and use of a propositional text base.* Boulder, Colo.: Institute for the Study of Intellectual Behavior, Technical Report No. 63, 1977.

Voss, J. F., & Bisanz, G. L. *Models and methods used in the study of prose comprehension and learning.* Paper presented at the Symposium on Expository Text, American Educational Research Association, Los Angeles, April 14, 1981.

Westfall, R. S. *The construction of modern science.* Cambridge: Cambridge University Press, 1977.

Wetmore, M. E. *Improving the comprehensibility of text.* Paper presented at the National Reading Conference, San Diego, December, 1980.

White, R. T., & Mayer, R.E. Understanding intellectual skills. *Instructional Science,* 1980, *9,* 101–127.

4 Thematic Processes in the Comprehension of Technical Prose

David E. Kieras

University of Arizona

This chapter is concerned with thematic processes in the comprehension of technical prose. Thematic processes are those which identify or derive the important content in a piece of prose, distinguishing it from the details or irrelevancies. Technical prose is a subtype of expository prose that is concerned with presenting information of a technical nature. Some examples: Table 4.1 is an excerpt from a military equipment manual; Table 4.2 is an excerpt from a biochemistry textbook; and Table 4.3 is an example of the simplified technical passages used in some of the experiments and modeling work summarized below.

Technical prose, and expository prose in general, have not been studied by cognitive psychologists as heavily as story materials. However, understanding how people comprehend technical prose is of immense practical importance in the educational domain. Most textbooks are technical prose. They present densely packed complex information that is usually highly novel to the reader. Oddly enough, much of the comprehension research done by educationally oriented researchers has focused on story-like materials, rather than on technical or expository prose. This could be a serious failure of scientific strategy, because

TABLE 4.1
Excerpt from a Military Equipment Manual

Two alternating current systems and one direct current system supply electrical power to the aircraft. The 115/200-volt ac power supply systems consist of two identical engine-driven ac generating systems and an external power receptacle. The dc power supply system consists of a dc bus powered either by a 24-volt 5-ampere-hour battery or two 28-volt dc transformer-rectifiers.

TABLE 4.2
Excerpt from a Biochemistry Text

Pancreatic RNase is a highly specific endonuclease which splits the bond between the phosphate residue at C-3′ in a pyrimidine nucleotide to C′5 in the next nucleotide in sequence. The basic feature of its actions is an intramolecular attack on the phosphodiester bond using the 2′-OH group to form an obligatory 2′:3′ cyclic phosphate intermediate, which is then hydrolysed by the enzyme to give pyrimidine 3′-phosphates either as free nucleotides or as a terminal nucleotide residue in an oligonucleotide.

there could be many important properties of technical prose that are only weakly represented by story materials.

A second area where technical prose is important is in technical documentation such as instruction or maintenance manuals. Almost every piece of technology, such as a computer, an automobile, a military airplane, or even a hand tool, is accompanied by one or more documents that describe how the device works, how to use it, and how to maintain it. The volume of this technical prose, which is vital to the functioning of our society, probably exceeds that of any other type of prose. Expert opinion seems to be that technical manuals are not very comprehensible. But given the paucity of scientific knowledge about how prose of this type is understood, it is hard for any agency or manufacturer to propose, justify, or enforce substantial standards.

So the study of technical prose is extremely important for practical reasons. It is also important for scientific reasons, in that technical prose could have its own distinctive features. The function of this chapter is to summarize a set of results on the properties of technical prose, with a focus on the thematic processes by which a reader abstracts the gist, or important content, from technical prose. The Bovair and Kieras Chapter in Part 2 of this book presents a detailed set of rules for the construction of propositional representations for technical prose materials.

TABLE 4.3
The *Metals* Passage

Different cultures have used metals for different purposes. The ancient Hellenes used bronze swords. The ancient Greeks used copper shields. The Hellenes invaded ancient Greece before the Trojan War. The bronze weapons that were used by the Hellenes could cut through the copper shields that were used by the Greeks. Because the color of gold is beautiful, the Incas used gold in religious ceremonies. The Incas lived in South America. However, the Spaniards craved the monetary value of gold. Therefore, the Spaniards conquered the Incas. Because aluminum does not rust and is light, modern Western culture values aluminum. Aluminum is used in camping equipment. Titanium is used in warplanes and is essential for spacecraft. Warplanes are extremely expensive. Titanium is the brilliant white pigment in oil paints that are used by artists.

THEORETICAL PROPERTIES OF TECHNICAL PROSE

Technical prose has several important properties that differ from the simple prose or story materials usually studied. One of course, is that technical prose abounds in novel concepts or terms that appear to require additional processing to understand (Just & Carpenter, 1980; Kintsch, Kozminsky, Streby, McKoon, & Keenan, 1975). Two other major features of technical prose are its distinctive referential forms and the relative unimportance of schemas compared to story materials.

Reference in Technical Prose

Technical prose follows some important syntactic rules that became obvious while applying the simulation reported in Kieras (1977, 1981b) to understanding technical prose (see Kieras, 1983). The most prominent has to do with noun phrase structure and the referential rules for given and new information (Clark & Haviland, 1977). Simple prose follows straightforward rules for the use of the determiners *a* and *the* to mark new and given referents (Kieras, 1977). In technical prose the classification of given and new information needs to be expanded to include the distinction between whether a referent is given or new with regard to not just the prior text, but the reader's knowledge as well. Consider in the following brief text how the status of referents is signaled syntactically:

> The corona is the outer atmosphere of the sun. The corona is a superheated gas that consists mostly of atoms of hydrogen. Scientists think that the corona expands away from the sun, forming the solar wind.

In the first sentence, despite the definite determiner, *corona* is completely new to most subjects, and so is the concept of the *outer atmosphere of the sun*, although it can be assembled from the concepts of the *atmosphere* and the *sun* which are known. Notice that the *sun* is a unique concept which can be presumed known to everybody, and so the definite determiner is appropriate. But the same determiner is used in *the corona* and *the outer atmosphere of the sun*, which are both *not* known. Perhaps the definite determiner on a knowledge-new item signals that the concept referred to is important enough to be presumed, meaning that the reader should immediately attempt to learn it. In contrast, *a superheated gas* is textually new and knowledge-new, although it, too, can be assembled from known concepts, but it has a "normal" indefinite determiner. Notice that *atmosphere, hydrogen,* and *scientists* lack determiners altogether, and are textually new and probably knowledge-given.

Thus, it appears that technical prose follows some definite, but complicated, rules in the use of determiners. First, technical prose contains many general concepts that are usually referred to with plural nouns with no determiners.

Second, indefinite noun phrases are relatively infrequent, and usually signal referents that are both textually new and knowledge-new. Third, definite noun phrases may mean any of the following: (a) textually-new knowledge-given items, such as *the sun;* (b) textually-new knowledge-new vocabulary terms that are important, such as *the corona;* (c) a textually new and knowledge-new assemblage of given concepts that is important, such as *the outer atmosphere of the sun;* (d) an ordinary reference to a textually given item, such as *the corona* in the second sentence of the above example.

The consistent use of determiners in simple prose makes referential processing of noun phrases relatively simple. In contrast, the multiple use of definite determiners in technical prose has made it difficult to devise simple parsing and reference rules for handling noun phrases. The overall implication is that the coherence and referential requirements of understanding technical prose are substantially more difficult than those of simple prose.

Some additional referential features of technical prose can be briefly listed; these are described in more detail in the Bovair and Kieras Chapter in Part 2 of this book. First, technical prose oftens refers to quantities and measurements whose semantic content can be very complex even though few words are involved. Second, references to *sets* of items are frequent and convey very complicated semantic content as well. Third, technical prose often uses complex names or labels for items whose meaning is not a simple combination of constituent meanings. For example, *X-ray star* could be propositionalized as (MOD STAR RAY) (MOD RAY X), but it seems that the actual semantic content is closer to *a star that has something to do with X-rays,* and the appropriate referential form is actually a single concept label: X-RAY-STAR. A more pointed example is the term *black hole* in the astronomical context. This is not simply a hole that is black. While there may be analogous problems in simple prose or in stories, they are very common and very distinctive in technical prose.

Facts, Schemas, and Text Grammars

A distinction can be made between three kinds of information involved in prose comprehension: *text grammars, content schemas,* and *content facts.* Content facts are the simple propositions conveyed by the prose, either explicitly, or implicitly. Since the propositions from connected discourse share arguments, the whole set of propositions from a passage will form a connected mass, in precisely the way described by the conventional theoretical notion of a semantic network. At this level information does not have any superordinate organizational content (cf. Anderson, 1980). An example of a passage full of such specific items from the domain of biochemistry is shown in Table 4.2. Notice the apparent lack of any higher-order structure in such material; rather it is just a series of facts.

A content schema represents a superordinate organization of a mass of possible content facts. It, like a schema in general, represents a commonly recurring configuration of things, but by a content schema is meant a configuration of facts, and not a configuration of textual elements, which is what a text grammar represents. For example, most biochemists probably have a content schema for the concept of an *enzyme,* in which the common facts that are known about specific enzymes are specified, such as the substrate, binding site, products, and so forth. If the reader has such a schema, it could be applied to the comprehension of the passage in Table 4.2.

A text grammar is a schema (in the general sense) that represents a frequent configuration of textual elements, defined independently of specific content, and thus operating at the level that van Dijk (1972) termed *textual surface structure.* For example, a paragraph may follow a pattern of first stating the topic, then expanding on it, and then stating a conclusion. Textbooks about writing give many such patterns. The important point is that facts in essentially any content area can be stated in these different forms, meaning that the text grammar forms are essentially independent of the passage content. This marks the distinction between content schemas and text grammars.

The major theoretical idea in the story-based comprehension research is that of the story grammar or schema (Kintsch, 1977; Mandler, 1978; Mandler & Johnson, 1977; Rumelhart, 1975, 1980). This notion captures the idea that a story conforms to a stereotypical pattern. The reader is supposed to be able to use knowledge of this pattern to make comprehension a very rapid and efficient process, consisting mostly of matching items in the input with "slots" in the schema-pattern.

It has not been clear whether a story grammar is a content schema or a text grammar. It could be argued that most stories follow certain content schemas having to do with events occurring over time, and there are text grammars that specify how to take these events and generate story passages (cf. Brewer & Lichtenstein, in press). There may be some modifications of event ordering, and other things, in order to produce different types of stories, but there is, nonetheless, a strong relationship between the order of the story events and the order that the events appear in the story text. This correlation between content schemas and text grammars in stories apparently has resulted in these two concepts being confused with each other, considerably diminishing the precision and theoretical value of the schema concept.

However, the major feature of technical prose is that it usually contains content that is mostly novel to the reader, as in a textbook, and so the reader cannot apply content schemas to any great extent. This suggests that comprehending technical prose is not primarily a matter of matching the content to a previously known pattern, but rather involves dealing with the passage content at the level of the individual propositions conveying the content. Once the reader has these propositions internally represented, he or she may go on to add inferred propositions to them, organize them into some more meaningful form, and delete and modify them. But such processes are much more "bottom-up" than the strongly "top-down" processing represented by the use of a schema. However, technical prose, like all prose, still follows some text-grammar rules that govern the placement and order of information within a piece of text.

So, the claim is that a piece of technical prose follows a text grammar, contains many novel content facts, and may or may not have a content schema that is available to the reader, but there need be no strong relationship between these three kinds of information. Even if a content schema is available to the reader, this schema provides no strong expectations about the text grammar form of the material that are of value to the reader. For example, there appear to be no textual rules that state in what order one must describe the facts about an enzyme. This relative independence of content facts, content schemas, and text grammar marks a major difference between technical prose and story materials.

A Theoretical Framework

The schema notion seems to have very little applicability to the comprehension of technical prose. A more appropriate theoretical approach would be one emphasizing those aspects of comprehension that work at the level of processing individual content facts. The best currently available theoretical framework is the macrostructure theory developed over the last decade by Kintsch and van Dijk (Kintsch, 1977; Kintsch & van Dijk, 1978; van Dijk, 1977a, 1977b, 1980). This framework, with some modifications, is used to organize the results summarized in this chapter.

The macrostructure theory can be summarized in its main content very briefly: When a reader comprehends a passage, he or she first extracts the *microstructure* of the passage, and then applies *macrorules* to derive a passage *macrostructure*. The microstructure represents the immediate content of the passage, while the macrostructure represents the gist, or important content, of the passage. The macrorules essentially "boil down" the large number of micropropositions to the relatively small number of macropropositions. The macrostructure propositions are then given priority for storage in memory. Upon recall, the macropropositions are expanded to produce a paraphrased, and possibly distorted, version of the original passage.

The focus of this chapter is on the process of abstracting the thematic content. In terms of the macrostructure theory, this process is that of building the passage macrostructure. However, to address this process more directly, it is necessary to modify the macrostructure framework, because the goal of the original Kintsch and van Dijk work has been to explain the properties of prose recall, and not explicate the process by which the macrostructure is built (but see van Dijk & Kintsch, 1983). As a result, the macrostructure building process has been studied only indirectly, with the mechanisms of memory storage and retrieval intervening. Also, the macrorules as defined thus far have not been worked out in any detail, and, more importantly, the macrorules operate only on the semantic, or propositional, content of the passage. Other influences, such as the textual surface structure, on the macrostructure-building process need to be included.

The framework proposed here is that the macrostructure-building process uses the propositional content of the passage primarily, but is guided by the passage surface structure. In particular, there seem to be common text grammars that specify where in the passage important information is likely to appear, and there are several surface-level signals that mark individual items of information that are important to the passage macrostructure. Thus, abstracting the main content from a passage depends not only on the semantic content of *what* is said, but also on the specifics of *how* it is said, both at the level of the whole passage, and at the level of individual sentences. Results that support this point of view are summarized below followed by a brief description of a simulation model that illustrates this view of the macrostructure-building process.

METHODS FOR STUDYING THEMATIC PROCESSES

The results summarized below concern how subjects identify the main content of a passage. They were obtained by using an experimental task that is substantially different from the usual recall task. The subject is given a paragraph-length passage to read, and then is asked to provide a statement of the important content of the passage. This is either a statement of the *main item,* which is required to be a title-like noun phrase that indicates what the passage is about, or a statement of the *main idea,* which is a brief complete sentence that states the point, or main idea, of the passage.

Of course, other measures could be used to assess what subjects think is the important content. Subjects could write summaries, but due to the relatively large size and lack of constraint on summaries, they would be very difficult to analyze rigorously and in detail. A very simple approach is to have subjects underline or otherwise indicate the important content in a passage (see Kieras, 1979a). But this response mode constrains subjects to choose only the explicit content, rather than being allowed to express inferred ideas. Hence the main idea and main item tasks strike a good balance between constraining the volume and form of a subject's response while leaving the content relatively free.

The details of the instructions for these response tasks are important. The main pitfall in asking subjects to produce any kind of summary for a passage is that many of them will produce responses that are uninterpretable and useless. These are of roughly three kinds: overgeneralized responses, such as *mankind has advanced* for the passage shown in Table 4.3; obscure responses, such as an actually observed one of *The superb practice force of any item may fail,* for a passage describing the Battle of Jutland (see Kieras, 1980b); and inappropriate responses, which are "flip," humorous, or "creative," such as *Wasting taxpayer money* for the biochemistry passage. While such useless responses occur to some extent regardless of the instructions, it is important to reduce their frequency to a low enough level to allow the underlying consistency between subjects to emerge.

A great deal of the useless variation between responses can be eliminated by insisting that subjects follow the constraints on form appropriate to the main item or main idea task, along with a constraint on length. By insisting on the correct grammatical form of the response, subjects are compelled to generate at least one whole proposition in the main idea task, or a single referent in the main item task. We have usually limited responses to 80 characters, which is the length of one line on the standard video computer terminal used in the experiments. By limiting the length of the response, subjects are forced to seriously pick out the important content, since they cannot simply put down everything they think of. The inappropriate responses can be mostly eliminated by instructions to state in the response something that was "actually mentioned" in the passage. This instruction appears just to encourage subjects to take the task seriously, because there are few cases of purely verbatim responses. Essentially the same result can be obtained with less apparently confining instructions by simply asking subjects to avoid generating the inappropriate type of useless response mentioned above, and to produce serious and thoughtful responses.

The main idea or main item responses can be analyzed for content, and then examined to determine what content of the passage is being used to produce the response. A simple way to analyze the response content is to sort the responses into rough categories. If this is done blind to a within-passage manipulation, the results will be reasonably reliable. However, there is no way to compare responses obtained for completely different passages with this simple method, since the grain of the categories cannot be controlled. A more detailed approach, based on a propositional analysis of the responses, is described in Part 2.

Reading times for the entire passage, or its individual sentences, can be collected and related to the passage structure and content of the responses. Reading times can reveal changes in the amount of macroprocessing required by a passage as a function of manipulations in the form or content of the passage. By using a sentence-at-a-time procedure, considerable detail can be obtained about effects of passage manipulations on reading time. However, such effects may not always appear (see Kieras, 1978, 1980a, 1981a), and so a theoretical analysis may not be clearly testable in terms of reading times. The basic problem is that a manipulation that changes the *outcome* of a mental process does not necessarily significantly alter the amount of time required to arrive at that outcome!

A final measure used in the work summarized here is importance ratings. Subjects engage in a main idea response task, but in addition, they rate the individual passage sentences for importance to the main idea. This can be done either with the entire passage present, or in a sentence-at-a-time paradigm.

RESULTS

Properties of Macrostructure

The Relation of Main Items and Main Ideas.   Theoretically, the main item is simply the most important referent in the passage, whereas the main idea is the most important proposition. Presumably, there should be an intimate relationship between these two response forms. In Kieras (1979b) subjects generated either main idea or main item responses for paragraphs taken from *Scientific American* articles. One way the two response types were related was that popular main items were also popular surface subjects of main idea responses, corresponding to the theoretical intuition that main ideas are *about* main items. A second result was that producing the main item of a passage is much easier than producing the main idea. The average completion time per paragraph for the main idea task was about 40 seconds longer than for the main item task. While subjects had to write more in the main idea task, it seems unlikely that this large amount of time was required simply to write a sentence as opposed to a noun phrase. Rather, the additional time must reflect a substantial difference in the processes involved. Identifying the main referent involves simply singling out the main argument of the mass of propositions, whereas finding the main proposition would require finding the set of arguments that is most important, and then picking the most important relation connecting them. A similar idea at a simpler level appears in the results of Manelis (1980) and Kieras (1978), which suggest that in simple passages thematic content responses may be determined by which proposition is "central" in the passage structure.

Global Coherence.   One of the defining features of a well-formed passage is global cohrence, the property of the passage being *about* one thing (van Dijk, 1979, 1980). Kieras (1981a) found that subjects could generate main item statements for passages that had a single major referent much faster and more consistently than for passages that had three major referents. While this is a simple result, examination of the content of the responses showed that when there is a single major referent, subjects show a strong tendency to simply report it as the main item. But when there is more than one major referent, many readers infer another referent that subsumes the three that were presented in the passage. Thus readers can arrive at a global topic even though the passage does not have an obvious explicit one. This extra macrolevel processing takes additional time, and its dependence on an individual reader's idiosyncratic inferences results in less consistency between subjects.

Different Types of Macrostructure.   Passages differ in the relationship of their macrostructure to the microstructure. This issue is best illustrated by referring to the rules that van Dijk (1977a, 1977b, 1980) proposed for the construction of macrostructure. The two most important rules are (1) *Generalization:* A set of propositions consisting of instances of a single general concept can be replaced by the single general proposition; (2) *Construction-Integration:* A series of propositions can be replaced by their consequence. For example, a passage describing the history of the Watergate affair can be summarized by the statement *Nixon resigned because of Watergate*. Van Dijk made a distinction between whether this consequence proposition was explicitly present in the passage and only had to be selected (integration), or had to be constructed by inference (construction). A further distinction concerns whether the macroproposition is entailed by, or entails, the micropropositions; but this distinction is not important here.

Kieras (1980b) examined several passages whose main ideas were based on either the generalization rule or the construction-integration rule. The conclusion was that subjects were faster, and more consistent, at producing main idea statements for the generalization passages than for the construction-integration ones. Moreover, if the main idea was explicitly stated in the passage, readers were generally faster and more consistent in their responding than if it were absent, and tended to reproduce the presented main idea in their responses. But this effect was considerably weaker in the construction-integration passages, suggesting that these macrostructures were considerably more difficult to identify than the generalization structures.

In terms of macroprocessing, in the generalization passages, the reader must simply recognize the pattern of instances of the same general concept. The macrostructure of such a passage is thus a rather simple single-layer tree. Providing the generalization explicitly almost guarantees that the pattern will be recognized. But, in the construction-integration passages, the reader must be able to deduce or recognize the chain of antecedents and consequences in the argument being presented, or the final outcome of a sequence of events. This reasoning is more complex compared to the generalization passages, and so is slower, and depends more on the idiosyncratic knowledge and reasoning process of the individual subjects, and so is less consistent. Even an explicit main idea may not be recognized as such by all subjects.

Signals for Thematic Content

Sentence Topic-Comment Assignment.   Whether a referent appears as the surface subject of passage sentences affects its thematic importance, since this syntactic position usually carries a marking of the sentence topic. Perfetti and Goldman (1974, 1975) found that readers assign the topical referent of a passage to the surface subject position of a sentence, and will use the passive voice, if necessary, to do so. Van Dijk (1979) also pointed out that the assignment of items to either the topic or the comment position in a sentence will be determined by the global topic of the passage. However, Kieras (1981a) showed that topic-comment assignment could influence main item responses by using passages in which the sentence topic-comment assignment could be reversed, while essentially preserving the propositional content. This result shows that sentence surface structure can influence the macrostructure-building process.

Weak Thematic Markers.   If the main idea is otherwise clear, marking it may have little or no effect. Some explicit markers of thematic content are titles, which name the main item explicitly, and marking phrases, such as *the important point is that . . . ,* which signal important propositions.

Effects of such markers on memory for passage content appears to be weak. By using passages with two possible global topics and manipulating the title of the passage, Schallert (1976) showed effects of titles on recognition memory, but not recall, and Kozminsky (1977) found recall effects that were fairly weak. Likewise, the reported effects of marking phrases on recall (Meyer, 1977) also appear to be weak.

These markers also appear to be weak in influencing thematic responses. In unpublished work, Kieras used passages that had already been used in main item and main idea tasks, and so a strong and a weak main idea or item could be chosen for each one. A comparison was done for both main idea and main item response tasks, using titles and marking phrases, with either no marker, marking the strong idea or item, or marking the weak item or idea. Although other effects appeared, such as the initial mention effect (see below), no effects of the marking condition on main idea or main item statements appeared at all. The conclusion is that when the thematic content is reasonably clear, the reader considers the markers as redundant, or simply ignores them.

Since the effectiveness of various forms of emphasis is an important practical question in document design (cf. Charrow & Redish, 1980; Swarts, Flower, & Hayes, 1980), further study of them would be worthwhile. But it could be that their effects, if any, are transient. That is, titles or marking phrases may influence which hypotheses about the main idea are considered before the final result is arrived at, but this final result may not reflect the markers at all. Of course, if the material were almost incomprehensible, the reader might be forced to rely much more heavily on these markers. But notice that the results described above were obtained using technical passages that were in fact very unfamiliar to readers. Apparently, the semantic content of the passages was usable, in spite of its unfamiliarity, and dominated the surface-level markers. This is an instance of the principle of "shallow semantics" discussed below.

The Role of Text Structure

Location of Important Information.   At the level of text structure the concern is where in the passage the important information appears, as opposed to the nature of the information itself. One question is whether there are standard locations for important information.

Kieras (1979a) reported one study in which subjects produced main idea statements for naturally occurring paragraphs from *Scientific American*. When the content of the responses was compared to the original paragraph sentences, it appeared that when the source of the main idea could be assigned to a single sentence, this source was mostly the beginning of the passage, and to some extent, the end, forming a U-shaped function with a very high peak on the first sentence. Another study in Kieras (1979a) had subjects underline the most important sentence in page-length passages. Again the bulk of the responses were on sentences that occurred first or early in the passage, then with another, smaller peak at the end of the passage. Finally, Kieras (1980b; Kieras & Bovair, 1981) collected importance ratings for individual sentences in paragraphs in which the main idea was either explicitly presented in the first sentence, or was absent. When present, this initially presented main idea sentence was very heavily chosen as the most important sentence. However, with some passages, sentences appearing at the end were also considered fairly important, especially if the initial main idea sentence was missing.

These results suggest that the initial position in a passage is the most popular location for important information. However, a second location is the end of the passage. As suggested in Kieras (1980b), some passages appear to have a structure consisting of an argument leading up to a conclusion.

The Function of Initial Mention.   The results summarized above, along with theoretical considerations (e.g., Carpenter & Just, 1977), suggest that the initial position in a passage is uniquely important. Serial position effects in prose recall have been observed (see Meyer, 1977), but these have usually been attributed to the fact that the important information tends to appear first; since important information is recalled better, then the first information will be recalled better than later information. However, the initial position could serve to mark information as important, making initially mentioned information thematically important to some extent just by virtue of its position.

This hypothesis was confirmed by the studies reported in Kieras (1980b), using the main idea and main item tasks. The approach was to keep passage content constant, and only vary what was marked as thematic by variations in order of mention. The results show that an item or idea is considered more thematically important if it is mentioned first than if mentioned later in the passage. Hence readers appear to expect the main idea or item to appear first in a passage, and so assign thematic importance to first-appearing items. Thematic effects produced by initial mention also appear in recall, and cannot be attributed to simple serial position effects (Kieras, 1981c).

Accompanying the thematic role of initial mention, there is also an important reading time effect of initial mention. The first sentence in a passage is usually read for a relatively long time. This has been demonstrated in two ways (see Kieras, 1981b, 1982; Kieras & Bovair, 1981). The first is studies manipulating the presence or position of an explicit initial main idea sentence in using a sentence-at-a-time paradigm. The sentence that follows the explicit initial main idea sentence is either the second sentence in the passage if the initial main idea is present, or it is the first sentence if the main idea is absent or elsewhere. The reading time on this sentence is longer if it appears first than if it appears second. The second demonstration is that the first sentence is read longer than would be predicted from its propositional content and its length. That is, using either a statistical model for sentence reading times, or a simulation model that represents parsing, referential, ad representational processes, the reading time on individual sentences can be predicted (see Kieras, 1981b, in press). Consistently, the first sentence in a passage is underpredicted by such variables; significantly better fits are obtained by including a variable that represents that a sentence occupies the first position. With the passages studied, the estimate thus obtained of the additional time required on the first sentence is about 1 to 2 seconds.

Hence, the first sentence of a passage appears to require more processing than one would expect based on its other properties. The model-based assessment rules out some of the simple explanations, such as the need to define many new referents in the first sentence. Rather, there seems to be a unique function of the first sentence, perhaps one of "setting the stage," or preparing the comprehension system to process a large body of information about a certain subject matter. If the first sentence actually contains the main idea, then this stage-setting function will be maximally successful.

A good example of the importance of a main idea appearing in the initial position is the results in Kieras (1982; Kieras & Bovair, 1981). These were obtained using passages based on the generalization macrorule presented in a sentence-at-a-time paradigm, and with main idea responses, reading times, importance ratings, and think-aloud protocols being collected. In these passages, the main idea was a generalization, either explicitly stated in the initial position, or absent, and the body of the passage consisted of a series of instances of the generalization with some irrelevant information present as well. The instances were ordered along some dimension, such as in chronological order. Table 4.3 is an example.

As mentioned above, these passages have a fairly simple macrostructure. But the initial appearance of the main idea can make a substantial difference in the processing that subjects do while reading through the passage. In brief, if an obvious candidate for the main idea appears first, then the reader need only adopt it, and then test if for adequacy while reading the remainder of the passage. If not, the reader must attempt to formulate a main idea while reading, and be prepared to reformulate it whenever a poor fit is noticed. As a result, some sentences may appear important when first read, but then later turn out to be merely details or irrelevant. Thus, the initially presented explicit main idea "protects" the reader against the irrelevant material or alternative possible main ideas, and so simplifies arriving at the main idea.

Shallow Semantics

Macrostructure processing can apparently proceed largely on the basis of only limited, or shallow, knowledge of the semantics of the subject matter. Given the nature of the technical prose materials studied in this work, one would suspect that the typical college student would be completely bewildered by the subject matter, and so be forced to rely almost exclusively on surface level cues to the important content. However, subjects display a marked ability to comprehend the propositional structure of a passage at a shallow level, and then use this information to identify the important content. This level of comprehension actually corresponds very closely in concept to the process engaged in by a prose researcher of constructing a propositional representation of a passage. Such a representation has many useful properties, such as its connectivity structure, even though it does not represent the full semantic content of the passage.

Subjects appear to be able to use the shallow semantic information to identify the main content even when the surface-level markers are inconsistent, or when the content is quite unfamiliar. This assertion is supported by the following observations: (1) Surface-level markers do not dominate subjects' responses; semantic considerations often override the surface markers. For example, in Kieras (1980a), initial mention influences the choice of main item, but usually about a third of responses were not of the marked item. As one subject commented during debriefing, of course the topic should appear first, but sometimes the obvious topic was elsewhere! (2) Even in very unfamiliar material, subjects are fairly consistent in assigning importance ratings to strongly relevant and irrelevant sentences, even if they are fairly inconsistent in their main idea responses (Kieras, 1980b, 1982; Kieras & Bovair, 1981). (3) Subjects can use some of the easily inferred semantic properties of sentence terms to relate an individual sentence to a main idea. For example, in an experiment using think-aloud protocol methods (Kieras, 1982; Kieras & Bovair, 1981), a subject read the sentence *A hydrogen maser clock has pico-second accuracy for 10 million years* in a passage about how modern timekeeping devices are extremely accurate, and commented, "I don't know what a hydrogen maser is, and I don't know what a pico-second is, but this is obviously a clock that is extremely accurate." (4) Subjects can use simple superordination relationships presented in a passage to choose main items, even when the terms are novel. For example, in Kieras (1980a, 1981c), a passage was used in which *biotransformation* was described as a general process, and *the liver* was introduced as an organ that performs biotransformation, and then further described. Subjects showed a very strong tendency to prefer the general, but unfamiliar, term as the passage topic, even though propositions about *the liver* were much better recalled.

Thus, it appears that at least a major portion of macrostructure processing can go on without full or deep understanding of the passage content. Hence, the role of general knowledge in these tasks is relatively limited; when subjects can pick out central propositions using only superficial or simple semantic relations, more detailed knowledge is not necessary. Note that the college students used as subjects in this and most prose research probably have developed during their long history of schooling a specialized skill for dealing with complex verbal material without fully understanding it.

A MODEL OF THEMATIC PROCESSES

Thematic content is specified by a combination of information at different levels and of different types. Overall, it seems that the most important information source is the propositional structure of the passage content. In the discussion above of shallow semantics, it was pointed out how people can deal with complex technical prose material without full comprehension of it. Apparently they make use of the superficial characteristics of the semantics and the propositional structure.

That the propositional and semantic content of a passage would be the most important determinant of macrostructure is in the spirit of the original macrostructure theory. But a major modification of the theory is that surface level features, both of individual sentences, and the passage as a whole, also influence the macrostructure-building process. This is an important point. Ever since Sachs's (1967) paradigmatic study showing the apparent unimportance of surface form, the cognitive psychology of comprehension has tended to ignore surface structure in favor of semantic content. However, it seems clear that surface structure is normally chosen by the writer in an attempt to convey a desired meaning most efficiently. The reader is expecting these conventional uses of surface structure, and so bases his or her meaning interpretation on them to some extent. Hence an adequate theory of comprehension must explain not only how readers derive the semantic content of sentences and relate them to already known information, but also how the surface form of the input is used to guide or streamline this process.

A model conforming to this theoretical approach is reported in Kieras (1982), and will be briefly described here. Although the model is rather limited, having been applied only to the generalization passages described above, it does illustrate the principle that main ideas can be derived with only shallow semantic knowledge, and through the use of textual and sentence surface structure as well as the propositional content.

The model takes the propositionalized form of the passage as input, and processes it one sentence at a time. It sets up and maintains a hypothesized or candidate main idea for the passage, and may modify this in the course of processing the passage. The final candidate is then reported as the main idea. For simplicity, the model uses only a single proposition as its main idea, which is supposed to correspond to the main proposition of a subject's main idea response.

The model adopts a candidate main idea usually after reading the first sentence, and then tests each succeeding sentence for being an instance of the main idea generalization. If so, the model proceeds to the next sentence. But if not, the model may, depending on a decision rule, compute a new candidate main idea. Different rules for this decision to revise the main idea are possible. For example, a revision attempt is indicated if a large sentence that is unrelated to the current main idea is encountered, or the model has accumulated more propositions that are unrelated to the main idea than are related.

The model implements van Dijk's generalization macrorule with rules for summarizing a set of specific propositions with a general one, basically by finding sets of propositions whose arguments are concepts that share supersets. Thus, the general knowledge required by the model is quite limited, consisting of little more than set-superset relations for the arguments. The fact that so little knowledge is required may explain much of the shallow semantics phenomena described above.

But detailed general knowledge seems to be quite important in the microlevel inferential process required before the macrolevel processing can be applied. For example, in the Table 4.3 passage, the sentence *The Hellenes used bronze swords* cannot be related to the main idea *cultures use metals* until an inference is made. The model performs this inference with a rule in general knowledge that if X uses Y, and Y is made of Z, then X uses Z. This rule yields *Hellenes used bronze*, which can be related to the main idea. Hence, before the macroprocesses can work, the microlevel elaboration and inferences must be done. Intuitively, such inferences should be driven by the current hypothesized main idea. But the model simply makes all inferences that its knowledge allows before proceeding, a simple, but rather inefficient and unrealistic process.

The model relies heavily on the surface structure of the passage and the sentences in arriving at a main idea. At the sentence level, the model makes use of the main proposition in a sentence more than the others, because the main propositions are usually more relevant to the global main idea. The designation of a proposition as a main proposition is done on the basis of the sentence surface structure; it is the one representing the main verb relating the surface subject to the surface object.

The role of textual surface structure is very important in that the initial mention convention is a central part of the model's processes. If the model determines that the first sentence main proposition contains general terms, it concludes that the first sentence contains a candidate main idea, and so adopts the main proposition as its first main idea. It then selects a relatively conservative criterion for deciding when to revise the main idea on subsequent sentences. Thus, if a passage has an explicit first sentence main idea, the model adopts it, and will keep it unless it encounters a severe degree of inconsistent information in the remainder of the passage. This corresponds to the general result in Kieras (1982; Kieras & Bovair, 1981) that the first sentence main idea is usually produced as the main idea response, with few revisions occurring along the way.

In contrast, if the first sentence is not general, the model either generalizes the first sentence to get a candidate main idea, or waits until the second sentence is processed, and then generates a main idea. These two strategies were observed in the think-aloud protocols reported in Kieras (1982; Kieras & Bovair, 1981). The model then selects a liberal, or "hair-trigger," criterion for revising the main idea. Since the model had to "guess" a main idea, it must be prepared to abandon its initial guess quickly in favor of another. As observed in human readers, the result is that when the main idea is not explicitly stated, the model changes its mind relatively often.

CONCLUSION

The model represents the combination of the use of both surface and semantic information in arriving at a main idea. The surface information acts to guide the process by which the semantic content is used. In Kicras (1982) more detail is provided on how the model conforms to human subjects in terms of reading times, importance ratings, and think-aloud protocols. While the model has some serious problems and limitations, its overall performance is encouraging.

It should be noted in closing that the model operates using only the text grammar knowledge of generalization passage structure, and the content facts in the passage and in its general knowledge. It does not make use of content schemas. Hence the most notable feature of the model is that without using the currently popular schema notion, it does a plausible job of accounting for an important form of prose comprehension. It is able to do this, of course, because schemas do not seem to be very important in technical prose. Perhaps the long-standing emphasis on the schema theory of comprehension has served its purpose, and now we will profit by developing a broader set of theoretical approaches to comprehension processes.

ACKNOWLEDGMENT

The work summarized in this paper was supported by the Office of Naval Research, Personnel and Training Research Programs, under Contract Number N00014-78-C-0509, NR 157-423.

REFERENCES

Anderson, J. R. *Concepts, propositions, and schemata: What are the cognitive units?* Technical Report 80-2, Carnegie-Mellon University, May, 1980.

Brewer, W. F., & Lichtenstein, E. H. Event schemas, story schemas, and story grammars. In J. Long & A. Baddeley (Eds.), *Attention and performance IX*. Hillsdale, N.J.: Lawrence Erlbaum Associates, 1981.

Carpenter, P. A., & Just, M. A. Integrative processes in comprehension. In D. LaBerge & S. J. Samuels (Eds.), *Basic processes in reading: Perception and comprehension*. Hillsdale, N.J.: Lawrence Erlbaum Associates, 1977, 217–241.

Charrow, V. R., & Redish, J. C. *A study of standardized headings for warranties*. Document Design Project Technical Report No. 6, American Institutes for Research, February, 1980.

Clark, H. H., & Haviland, S. E. Comprehension and the given-new contract. In R. O. Freedle (Ed.), *Discourse processes: Advances in research and theory* (Vol. 1). Norwood, N.J.: Ablex, 1977.

Just, A. M., & Carpenter, P. A. A theory of reading: From eye fixations to comprehension. *Psychological Review*, 1980, *87*, 329–354.

Kieras, D. E. Problems of reference in text comprehension. In M. Just & P. Carpenter (Eds.), *Cognitive processes in comprehension*. Hillsdale, N.J.: Lawrence Erlbaum Associates, 1977.

Kieras, D. E. Good and bad structure in simple paragraphs: Effects on apparent theme, reading time, and recall. *Journal of Verbal Learning and Verbal Behavior*, 1978, *17*, 13–28.

Kieras, D. E. *Initial mention as a cue to the main idea and main item of a technical passage*. Technical Report No. 3, University of Arizona, July, 1979. (a)

Kieras, D. E. *The relation of topics and themes in naturally occurring technical paragraphs*. Technical Report No. 1, University of Arizona, January, 1979. (b)

Kieras, D. E. Initial mention as a signal to thematic content in technical passages. *Memory & Cognition*, 1980, *8*, 345–353. (a)

Kieras, D. E. *Abstracting main ideas from technical prose: A preliminary study of six passages*. Technical Report No. 5, University of Arizona, August, 1980. (b)

Kieras, D. E. The role of major referents and sentence topics in the construction of passage macrostructure. *Discourse Processes*, 1981, *4*, 1–15. (a)

Kieras, D. E. Component processes in the comprehension of simple prose. *Journal of Verbal Learning and Verbal Behavior*, 1981, *20*, 1–23. (b)

Kieras, D. E. Topicalization effects in cued recall of technical prose. *Memory and Cognition*, 1981, *9*, 541–549. (c)

Kieras, D. E. A model of reader strategy for abstracting main ideas from simple technical prose. *Text*, 1982, *2*, 47–82.

Kieras, D. A simulation model for the comprehension of technical prose. In G. H. Bower (Ed.), *The Psychology of Learning and motivation*, Vol. 17. New York: Academic Press, 1983.

Kieras, D. E. A method for comparing a simulation model to reading time data. In D. Kieras & M. Just (Eds.), *New methods in reading research*. Hillsdale, N.J.: Lawrence Erlbaum Associates, in press.

Kieras, D.. & Bovair, S. *Strategies for abstracting main ideas from simple technical prose*. Technical Report No. 9 (UARZ/DP/TR-81/9), University of Arizona, November, 1981.

Kintsch, W. On recalling stories. In M. Just & P. Carpenter (Eds.), *Cognitive processes in comprehension*. Hillsdale, N.J.: Lawrence Erlbaum Associates, 1977.

Kintsch, W., Kozminsky, E., Streby, W. J., McKoon, G., & Keenan, J. M. Comprehension and recall of text as a function of a content variable. *Journal of Verbal Learning and Verbal Behavior*, 1975, *14*, 196–214.

Kintsch, W., & van Dijk, T. A. Toward a model of discourse comprehension and production. *Psychological Review*, 1978, *85*, 363–394.

Kozminsky, E. Altering comprehension: The effect of biasing titles on text comprehension. *Memory and Cognition*, 1977, *5*, 482–490.

Mandler, J. M. A code in the node: The use of a story schema in retrieval. *Discourse Processes*, 1978, *1*, 1–13.

Mandler, J. M., & Johnson, N. S. Remembrance of things parsed: Story structure and recall. *Cognitive Psychology*, 1977, *9*, 111–151.

Manelis, L. Determinants of processing for a propositional structure. *Memory & Cognition*, 1980, *8*, 49–57.

Meyer, B. J. F. What is remembered from prose: A function of passage structure. In R. O. Freedle (Ed.), *Discourse production and comprehension: Advances in research and theory*, (Vol. 1). Norwood, N.J.: Ablex, 1977.

Perfetti, C. A., & Goldman, S. R. Thematization and sentence retrieval. *Journal of Verbal Learning and Verbal Behavior*, 1974, *13*, 70–79.

Perfetti, C. A., & Goldman, S. R. Discourse functions of thematization and topicalization. *Journal of Psycholinquistic Research*, 1975, *4*, 257–271.

Rumelhart, D. E. Notes on schema for stories. In D. G. Bobrow & A. Collins (Eds.), *Representation and understanding: Studies in cognitive science*. New York: Academic Press, 1975.

Rumelhart, D. E. Schemata: The building blocks of cognition. In R. Spiro, B. Bruce, & W. Brewer (Eds.), *Theoretical issues in reading comprehension*. Hillsdale, N.J.: Lawrence Erlbaum Associates, 1980.

Sachs, J. S. Recognition memory for syntactic and semantic aspects of connected discourse. *Perception and Psychophysics*, 1967, *2*, 437–442.

Schallert, D. L. Improving memory for prose: The relationship between depth of processing and context. *Journal of Verbal Learning and Verbal Behavior*, 1976, *15*, 621–632.

Swarts, H., Flower, L. S., & Hayes, J. R. *How headings in documents can mislead readers*. Document Design Project Technical Report No. 9, Carnegie-Mellon University, April, 1980.

van Dijk, T. A. *Some aspects of text grammars*. The Hague: Mouton, 1972.

van Dijk, T. A. *Text and context*. London: Longman, 1977. (a)

van Dijk, T. A. Semantic macro-structures and knowledge frames in discourse comprehension. In M. Just & P. Carpenter (Eds.), *Cognitive processes in comprehension*. Hillsdale, N.J.: Lawrence Erlbaum Associates, 1977. (b)

van Dijk, T. A. Relevance assignment in discourse comprehension. *Discourse Processes*, 1979, *2*, 113–126.

van Dijk, T. A. *Macrostructures*. Hillsdale, N.J.: Lawrence Erlbaum Associates, 1980.

van Dijk, T. A., & Kintsch, W. *Strategies of discourse comprehension*. New York: Academic Press, 1983.

5

Implicit Knowledge, Question Answering, and the Representation of Expository Text

Arthur C. Graesser
Sharon M. Goodman

California State University, Fullerton

When a statement is interpreted in the context of a passage, the comprehender generates inferences and expectations. This is rather obvious. However, an explanation of inference generation seems open-ended and mysterious. What inferences are generated? How are inferences generated? In this chapter we describe a representational system that incorporates implicit knowledge into passage representations.

There was a time when psychologists were squeamish about investigating inferences. Since inferences do not reside in the text and most inferences cannot be formally derived from the text, psychologists postponed the study of inferencing. Psychological theories of text representation focused primarily on the assignment of explicit information to structural hierarchies (Crothers, 1972; Kintsch & Keenan, 1973; Mandler & Johnson, 1977; Meyer, 1975; Thorndyke, 1977). Times have changed. Psychologists have recently been exploring inference mechanisms quite vigorously. It is well acknowledged that inferences and expectations are generated from several sources of information: (1) the semantics of isolated statements and sets of statements (for reviews, see Clark & Clark, 1977; Harris & Monaco, 1978; Kintsch, 1974; Miller & Johnson-Laird, 1976; Norman & Rumelhart, 1975; Revlin & Mayer, 1978), (2) passage context (Beaugrande, 1980; Crothers, 1979; Graesser, 1981; Just & Carpenter, 1978; Kintsch & van Dijk, 1978; Nicholas & Trabasso, 1980; Singer, 1980; den Uyl, 1980; Warren, Nicholas, & Trabasso, 1979), (3) the pragmatic context between the writer and reader or speaker and listener (Beaugrande, 1980; Bower, 1978; Corsaro, 1981; Morgan & Green, 1980; Schweller, Brewer, & Dahl, 1976; van Dijk, 1980), (4) generic knowledge structures (schemas) that are activated by virtue of individual statements, the passage context, and the pragmatic context (Adams & Collins, 1979; Anderson, 1977; Bower, Black, & Turner, 1979; Bransford & Johnson, 1973; Bransford & McCarrell, 1974; Graesser, 1981; Graesser, Gordon, & Sawyer, 1979; Graesser & Nakamura, 1982; Rumelhart, 1980; Rumelhart & Ortony, 1977; Schank & Abelson, 1977), and (5) the goals of the comprehender (Black, 1981; Frederiksen, 1975; Goetz & Armbruster, 1980; Mandl, Schnotz, & Ballstaedt, 1980; Mosenthal, 1983).

An adequate psychological theory of text representation and comprehension should not be confined to an analysis of the text, per se. The conceptual-psychological representation of text is a product of a complex interaction between the text and the comprehender.

Quasiformalists and Schematicians

How should inferences be incorporated into theories of text representation? This question has engendered some disagreement. Psychologists seem to vary along a continuum ranging from the quasiformalists to the schematicians. How do the quasiformalists differ from the schematicians?

Quasiformalists are primarily interested in analyzing explicitly stated information. Inferences have a secondary status. Inferences usually attract the quasiformalist's attention when there is some problem in representing explicit information. Quasiformalists have borrowed many ideas from linguistic theories of sentence structure (Chomsky, 1965; Fillmore, 1968) and text structure (Grimes, 1975; Halliday & Hasan, 1976). Generally speaking, linguists are in the enterprise of explaining language structure and usage rather than explaining inference mechanisms and the representation of world knowledge.

Most quasiformal theories in psychology include the following assumptions and analyses.

1. Sentences are segmented into idea units. The units are usually propositions.
2. Idea units within sentences or clauses are structurally related. The structures are usually hierarchical.
3. Idea units and/or sentences are interrelated in a structurally coherent manner. A structure is coherent if every idea unit is directly related to at least one other idea unit.
4. Higher-order structures are formed from sets of sentences or idea units.

With regard to the first two analyses, the researcher usually specifies a formal or quasiformal symbolic system. For example, predicate calculus is sometimes adopted in the first analysis. Linguistic theories have had a substantial impact on analyses 1 and 2. However, linguistic theories and formal systems have been either uninformative or incomplete when applied to analyses 3 and 4. Quasiformalists usually rely on their intuitions or a handful of rules when explaining text coherence and the formation of higher-order idea units. Sometimes inferences must be incorporated into a passage representation in order to complete analyses 3 and 4. Thus, the quasiformalists are indeed concerned with inferences. However, their concern is restricted to those inferences that are needed for completing the above four analyses.

Who are some typical quasiformalists? The chapters in this book by Meyer, Miller, and Kieras lean toward the quasiformal end of the continuum. The quasiformal approach is quite visible in several theories of text representation in psychology (Crothers, 1972, 1979; Kieras, 1981; Kintsch, 1974; Kintsch, Kozminsky, Streby, McKoon, & Keenan, 1975; Meyer, 1975, 1977a, 1977b; Miller & Kintsch, 1980; van Dijk, 1980; Vipond, 1980).

According to the schematicians, implicit knowledge structures are just as important as explicit information. Schematicians investigate the representation and use of generic knowledge structures called schemas. Schemas guide the interpretation of explicit input, the generation of inferences, and the formation of expectations. Schemas impose structure on the explicit and implicit information. Without these schemas, prose has no meaning and structure.

In this chapter, we adopt a relatively broad, and widely accepted definition of schema (Minsky, 1975; Rumelhart, 1980; Rumelhart & Ortony, 1977). Schemas are natural packets of generic knowledge that are highly structured. Schemas correspond to different knowledge domains, including people, objects, action sequences, event sequences, rhetorical patterns, and so on. There are schemas that incorporate world knowledge, pragmatic knowledge, and language. Cognitive scientists have identified many different types of schemas and have introduced several schema-base constructs, e.g., scripts (Abelson, 1981; Schank & Abelson, 1977), stereotypes (Hamilton, 1981; Taylor & Crocker, 1981), themes (Agar, 1979; Schank & Abelson, 1977), models (Johnson-Laird, 1980), frames (Charniak, 1978; Minsky, 1975), and memory organization packets (Schank, 1980).

Schematicians address a number of questions about implicit knowledge when investigating prose comprehension and representation. What schemas are activated when a passage is comprehended? To what extent can the activated schemas "explain" information that is explicitly stated? When a schema is activated, what information is passed to the specific passage representation? How are inferences and expectations generated? How are erroneous inferences and expectations disconfirmed? How does the comprehender deal with information that is inconsistent or irrelevant to an underlying schema?

Schematicians have sometimes been lax when it comes to the details of representing explicit information in prose. Since comprehension is viewed as a complex interaction between incoming passage information and generic schemas, many schematicians have not become bogged down in linguistic details of prose representations (of course, there are exceptions). The schematicians have been influenced by theories of world knowledge representation and natural language comprehension which are not intimately related to linguistic theories. Psychologists have reported experiments that demonstrate the importance of the schema construct, but they have rarely specified the representations of the relevant schemas in detail. When detailed representations are proposed, they are restricted to a specific topic matter or knowledge domain. The problem of representing world knowledge is indeed open-ended.

Who are the schematicians? The chapters by Mayer and Voss in this book come closest to the schematician positions. Like the quasiformalists, the schematicians are quite visible in contemporary psychology (Anderson, Spiro, & Anderson, 1978; Bisanz & Voss, 1981; Bower, Black, & Turner, 1979; Collins, Brown, & Larkin, 1980; Graesser, 1981; Graesser & Nakamura, 1982; Spiro, 1977, 1980).

Both the quasiformalists and the schematicians enjoy certain benefits and suffer certain shortcomings. The representations generated by the quasiformalists are very detailed and faithfully close to what is explicitly stated in prose. The representational theories of the quasiformalists can be applied to all or many types of passages. However, the quasiformalists have not adequately advanced our theoretical understanding of inference mechanisms and global levels of conceptual structure. The schematicians have had more to contribute to these latter issues, but usually at the expense of glossing over some linguistic details.

In this chapter we attempt to be "quasiformalschematicians." According to our proposed representational system, the representation of a passage includes inferences that are generated from generic schemas. Thus, passage representations include both implicit and explicit information. We represent schematic knowledge and the information in passages by a common, quasiformal system.

GOALS OF THE PROPOSED REPRESENTATIONAL SYSTEM

One objective of this chapter is to describe our system for representing expository passages. We refer to our representational system as a theory, even though other terms may be more accurate, i.e., symbolic language, categorical system, text analysis, and so forth. In order to appreciate a representational theory, one must first understand the goals of the theory. There were six goals underlying our proposed representational theory:

1. The passage representations generated by the theory should approximate the content and structure of the conceptualizations that human comprehenders construct.
2. The passage representations should include inferences as well as explicitly stated information.

3. The passage representations should specify how knowledge is cognitively represented at the semantic conceptual level.
4. The theory should be useful for representing generic schemas in addition to specific passages.
5. The theory should apply to many different types of schemas and many different types of passages.
6. The theory should be simple enough for moderately trained judges to use.

In the remainder of this section we briefly comment on each of these goals.

According to the first goal, the theory should correspond closely to the psychological conceptualizations that humans create. Therefore, the representations should explain performance that humans exhibit in behavioral tasks, such as prose recall, prose summarization, and question answering. The theory does not consist of a formal representation of text, per se. Rather, the theory consists of a quasiformal representation of cognitive conceptualizations and structures.

According to the second goal, passage representations should capture inferences as well as explicitly stated information. In previous studies, a question-answering method has been adopted for exposing inferences that are potentially generated during comprehension (Graesser, 1978, 1981; Graesser, Robertson, & Anderson, 1981; Graesser, Robertson, & Clark, 1983; Graesser, Robertson, Lovelace, & Swinehart, 1980). For each statement in a passage, subjects were probed with questions either during or after passage comprehension. The answers included a large number of inferences. The explicit information and the empirically derived inferences were related structurally according to the constraints of the representational theory. The question-answering method is discussed further in a later section.

According to the third goal, the theory should specify how information is represented at a semantic or conceptual level. With regard to prose, the theory captures the *conceptual connectivity* among explicit and inferred idea units. The theory has not been developed to the point of explaining *sequential connectivity* in text, i.e., the order in which explicit idea units are mentioned in a passage. The theory has also not yet been developed to capture *pragmatic coherence,* i.e., the significance and coherence of the text with respect to the writer/reader relationship or the speaker/listener relationship. In principle, the theory could be expanded to account for sequential connectivity and pragmatic coherence. However, these two avenues have not yet been explored in much detail.

According to the fourth goal, the theory should be useful for representing knowledge in generic schemas. Thus, the passage representations are similar to the representations of world knowledge. Indeed, the proposed theory has been used to represent goal-oriented action sequences, causal chains, social knowledge, and static, descriptive information. Since passages are written to transmit information about the world, it makes sense to have a common representational system for both prose and schemas.

According to the fifth goal, the theory should apply to a variety of schemas and passages. So far, we have analyzed 117 different schemas that apply to people, objects, goal-oriented activities, and causally driven event sequences. Regarding passages, the theory has been used to analyze 26 narrative passages, 5 expository passages, and 1 persuasive passage.

According to the last goal, the theory should be simple enough for a moderately trained colleague to use. This is a rather controversial goal that we have chosen to adopt. Many representational systems are so complex that they have alienated virtually all researchers except for the one who invented the theory. Problems arise when a system has a large number of categories, rules, relationships, and constraints that are not understood and appreciated by colleagues. We chose to seek simplicity. At the same time, we acknowledge that our theory glosses over some distinctions that are potentially important, but not frequently encountered. We believe that the proposed theory captures important categories of knowledge that are often functional in human symbolic mechanisms. A graduate student can acquire and use our theory within 5 to 10 hours of training. The theory could be expanded to capture finer distinctions, perhaps at the cost of alienating colleagues.

REPRESENTING PASSAGES AND SCHEMAS

This section is an overview of our representational theory. A more detailed discussion of the theory is presented in Graesser (1981) and Part 2 of this book.

In the proposed theory, knowledge is represented as a network of labeled statement nodes that are interrelated by labeled, directed arcs. We call these knowledge structures *conceptual graph structures*. Conceptual graph structures represent specific schemas and specific passages. The statement nodes are idea units that correspond to an event, state, process, action, or to what van Dijk (1980) has called a FACT node. The proposed theory has some striking similarities to some theories in psychology (Black & Bower, 1980; Nicholas & Trabasso, 1980; Warren, Nicholas, & Trabasso, 1979), in linguistics (Beaugrande, 1980, Beaugrande & Colby, 1979), and to Schank's Conceptual Dependency Theory (Lehnert, 1978; Schank, 1973, 1975; Schank & Abelson, 1977).

Suppose that a researcher had access to most or all of the knowledge that is relevant to a specific passage or a specific schema. The researcher would organize this knowledge by constructing a conceptual graph structure. Constructing a conceptual graph structure involves three major steps:

Step 1. Segmenting information into statement nodes.
Step 2. Assigning statement nodes to node categories.
Step 3. Interrelating nodes by labeled directed arcs.

Some discussion is devoted to each of these three steps.

Statement Nodes.   A statement node is very similar but not equivalent to a proposition (Clark & Clark, 1977; Kintsch, 1974; Norman & Rumelhart, 1975). Like a proposition, a statement node contains a predicate and one or more arguments. The sentence *wagons have round wheels,* for example, has two statement nodes.

Node 1: Wagons have wheels
Node 2: Wheels are round

However, a statement node is not strictly equivalent to a proposition for reasons that are discussed in Part II of this book (see also Graesser, 1981). A statement node may contain more than one proposition. For example, according to some propositional analyses (Clark & Clark, 1977; van Dijk, 1980), nouns are predicates that ascribe properties to a contextually or referentially specific person, object, location, or concept. Consider the following example sentences and propositional analyses:

Sentence 1: Wagons have wheels
    Proposition 1: Possess (X1, X2)
    Proposition 2: Wagons (X1)
    Proposition 3: Wheels (X2)
Sentence 2: Scythians developed the wheel
    Proposition 1: Develop (A1, X1)
    Proposition 2: Scythian (A1)
    Proposition 3: Wheel (X1)

The example sentences have three propositions but only one statement node. The propositions with noun predicates are not coded as separate statement nodes.

According to most propositional theories, there are verb predicates that require propositional arguments. Many of these verbs denote cognition (*know, believe*), perception (*see, hear*), intentions (*want, desire*), and communication (*tell, ask*). For example, consider the following sentences and propositional analyses:

Sentence 3: The Egyptian knew that wagons have wheels.
    Proposition 1: Knew (A1, Proposition 2)
    Proposition 2: Possess (X1, X2)
    Proposition 3: Egyptian (A1)
    Proposition 4: Wagons (X1)
    Proposition 5: Wheels (X2)
Sentence 4: Egyptians wanted the wagons to have wheels.
    Proposition 1: Want (A1, Proposition 2)
    Proposition 2: Possess (X1, X2)
    Proposition 3: Egyptians (A1)

Proposition 4: Wagons (X1)
Proposition 5: Wheels (X2)

Sentences 3 and 4 contain five propositions but only one statement node. In these sentences one proposition is embedded in another proposition; the compound is represented as only one statement node.

As we mentioned earlier, a statement node is similar to what van Dijk (1980) has called a FACT. A FACT is a cognitive representation of one state, event, process, or action. In van Dijk's theory, there are "FACT sequencies" that must be connected in a coherent manner. Analogously, our conceptual graph structures contain statement nodes that are interrelated in a connected, coherent manner. We believe that statement nodes and van Dijk's FACTS are more natural psychological units than are propositions (see also Chafe, 1980).

Node Categories. Each statement node is assigned to one of six node categories:

Physical State (PS)
Physical Event (PE)
Internal State (IS)
Internal Event (IE)
Goal (G)
Style (S)

Table 5.1 describes each node category and gives example statement nodes. For a detailed specification, see Part II of this book.

For the most part, the node categories are self explanatory. However, there are a few points that need clarification. One point deals with the Goal node. Goal nodes are assigned values of G+, G−, or G?. A G+ is a Goal that has been achieved. Intentional actions are categorized as G+. A Goal node that is not achieved is categorized as G−. When a researcher is uncertain as to whether a Goal is achieved, the node is categorized as a G?. It is apparent from this analysis that an action is defined primarily in terms of its underlying intention and whether the goal state is achieved. The behavior that is executed during the action is often of secondary importance or of uncertain status. Consider the following intentional action, which is categorized as Goal+.

Someone put wheels on an axle.

In this Goal statement, the agent did something which caused the achievement of the intended Goal of wheels being on an axle. The exact behaviors are not specified. Sometimes Goal nodes somewhat specify the behavior, as shown by the examples below.

Someone lifted the wheels on the axle.
Someone hammered the wheels on the axle.

The behavioral aspect of an intentional action may be unspecified (A do something) or weakly specified by virtue of the semantic features of the verb. However, the intention (goal) is the same.

The categorization of some statement nodes is entirely ambiguous unless the passage context is known. Sometimes there is an ambiguity as to whether a node is a state or an event. For example, consider *the wagon was broken* in the following two contexts.

TABLE 5.1
Six Node Categories in the Proposed Representational System

Node Category	Identification Criterion	Examples
Physical State (PS)	Statement refers to an ongoing state in the physical or social world	*The dragon was large.* *The ant was unable to swim.* *The heroes were not married.*
Physical Event (PE)	Statement refers to a state change in the physical or social world	*The boy fell.* *The stream carried away the ant.* *The man became an uncle.*
Internal State (IS)	Statement refers to an ongoing state of knowledge, attitude, sentiment, belief, or emotion in a character	*The heroes knew about the dragon.* *The mother loved roses.* *The boy did not believe in God.*
Internal Event (IE)	Statement refers to a state change in knowledge, attitude, sentiment, belief, or emotion in a character	*The heroes became angry.* *The heroes heard the cries.* *The man recognized the ring.*
Goal (G)	Statement refers to an achieved or unachieved state that a character wants, needs, or desires. An *action* involves a character executing behavior and achieving a goal; there may be goals that are not achieved and plans that are not applied by executing behavior	*The dragon kidnapped the daughters.* *The lady told the man to stop.* *The ant stung the birdcatcher.* *The baby wanted to eat.* *The father watched television.*
Style (S)	Statement or phrase that refers to details about the style in which an action or event occurred	*X occurred quickly.* *C did something with a knife.* *C moved one foot at a time.*

Adapted from Graesser (1981).

When the tornado came, the wagon was broken.
Before the tornado came, the wagon was broken.

The wagon was broken is a Physical Event in the first context and a Physical State in the second. Ambiguities also occur when deciding whether a node is an event or an intentional action (Goal+). Consider the following examples.

In order to immobilize the enemy, the Egyptians broke the axles.
After driving for 30 days, the Egyptians broke the axles.

Egyptians broke axles is a Goal+ in the first sentence and probably an unintended Physical Event in the second. Again, context is needed to disambiguate nodes that would otherwise be ambiguous.

Arc Categories.   The labeled nodes are interrelated by the following five categories of labeled, directed arcs:

Reason (R)
Intiate (I)
Manner (M)
Consequence (C)
Property (P)

Table 5.2 defines each arc category and provides some examples. A more complete description is presented in Part II of this book and in Graesser (1981).

A few comments should be made about the arcs. One point is that each arc category has specific constraints as to what node categories are to be connected. Table 5.3 summarizes the rules for interrelating the nodes with arcs. Each rule in Table 5.3 specifies the categories of nodes that a specific type of arc may interrelate. According to rule 1, Reason arcs relate only Goal nodes. According to rule 2, the Initiate arc relates any category of node to a Goal node. According to rule 6, the Property arc relates an argument of any type of node to a Physical State node or an Internal State node. The rules in Table 5.3 impose definite constraints on the manner of interelating nodes with arcs. Part II presents a more complete discussion of these rules for composing conceptual graph structures.

A second point is that each arc has a designated direction. The direction is not arbitrary. Consider the example below.

⟨Goal 1: Someone puts wheel on axle⟩

$\uparrow$ R

⟨Goal 2: Someone lifts wheel⟩

In this example, Goal 1 is superordinate to Goal 2; lifting the wheel is a subgoal of putting a wheel on an axle. Subgoals are linked to Goals by *forward* Reason arcs. This directionality reflects the fact that the subgoal is accomplished prior to the Goal. If all the subgoals for Goal X are achieved, then the result is that Goal X is achieved. Consider the following example.

⟨Physical Event 1: Wagon moves⟩

$\left. \downarrow \right|$ C

⟨Physical Event 2: Wheels wear out⟩

In this example, Physical Event 1 occurs before Physical Event 2, rather than vice versa.

TABLE 5.2
Arc Categories That Interrelate Nodes

Arc Category	Definition	Example
Reason (R)	One Goal node is a reason for another Goal node	*The dragon's kidnapping the daughters* (G1) is a reason for *the dragon's carrying off the daughters* (G2) R <G2> → <G1>
Initiate (I)	A State or Event node initiates a Goal node	The state of *being hungry* (PS) initiates the goal of *ingesting food* (G) I <PS> → <G>
Consequence (C)	A State, Event, or action (Goal+) node has the consequence of another State or Event node	*The ant being pulled under water* (PE1) has the consequence of *the ant drowning* (PE2) C <PE1> → <PE2>
Manner (M)	An Event or action (Goal+) node occurs with some style (Style or Goal node)	*The man walked* (G+) *in a manner that was quick* (S) M <G+> → <S>
Property (P)	A character, object, or entity has some property that is a State node	*The man owned a jacket* (PS1) *that was red* (PS2) D <argument of PS1> → <PS2>

Adapted from Graesser (1981).

TABLE 5.3
Rules for Interrelating Nodes
with Arcs

Rule 1: <Goal> $\xrightarrow{R}$ <Goal>

Rule 2: < > $\xrightarrow{I}$ <Goal>

Rule 3: < > $\xrightarrow{C}$ <{State/Event}>

Rule 4: <{Event/Goal}> $\xrightarrow{M}$ <Style>

Rule 5: <Goal> $\xrightarrow{M}$ <Goal>

Rule 6: <Argument of Node> $\xrightarrow{P}$ <State>

A third point is that the arcs may be articulated verbally by higher order predicates and connectives. For example, suppose that two Goal nodes are connected by a Reason arc as follows: $\langle$Goal 1$\rangle \xrightarrow{R} \langle$Goal 2$\rangle$. Then the following connectives are appropriate.

$\langle$Goal 1$\rangle$ in order to $\langle$Goal 2$\rangle$
$\langle$Goal 1$\rangle$ so that $\langle$Goal 2$\rangle$
$\langle$Goal 2$\rangle$ by $\langle$Goal 1$\rangle$

Table 5.4 shows some connectives for the Reason, Initiate, and Consequence arcs.

Conceptual Graph Structures.   It is convenient to segregate graph structures or portions of graph structures into three types:

Goal-oriented structures
Cause-oriented structures
Static, descriptive structures

An example of each of these types of structures should help convey the highlights of our representational theory.

A goal-oriented structure is shown in Fig. 5.1. In a goal-oriented structure an agent enacts a number of actions that achieve certain goals. From the perspective of the agent, goal-oriented structures are normally organized in a hierarchical fashion. Subgoals are embedded within goals in a subordinate fashion; sub-

subgoals are subordinate to subgoals (Becker, 1975; Black & Bower, 1980; Charniak, 1977; Graesser, 1978, 1981; Miller, Galanter, & Pribram, 1960; Newell & Simon, 1972). In addition to the hierarchical characteristic, goal-oriented structures tend to have the following characteristics.

1. Goal nodes that are interrelated with Reason and Manner arcs.
2. Goal nodes that are initiated by state and event nodes via the Initiate arcs.
3. Style nodes that are linked to Goal nodes via Manner arcs.

The nodes and arcs in Fig. 5.1 are quite consistent with these characteristics of goal-oriented structures.

The content of a conceptual graph structure may be verbally articulated in several ways. There are many paraphrases for a graph structure. The following paragraphs are two different verbal descriptions of the structure in Fig. 5.1.

TABLE 5.4
Some Higher Order Predicates for Reason, Initiate,
and Consequence Arcs

Arc Category	Arc with Node Category	Predicates with Examples
Reason	R <Goal 1> -----> <Goal 2>	Someone lifted the wheel *in order to* put the wheel on the wagon. Someone lifted the wheel *so that* the wheel would be on the wagon. Someone put the wheel on the wagon *by* lifting the wheel.
Initiate	I < > -----> <Goal>	Someone cut down trees *because* trees have wood. Trees have wood *so* someone cut down the trees.
Consequence	C < > -----> { State / Event }	The wheels wore out *because* the wagon rolled. The wagon rolled *so* the wheels wore out. The wagon rolled; *therefore* the wheels wore out. The wheels wore out after the wagon rolled. The wagon's rolling caused the wheels to wear out. The wagon's rolling *lead to* the wheels wearing out.

a. Pulling sledges was difficult so people wanted to make it easier. People put wheels on sledges by making wheels, attaching wheels to the axles, and attaching the axles to the sledge. People made wheels out of wood because wood is solid, wood was the only solid material around, and because solid wheels are easier to pull. People cut trees because trees are made out of wood.

b. People cut trees in order to make wheels out of wood. Trees were made out of wood and wood was solid. In fact, wood was the only solid material around. Of course, solid wheels are easier to pull. After the wheels were made, people attached wheels to axles and the axles to sledges in order to put wheels on the sledges. The reason for putting wheels on sledges was to make pulling sledges easier. Pulling sledges was difficult at that time.

There are still other ways to articulate the structure in Fig. 5.1. The fact that there are several verbal descriptions for one structure should not be construed as a weakness. The goal of the proposed theory is to capture conceptual connectivity as opposed to sequential connectivity and other surface structure properties.

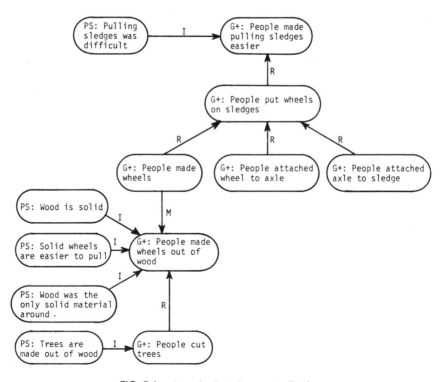

FIG. 5.1.   A goal-oriented conceptualization.

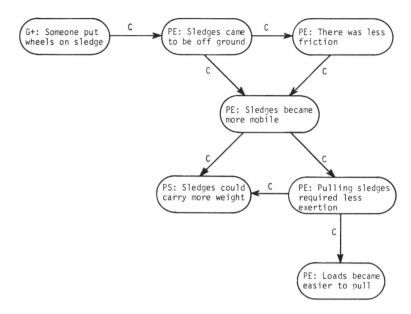

FIG. 5.2.   A cause-oriented conceptualization.

Figure 5.2 shows an example of a cause-oriented structure. Cause-oriented structures are organized in a network fashion with causal chains. Generally speaking, there is a chain of events that unfold over time and each event requires certain enabling states. These events and states are driven by a causal mechanism that exists in nature. A given state may enable several events. An event may have several consequences and may have several causes. Cause-oriented structures are usually complex networks of state and event nodes that are interrelated by Consequence arcs.

Cause-oriented structures are not perfect representations of the causal systems that they capture. Most comprehenders do not fully understand the complex nuances and mysteries of physical mechanisms. The psychological structure is a simplification of the true causal mechanism. Also, the Consequence arc does not usually mean *cause* in a strict sense. One event or state leads to another event or state, but is not a necessary and sufficient cause. Suppose that PE1 and PE2 are related by a Consequence arc as follows: $\langle \text{PE1} \rangle \xrightarrow{C} \langle \text{PE2} \rangle$. Such an expression does not necessarily mean that PE1 causes PE2. Instead it means that (a) PE1 occurred or existed prior to PE2, (b) there is a close conceptual link between PE1 and PE2, and (c) PE1 leads to PE2 by virtue of a causal mechanism rather than a goal-oriented plan. We believe that cause-oriented structures are fundamentally different from goal-oriented structures (see Wilks, 1977).

Figure 5.3 shows a static, descriptive conceptualization. Static concepts have properties, attributes, and features. These properties are ascribed to static con-

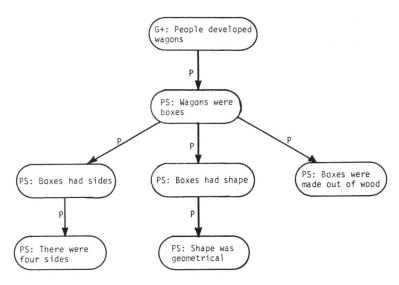

FIG. 5.3.   A descriptive conceptualization.

cepts by linking a state node to the concept by a Property arc. Suppose that a statement node N has an argument, *a*. The argument *a* is modified by linking it to statement node M by a Property arc. It should be noted that node M must also have the argument *a*, and therefore argument *a* is in nodes N and M. Kintsch's argument repetition rule (Kintsch, 1979; Kintsch & van Dijk, 1978; see also Miller's chapter) would be adopted directly when mapping out static descriptive structures. We should also mention that nearly all of the static structures we have analyzed have been hierarchical with respect to the Property arc.

A QUESTION-ANSWERING METHOD FOR EMPIRICALLY EXPOSING PASSAGE INFERENCES

One goal of our proposed theory is to include inferences in the passage representations. How does an investigator obtain these inferences? We have used an empirical method of exposing prose inferences. The comprehender reads a passage and later answers questions about the explicit passage statements. The answers include inferences that are ultimately preserved in the final passage structure. We call this method of exposing implicit knowledge the question-answering method.

Researchers have recently come to appreciate the insights that can be gained by collecting think-aloud protocols or question-answering protocols. Verbal protocols have been collected to investigate prose comprehension (Bisanz & Voss, 1981; Collins et al., 1980; Graesser, 1981; Miller & Kintsch, 1980; Olson,

Mack, & Duffy, 1980), writing processes (Collins & Gentner, 1980; Flower & Hayes, 1980; Hayes & Flower, 1980), and problem solving (Ericsson & Simon, 1979; Newell & Simon, 1972). During the last 5 years we have developed a question-answering (Q/A) method for exploring several issues regarding prose comprehension. So far, the Q/A method has been applied to passages describing common procedures and scripts (Graesser, 1978), to relatively long familiar fairy tales (Graesser, Robertson, Lovelace, & Swinehart, 1980), to short narrative passages (Graesser, 1981; Graesser, Robertson, & Anderson, 1981; Graesser, Robertson, & Clark, 1983), and to short expository passages (Graesser, 1981; Graesser et al. 1983). In this section we review the procedures and analyses we have used in our Q/A method. In subsequent sections we give an overview of what we have learned from Q/A research.

In previous applications of the Q/A method, the comprehender has been probed with why questions and/or how questions after reading or listening to a passage. Each explicit statement node in the passage is probed with questions. For example, if the passage states that *people pulled sledges,* then the comprehender would answer two questions: *Why did people pull sledges?* and *How did people pull sledges?* Of course, subjects could be probed with other types of questions, such as *who, what, when, where, how many, what kind,* and *so what.* In most of our experiments we have collected answers to why questions and how questions because these questions elicit many inferences and expose much of the underlying passage structure for narrative and expository prose. Other types of questions may be more suitable for passages in the persuasion and description genres.

We have used two types of Q/A methods in order to vary the amount of inferences that are exposed. In the *standard* Q/A task, the subjects write down whatever answers seem relevant and come to mind. In the *extended* Q/A task, subjects are encouraged to give very detailed answers and to include very obvious information. Subjects are asked to write down at least four lines of information per answer. The extended Q/A task probes roughly three times as many answers as the standard task. However, the quality or truth of the answers does not decline when subjects are probed more extensively. In the Graesser et al. (1981) study, a separate group of subjects rated the empirically generated inferences on a 4-point verification scale after reading the passages. The mean verification ratings did not differ significantly between inferences generated in the standard Q/A task and those inferences generated only in the extended Q/A task.

An analysis of the Q/A protocols includes three phases. In phase 1 trained judges segment the answer protocols into statement nodes. As long as the judges are trained, there is a high interjudge reliability in segmenting answer protocols into statement nodes. The proportion of statement nodes that are common between any two judges' analyses has been .92 or higher. In phases 2 and 3 judges decide which statement nodes have the same gist or a very similar meaning. In phase 2, judges decide which answer nodes have the same meaning when analyzing the various subjects' protocols for a specific statement and question. In our previous estimates, .90 or more of these decisions have agreed for any two judges. In phase 3, judges decide which nodes generated from different statements and questions capture the same meaning. The product of these analyses includes a listing of all distinct statement nodes that were generated as an answer to at least one of the questions. Approximately 85% of the answer nodes are inferences, whereas 15% are explicit statements in the passage.

Subjects are occasionally off the wall when answering questions. Fortunately, there is a way to eliminate these bizarre answers. An answer is included in subsequent analyses only if it was generated by at least two subjects. In previous studies, only 5% of the statement nodes have been bizarre, and these answers were eliminated by the criterion of being generated by only one subject.

The judges prepare a final list of n explicit nodes and m inference nodes, yielding a total of $m + n$ unique nodes. After this list is prepared, the judges construct a conceptual graph structure from the $m + n$ nodes. The trained judges assign the nodes to node categories. In previous studies, a given pair of judges have agreed on .70 or more (usually more) of the decisions. The judges then interrelate the nodes with labeled, directed arcs. This is the most challenging phase of the analysis. It is possible to assess the interjudge agreement by computing the proportion of arcs that are common for any two judges. These proportions have varied from .52 to 1.00 depending on the judges and the passages. It is important to point out that the judges need to be highly trained when they interrelate the nodes with arcs. Sometimes discrepancies arise when the graph structures are composed. Conflicts are resolved by judges meeting and discussing why they made their decision. After the discussion, conflicts are resolved by a majority rule.

Previous applications of the Q/A method suggest that comprehenders construct a large number of inferences. In the Graesser et al. (1981) study we analyzed four short narrative passages with 15 to 20 explicit nodes per passage. For every explicit statement there were over eight distinct inference nodes. For expository passages of comparable length and difficulty, the ratio was 2.4 unique inference nodes per explicit node (Graesser, 1981). It appears that nearly four times as many inferences are generated in narrative prose as in expository prose. These data suggest that the conceptual organization of expository prose is constrained substantially by explicit information. Theories of representation that dwell on explicit information should provide a closer correspondence to the cognitive representations of expository passages than to those of narrative passages.

The inference nodes that are extracted by the Q/A method are regarded as *potential* inferences that comprehenders generate during comprehension. Some of the inference nodes would be generated by all comprehenders whereas other inference nodes would be generated by only some individuals. Some of the inferences would probably not be generated at comprehension, but rather, they would be dragged out only during the question-answering task. At this point, we are uncertain about the status of the inference nodes extracted by the Q/A method. We are presently conducting experiments that assess which inferences tend to be generated during comprehension versus at question answering. Until these studies are completed, we must be tentative about our conclusions regarding inference processes during comprehension. At the same time, we believe that comprehension involves the construction of many inferences and that the Q/A method is a reasonable method for uncovering these inferences.

UTILIZATION OF CONCEPTUAL GRAPH STRUCTURES IN BEHAVIORAL TASKS

According to the first goal of our proposed theory, the theoretical representations should approximate the conceptual structures of comprehenders. What evidence is there that the conceptual graph structures correspond to conceptualizations that comprehenders construct? At present there is no absolute answer to this question and there is no perfect experimental method for arriving at an answer. However, there are indirect ways of assessing whether the conceptual graph structures have some correspondence to comprehenders' conceptualizations. If the graph structures play an explanatory role in a variety of behavioral tasks, then the investigator has some confidence that the structures are useful and viable approximations to the representations that humans construct. If, however, graph structures are unable to account for performance in many behavioral tasks, then the representations are not useful and would eventually be abandoned. This was the approach to testing the graph structures in our previous research (Graesser, 1981; Graesser et al., 1981). We were encouraged to find that the conceptual graph structures explained performance in a number of behavioral tasks including: question answering; goodness-of-answer ratings; verification ratings of inferences and explicit nodes; and recall of explicit nodes.

It is beyond the scope of this chapter to review all of the empirical evidence that supports the usefulness and validity of the conceptual graph structures. However, we will point out some of the informative highlights. Graesser (1981) reviews the evidence in more detail.

In order to explain performance in each behavioral task, we assumed the distinction between knowledge structures and symbolic procedures that operate on the knowledge structures. The knowledge structures consisted of the conceptual graph structures that we have already described. The symbolic procedures consisted of procedural structures, usually in the form of a *production system* (Anderson, 1976; Collins, 1977; Hayes-Roth & Hayes-Roth, 1979; Hayes-Roth,

Waterman, & Lenat, 1978; Newell, 1973, 1980; Newell & Simon, 1972; Stevens & Collins, 1979) or ordered rule sets (Lehnert, 1978; van Dijk, 1980). There is a specific symbolic procedure or set of procedures associated with each behavioral task. When the appropriate symbolic procedure is applied to a conceptual graph structure, theoretical output is generated. Hopefully, the theoretical output closely matches the empirical output obtained in the behavioral task.

Question Answering. Symbolic procedures have been specified for the following four types of questions:

Why ⟨action⟩
How ⟨action⟩
Why ⟨event⟩
How ⟨event⟩

The symbolic procedures are summarized in Table 5.5. Actions correspond to Goal nodes and events correspond to Physical Events and Internal Events. We have also specified symbolic procedures for Why ⟨state⟩ and How ⟨state⟩ questions, but these will not be discussed here.

We assumed that the symbolic procedures in Table 5.5 operate on conceptual graph structures when individuals answer why and how questions about actions and events in a passage. Consider the why ⟨action⟩ question, which is sometimes called a "goal-orientation" question (Lehnert, 1978). When such a question is

TABLE 5.5
Symbolic Procedures for Generating Answers
to Four Types of Questions

Why <action> (goal orientation)

   (1) Output nodes radiating from the action node via $\vec{R}$ *.

   (2) Output nodes radiating from the action node via $\vec{I}$ and the nodes in step 1 via $\overleftarrow{I}$.

How <action> (instrumental/procedural)

   (1) Output nodes radiating from the action node via $\overleftarrow{R}$ *.

   (2) Output nodes radiating from the action node via $\vec{M}$ * and the nodes in step 1 via $\vec{M}$ *.

Why <event> and how <event> (causal antecedent)

   (1) Output nodes radiating from the event node via $\overleftarrow{C}$ *.

Adapted from Graesser, Robertson, and Anderson (1981).[a]
[a]An asterisk (*) signifies a path of links with the designated label.

asked, the answerer accesses the action node in the structure and then produces as answers the following nodes in the conceptual graph structure:

1. Goal nodes that radiate from the probed action via paths of forward Reason arcs.
2. Nodes that are connected to the probed action and the superordinate Goal nodes via backward Initiate arcs.

For example, suppose that the structure in Fig. 5.1 was the relevant knowledge structure and that the subject was asked *Why did people make wheels?* The theoretically generated answers for this question are listed below.

in order to put wheels on sledges
so that people could make pulling sledges easier
because pulling sledges was difficult.

These answers seem quite sensible and appropriate. The theoretical answers generated from a how ⟨action⟩ question would be quite different. Suppose the subject was asked *How did people make wheels?* According to the symbolic procedure for how ⟨action⟩ questions in Table 5.5, the answers below would be generated theoretically.

by making wheels out of wood.
by cutting trees.

When the symbolic procedures for question answering (in Table 5.5) are applied to the conceptual graph structures, it is possible to specify the sets of permissible answers that would theoretically be generated when specific nodes are probed with specific questions. The *theoretical* set of permissible answers could potentially be different from the *obtained* answers to specific questions. However, the results from two studies revealed that nearly all of the obtained answers to specific questions were theoretically permissible answers (Graesser, 1981; Graesser et al., 1981). The percentage was 91% for narrative prose, whereas the percentage was 81% for the expository prose.

An observant reader may have detected a problem of circularity in the above data that support the validity of the Q/A procedures. The Q/A method was used to generate the nodes in the conceptual graph structures. Then the graph structures and Q/A procedures were used to explain the obtained answers in the Q/A task. In fact, the reported analyses are not completely circular. The Q/A analyses were used to generate a pool of inferences about a passage. These inferences were subsequently organized into a graph structure by judges who were not completely informed as to how these graph structures would be analyzed. The composition of each graph structure was also constrained by the rules of composition shown in Table 5.3. The nodes could be interrelated in an exponentially horrendous number of ways, but only a few configurations would meet the constraints imposed by the composition rules. The Q/A procedures in Table 5.5 were then applied to the conceptual graph structures in order to obtain a set of theoretical answers to specific questions. We found that most of the obtained answers to specific questions would also be generated theoretically. This findings is not entirely trivial because there are substantial theortical constraints on the rules for composing graph structures and the symbolic components in the question-answering procedures. In any event, the potential problem of circularity was addressed more directly in some experiments involving goodness-of-answer ratings.

Goodness-of-Answer Ratings.   In this task subjects read passages and then rated the "goodness" of specific answers to specific questions. For some question-answer items, the answers would be generated theoretically (i.e., it was a permissible answer when the appropriate symbolic procedure was applied to the conceptual graph structure). Goodness-of-answer ratings were substantially higher for items with theoretically permissible answers then items that did not have permissible answers. A more informative finding was that the goodness-of-answer ratings were almost the same for the following two sets of items:

1. Question-answer items with two constraints. First, the specific answer would be generated theoretically from the specific question. Second, the specific answer was generated empirically from the specific question in the Q/A protocols.

2. Question-answer items in which the specific answer would be generated theoretically from the specific question. However, the specific answer was *not* generated empirically from the specific question in the Q/A protocols; the answer was generated empirically from a different question.

This latter finding provided rather strong support for the validity of the conceptual graph structures and also the symbolic procedures for question answering. These theoretical structures were substantial predictors of goodness-of- answer ratings. By contrast, the ratings were not strongly predicted by the empirical likelihood of generating a specific answer to a specific question in a Q/A protocol. (It should be noted that different subjects participated in the goodness-of-answer study than in the study that collected Q/A protocols).

Verification Ratings.   After reading a passage, subjects rated passage inferences on a verification (truth) scale. Verification ratings were higher for nodes with higher structural centrality. Structural centrality was measured as the number of arcs that directly radiate from a node in the graph structure. Multiple regression analyses supported this outcome after partialling out a number of obvious variables, including prior knowledge and the number of subjects who produced the node in the Q/A task. A production system was proposed to account for the verification ratings (see Graesser, 1981).

Recall of Explicit Nodes.   Prose recall has been one of the most popular tasks used to test a representational theory. In earlier studies (see Graesser, 1981) we argued that abstraction and summarization processes occur during recall and that specific abstraction/summarization rules can predict which statements in passages tend to be recalled. The rules differ for different categories of nodes and different types of conceptualizations. For example, superordinate actions (Goals) in a goal-oriented hierarchy tend to be recalled more often than relatively subordinate actions (see also Graesser, 1978; Graesser, Robertson, Lovelace & Swinehart, 1980). Also, Goal nodes tend to be recalled when they are connected directly to many other Goal nodes. Events and states do not show such systematic trends. Many events and states are part of cause-oriented conceptualizations that are not organized in a strictly hierarchical manner.

The conceptual graph structures were explanatory when accounting for data in diverse behavioral tasks. This outcome provided encouraging support for the conceptual graph structures, but did not unequivocally establish the validity of these structures. Of course, it can be argued that *all* representational theories suffer from indeterminacy because many alternative structures can account for any given set of behavioral data (Anderson, 1978). The problem of testing the proposed theory of prose representation is in principle not different from the problems associated with testing other theories of representation. Moreover, there is evidence that the proposed representational system is useful and natural because it provided a foundation for explaining behavioral data in different tasks.

THE CONTENT AND STRUCTURE OF SCHEMAS

In a previous section we described a Q/A method for exposing the inferences that may be generated when specific passages are comprehended. Where do these passage inferences come from? We believe that schemas provide the background knowledge that is needed for interpreting prose and generating inferences. Schemas are generic knowledge structures that guide comprehension in a conceptually driven fashion. Several schemas are identified when a specific passage is comprehended. These schemas correspond to different knowledge domains and levels of structure.

The representational system described in this chapter may be used for representing knowledge in schemas. There are computational advantages to having passages and schemas being represented in a common format. We believe, moreover, there is a close correspondence between the cognitive representation of passages and the cognitive representation of world knowledge schemas.

We have developed a method of mapping out the content and structure of schemas. The method involves two phases: a *free generation* phase and a *Q/A* phase. In the free generation phase, subjects write down attributes, events, and actions that are typical of a specific schema. This free generation task has been used by other researchers as a method of exposing schema content (Bower, Black, & Turner, 1979; Cantor, 1978). Trained judges then prepare a list of nodes that are generated by at least two subjects in the free generation phase. These free generation nodes are subsequently presented to a separate group of subjects who participate in a Q/A task. In the Q/A task, subjects answer a why-question and a how-question (or other questions) about each of the free generation nodes. The judges prepare a final list of nodes that are emitted by at least two subjects in either the free generation phase or the Q/A phase. Conceptual graph structures are composed from this final set of nodes.

We recently completed a study in which the content of 117 schemas was exposed by the "free generation + Q/A" method. For each schema, 8 subjects participated in the free generation task and another 8 subjects completed the Q/A task that included why and how questions. Although conceptual graph structures have not yet been composed, the node lists have been analyzed. Among the 117 schemas, the number of distinct nodes varied from 37 for FORGETTING to 216 nodes for RESTAURANT, with a mean of 95 nodes. The number of free generation nodes varied from three nodes for FORGETTING to 32 for RESTAURANT, with a mean of 13 nodes. These data suggest that schemas contain a wealth of information and also that the Q/A phase exposes most of this information. We should point out that the method does not usually tap aspects of a schema that are associated with infrequent states of the world, misfires, accidents, and correction mechanisms.

A QUESTION-ANSWERING METHOD OF EXPLORING THE CONSTRUCTION OF PROSE REPRESENTATIONS

Researchers have come to appreciate the importance of investigating the process of constructing prose representations (Bock, 1980; Collins et al., 1980; Graesser, 1981; Kieras, 1981; Kintsch & van Dijk, 1978; Spilich, Vesonder, Chiesi, & Voss, 1979; Vipond, 1980). A representation-based theory of comprehension is incomplete if it merely assigns theoretical representations to texts. A psychological theory also needs to specify how the representations are dynamically created during comprehension.

Our Q/A methodology has been adopted for tracing the construction of conceptual graph structures during comprehension (Graesser, 1981; Graesser et al. 1983). So far, we have explored the construction of narrative passages, but not expository passages. The purpose of this section is to outline the Q/A methodology and to summarize some of the conclusions that our previous studies have supported.

How might the Q/A method be used for exploring the process of constructing passage structures? In the basic manipulation, we probe comprehenders with questions about passage statements after comprehenders receive varying amounts of passage context. In the study to be described, there were three context conditions (see Table 5.6). In all three conditions, passage statements were probed with a why question, a how question, and a what-happened-next (WHN) question. Answers to why and how questions provide a profile of the inferences associated with a probed statement, whereas answers to WHN questions provided a profile of the expectations. In the *No Context* condition statements were probed out of the context of the passage. In the *Prior Context* condition, statements were probed during comprehension, that is, subjects knew about the passage up through a probed statement, but did not know about the subsequent

TABLE 5.6
Three Context Conditions Imposed for Examining the Construction
of Prose Representations

1. No Context
   Presented information:
     The dragon kidnapped the daughters.
   Questions:
     Why did the dragon kidnap the daughters?
     How did the dragon kidnap the daughters?
     What happened next?
2. Prior Context
   Presented Information:
     Once there was a Czar who had three lovely daughters. One day the three daughters went walking in the woods. They were enjoying themselves so much that they forgot the time and stayed too long. A dragon kidnapped them.
   Questions
     Why did the dragon kidnap the daughters?
     How did the dragon kidnap the daughters?
     What happened next?
3. Full Context
   Presented information:
     Once there was a Czar who had three lovely daughters. One day the three daughters went walking in the woods. They were enjoying themselves so much that they forgot the time and stayed too long. A dragon kidnapped the three daughters. As they were being dragged off they cried for help. The three heroes heard the cries and set off to rescue them. The heroes came and fought the dragon and rescued the maidens. Then the heroes returned the daughters to their palace. When the Czar heard of the rescue, he rewarded the heroes.
   Questions:
     Why did the dragon kidnap the daughters?
     How did the dragon kidnap the daughters?
     What happened next (after the dragon kidnapped the daughters)?

TABLE 5.7
Criteria for Identifying Six Categories of Inferences and Expectations

Category of Answer	Context Condition		
	None	Prior	Full
A. Statement-driven nodes that are preserved	+	+/−	+
B. Statement-driven nodes that are disconfirmed by prior context	+	−	−
C. Statement-driven nodes that are disconfirmed by subsequent context	+	+	−
D. Prior-context-driven nodes that are preserved	−	+	+
E. Prior-context-driven nodes that are disconfirmed by subsequent context	−	+	−
F. Subsequent-context-driven nodes	−	−	+

Symbols: +, answer is present in Q/A protocols; −, answer is not present in Q/A protocols.
Adapted from Graesser (1981).

passage context. In the *Full Context* condition, subjects read the entire passage before any of the statements were probed. With these three context conditions it was possible to trace much of the history of creating, preserving, and possibly disconfirming inferences and expectations. A node was recorded as *preserved* if it was an answer in the Full Context condition, and *disconfirmed* if it was not an answer in the Full Context condition.

Six node categories can be identified from the way in which an answer node (inference) is distributed among the three context conditions (see Table 5.7). A plus (+) signifies that the node was an answer to a particular questioned statement in a specific context condition. A minus (−) signifies that a particular node was not an answer in the specific condition. A node is classified as *statement-driven* when it was generated by the probed statement in isolation, i.e., the *No Context* condition. A statement-driven node could be disconfirmed by either prior passage context (category B) or by subsequent passage context (category C); alternatively, the statement-driven node might be preserved (category A). A *prior context-driven* node is not generated by a statement in isolation, but rather by a statement together with prior passage context. A prior-context-driven node may be either preserved (category D) or eventually disconfirmed by subsequent passage context (category E). A *subsequent-context-driven* node is generated by virtue of a statement together with passage context that occurs after the statement (category F). Categories A, D, and F are preserved nodes, whereas categories B, C, and E are disconfirmed. With this classification it is possible to examine the process of constructing structures from several perspectives.

The Q/A Profiles for Specific Passage Statements. Passage statements may be analyzed with respect to the answers to how, why, and WHN questions when particular statements are probed. Consider the preserved nodes that are statement-driven, prior-context-driven, and subsequent-context-driven. Suppose that the relative proportions were .10, .10, and .80 for categories A, D, and F. If this pattern of proportions occurred, then a given statement would not be fully interpreted until subsequent passage context is received. Comprehension would be difficult because very little could be concluded about a given statement until the entire passage is known. Suppose the relative proportions were .80, .10, and .10 for categories A, D, and F, respectively. This distribution would suggest a building-block analogy leading one to conclude that a passage is little more than the sum of the explicitly stated nodes. A .10, .80, and .10 set of relative proportions would suggest that prior context is primarily responsible for the interpretation of a statement.

Construction Charts for Specific Inference and Expectation Nodes. It is possible to trace the constructive history of implicit nodes by examining which passage statements, questions, and context conditions generate the node in the Q/A task. Construction charts were prepared for each implicit node that was generated by at least two subjects. Table 5.8A and Table 5.8B show two construction charts, one for the preserved node *the daughters became frightened* and one for the disconfirmed node *the daughters slept*. These nodes were generated from statements in *The Czar and his Daughters* (see Table 5.6).

TABLE 5.8A
Constructive History of the Inference Node *The Daughters
became frightened*

| | *Type of Questions and Context Condition* | | | | | | | | |
| | *Why* | | | *How* | | | *What Happened Next* | | |
Target Statements	*No*	*Prior*	*Full*	*No*	*Prior*	*Full*	*No*	*Prior*	*Full*
Daughters walked in woods									
Daughters enjoyed themselves									
Daughters forgot time									
Daughters stayed too long									
Dragon kidnapped daughters							2	1	2
Dragon dragged off daughters							1	10	1
Daughters cried	2	9	6	1	2	2			
Heroes heard cries									
Heroes went to the daughters									
Heroes fought dragon									
Heroes rescued daughters									
Heroes returned daughters to palace									
Czar heard of rescue									
Czar rewarded heroes									

TABLE 5.8B
Constructive History of the Inference Node *The Daughters slept*

| | Type of Questions and Context Condition | | | | | | | | |
| | *Why* | | | *How* | | | *What Happened Next* | | |
Target Statements	No	Prior	Full	No	Prior	Full	No	Prior	Full
Daughters walked in woods									
Daughters enjoyed themselves							1	1	0
Daughters forgot time				2	0	0			
Daughters stayed too long							1	1	0
Dragon kidnapped daughters									
Dragon dragged off daughters									
Daughters cried									
Heroes heard cries									
Heroes went to daughters									
Heroes fought dragon									
Heroes rescued daughters									
Heroes returned daughters to palace									
Czar heard of rescue									
Czar rewarded heroes									

Adapted from Graesser (1981).

The daughters became frightened was first generated as an expectation (answer to a WHN question) when *the dragon kidnapped the daughters* was interpreted in the story. This expectation was statement-driven because it was generated by some subjects in the No Context condition; the expectation was preserved because it was generated by some subjects in the Full Context condition. *The daughters became frightened* eventually became an inference because it was generated as an answer to a why question and a how question when *the daughters cried* was probed.

The daughters slept was first generated as an expectation when the statement *the daughters enjoyed themselves* was interpreted. The expectation was statement-driven, but eventually disconfirmed because no subjects generated the expectation in the Full Context condition. *The daughters slept* was a statement-driven inference generated from *the daughters forgot the time*. Again, however, this inference was ultimately disconfirmed because no subjects generated the item in the Full Context condition.

Construction charts were prepared for 1790 distinct inference or expectation nodes that had been generated as answers in four different narrative passages, with 15 to 20 explicit nodes per passage. Of these 1790 unstated nodes, 58% were preserved in the conceptual graph structure whereas 42% were disconfirmed. The construction charts provided critical data for exploring the process of constructing structures. The first passage statement that generated a particular node was informative because it marked the point where the node was first constructed.

Structural Transformations.   If a set of n statements produces some structure S, then S is transformed to a new structure S' when statement $n + 1$ is interpreted. How do structures S and S' differ? There are four ways that a structure S may be transformed to structure S' after an additional statement is comprehended in a passage. New nodes are added to the structure by either *appending* or *inserting*. Appending occurs when a new node is adjoined by an arc to some node in structure S. Inserting occurs when a new node is "sandwiched" in between two existing nodes in structure S. Analogously, there are two ways that nodes may be removed from structure S. *Pruning* occurs when there is a removal of some node m in structure S; when applicable, all nodes that radiate from node m (away from the main structure) are also removed. *Deleting and compressing* involves a more complex structural change. A node n is removed from structure S, and then the nodes that were directly connected to n are joined together (compressed). The inserting and the deleting + compressing modifications involve a restructuring of a graph, whereas appending and pruning modifications simply add or delete nodes from the structure S. A structural analysis was performed on narrative passages by tracing structural transformations that occurred as statements were incrementally interpreted in a passage.

We have explored the process of constructing passage structures by examining (a) the Q/A profiles for specific passage statements, (b) the construction charts for specific inferences and expectations, and (c) structural transformations. These analyses led to 29 observations about the process of constructing conceptual structures (see Graesser, 1981). A few of the outcomes and conclusions are described below.

Amount of Information.   Consider the likelihood that an inference or expectation node is preserved, given that it was generated by a statement. The likelihood that a generated node is preserved increases with the amount of information in the knowledge source that generated the node. Thus, statement-driven nodes are preserved less often than are prior-context-driven nodes. Prior-context-driven nodes have a higher likelihood of being preserved when they are activated later and later in the passage (i.e., when more prior context has accumulated). Prior-context-driven nodes have a higher likelihood of being preserved when they are generated by a global prior context than a local prior context.

The Impact of Prior Versus Subsequent Context.   Prior passage context carries the burden of generating inferences that are associated with a statement, whereas subsequent context carries the burden of disconfirming erroneous nodes. Consider the process of constructing inferences that are closely associated with a target statement. Whereas prior context was critical in generating these inferences, only 7% of the preserved inference nodes were subsequent-context-driven. Erroneous statement-driven inferences were disconfirmed by subsequent context more often than they were blocked by prior context.

Expectations.   Inference nodes that are preserved in conceptual graph structures are rarely confirmed expectations. Only 9% of the preserved inference nodes had been expected by virtue of previous passage context. Of course, this does not mean that expectations play a negligible role in comprehension. It does mean, however, the comprehension is better characterized by a mechanism that accommodates unpredicted input than a mechanism that confirms expected input.

Restructuring.   An incoming passage statement modifies the structure that is available just before the incoming statement is interpreted. The modification of old structures nearly always involves the simpler transformations of pruning and appending, rather than inserting and deleting + compressing. In other words, old nodes are rarely restructured when new information is interpreted. If restructuring is required, then the comprehender probably rereads the text from a different perspective.

The Lamination Effect.   The preserved inference nodes that radiate from a particular passage statement are layered, much like an onion. Statement-driven nodes form the inner layer that is closest to the target statement; prior-context-driven nodes form the middle layer; and subsequent-context-driven nodes form the outer layer. We call this layering of nodes the lamination effect. The lamination effect is violated when the nodes radiating from a target statement show a haphazard pattern, i.e., the statement-driven, prior-context-driven, and subsequent-context-driven nodes are distributed unsystematically in the structure associated with a target statement. Violations of this lamination effect were rare (less than 6% of the observed nodes).

The laminated composition simplifies of course of comprehension. The information associated with a knowledge source (schema) is compartmentalized with substructures being embedded within other structures. Deviations from lamination would suggest a more complicated process in which nodes from different schemas are heterogeneously distributed in the conceptual graph structures.

The Q/A method described so far provided a useful approach for exploring the process of constructing conceptual graph structures. However, the method is incomplete in one very important respect. The method reveals which passage statements invoke specific inferences and expectations, but it does not tap the generic schemas from which the implicit knowledge is generated. The method does not reveal how schemas interact with the passage information during comprehension. What mechanisms determine which nodes in a schema are passed to the conceptual graph structure for a passage? How do schemas communicate with one another during the process of passing nodes to the passage representations?

We are presently conducting a study that explores how schemas pass information to narrative conceptualizations. The narrative passages were the same passages that were investigated in some previous Q/A studies (Graesser, 1981; Graesser et al., 1981; Graesser et al., 1983). For each passage we identified a number of schemas that would be foregrounded during comprehension. For example, Table 5.9 shows a narrative passage, *The Czar and his Daughters* and 31 schemas that are associated with the passage. Microstructure schemas were identified on the basis of verbs, nouns, and adjectives that are explicitly stated in the passage. There were 20 microstructure schemas in the Czar story. Macrostructure schemas were identified on the basis of our intuitions. We identified 11 macrostructure schemas. The content of these 31 schemas had been empirically generated using the free generation + Q/A method described earlier.

TABLE 5.9
The Czar and his Daughters and 31 Schemas

Once there was a Czar who had three lovely daughters. One day the three daughters went walking in the woods. They were enjoying themselves so much that they forgot the time and stayed too long. A dragon kidnapped the three daughters. As they were being dragged off they cried for help. Three heroes heard the cries and set off to rescue the daughters. The heroes came and fought the dragon and rescued the maidens. Then the heroes returned the daughters to their palace. When the Czar heard of the rescue, he rewarded the heroes.

Microstructure Schemas	Macrostructure Schemas
Czar	Listening
Daughter	Marriage
Forest	Goodness
Dragon	Badness
Hero	Fairy Tale
Time	Finding
Palace	Lateness
Walking	Thanking
Enjoying	Returning Favor
Forgetting	Seeing
Dragging off	Fearing
Kidnapping	
Crying	
Hearing	
Moving	
Fighting	
Returning	
Rescuing	
Rewarding	
Loveliness	

At this point it would be useful to review some Q/A data that are available for exploring the process of constructing passage structures. For the present purposes we focus on an analysis of the Czar story. The Q/A data have provided the following knowledge structures.

1. The final conceptual graph structure that is available after a passage has been comprehended. The nodes in the structure include categories A, D, and F in Table 5.7. In the Czar story there were 93, 51, and 8 inference nodes in categories A, D, and F, respectively.

2. A set of intermediate conceptual graph structures which are created and modified dynamically as statements are incrementally interpreted in a passage. The intermediate structures contain preserved nodes (categories A, D, and F in Table 5.7) and nodes that are eventually disconfirmed (categories B, C, and E in Table 5.7). In the Czar story, there were 93, 19, 29, 51, 23, and 8 inference nodes in categories A, B, C, D, E, and F, respectively. In addition, there were 74 expectation nodes. An expectation node was defined as an answer to a WHN question for some passage statement N, but not an answer to a why question or a how question for passage statements 1 through N.

3. A set of schema representations. There is a conceptual graph structure for each microstructure and macrostructure schema that is relevant to a passage. In the Czar story we identified 31 schemas. Among these 31 schemas, there were 2893 schema nodes.

With the above nodes and structures we could explore the role of schemas in guiding comprehension processes and the construction of graph structures. In one analysis, we examined the extent to which passage nodes were activated by the 31 schemas. For each of the 223 passage inferences, we identified all of the schemas that contained a node that matched the inference node. Three types of matches were considered. An *exact match* is pretty much self-explanatory. The inference *it was a nice day* is an example of an exact match. This node was an inference generated from the statement *the daughters were walking in the woods* and also was a node in the WALKING schema. The second type of match involved *argument substitution;* the schema node contained an abstract argument (someone, something, someplace) whereas the passage inference contained a specific argument (daughters, sword, woods). For example, a Goal node in the WALKING schema was *person get exercise* whereas the corresponding passage inference node was *daughters get exercise*. The third type of match involved a *complex match* because at least two schemas were needed to achieve a match. For example, consider the Goal inference *daughters look at animals,* which was activated from the passage statement *the daughters went walking in the woods.* The inference could be derived from a Goal node in the WALKING schema (person look at surroundings) and a Physical State node in the FOREST schema (animals are in forests). Of all the matches that were scored, 9% were exact matches, 86% involved argument substitution, and 5% involved a complex match.

For 176 of the 223 inference nodes, there was a match with a node in at least one schema. Thus, the schemas accounted for 79% of the inference nodes. Of the 176 matching nodes, there were 92, 58, 26, and 10 nodes that matched with a node in 1, 2, 3, versus 4-6 schemas, respectively. The average inference node had a match with a node in 1.7 schemas. The microstructure schemas accounted for a great deal of the passages inferences. For 74% of the passage inferences, there was a match with a node in at least one microstructure schema. There was a match with a node in at least one macrostructure schema for 31% of the inferences. It is inappropriate, however, to compare percentages for the microstructure schemas versus the macrostructure schemas.

A subset (21%) of the inference nodes did not match a node from any of the schemas. These nonmatching nodes are interesting because they involve novel configurations. One of these inference nodes was the Style node, the daughters walked *between the trees*. There are trees in the FOREST schema, but none of the schema nodes specified that a person walks between trees. This Style inference suggests that there are more abstract schemas inherent in planning and problem solving.

Expectation nodes were analyzed in the same way that passage inferences were analyzed. In the Czar story there were 74 expectation nodes. There were 42 expectations (56%) with matches to a node in at least one schema. Of the 74 nodes, 52% matched a node in at least one microstructure schema, and 38% matched a node in at least one macrostructure schema.

How many schema nodes are ultimately passed to the passage structure? Among the 31 schemas that were relevant to the Czar story, there were 2893 nodes. Only 362 of these nodes matched an inference or expectation node in the passage. Therefore, only 13% of the schema nodes were passed to the conceptual graph structure for a passage. This outcome suggests that a substantial number of schema nodes are not relevant to a specific passage.

What mechanisms account for the process of narrowing down the schema nodes to the set that is incorporated in the passage representation? Presumably there is a systematic symbolic interaction among the nodes from (a) a foregrounded schemas, (b) prior passage context, and (c) an incoming statement. We are presently exploring mechanisms for pruning irrelevant schema nodes.

A large number of structures are available for exploring the process of constructing the conceptual graph structures. The structures include (1) graph structures for schemas that are relevant to the passage, (2) the final graph structure that is preserved when the passage is finished being comprehended, and (3) graph structures at intermediate points during comprehension as the passage is interpreted statement by statement in an incremental fashion. How are the passage structures dynamically created and modified? How are the nodes in the schema structures incorporated into the passage studied? What sorts of transformations are imposed on the intermediate passage structures? When schema nodes are passed to the passage structure, to what extent are schema nodes removed by pruning versus deleting + compressing? In general, how are structures transformed and how are different structures synchronized with one another?

There are many other analyses that could be performed on the available data. It should be apparent that the data base is sufficiently rich and detailed to explore the process of constructing structures from many angles and perspectives. In the near future we plan on using the Q/A methodology for expository passages.

DIFFERENCES BETWEEN NARRATIVE AND EXPOSITORY PROSE

Passages can be categorized into different classes, or genres. Those who have classified prose in English composition and literary criticism have usually proposed four major categories: narrative, expository, persuasive, and descriptive (Brooks & Warren, 1972; Decker, 1974; Nicholas & Nicholl, 1978; Sanderson & Gordon, 1963). In psychology, Brewer (1980) has categorized prose somewhat differently. According to Brewer, passages can be classified by structure (descriptive, expository, and narrative) and by force (informing, persuading, entertaining, and the "literary-aesthetic"), yielding a total of 12 categories. Of course, specific passages may have properties that are associated with more than one category. A novel is ordinarily narrative, but there may be a description of a setting or an exposition of why a society is the way it is. Encyclopedia articles are usually expository, but a passage may have a narrative excerpt that illustrates an important point. Genres may be viewed as fuzzy sets, just as most categories of knowledge.

According to Decker (1974) the primary purpose of expository text is to expose information or ideas. Although some expository passages may be used to entertain, to persuade, or to have an aesthetic impact, the primary purpose of expository prose is to inform the reader by exposing ideas. On the other hand, most narrative passages are written to entertain more than to inform.

In this section we describe some differences between narrative and expository prose. The following properties are characteristic of one genre or the other rather that definitional. There are two reasons for comparing the two types of prose. First, there is some evidence that narrative is much easier to comprehend and retain than expository prose. Compared to expository prose, narrative is read faster (Graesser, 1981; Graesser, Hoffman, & Clark 1980), is more absorbing (Britton, Graesser, Glynn, Hamilton, & Penland, 1983), is easier to comprehend (Graesser, Hauft-Smith, Cohen, & Pyles, 1980), is easier to recall (Cohen & Graesser, 1980; Graesser, Hauft-Smith, Cohen, & Pyles, 1980), and is selectively encoded when readers genuinely want to read in ecologically valid settings (Graesser, Higginbotham, Robertson, & Smith, 1978). Why does narrative prose have such a privileged status in the information-processing system? In order to answer this question we need to examine some differences at the conceptual and structural levels.

The second reason for comparing expository and narrative prose reflects the history and development of the proposed representational theory. Our representational system was first developed for narrative prose. As soon as the theory was developed to satisfaction for narrative prose, we decided to apply it to expository prose. In many ways the representational system generalized to expository prose. However, in other ways, the extension required a revision of our theory. In order to point out the successes and problems, it is important to enumerate potential differences between expository and narrative prose.

1. *Suspension of Disbelief.*   Whereas the reader assumes that information in expository prose is true, the information in narrative may be fictitious. In narrative prose, the reader does not constantly evaluate the truth of statements in relation to the reader's world knowledge. Coleridge (1967) has called this "the willing suspension of disbelief." The purpose of expository prose is to update the comprehender's general knowledge of well-accepted truths.

2. *Temporal and Spatial Referents.*   The episodes in narrative take place at a specific time and place. Of course the time and place may be fictitious. The time and place indices tend to be generic in expository prose. Statements in expository prose are regarded as universally true at relevant times and locations (Brown, 1966). Statements in narrative are true for the specific time and location in the narrative.

3. *Literate Prose Versus Mother Tongue.*   When people talk in everyday conversation, the discourse is normally narrative rather than expository. People talk about their experiences. This information conveys what happened. Expository prose is different from the language of the mother tongue (see Brown, 1966; Olson, 1977). Expository is a special genre that is normally reserved for text books and other written documents.

4. *Conceptual Structures.*   Sequences of episodes in narrative unfold in a chronological order, whereas information in expository prose may not follow any temporal order. According to Colby (1973), narrative prose contains eidochronic sequences, with chains of episodes that unfold according to causal or goal-oriented relationships.

When comparing the arc categories and node categories of narrative and expository prose, there are systematic differences (Graesser, 1981). First, expository prose has more descriptive conceptualizations than does narrative. There are more Internal State nodes, Physical State nodes, and Property arcs in expository than in narrative prose. Relative to expository prose, narrative has more goal-oriented conceptualizations with more Goal nodes, Style nodes, Reason arcs, and Initiate arcs.

5. *Number of Inferences.*   Comprehenders draw more inferences in narrative prose than expository prose. The Q/A method has revealed that roughly three or four times as many inferences are generated in narrative passages than expository passages (Graesser, 1981). This may be a consequence of the fact that more inferences are drawn from goal-oriented conceptualizations than cause-oriented and descriptive conceptualizations. Alternatively, the schemas that are invoked in narrative may be richer and more developed than those in expository prose.

From one perspective, the fact that narrative passages invoke more inferences than expository passages seems inconsistent with the finding that narrative passages are read faster. Specifically, there is some evidence that reading times for sentences increase with the number of inferences that sentences generate (Olson et al., 1980). This apparent discrepancy can perhaps be resolved when an alternative perspective is considered. Some sentences and passages may require longer reading times because the comprehender does not have an adequate knowledge base to guide comprehension and to generate inferences. Narrative passages might impose more demands on processing time than expository passages when considering the number of generated inferences; at the same time, however, narrative passages may invoke rich and well-developed schemas that facilitate comprehension speed.

6. *The Communication Function of Prose.*   The primary purpose of expository prose is to inform the reader about truths in the world. The primary function for narrative is to entertain the listener. Of course, these different goals are tendencies rather than necessities (Brewer, 1980).

7. *Rhetorical Features.*   Given that an important feature of narrative is to entertain, writers of narrative adopt specific rhetorical devices that are entertaining, such as suspense, surprise, and irony (Brewer & Lichtenstein, 1981). Narrative often builds up to a climax with a plot that involves interaction of goals among characters (Beaugrande & Colby, 1979; Bruce, 1978; Wilensky, 1978). The episodes in narrative normally follow a chronological order (Mandler, 1979; Stein & Nezworksi, 1978) although there can be entertaining deviations from a chronological order. In narrative, the plot is usually preceded by a setting that describes the time, place, and characters. Sometimes, aspects of the setting are distributed among episodes in the plot (see Black & Bower, 1980).

Expository prose often has a pyramid development. The passage first provides the overall elements of a topic and these elements are embellished with further paragraphs (Collins & Gentner, 1980). Within paragraphs, the first sentence sets up the theme or the topic of the paragraph and subsequent sentences embellish the theme or topic (Brown, 1966; Kieras, 1978, 1980). In expository prose the writer gets to the main point as soon as possible.

There are many different rhetorical devices that a writer may use to convey information in expository prose. Decker (1974) has enumerated the following rhetorical devices:

1. classification
2. comparison and contrast
3. illustration and concretizing
4. analogies
5. process analysis
6. cause/effect analysis
7. definition
8. induction/deduction
9. description
10. embedded narratives

Each of these rhetorical devices has its special set of constraints and conventions. The fact that expository prose has such a wide diversity in content and rhetorical devices has important implications for our representational theory and our Q/A method of exploring prose inferences. Regarding the Q/A method, why questions and how questions may not tap certain conceptualizations that are central to the organization and development of some expository passages. Regarding our representational theory, we may need to introduce additional node categories and arc categories in order to accommodate some expository passages. We have more to say about these issues in a later section.

8. *Connectives, Transitional Words, and Signaling Devices.*   In narrative, transitional phrases and signaling devices play a less critical role than in expository. Transitional words and connectives help the reader keep track of the logical flow in expository passages (Grimes, 1975; Halliday & Hasan, 1976). For example, there are additive relations that signal the reader that some information should be added (*in addition, furthermore, moreover*). A temporal relation signals readers about the sequential or temporal order (*then, soon, before*). A *causal* relation clarifies the logical development (*therefore, because, consequently*). An adversative relation signals that there is a contrast or comparison (*but, however, on the other hand*). These signaling devices are important for understanding expository prose (Britton, Meyer, Hodge, & Glynn, 1980). They are less critical in narrative passages in which the chronology is important. In a narrative plot, a vague connective like *and then* may be sufficient for comprehension.

THE REPRESENTATION OF EXPOSITORY PROSE

Our previous investigation of expository prose focused on four short passages with roughly 25 explicit statement nodes per passage. These passages are presented in Table 5.10. We have used a Q/A method to expose the inferences that are potentially constructed when these passages are comprehended. After listening to each passage, subjects answered a why question and a how question about each explicit statement node. A conceptual graph structure has been constructed for each passage, which includes the explicit nodes and all inference nodes that were generated by at least two subjects in the Q/A task. The conceptual graph structure for the *Development of the Wagon* is provided in Part 2 of this book.

TABLE 5.10
Expository Passages Studied

Development of the Wagon

The wheel and the wagon developed at the same time, approximately 5000 years ago. At that time, human beings found that they could pull their sledges more easily if they fitted them with wheels of solid wood. The Egyptians were among the earliest people to use wagons. The Scythians wandered over the plains of southeastern Europe as early as 700 B.C., carrying their possessions on two-wheeled carts covered with reeds. However, until the middle ages, the wagons were no more than boxes set upon axles between wheels. Then the four-wheeled coach was developed in Germany.

Social Origins

Socially, the hunting ape had to increase his urge to communicate and to cooperate with his fellows. Facial expressions and vocalizations had to become more complicated. With all the new weapons available, he had to develop powerful signals that would inhibit attacks within the social group. On the other hand, with a fixed home base to defend, he had to develop stronger aggressive responses to members of rival groups.

The Placenta

The placenta is the organ through which the growing embryo obtains food and eliminates wastes. Blood vessels in the embryo go through the umbilical cord to the placenta and back again to the embryo. Nutrients from the mother animal are absorbed into the placenta. From it they flow into the blood vessels of the cord, and are taken to the growing embryo. Embryonic wastes flow from the embryo, through the umbilical cord, to the placenta, through the mother's blood stream, and are then eliminated by the mother's kidneys.

The Zeeman Effect

The Zeeman Effect is the splitting up of spectrum lines into two or more components. It is caused by placing a light source in a strong magnetic field. The components from any one line have a set of frequencies that are different for every known chemical element. These components make a symmetrical pattern around the original source of light. The patterns vary from line to line, and are plane, elliptical, or circularly polarized. By using the Zeeman Effect, astronomers can measure the strength of the magnetic field on the surface of the stars.

For the most part, we found the six node categories and the five arc categories to be adequate when constructing conceptual graph structures for the four passages. Although our representational system was originally developed for narrative prose, the system proved to be useful when we attempted to tackle expository prose. In some respects, however, the original representational system seems incomplete. Some additional node categories and arc categories would improve our theory in its application to expository passages.

One way to improve our theory is to add an ''Implies'' arc. Sometimes a state node was an implication of one or more nodes. For example, consider the three statement nodes below.

1. The Egyptians invented the wagon
2. people used wagons
3. The Egyptians were the first people to use wagons

Node 3 would be a logical implication of Nodes 1 and 2. In our present representational system, the Consequence arc is used to capture implication, as shown below.

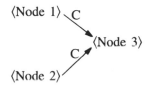

Our theory could be improved by introducing the Implies arc; the Implies arc would interrelate the above three nodes rather than the Consequence arc. Consequence arcs would be reserved for node sets that capture a causal sequence of events and states that unfold in a chronological order. The Implies arc would be reserved for node sets that involve atemporal, logical implications. A passage about mathematics or logic would contain many Implies arcs. A passage about the operation of a nuclear power plant would contain many Consequence arcs.

In order to evaluate the scope of our representational theory, we need to examine many more expository passages than the four passages in Table 5.10. Unfortunately, the collection of Q/A protocols has been very time consuming. One way of circumventing the time-consuming collection of verbal protocols is to analyze the explicit content of several passages. We do not really need to expose passage inferences in order to apply our representational theory to different passages. The purpose of exposing these inferences was to arrive at a closer correspondence to the conceptual structures that comprehenders construct. Explicit information can be submitted to our theoretical system in the same way that we have submitted explicit plus implicit information. Of course, there may be some problems in analyzing explicit information alone. The explicit content of a passage may have many gaps in conceptual development; these gaps would normally be filled by the comprehender's inference mechanisms.

We have applied our representational theory to the explicit content of passages chosen by other contributors in this volume. In order to illustrate the product of these efforts, the conceptual graph structure of Miller and Kintsch's *Saint* passage is presented in Table 5.11. We identified 32 statement nodes in the *Saint* passage. The nodes are listed in the left column of Table 5.11. The nodes were interrelated by 38 arcs. The arcs are listed in the right column of Table 5.11.

We will not present conceptual graph structures for the other passages that contributors in this volume have chosen. Some of their passages were rather long. Moreover, a detailed node and arc list (e.g., Table 5.11) would not reveal

TABLE 5.11
Conceptual Graph Structure for Miller and Kintsch's Saint Passage

The Saint

In the request to canonize the "frontier priest," John Neumann, bishop of Philadelphia in the 19th century, two miracles were attributed to him in this century. In 1923, Eva Benassi, dying from peritonitis, dramatically recovered after her nurse prayed to the bishop. In 1949, Kent Lenahan, hospitalized with two skull fractures, smashed bones and a pierced lung after a traffic accident, rose from his deathbed and resumed a normal life after his mother had prayed ardently to Neumann.

Nodes	*Arcs*
	R
1. G+: Someone get John Neumann canonized	$<G+2>$ -----> $<G+1>$
	P
2. G+: Someone request that John Neumann be canonized	$<G+2>$ -----> $<PS3>$
	P
3. PS: John Neumann was frontier priest	$<G+2>$ -----> $<PS4>$
	P
4. PS: John Neumann was bishop at Location L1 at Time T1	$<PS4>$ -----> $<PS5>$
	P
5. PS: Location L1 was in Philadelphia	$<PS4>$ -----> $<PS6>$
	I
6. PS: Time T1 was in 19th century	$<IE7>$ -----> $<G+1>$
	P
7. IE: Someone attributes miracles to John Neumann at Time T2	$<IE7>$ -----> $<PS8>$
	P
	$<IE7>$ -----> $<PS9>$

(*continued*)

TABLE 5.11   (*Continued*)

Nodes	Arcs
8. PS: time T2 is in this century	C <G+10> -----> <IE7>
9. PS: There were two miracles	C <G+10> -----> <PS9>
10. G+: John Neumann performed a miracle	C <G+11> -----> <IE7>
11. G+: John Neumann performed a miracle	C <G+11> -----> <PS9>
12. PS: Eva Benassi had peritonitis	C <PS12> -----> <PE13> I <PE13> -----> <G+15>
13. PE: Eva Benassi was dying	P <PE13> -----> <PS14>
14. PS: Eva Benassi had a nurse	I <PS14> -----> <G+15>
15. G+: The nurse prayed to John Neumann	I <G+15> -----> <G+10>
16. PE: Eva Benassi recovered at Time T3	C <G+10> -----> <PE16>
17. S: Recovery was dramatic	M <PE16> -----> <S17>
18. PS: Time T3 was in 1923	P <PE16> -----> <PS18>
19. PE: A traffic accident occurred	C <PE19> -----> <PE20>
20. PE: Kent Lenahan's skull was fractured	P <PE20> -----> <PS21>
21. PS: Skull had fracture in two locations	C <PE19> -----> <PE22>
22. PE: Kent Lenahan's bones were smashed	C <PE19> -----> <PE23>
23. PE: Kent Lenahan's lung was pierced	C <PE20> -----> <PE24> C <PE22> -----> <PE24>
24. PE: Kent Lenahan was dying	C <PE23> -----> <PE24> I <PE19> -----> <G+25>
25. G+: Someone hospitalized Kent Lenahan	I <PE24> -----> <G+25>

(*continued*)

TABLE 5.11   (*Continued*)

Nodes	Arcs
26. PS: Kent Lenahan had a mother	P <PE24> -----> <PS26>
27. G+: The mother prayed to John Neumann	I <PE24> -----> <G+27>
	I <PS26> -----> <G+27>
28. S: Praying was ardent	I <G+27> -----> <G+11>
	M <G+27> -----> <S28>
29. PE: Kent Lenahan rose from the deathbed at Time T4	C <G+11> -----> <PE29>
30. PS: Time T4 was in 1949	P <PE29> -----> >PS30>
31. PE: Kent Lenahan's life resumed	C <PE29> -----> <PE31>
32. PS: The life was normal	P <PE31> -----> <PS32>

the issues that we confronted when we constructed conceptual graph structures for their passages. In the remainder of this section, we address some of the problems and issues at a more general level.

Information That is Not Captured by Our Conceptual Graph Structures.   It is important to restate which levels of information our representational theory is not designed to capture. Earlier in this chapter we specified six goals that motivated the development of our representational theory. Not surprisingly, our theory was not designed to explain all of the knowledge that a comprehender invokes during comprehension.

The representational theory was not designed to capture the global rhetorical levels of text organization. Psychologists have identified a number of rhetorical schemas for expository passages, such as a schema for passages involving definitions (Munro, Lutz, & Gordon, 1979), a schema for psychological research reports (Kintsch & van Dijk, 1978), a schema for newspaper articles (Thorndyke, 1979), and a schema for expository passages that introduce and elaborate on a topic (van Dijk, 1980). Expository passages could be subdivided into a number of subcategories with unique rhetorical properties within each subcategory. The rhetorical organization of a research report is clearly different from that of a newspaper article. Similarly there are rhetorical conventions for narrative prose (Mandler & Johnson, 1977; Rumelhart, 1975; Stein & Glenn, 1979; Thorndyke, 1977). The global rhetorical organization of narrative and expository prose is best construed as a level of structure that is different from that of our conceptual graph structures. The rules for mapping the rhetorical structures onto the conceptual graph structures have not been delineated. We intend to investigate these rules in future research.

Our representational theory has not been developed to the point of completely explaining *sequential* connectivity (Beaugrande, 1980), i.e., the order in which statements are presented in prose. We have identified some of the rules that would probably be part of a symbolic device that generates coherent sequential orderings from conceptual graph structures (see Graesser, 1981). For example, if two events, E1 and E2, are related by forward Consequence arc (i.e., $E1 \xrightarrow{C}$ E2), then Event E1 is usually stated before Event E2. According to this simple rule, events are mentioned in a chronological order when they are connected by Consequence arcs. Exceptions to this rule require the linguistic transformation of verb tense (e.g., E2 occurred-E1 *had* occurred) or the inclusion of a special connective (e.g., E2 *after* E1). However, we have not enumerated all of the rules that generate coherent sequences of statement nodes from the conceptual graph structures.

Our conceptual graph structures do not carry enough information to determine unique *surface structures*. A single graph structure can be articulated linguistically in many different ways, as we discussed earlier in this chapter. In order to account for the acceptable paraphrases of a conceptual graph structure, we would need to specify a set of rules that generate linguistic descriptions from the conceptual graph structures. These rules have not yet been worked out.

Our representational theory does not explain *pragmatic coherence* (Beaugrande, 1980), i.e., whether a passage is a coherent message in a communicative interchange between the writer and reader. The formulation of pragmatic coherence rules would be a very challenging project at this state of the science. One way to approach this problem is to build a conceptual graph structure for the writer/reader interaction; this pragmatic graph structure would be separate from the conceptual graph structure of the message content. Sometimes the message content addresses the pragmatic graph structure. For example, suppose that a passage about a nuclear reactor began as follows:

The purpose of this document is to inform you about the operation and safety of nuclear reactors . . .

This excerpt addresses the pragmatic graph structure involving the writer and reader rather than the conceptual graph structure that explains the mechanism of a nuclear reactor.

The fact that our representational theory does not explain the above phenomena should not be construed as a weakness. Our theory was designed to capture the organization of knowledge at the semantic-conceptual level. Moreover, the other representational theories in this volume have also not been able to explain the global rhetorical organization of prose, sequential coherence, pragmatic coherence, and the linguistic rules for generating surface structures from the underlying semantic structures.

Connectives.   Connectives include (a) transitional phrases in text that relate sentences and clauses (*however, therefore, but,* etc.), (b) higher-order predicates that interrelate propositions (*in order to, resulted in, lead to*), and logical operators (*and, or*). Meyer calls many of these connectives "rhetorical predicates." Connectives are important elements to study for a number of reasons. First, many connectives designate the arc categories that interrelate statement nodes in the graph structures. In Table 5.4 we listed some of the connectives that are associated with Reason, Consequence, and Initiate arcs, e.g., *in order to, because, so that,* and so forth. Second, connectives are used prevalently in expository prose in order to clarify the logical development of a topic. As we pointed out earlier, many connectives are signaling devices for different types of relationships. For example, an additive relation would have connectives such as *in addition, furthermore,* and *moreover,* whereas an adversative relation would have connectives such as *but, however,* and *on the other hand* (Halliday & Hasan, 1976). Third, connectives are not handled by our representational theory in a single, elegant manner.

Some connectives correspond directly to the arcs in our representational theory (i.e., Table 5.4). There are connectives associated with Reason arcs (*in order to, so that, by*), Consequence arcs (*because, led to, enabled, caused, and then, before, after, as a consequence of, implies*), Initiate arcs (*because, so*), Manner arcs (*by means of, in a manner that*) and Property arcs (*property of, attribute of*). Some connectives signal more than one arc category. For example, the connective *because* may signal either a Consequence or an Initiate arc.

The passages of other contributors in this volume contain connectives that are associated with the various arc categories. A few examples should reinforce this point. Meyer's *Supertanker* passage contained the following sentence.

As a result of spillage [oil was spilled in the ocean] the environment was damaged.

The excerpt involves Physical Event nodes and a Consequence arc as shown below.

⟨PE: Oil was spilled in the ocean⟩

$\Big|$ C

⟨PE: the environment was damaged⟩

Mayer's *Radar* passage contains the following excerpt.

Pulse transmission is suppressed in order to receive echo pulses.

This excerpt invokes two Goal nodes and a Reason arc, as shown below.

⟨Goal+: X suppresses pulse transmission⟩

|R

⟨Goal+: X receives echo pulses⟩

Voss's *Lion* passage had the following excerpt.

We . . . help each other by warning of danger.

This excerpt contains two Goal nodes and a Reason arc.

⟨Goal+: X warns Y of danger⟩

|R

⟨Goal+: X helps Y⟩

Some connectives do not signal a single arc in a conceptual graph structure. Instead, the significance of these connectives is related to a substructure of nodes and arcs. For example, consider following excerpt in Meyer's *Supertanker* passage.

the solution lies in the following three tactics.
First, . . . Second, . . . Third, . . .

There is a general Goal node, ⟨Goal: X solve problem⟩, and three tactics that constitute separate subgoals for achieving the goal. Each subgoal is linked to the main goal by a Reason arc. The connectives (First, Second, Third) enumerate the three different subgoals.

Consider the following excerpt from the *Supertanker* passage.

The Tanker . . . crashed off the coast . . . and resulted in the washing ashore of 200,000 dead seabirds. Oil spills also kill . . . plant life.

In this example, an oil spill has two consequences, namely the death of seabirds and the death of plant life. The connective *also* signifies that the death of plant life is the second consequence; the death of seabirds is the first consequence.

Events may have multiple consequences and multiple enabling states. Similarly, Goals may be accomplished by enacting several different plans and achieving several subgoals; intentional actions may be executed for more than one reason. Additive connectives (*in addition, moreover, furthermore*) occur when a particular node had multiple arcs directly emanating from it and two or more of these arcs are in the same direction and category. In the structure below there are multiple reasons for Goal 1.

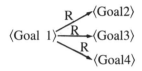

If the arcs were in the opposite direction, there would be multiple methods. In the structure below there are multiple consequences to Event 1.

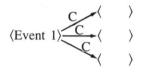

If these Consequence arcs were in the opposite direction, then Event 1 would have multiple causes or multiple enabling states.

The occurrence of some events are contingent on states of the world. Consider the following excerpt from Mayer's *Radar* passage.

When an object is present, it leaves a bright spot on . . . the screen.

This excerpt would include the following two nodes connected by a Consequence arc.

$$\langle \text{PS: object is present} \rangle \xrightarrow{\text{C}} \langle \text{PE: bright spot occurs on screen} \rangle$$

Of course, one would also infer the following configuration.

$$\text{PS: object is not} \xrightarrow{\text{C}} \text{PS: bright spot is not on}$$
$$\text{present} \qquad\qquad \text{screen}$$

There are a variety of connectives that signal contingencies: *if-then, when, whenever, as long as*. Expository passages often convey several different contingencies that are relevant to the topic under discussion. Some connectives signal adversative relations, (e.g., *however, on the other hand*). These would apply when there are a set of contingencies and some antecedent states of the world are incompatible. Our example contingency could be articulated as follows.

When an object is present, a bright spot occurs on the screen. However, when there is no object present, there is no bright spot on the screen.

Nouns Referring to Nodes and Arcs.   Nouns often refer to statement nodes or to arcs in conceptual graph structures. For example, in Meyer's *Supertanker* passage, *supertanker spills oil* is a Physical Event node at the beginning of the passage. A later reference to the node was the noun phrase *oil spill*. In the same passage there is a sentence that begins: *Attributes of a typical supertanker include. . . .* The noun *attributes* refers to a number of Property arcs that relate *supertanker* to some Physical State nodes.

Some nouns refer to a configuration of nodes and arcs. For example, consider the first sentence in Mayer's *Radar* passage.

Radar means the detection and location of remote objects by the reflection of radio waves.

Radar refers to a number of Physical Event nodes—e.g., *objects are detected, objects are located,* and *waves are reflected*—and a number of Physical State nodes. The statement node *Radar means X* would be difficult to accommodate by our representational theory. If *Radar means X* is a node, what other node or nodes would it be linked to? It appears that our theory needs to be modified. One solution is to assign X an abstract referent such as *PROCESS* and to embellish the PROCESS argument with the relevant Physical Events and States via a Property arc (or alternatively, a Manner arc). If this solution is adopted, then we would need to add the following composition rule to those listed in Table 5.3.

$$\text{Rule 7: } \langle \text{PROCESS argument of node} \rangle \xrightarrow{\text{P}} \langle \text{Event} \rangle$$

Causatives.   Most comprehenders do not have a scientifically or philosophically rigorous framework for interpreting causality. Cause-driven mechanisms are very complicated systems. How does the comprehender reduce the complexity of a cause-driven system? One way is to assume that a specific event in a system is caused by an animate agent or a static component in the system. For example, myths provided one way of understanding natural phenomena; animate beings intentionally create the events in a natural system such as the weather. Of course, attributing a cause to an animate agent does not reveal the details of how a system operates.

Expository passages often contain linguistic expressions with inanimate agents. In Mayer's *Radar* passage, for example, the excerpt *an antenna sends out a stream of short pulses* contains an inanimate agent. The antenna does not really create and send out the stream of pulses. Instead, waves travel to the antenna and are modified by virtue of the physical properties of the antenna.

Expressions with inanimate agents can be analyzed in two ways in our representational system. One analysis treats the inanimate agents as if they were animate agents. Thus, *an antenna sends out a stream of pulses* would be a Goal+ node. Many comprehenders may indeed construct Goal structures when they interpret causal systems. A second, alternative analysis would contain Physical Events and States interrelated by Consequence arcs as shown below.

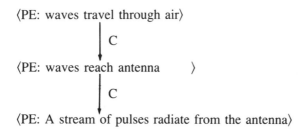

⟨PE: waves travel through air⟩

C

⟨PE: waves reach antenna   ⟩

C

⟨PE: A stream of pulses radiate from the antenna⟩

Expository passages sometimes contain linguistic expressions with a hidden agent, that is, an agent is elliptically deleted. The *Radar* passage contains the excerpt *a transmitter and a receiver are employed separately*. Someone or something *employs* these components, but the agent is not explicitly stated. In our analyses we fill in the hidden agent with a "dummy" argument, e.g., *X*.

Speech acts.   A speech act is performed whenever one person says something to another person. Speech acts may occur on two levels when a passage is comprehended. First, there is the pragmatic level which involves the communicative interchange between the writer and the reader of the passage. Second, there is the message level when the passage conveys what one character says to another character. In the present context we will be discussing speech acts at the message level.

Speech acts are considered Goal nodes in our analysis. Just as characters execute physical behavior to achieve goals, characters perform speech acts to achieve goals. When a Goal node is a speech act, the statement node contains a verb that specifies the "performative aspect" of the speech act (Austin, 1962; Searle, 1969). There are many types of performatives: informing, requesting, questioning, promising, and so forth. Voss's *Lion* passage contains many speech acts. The statements below were extracted from the *Lion* passage. Each statement is a Goal node that involves a speech act; the performative aspect of each statement should be obvious.

The mouse informed the other animals that he agreed with the tiger.
The tiger asked the rat whether the rat would join the other animals.
The tiger requested the animals to raise their paws.

These Goal nodes were expressed in the form of direct quotes in Voss's *Lion* passage.

The mouse said "I agree with tiger."
The tiger said . . . "Will you join us?"
The tiger said . . . "raise your paw."

Speech acts are performed to achieve higher level goals. When a character wants to obtain some information, the speech act is a question.

⟨Goal 1: character 1 get some information⟩

$\uparrow$ R

⟨Goal 2: character 1 asks character 2 about X⟩

When a character wants another character to do something, the speech act is a request.

⟨Goal 1: character 1 get character 2 to do X⟩

$\uparrow$ R

⟨Goal 2: character 1 request X from character 2⟩

The notion that speech acts are interrelated with a person's Goals would be accepted by a number of researchers (see Cohen & Perrault, 1979; Schmidt, 1976).

SOME REPRESENTATIONAL ISSUES THAT CONFRONT A THEORY WITH CONCEPTUAL GRAPH STRUCTURES

Our proposed representational system is not perfect and complete. There are a number of representational problems that need to be solved. In this section we will point out some of these problems and suggest some tentative but reasonable solutions.

Our proposed representational system was originally developed for narrative prose. Indeed, we were encouraged to learn that the conceptual graph structures for narrative passages explained data in a variety of behavioral tasks. Then we decided to tackle expository passages. The conceptual graph structures for expository prose continued to explain empirical trends in question-answering experiments and inference verification experiments. When applied to expository prose, we were satisfied with the representational system in many ways. However, for reasons discussed in the last section, the original representational system seemed incomplete.

The proposed representational system can obviously be expanded. We could introduce additional node and arc categories. For example, we could subclassify Consequence arcs into several subcategories, such as *leads to, causes, enables, results, implies*. We could subclassify Physical State nodes into social states, physical states, agent's abilities, normative obligations, and so forth. We could unpack nodes themselves into substructures containing primitive predicates (see Miller & Johnson-Laird, 1976; Norman & Rumelhart, 1975; Schank, 1972, 1973). However, there are practical disadvantages to bogging down the system with more distinctions and detail. First, the representation system needs to be simple if we want moderately trained individuals to use the system. Simplicity implies glossing over some distinctions that are potentially important. Second, the symbolic procedures that operate on graph structures grow in complexity as we introduce more arc and node categories. Some level of complexity is desired for an accurate explanation of the data. However, it is easy to become buried in esoteric problems of representation that are specific to the knowledge structures under investigation. We have decided to take a cautious approach. We have adopted node and arc categories only if they introduce important distinctions in many different knowledge structures.

Psychologists have sometimes pointed out problems with theories that map out representational structures for passages. The arguments on this matter are complex and we do not believe they need to be resolved entirely at this point in the science. For example, it is often said that it is hopeless to propose a representational structure for a passage and to say that the representation corresponds closely to the structure that humans construct. Why is such an enterprise hopeless? The true cognitive structures could vary from person to person depending on the comprehender's goals and prior knowledge. Indeed, all of the representation systems in this book would be subject to this criticism.

We acknowledge that the true cognitive representation of a passage varies from individual to individual. For a number of reasons, however, this fact alone is not sufficient to undermine the enterprise of composing theoretical representations for passages. A representational structure for a passage or schema is an idealized representation that may be a useful and valid predictor of human behavior. For example, we may view a theoretical structure as an ideal representation that captures the passage content and structure for an ideal comprehender. When an individual's true cognitive structure deviates from the theoretical ideal representation, the individual's performance in experimental tasks may suffer in specific and systematic ways. In this sense, the ideal representation is a useful and valid theoretical construct. In the same breath, we should emphasize that an acknowledgment of individual differences is not an explanation of individual differences. Indeed, theoretical passage representations may be a useful or necessary component of a theory that explains individual differences.

There is another reason why the problem of individual differences does not undermine the enterprise of constructing passage representations. The representational theory might be sufficiently flexible and complete to provide for several alternative representations of a passage. For example, we might propose a conceptual graph structure for a passage and claim that the structure is a typical structure. Alternatively, the structure might embody the conceptualizations that different individuals construct. We might claim, for example, that the theoretical graph structure for a passage may account for several substructures that specific individuals construct depending on their unique goals and prior knowledge. If we know (a) the comprehender's goals, (b) the comprehender's prior knowledge (i.e., schema content and structure), and (c) the conceptual graph structure for the passage, then we would predict some substructure to be the true passage representation for that individual. Thus, a conceptual graph structure would be useful if it could account for individual differences by transforming it and viewing it from alternative perspectives.

The issue of multiple perspectives became important when we tried to represent expository passages with our representational system. Graesser (1981) presented some evidence that there are more individual differences when individuals comprehend expository prose than narrative prose. To caricature the problem just a bit, when 20 individuals interpret an expository passage there are 13 different passage structures, whereas there are only 3 different passage structures for a narrative passage. The problem of multiple perspectives became even more salient when we started analyzing schema structures. A central property of a schema is to provide a conceptual framework for interpreting some common input when the input is viewed from alternative perspectives (Minsky, 1975; Norman & Bobrow, 1979).

We recently have been exploring how conceptual graph structures can be viewed from different perspectives. A particular perspective would presumably be manifested in a comprehender's summary protocol or recall protocol of a passage. What are some of the alternative perspectives of interpretation? A few of the alternative perspectives are discussed below.

Goal-Oriented Versus Cause-Oriented Structures.   It was sometimes difficult to decide whether a set of nodes should be embedded in a goal-oriented structure or a cause-oriented structure. For example, consider the structures in Figs. 5.4 and 5.5. The two structures capture the same content. However, Fig. 5.4 is a cause-oriented structure and Fig. 5.5 is a goal-oriented structure. Which structure is most appropriate?

One might argue that Fig. 5.4 is correct because it captures the fact that man had to *discover* an effective way for wheels to roll on a surface. By happenstance, wood was shaped in a smooth way; the smoothness of the wheel allowed the wheels to roll more easily. By happenstance, man cut at the base of a tree. Since the base of a tree is round, the wheel ended up round. Much to man's

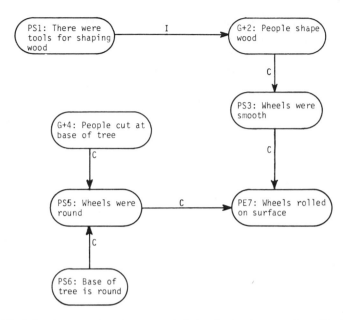

FIG. 5.4. A cause-oriented structure depicting the development of an effective wheel.

surprise, the round wheels rolled better than the square ones. Figure 5.4 embodies man's rocky road to the discovery of an effective wheel.

On the other hand, one might argue that Fig. 5.5 is correct because it captures man's *planning* when man created an effective wheel. Perhaps man started with the goal of having a wheel roll on a surface. In order to do this, man created two subgoals: to get the wheel round and to get the wheel smooth. In order to get a round wheel, man created the subgoal of cutting at the base of trees, because man knew that the base of trees are round. In order to get a smooth wheel, man had the subgoal of shaping wood, knowing that there were tools around for shaping. Figure 5.5 embodies man's rational planning of an effective wheel.

Perhaps both structures would be desired in the representational theory. Some comprehenders might construct the information in a cause-oriented fashion and others in a goal-oriented fashion. The orientation may depend on the goals of the comprehender (Black, 1981). Alternatively, all comprehenders may interpret the information in both ways. From some perspectives, the information would be constructed in a causal sense, whereas from other perspectives the information may be viewed in a goal-oriented sense. Consider the following two questions.

1. How did wheels come to roll on surfaces?
2. How did man get wheels to roll on surfaces?

When answering the first question, Fig. 5.4 may provide the most natural answer. For the second question, Fig. 5.5 might provide the most natural answer.

It is important to mention that goal-oriented structures map systematically onto causal sequences. Consider the following structural chain and the connectives.

Cause-oriented chains

Wheels rolled on surfaces *because* the wheels were round; the wheels were round *because* the people cut at the base of trees.

The fact that people cut at the base of trees had the *consequence* that the wheels were round; the fact that the wheels were round had the *consequence* that the wheels rolled on surfaces.

Goal-oriented chains

Man caused wheels to roll on surfaces *by* making round wheels; man made round wheels *by* cutting at the base of trees.

Man cut at the base of trees *in order to* make wheels round; man made round wheels *in order to* have the wheels roll on surfaces.

In some sense, all of these chains capture the same events despite the fact that the connectives are different, the orderings are different, and the emphasis is different. It is obviously important for man to arrange goal-structures to synchronize with physical constraints and causal necessity.

One way of handling the problem is to revise the representational system so that Goal nodes are decomposed into two subunits: (*1*) *Goals* and (*2*) *intended*

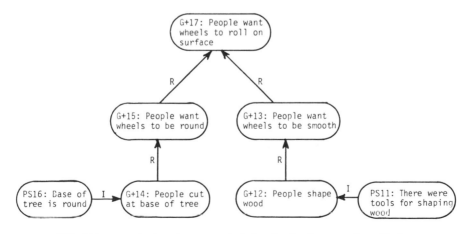

FIG. 5.5.   A goal-oriented structure depicting the development of an effective wheel.

outcomes that would be categorized as Physical Events. The revised conceptual graph structure in Fig. 5.6 would accommodate both the goal-oriented perspective and the cause-oriented perspective. This solution is compatible with Schank's Conceptual Dependancy Theory (Schank, 1975; Schank & Ableson, 1977). At the same time, however, there would be certain repercussions on (a) the symbolic procedures for question answering, (b) the ability of the graph structure to explain data collected in behavioral tasks, and (c) the ease with which the revised representational theory could be acquired and used by moderately trained judges.

Comprehenders sometimes impose goal-oriented structures on mechanisms that are strictly causal from the point of view of scientists. This occurs in mythology when natural phenomena (weather, the creation of the world, etc.) are understood as goal-oriented conceptualizations with gods, intentions of gods, and conflicts among gods. One way of understanding a cause-driven mechanism is to make an interesting story about it and thereby embellish the structure with Goal nodes and goal hierarchies.

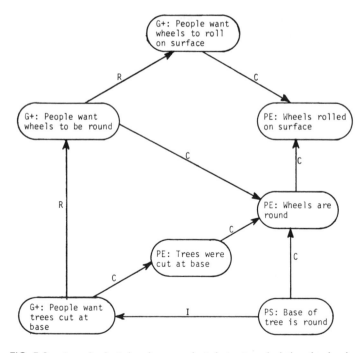

FIG. 5.6.   A goal-oriented and cause-oriented structure depicting the development of an effective wheel.

Descriptive Structures Versus Goal-Oriented Structures.   Descriptive conceptualizations contain a high density of State nodes and Property arcs. A descriptive structure would depict an object or scenario in a static way. Such a static description would not capture the functional, goal-oriented knowledge that often explains why specific states exist. For example, consider the following excerpt:

1. The four-wheeled coach developed in Germany.

There would be the following four explicit nodes in this excerpt.

PE1:   People developed coach at some location.
PE2:   The location was in Germany.
PE3:   The coach had wheels.
PE4:   There were four wheels.

The structure below interrelates these four nodes.

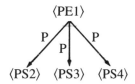

The above content and structure of the excerpt does not capture the goal-oriented knowledge that explains the existing states. Each of the Physical States or Events was presumably created with certain goals in mind. For example, the following goals would be relevant.

People wanted to transport people.
People wanted carts to be stable.
People wanted carts to move.

These goals would motivate and interrelate the Physical States and Events. Such functional knowledge would need to be incorporated in conceptual graph structures depicting Physical States that man manufactures. Some comprehenders would adopt a functional perspective whereas others would be satisfied with a descriptive, pictorial perspective. The goals and knowledge of the comprehender would be an obvious factor determining the comprehender's perspective. An artist would probably be satisfied with the descriptive perspective without seeking the functional underpinnings. An anthropologist would presumably seek a functional explanation of the static properties.

Perspectives of Alternative Agents.   The information in a passage may involve several animate agents. Each animate agent has his/her specific goal-oriented structure. Consider the following excerpt.

The Scythians fought enemies in Europe

This single excerpt would engender a number of goal structures, including the following.

The Scythians' goal structure
The enemies' goal structure
The goal structure of the writer
The goal structure of the comprehender

The goals of the comprehender and the writer presumably have some impact on the conceptual graph structure. Sometimes the comprehender analyzes the author's intentions and sometimes not. However, in this chapter we have made only passing reference to the pragmatic interaction between the writer and reader, or speaker and listener. In future research, we will be exploring the symbolic interaction between pragmatic levels of analysis and the conceptual graph structures of the passages.

The comprehender may take the perspective of one or more agents that are referenced in a passage. The two agents that are referred to in the example sentence are *the Scythians* and *the enemies*. There is a goal structure for the Scythians and another for the enemies. The comprehender might construct a detailed goal structure for the Scythians but a rarefied goal structure for the enemies. Indeed, the enemy structure might be so rarefied that the behavior of the enemies may be construed as Physical Events rather than goal-oriented actions. The comprehender may empathize with a specific character in a story and such a perspective would expand or enrich the goal structures of that character at the expense of the other characters. Recall protocols for stories vary systematically depending on the character with which the comprehender identifies or emphathizes (Anderson & Pichert, 1978; Bower, 1978). Reading times for sentences increase when comprehenders shift their point of view from one character to another character (Black, Turner, & Bower, 1979).

We believe that an important goal for a representational theory is to accommodate alternative structures that occur when the comprehender adopts different perspectives. The proposed conceptual graph structures do not depict the true cognitive representation of all comprehenders. Instead, the conceptual graph structures are theoretical representations that capture the knowledge that comprehenders may potentially construct. Thus, if we know the goals of a specific comprehender and the generic knowledge structures (schemas) of the specific comprehender, then in principle, we should be able to predict the comprehender's cognitive structure for a passage.

FINAL COMMENTS

At this point in time, our representational system is not perfect and complete. However, we believe that our representational system and our methodological approach is leading in the right direction. Unlike most theories of representation and comprehension, our research is scratching beneath the surface of explicit code and penetrating the mysteries of implicit knowledge.

ACKNOWLEDGMENTS

The research reported in this chapter was supported by a National Institute of Mental Health grant (MH-33491) awarded to the first author. We would like to thank the following members of the Cognitive Research Group at California State University at Fullerton who assisted us in conducting the reported studies: Lea Adams, John Bergeson, Leslie Clark, Scott Elofson, Tami Murachver, Glenn Nakamura, James Riha, and Judy Zimmerman. We are indebted to John Black for his helpful comments on an earlier draft.

REFERENCES

Abelson, R. P. The psychological status of the script concept. *American Psychologist,* 1981, *36,* 715–729.

Adams. M. J., & Collins, A. A schema-theoretic view of reading. In R. O. Freedle (Ed.), *New directions in discourse processing* (Vol. 2). Norwood, NJ: Ablex, 1979.

Agar, M. Themes revisited: Some problems in cognitive anthropology. *Discourse Processes,* 1979, *2,* 11–31.

Anderson, J. R. *Language, memory, and thought.* Hillsdale, NJ: Lawrence Erlbaum Associates, 1976.

Anderson, J. R. Arguments concerning representation for mental imagery. *Psychological Review,* 1978, *85,* 249–277.

Anderson, R. C. The notion of schemata and the educational enterprise: General discussion of the conference. In R. C. Anderson, R.J. Spiro, & W. E. Montague (Eds.), *Schooling and the acquisition of knowledge.* Hillsdale, NJ: Lawrence Erlbaum Associates, 1977.

Anderson, R. C., & Pichert, J. W. Recall of previously unrecallable information following shift in perspective. *Journal of Verbal Learning and Verbal Behavior,* 1978, *17,* 1–12.

Anderson, R. C., Spiro, R. J., & Anderson, M. C. Schemata as scaffolding for the representation of information in connected discourse. *American Education Research Journal,* 1978, *15,* 433–440.

Austin, J. L. *How to do things with words.* Oxford: Oxford University Press, 1962.

Beaugrande, R. *Text, discourse, and process.* Norwood, NJ: Ablex, 1980.

Beaugrande, R., & Colby, B. N. Narrative models of action and interaction. *Cognitive Science,* 1979, *3,* 46–66.

Becker, J. D. Reflections on the formal description of behavior. In D. G. Bobrow, & A. Collins (Eds.), *Representation and understanding.* New York: Academic Press, 1975.

Bisanz, G. L., & Voss, J. F. Sources of knowledge in reading comprehension: Cognitive development and expertise in a context domain. In A. M. Lesgold & C. A. Perfetti (Eds.), *Interactive processes in reading.* Hillsdale, NJ: Lawrence Erlbaum Associates, 1981.

Black, J. B. The effects of reading purpose on memory for text. In J. Long & A. Baddeley (Eds.), *Attention and performance IX.* Hillsdale, NJ: Lawrence Erlbaum Associates, 1981.

Black, J. B., & Bower, G. H. Story understanding and problem solving. *Poetics,* 1980, *9,* 223–250.

Black, J. B., Turner, T. J.,& Bower, G. H. Point of view in narrative comprehension, memory, and production. *Journal of Verbal Learning and Verbal Behavior,* 1979, *18,* 187–198.

Bock, M. Some effects of titles on building and recalling prose structures. *Discourse Processes,* 1980, *3,* 301–311.

Bower, G. H. Experiments on story comprehension and recall.*Discourse Processes,*1978,*1,*211–232.

Bower, G. H., Black, J. B., & Turner, T. J. Scripts in memory for text. *Cognitive Psychology,* 1979, *11,* 177–220.

Bransford, J. D., & Johnson, M. K. Consideration of some problems of comprehension. In W. G. Chase (Ed.), *Visual information processing.* New York: Academic Press, 1973.

Bransford, J. D., & McCarrell, N. S. A sketch of a cognitive approach to comprehension: Some thought about understanding what it means to comprehend. In W. B. Weimer & D. S. Palermo (Eds.), *Cognition and the symbolic processes.* Hillsdale, NJ: Lawrence Erlbaum Associates, 1974.

Brewer, W. F. Literary theory, rhetoric, and stylistics: Implications for psychology. In R. J. Spiro, B. C. Bruce, & W. F. Brewer (Eds.), *Theoretical issues in reading comprehension.* Hillsdale, NJ: Lawrence Erlbaum Associates, 1980.

Brewer, W. F., & Lichtenstein, E. H. Event schemas, story schemas, and story grammars. In J. Long & A. Baddeley (Eds.), *Attention and performance IX.* Hillsdale, NJ: Lawrence Erlbaum Associates, 1981.

Britton, B. K., Graesser, A. C., Glynn, S. M., Hamilton, T., & Penland, M. Use of cognitive capacity in reading: Effects of content features of text. *Discourse Processes,* 1983, *6,* 39–58.

Britton, B. K., Meyer, B. J. F., Hodge, M. H., & Glynn, S. Effects of the organization of text on memory: Tests of retrieval and response criterion hypotheses. *Journal of Experimental Psychology: Human Learning and Memory,* 1980, *6,* 620–629.

Brooks, C., & Warren, R. P. *Modern rhetoric.* New York: Harcourt Brace Jovanovich, 1972.

Brown, H. *Prose styles: Five primary types.* Minneapolis, MN: University of Minnesota Press, 1966.

Bruce, B. C. What makes a good story? *Language Acts,* 1978, *55,* 460–466.

Cantor, N. *Prototypicality and personality judgments.* Unpublished doctoral dissertation, Stanford University, 1978.

Chafe, W. L. *The pear stories: Advances in discourse processes,* Norwood, NJ: Ablex, 1980.

Charniak, E. A framed PAINTING: The representation of a common sense knowledge fragment. *Cognitive Science,* 1977, *1,* 355–394.

Charniak, E. On the use of framed knowledge in language comprehension. *Artificial Intelligence,* 1978, *11,* 225–266.

Chomsky, N. *Aspects of the theory of syntax.* Cambridge, MA: MIT Press, 1965.

Clark, H., & Clark, E. V. *Psychology and language.* New York: Harcourt Brace Jovanovich, 1977.

Cohen, A. D., & Graesser, A. C. The influence of advanced outlines on the free recall of prose. *Psychonomic Society,* 1980, *15,* 348–350.

Cohen, P. R., & Perrault, C. R. Elements of a plan-based theory of speech acts. *Cognitive Science,* 1979, *3,* 177–212.

Colby, B. N. A partial grammar of Eskimo folktales. *American Anthropologist,* 1973, *25,* 645–662.

Coleridge, S. T. Biographia literaria. In D. Perkins (Ed.), *English romantic writers.* New York: Harcourt, Brace, & World, 1967.

Collins, A. M. Processes in acquiring knowledge. In R. C. Anderson, R. J. Spiro, & W. E. Montague (Eds.), *Schooling and the acquisition of knowledge.* Hillsdale, NJ: Lawrence Erlbaum Associates, 1977.

Collins, A. M., Brown, J. S., & Larkin, K. M. Inference in text understanding. In R. J. Spiro, B. C. Bruce, & W. F. Brewer (Eds.), *Theoretical issues in reading comprehension.* Hillsdale, NJ: Lawrence Erlbaum Associates, 1980.

Collins, A. M., & Gentner, D. A framework for a cognitive theory of writing. In L. W. Gregg & E. Steinberg (Eds.), *Cognitive processes in writing: An interdisciplinary approach.* Hillsdale, NJ: Lawrence Erlbaum Associates, 1980.

Corsaro, W. A. Communicative processes in studies of social organization: Sociological approaches to discourse analysis. *Text,* 1981, *1,* 5–64.

Crothers, E. J. Memory structure and the recall of discourse. In J. B. Carroll & R. O. Freedle (Eds.), *Language comprehension and the acquisition of knowledge.* Washington, DC: Winston, 1972.

Crothers, E. J. *Paragraph structure inference.* Norwood, NJ: Ablex, 1979.

Decker, R. E. *Patterns of exposition IV.* Boston, MA: Little, Brown, & Company, 1974.

den Uyl, M. J. *Controlling inferences by semantic cohesion.* Paper presented at the second annual Cognitive Science Conference, New Haven, CT: 1980.

Ericsson, K. A., & Simon, H. A. *Thinking aloud protocols as data.* (C.I.P. working paper No. 397). Pittsburgh, PA: Carnegie-Mellon University, 1979.

Fillmore, C. J. The case for case. In E. Bach & R. J. Harms (Eds.), *Universals in linguistic theory.* New York: Holt, Rinehart & Winston, 1968.

Flower, L. S., & Hayes, J. R. The dynamics of composing: Making plans and juggling constraints. In L. Gregg & E. R. Steinberg (Eds.), *Cognitive processes in writing.* Hillsdale, NJ: Lawrence Erlbaum Associates, 1980.

Frederiksen, C. H. Effects of context-induced processing operation on semantic information acquired from discourse. *Cognitive Psychology,* 1975, *7,* 139–166.

Goetz, E. T., & Armbruster, B. B. Psychological correlates of text structure. In R. J. Spiro, B. C. Bruce, & W. F. Brewer (Eds.), *Theoretical issues in reading comprehension.* Hillsdale, NJ: Lawrence Erlbaum Associates, 1980.

Graesser, A. C. How to catch a fish: The representation and memory of common procedures. *Discourse Processes,* 1978, *1,* 72–89.

Graesser, A. C. *Prose comprehension beyond the word.* New York: Springer-Verlag, 1981.

Graesser, A. C., Gordon, S. E., & Sawyer, J. D. Memory for typical and atypical actions in scripted activities: Test of a script pointer + tag hypothesis. *Journal of Verbal Learning and Verbal Behavior,* 1979, *18,* 319–332.

Graesser, A. C., Hauft-Smith, K., Cohen, A. D., & Pyles, L. D. Advanced outlines, familiarity, text genre, and retention of prose. *Journal of Verbal Learning and Verbal Behavior,* 1980, *48,* 209–220.

Graesser, A. C., Higginbotham, M. W., Robertson, S. P., & Smith, W. R. A natural inquiry into the National Enquirer: Self-induced versus task-induced reading comprehension. *Discourse Processes,* 1978, *1,* 355–372.

Graesser, A. C., Hoffman, N. L., & Clark, L. F. Structural components of reading time. *Journal of Verbal Learning and Verbal Behavior,* 1980, *19,* 131–151.

Graesser, A. C., & Nakamura, G. The impact of a schema on comprehension and memory. In G. H. Bower (Ed.), *The psychology of learning and motivation* (Vol. 16), New York: Academic Press, 1982.

Graesser, A. C., Robertson, S. P., & Anderson, P. A. Incorporating inferences in narrative representations: A study of how and why. *Cognitive Psychology*, 1981, *13*, 1–26.

Graesser, A. C., Robertson, S. P., & Clark, L. F. A Q/A method of exploring on-line construction of prose representations. In J. Fine & R. O. Freedle (Eds.), *New directions in discourse processing*. Norwood, NJ: Ablex, 1983.

Graesser, A. C., Robertson, S. P., Lovelace, E., & Swinehart, D. Answers to why-questions expose the organization of story plot and predict recall of actions. *Journal of Verbal Learning and Verbal Behavior*, 1980, *19*, 110–119.

Grimes, J. *The thread of discourse*. The Hague: Mouton, 1975.

Halliday, M. A., & Hasan, R. *Cohesion in English*. London, Longman, 1976.

Hamilton, D. L. Illusory correlations as a basis for stereotyping. In D. L. Hamilton (Ed.), *Cognitive processes in stereotyping and intergroup behavior*. Hillsdale, NJ: Lawrence Erlbaum Associates, 1981.

Harris, R. J., & Monaco, G. E. Psychology of pragmatic implications: Information processing between the lines. *Journal of Experimental Psychology: General*, 1978, *107*, 1–22.

Hayes, J. R., & Flower, L. S. Identifying the organization of writing processes. In L. W. Gregg & E. Steinberg (Eds.), *Cognitive processes in writing*. Hillsdale, NJ: Lawrence Erlbaum Associates, 1980.

Hayes-Roth, B., & Hayes-Roth, F. A cognitive model of planning. *Cognitive Science*, 1979, *3*, 275–310.

Hayes-Roth, F., Waterman, D. A., & Lenat, D. E. Principles of pattern-directed inference systems. In D. A. Waterman & F. Hayes-Roth (Eds.), *Pattern-directed inference systems*. New York: Academic Press, 1978.

Johnson-Laird, P. N. Mental models in cognitive science. *Cognitive Science*, 1980, *4*, 71–115.

Just, M. A., & Carpenter, P. A. Inference processes during reading: Reflections from eye fixations. In J. W. Senders, D. F. Fisher, & R. A. Monty (Eds.), *Eye movements and higher psychological functions*. Hillsdale, NJ: Lawrence Erlbaum Associates, 1978.

Kieras, D. E. Good and bad structure in simple paragraphs: Effects on apparent theme, reading time, and recall. *Journal of Verbal Learning and Verbal Behavior*, 1978, *17*, 13–28.

Kieras, D. E. Initial mention as a signal to thematic content in technical passages. *Memory and Cognition*, 1980, *8*, 345–353.

Kieras, D. E. Component processes in the comprehension of simple prose. *Journal of Verbal Learning and Verbal Behavior*, 1981, *20*, 1–23.

Kintsch, W. *The representation of meaning in memory*. Hillsdale, NJ: Lawrence Erlbaum Associates, 1974.

Kintsch, W. On modeling comprehension. *Educational Psychologist*, 1979, *14*, 3–14.

Kintsch, W., & van Dijk, T. A. Toward a model of text comprehension and production. *Psychological Review*, 1978, *85*, 363–394.

Kintsch, W., & Keenan, J. Reading rate and retention as a function of the number of propositions in the base structure of sentences. *Cognitive Psychology*, 1973, *5*, 257–274.

Kintsch, W., Kozminsky, E., Streby, W. J., McKoon, G., & Keenan, J. M. Comprehension and recall of text as a function of content variables. *Journal of Verbal Learning and Verbal Behavior*, 1975, *14*, 196–214.

Lehnert, W. *The process of question answering*. Hillsdale, NJ: Lawrence Erlbaum Associates, 1978.

Mandl, H., Schnotz, W., & Ballstaedt, S. *Learning from text: Seen from the perspective of action theories*. Paper presented at the twenty-second International Congress of Psychology, Leipzig, Germany, Deutscheland Democratic Republic, 1980.

Mandler, J. M. Categorical and schematic organization in memory. In C. R. Puff (Ed.), *Memory organization and structure*. New York: Academic Press, 1979.

Mandler, J. M., & Johnson, N. S. Remembrance of things parsed: Story structure and recall. *Cognitive Psychology*, 1977, *9*, 11–151.

Meyer, B. J. F. *The organization of prose and its effects on memory*. New York: American Elsevier, 1975.

Meyer, B. J. F. The structure of prose: Effects on learning and memory and implications for educational practice. In R. C. Anderson, R. J. Spiro, & W. E. Montague (Eds.), *Schooling and the acquisition of knowledge*. Hillsdale, NJ: Lawrence Erlbaum Associates, 1977. (a)

Meyer, B. J. F. What is remembered from prose: A function of passage structure. In R. O. Freedle (Ed.), *Discourse processes: Advances in research and theory* (Vol. 1). Norwood, NJ: Ablex, 1977. (b)

Miller, G. A., Galanter, E., & Pribram, K. H. *Plans and the structure of behavior*. New York: Holt, Rinehart, & Winston, 1960.

Miller, G. A., & Johnson-Laird, P. N. *Language and perception*. Cambridge, MA: Harvard University Press, 1976.

Miller, J. R., & Kintsch, W. Readability and recall of short prose passages: A theoretical analysis. *Journal of Experimental Psychology: Human Learning and Memory*, 1980, *6*, 335–354.

Minsky, M. A framework for representing knowledge. In P. H. Winston (Ed.), *The psychology of computer vision*. New York: McGraw-Hill, 1975.

Morgan, J. L., & Green, G. M. Pragmatics and reading comprehension. In R. J. Spiro, B. C. Bruce, & W. F. Brewer (Eds.), *Theoretical issues in reading comprehension*. Hillsdale, NJ: Lawrence Erlbaum Associates, 1980.

Mosenthal, P. Reading comprehension research from a classroom perspective. In J. Flood (Ed.), *Understanding reading comprehension*. Newark, Delaware: International Reading Association, 1983.

Munro, A., Lutz, K. A., & Gordon, L. *On the psychological reality of text types*. Unpublished manuscript, University of Southern California, 1979.

Newell, A. Production systems: Model of control structures. In W. G. Chase (Ed.), *Visual information processing*. New York: Academic Press, 1973.

Newell, A. Harpy, production systems and human cognition. In R. Cole (Ed.), *Perception and production of fluent speech*. Hillsdale, NJ: Lawrence Erlbaum Associates, 1980.

Newell, A., & Simon, H. A. *Human problem solving*. Englewood Cliffs, NJ: Prentice-Hall, 1972.

Nicholas, D. W., & Trabasso, T. Towards a taxonomy of inferences. In F. Wilkening, J. Becker, & T. Trabasso (Eds.), *Information integration by children*. Hillsdale, NJ: Lawrence Erlbaum Associates, 1980.

Nicholas, J. K., & Nicholl, J. R. *Rhetorical models for effective writing*. Cambridge, MA: Winthrop Publishers, Inc., 1978.

Norman, D. A., & Bobrow, D. Descriptions: An intermediate stage in memory retrieval. *Cognitive Psychology*, 1979, *11*, 107–123.

Norman, D. A., & Rumelhart, D. E. *Explorations in cognition*. San Francisco: Freeman, 1975.

Olson, D. R. The language of instruction: On the literate bias of schooling. In R. C. Anderson, R. J. Spiro, & W. F. Montague (Eds.), *Schooling and the acquisition of knowledge*. Hillsdale, NJ: Lawrence Erlbaum Associates, 1977.

Olson, G. M., Mack, R., & Duffy, S. *Strategies for story understanding*. Paper presented at the meeting of the Cognitive Science Society, Yale University, New Haven, 1980.

Revlin, R., & Mayer, R. E. (Eds.) *Human reasoning*. New York: Wiley, 1978.

Rumelhart, D. E. Notes on a schema for stories. In D. G. Bobrow & A. Collins (Eds.) *Representation and understanding*. New York: Academic Press, 1975.

Rumelhart, D. E. Schemata: The building blocks of cognition. In R. J. Spiro, B. C. Bruce, & W. F. Brewer (Eds.), *Theoretical issues in reading comprehension*. Hillsdale, NJ: Lawrence Erlbaum Associates, 1980.

Rumelhart, D. E., & Ortony, A. The representation of knowledge in memory. In R. C. Anderson, R. J. Spiro, & W. E. Montague (Eds.), *Schooling and the acquisition of knowledge*. Hillsdale, NJ: Lawrence Erlbaum Associates, 1977.

Sanderson, J. L., & Gordon, W. K. (Eds.) *Exposition and the English language*. New York: Appleton-Century-Crofts, 1963.

Schank, R. C. Conceptual dependancy: A theory of natural language and understanding. *Cognitive Psychology*, 1972, *3*, 552–631.

Schank, R. C. Identification of conceptualizations underlying natural language. In R. C. Schank, & K. M. Colby (Eds.), *Computer models of thought and language*. San Francisco: Freeman, 1973.

Schank, R. C. The structure of episodes in memory. In D. G. Bobrow & A. Collins (Eds.), *Representation and understanding*. New York: Academic Press, 1975.

Schank, R. C. Language and Memory. *Cognitive Science*, 1980, *4*, 243–284.

Schank, R. C., & Abelson, R. *Scripts, plans, goals, and understanding*. Hillsdale, NJ: Lawrence Erlbaum Associates, 1977.

Schmidt, C. F. Understanding human action: Recognizing the plans and motives of other persons. In J. S. Carroll & J. W. Payne (Eds.), *Cognition and social behavior*. Hillsdale, NJ: Lawrence Erlbaum Associates, 1976.

Schweller, K. G., Brewer, W. F., & Dahl, D. A. Memory for illocutionary effects of utterances. *Journal of Verbal Learning and Verbal Behavior*, 1976, *15*, 325–334.

Searle, J. R. *Speech acts*. London: Cambridge University Press, 1969.

Singer, M. The role of case-filling inferences in the coherence of brief passages. *Discourse Processes*, 1980, *3*, 185–201.

Spilich, G. J., Vesonder, G. T., Chiesi, H. L., & Voss, J. F. Text processing of domain related information for individuals with high and low domain knowledge. *Journal of Verbal Learning and Verbal Behavior*, 1979, *18*, 275–290.

Spiro, R. J. Remembering information from text: Theoretical and empirical issues concerning the "state of schema" reconstruction hypothesis. In R. C. Anderson, R. J. Spiro, & W. E. Montague (Eds.), *Schooling and the acquisition of knowledge*. Hillsdale, NJ: Lawrence Erlbaum Associates, 1977.

Spiro, R. J. Constructive processes in prose comprehension and recall. In R. J. Spiro, B. C. Bruce, & W. F. Brewer (Eds.), *Theoretical issues in reading comprehension*. Hillsdale, NJ: Lawrence Erlbaum Associates, 1980.

Stein, N. L., & Glenn, G. G. An analysis of story comprehension in elementary school children. In R. O. Freedle (Ed.), *New directions in discourse processing* (Vol. 2). Norwood, NJ: Ablex, 1979.

Stein, N. L., & Nezworski, T. The effect of organization and instructional set on story memory. *Discourse Processes*, 1978, *1*, 177–193.

Stevens, A. L., & Collins, A. Multiple conceptual models of a complex system. In R. E. Snow, P. A. Frederico & W. E. Montague (Eds.), *Aptitude, learning, and instruction: Cognitive process analysis*. Hillsdale, NJ: Lawrence Erlbaum Associates, 1979.

Taylor, S. E., & Crocker, J. Schematic bases of social information processing. In E. T. Higgins, P. Herman, & M. P. Zanna (Eds.), *The Ontario symposium on personality and social psychology*. Hillsdale, NJ: Lawrence Erlbaum Associates, 1981.

Thorndyke, P. W. Cognitive structures in comprehension and memory of narrative discourse. *Cognitive Psychology*, 1977, *9*, 77–110.

Thorndyke, P. W. Knowledge acquisition from newspaper stories. *Discourse Processes*, 1979, *2*, 95–112.

van Dijk, T. A. *Macrostructures: An interdisciplinary study of global structures in discourse, interaction, and cognition*. Hillsdale, NJ: Lawrence Erlbaum Associates, 1980.

Vipond, D. Micro- and macroprocesses in text comprehension. *Journal of Verbal Learning and Verbal Behavior*, 1980, *19*, 276–296.

Warren, W. H., Nicholas, D. W., & Trabasso, T. Event chains and inferences in understanding narratives. In R. O. Freedle (Ed.), *New directions in discourse processing* (Vol. 2). Norwood, NJ: Ablex, 1979.

Wilensky, R. Why John married Mary: Understanding stories involving recurring goals. *Cognitive Science*, 1978, *2*, 235–266.

Wilks, Y. What sort of taxonomy of causation do we need for language understanding. *Cognitive Science*, 1977, *1*, 235–264.

6

Knowledge and the Processing of Narrative and Expository Texts

James F. Voss
University of Pittsburgh

Gay L. Bisanz
University of Alberta

In the last decade considerable research has been devoted to the question of how text is processed. In these investigations, narrative texts have received most of the attention, expository texts have received somewhat less study, and other types of text have received virtually no study at all. Viewed in general terms, research on how text is comprehended and remembered has shown that it is a function of two factors, the structure of the text itself and the knowledge utilized by the individual. Interestingly, research on narrative text has tended to focus upon the role of knowledge while research on expository text has tended to focus on the role of text structure. The present paper is concerned with assessing the current state of research on how knowledge influences text processing. Because of the differential emphasis in research on narrative and expository texts, this chapter begins with a discussion of studies on knowledge and the processing of narrative text. The second part focuses upon the role of knowledge in processing expository text, drawing comparisons to narrative when appropriate. Finally, there is a brief concluding section.

KNOWLEDGE AND THE PROCESSING OF NARRATIVE TEXT

Virtually all recent studies that have focused on the role of knowledge in processing narratives have been formulated within what Rumelhart (1977) has termed "the modal model." Within this framework, knowledge is assumed to be organized into units often called "schemata" (see Adams & Collins, 1979; Rumelhart, 1980b; Rumelhart & Ortony, 1977; and Thorndyke & Yekovich, 1980, for general discussions of this concept). Text processing is hypothesized to involve the construction of a coherent representation of a passage through the activation and verification of schemata at various levels of abstraction. These schemata allow the reader to account for and interpret information explicitly mentioned in the text and also to make inferences about information not mentioned. In addition, Graesser, Gordon and Sawyer (1979) have proposed a "schema-plus-tag" hypothesis which has a provision for tagging information that is uncommon to schemata. In general, it is assumed that schemata play an important role in encoding, recalling, summarizing, producing, and learning from narratives.

Knowledge of Text Structure

Much research has been focused on the role of knowledge of story structure in recalling and summarizing simple stories (Black & Bower, 1979; Glenn, 1978; Kintsch & Greene, 1978; Kintsch, Mandel, & Kozminsky, 1977; Kintsch & van Dijk, 1975; Mandler, 1978; Mandler & De Forest, 1979; Mandler & Johnson, 1977; Mandler, Scribner, Cole & De Forest, 1980; Rumelhart, 1975, 1977; Stein & Glenn, 1979; Stein & Nezworski, 1978; Thorndyke, 1977). The simple stories that have been studied include a subclass of narratives that focus on the problem-solving behavior of a single protagonist. Investigators have argued that with exposure to these stories, individuals develop a schema that incorporates knowledge about prototypical sequences of story events (cf. Mandler & Johnson, 1977).

There have been at least two ways in which knowledge of such sequential structure has been described. The "story grammar" approach has been used to characterize the individual's knowledge of story structure as constituent events that can be established by a set of re-write rules. The terminal nodes derived by applying these rules represent the structural components of the narratives, and successive nodes are assumed to be related by connectives such as AND, CAUSE, and ALLOW. (For discussion of the merits of this approach see Black & Wilensky, 1979; Mandler & Johnson, 1980; and Rumelhart, 1980b.) A second, less frequently employed, approach has been to characterize individuals' knowledge of story structure in terms of "systems of schemata" that parse stories as if they were goal-directed problem-solving episodes (Rumelhart, 1977).[1]

Researchers who have focused on the individual's knowledge of story structure have not denied the importance of other types of knowledge. For example,

---

[1]Kintsch and van Dijk (1975; Kintsch, 1977) have also characterized knowledge of story structure in the context of developing a general theory of text macrostructure.

Mandler and Johnson (1977) acknowledged that the individual's knowledge of causal relations and various types of action sequences is important in story understanding. Likewise, Poulsen, Kintsch, Kintsch, and Premack (1979) have discussed children's description and recall of picture stories in relation to knowledge of story components as well as knowledge of principles and rules of human action. Similarly, the existence of and need to characterize story schemata relevant to genre other than the simple problem-solving story has been acknowledged. For example, Mandler (1978) has indicated that people have experienced many types of stories and could draw on a number of schemata to fit them. Thus, *research focused on knowledge of the structure of simple stories reflects pragmatic decisions about how to begin studying the retention and summarization of narrative texts,* rather than reflecting a commitment to the centrality of such knowledge in general theories of knowledge application and text processing.[2] We shall briefly describe some of the insights that have been derived from this approach.

Studies of Story Recall.   In initial attempts to demonstrate that story schemata influence retrieval, individuals have been asked to recall stories with disrupted plot structure or told to recall them in an order other than the canonical sequence (e.g., Mandler, 1978; Mandler & De Forest, 1979; Stein & Nezworski, 1978; Thorndyke, 1977). These studies show that there is a strong tendency to recall stories in prototypical order regardless of how stories have been presented or how subjects have been instructed to recall them (Mandler, 1978; Mandler & De Forest, 1979). The studies also have demonstrated that disrupted plot structure can lead to decrements in the quantity of recall (e.g., Stein & Nezworski, 1978; Thorndyke, 1977). Furthermore, Thorndyke (1977) showed that repeating story structure across successively presented stories can enhance recall, whereas repeating story content can cause proactive interference.

Other research has examined the effects of specific components of the hypothesized story schema upon recall. For example, through manipulations of episode length, results have been obtained indicating that "the episode" serves as a basic unit in organizing story recall (Black & Bower, 1979; Glenn, 1978). More recently, Mandler and Goodman (1980) have demonstrated the psychological validity of even lower-level components. Their method involved measuring the speed of retrieving adjacent sentence pairs when these pairs were both within and outside the boundaries of story grammar categories.

Analyses of story structure have also contributed to the understanding of issues that have arisen in cross-cultural research (e.g., Kintsch & Greene, 1978; Mandler, Scribner, Cole, & DeForest, 1980) and especially in developmental studies of memory (e.g., Mandler & Johnson, 1977; Stein & Glenn, 1979). For

---

[2]This point is important to emphasize because the goals of this line of research, particularly as it relates to story grammars, are often misunderstood (see for example, Mandler in press).

example, within the developmental literature, an important question has been whether or not young children's recall reflects temporal order and cause and effect relations. Both Piaget (1926/1960) and Fraisse (1963) claimed that it does not. Prior to story grammar analyses, the issue had been investigated within the context of research on children's memory. However, the stimuli used in these studies more closely resembled word lists than actual narratives (e.g., Brown, 1975). By using story grammars to examine the relationship between text structure and recall, it has been demonstrated that children as young as six have little trouble recalling temporal and causal relations in "well-formed" stories (Mandler & Johnson, 1977; Stein & Glenn, 1979). Initial speculation about the conflicting evidence derived from these recent studies and those of Piaget centered around the unusual structural features or complexity of the narratives employed by Piaget (see Mandler & Johnson, 1977; Stein & Glenn, 1979). However, a recent reanalysis of Piaget's *own* data, using the categories and relations identified in grammars, speaks directly to the need for analytical tools like the story grammar: The analysis simply failed to provide evidence supporting Piaget's claim about deficiencies in young children's recall (Stein & Trabasso, in press).

Studies of Story Summarization.   Research on summarization has lead to the development of models that try to explain how individuals are able to select and summarize the important aspects of a story. Studies have shown that while the information contained in summaries is nearly always included in recall protocols, such protocols differ from summaries in that they contain more details of the plot (Kintsch & van Dijk, 1975; Rumelhart, 1977; Thorndyke, 1977). This relationship is explained within Rumelhart's (1977) framework as follows: Systems of schemata assign a structure to the events of a story. The outcome is a hierarchical representation that provides a way to distinguish between the important parts of a story and relatively unimportant details, namely, the higher the information in the representation, the more central and important it is (cf. Thorndyke, 1977). The summarization process then involves (a) selecting a level of summarization and (b) removing nodes in the representation below the chosen level. Generation of a summary is then handled by a set of summarization rules that are associated with specific nodes of the hierarchy and are able to generate a sequence of appropriate sentences. While remembering just the information at the higher nodes is equivalent to providing a summary of a story, recall within this framework involves locating the traces of a story in memory and using the story schemata to reconstruct the original message in a top-down fashion. Thus, summarizing and recalling are related in that nodes higher in the structure are of primary importance to both.

In contrast, the Kintsch and van Dijk model (1975, 1978; Kintsch, 1977) incorporates a more general mechanism of summarization that is not necessarily dependent upon, but definitely enhanced by, the operation of a story schema. In this theory, the semantic structure of text is assumed to have two general levels.

The *microstructure* level consists of propositions and their relations, while the *macrostructure* level consists of propositions that characterize the text as a whole. The macrostructure is derived through the application of macrorules to the text microstructure, with the rules producing deletion of some micropropositions, generalization of others, and/or construction of new macropropositions that subsume several micropropositions. The operation of macrorules thus acts to create a more abstract representation that preserves the essential meaning of a text. The macrorules are assumed to operate under the control of a schema, which, in the case of simple stories, is the schema characterized by story grammar theories. As the macro-operators are applied, their products are classified in terms of their relevance or irrelevance to the controlling schema, and it is this process that determines the parts of the text that will be used in producing summaries (cf. Kintsch & van Dijk, 1975).

Within the Kintsch and van Dijk model, propositions occurring in summaries and in recall protocols are hypothesized to be related because one's memory representation for stories consists of macropropositions and associated micropropositions. When asked to recall, it is assumed that subjects use the macrostructure as a cue producing both this information and any related micropropositions that are still in memory. When asked to summarize, subjects are assumed to base their responses on macrostructure information (Kintsch & van Dijk, 1975). Thus, this view is quite similar to that of Rumelhart's (1977) in that summarization is the result of information stored at a relatively high level and information at this level is used to recall more detailed information. The primary difference in the positions is in the means by which the higher-level information is generated.

A Caveat.   The intention of our discussion thus far has been to illustrate the usefulness of an approach focused on knowledge of story structure. We have not attempted to describe all the findings related to recall and summarization, nor have we even begun to discuss research focused on the role of story schemata in encoding, producing or learning from narratives (see for example, Botvin & Sutton-Smith, 1977; Feedle & Hale, 1979; Mandler & Goodman, 1980). While there is little doubt that the focus on knowledge of story structure has been fruitful, we would suggest that such a narrow focus may be reaching a point of diminishing returns. Indeed, research must now be broadened to consider other types of knowledge that a comprehender uses in understanding texts. This need derives from the fact that many interesting questions about the development and application of story schemata cannot be answered without making reference to such knowledge. We use examples from our own research to illustrate this point.

Perhaps because work on knowledge of story structure has been confined to a schema that even young children have acquired, questions about knowledge important to the development and application of story schemata have been largely ignored. These questions became highlighted when we began to examine children's knowledge of *Protagonist-Antagonist* (P-A) stories. For example, in a recent protocol study, Bisanz (see Bisanz & Voss, 1981) had children in grades 2, 4, 6 as well as college students listen to a P-A story about nine animal characters. The story was stopped at certain points and subjects were asked to anticipate the next event. The study was designed to assess subjects' expectations about P-A stories. Two developmental trends are of relevance to this discussion.

The first trend relates to the question of whether or not subjects were making reference to a P-A story schema in generating their expectations. For grade 2 and 4 students the answer appears to be negative. In fact, the data indicated that they were applying their knowledge of *single* protagonist stories in conjunction with their knowledge of human behavior, rather than making reference to a P-A story schema. This hypothesis was derived largely from their inability to anticipate the actions of the story antagonist. However, the expectations of students in grade 6 were consistent with the hypothesis that they were making reference to a P-A story schema. The college student data yielded yet another pattern. In many cases college students were less likely than the sixth-grade children to generate problem-solving attempts for the characters, giving as a reason for not generating attempts the possible motives of the characters. Such findings led to the hypothesis that college students were jointly applying their knowledge of a schema for P-A stories and their knowledge of social human behavior. This is not to say that grade 6 students were not using the latter, but somehow it was more subordinate to their story schema.

The second trend pertains to the number of text schemata that individuals become familiar with as they grow older. At one point in the story, where a major character's problem-solving attempt had just ended in failure, subjects were repeatedly probed about what might happen next. Overall there was a significant increase in the number of alternatives generated as a function of age. Grade 6 students generated the most alternatives consistent with a P-A story schema, whereas the number and nature of alternatives generated by college students suggested that their expectations were being influenced not only by a P-A story schema, but also by their broader experience with a wide range of text types. For example, one college student, when asked to justify why he had anticipated that the story would end happily, said, "Stories usually end in a happy way, [but] a lot of them that I've read haven't like *Animal Farm.*"

This study brings into focus a number of questions about the role of knowledge in the development and application of narrative schemata. First, *is there a default strategy that can be used to understand narratives when no clear story schema applies or when it is ambiguous as to whether a currently activated schema will account for story events?* Given data from the study just described, we would suggest that the answer is affirmative, and that the strategy involves application of general knowledge about human actions. In fact, a number of theories of narrative comprehension have focused on knowledge of human actions as a primary factor in the understanding process. These theories are the subject of the next section. Second, *how might deficiencies in knowledge about human behavior affect the development and application of story schemata?* It may be that the younger children in this study did not apply a P-A story schema because it was simply not available: Deficiencies in their knowledge of social actions may have prevented them from abstracting the sequences of behavioral interactions necessary to schema development. Likewise, such knowledge deficiencies could decrease the chances that younger children will recognize cues relevant to the application of story schemata that they have already acquired (cf. Bisanz, in press). Third, *how does the individual decide whether he is reading a fairy tale, a social commentary like Animal Farm, science fiction, or any other type of text?* The answer would appear to lie in the contents of the passage as it unfolds. There may well be linguistic cues, but for other cues the individual will rely on other types of knowledge, like knowledge of social actions, to recognize and classify physical and human events.

In addition to these questions, Bisanz and Voss (in preparation) raise a more sensitive question: How much does a story schema really account for memory performance even if it is known to be operative? Bisanz and Voss (1981b) conducted an experiment in which children in grades 1 and 4, as well as college students, recalled a P-A story. The Kintsch and van Dijk (1978) model was applied to the data. This model assumes that text processing occurs in cycles of n propositions, which Kintsch and van Dijk (1978) initially defined as the number of propositions in a sentence. A similar assumption was made in the Bisanz and Voss analysis. Another assumption of the Kintsch and van Dijk model is that each set of n propositions is checked for referential coherence. This process is represented by constructing connected graphs, and arranging the graphs into levels using a simplicity criterion. Our graphs were arranged into levels by letting the proposition determined to be the focus of the sentence head the graph.

The Kintsch and van Dijk (1978) model also incorporates four parameters, s, p, m, and g. The g parameter was not considered in this analysis and thus will not be discussed. The s parameter denotes a working memory buffer that carries s propositions over from one cycle to the next. In our analysis, the value of s was assumed to be 2, since Spilich, Vesonder, Chiesi and Voss (1979) found this value to provide the best fit even when individuals differed in knowledge. In addition, propositions from the leading edge of the graphs were assumed to be carried over between cycles (Kintsch & Vipond, 1979). The p and m parameters denote the probability of recalling a microproposition and macroproposition, respectively. Macropropositions and micropropositions were designated based upon hypotheses about the type of schema controlling comprehension and recall at each age. Among the candidate schemata examined were those for single protagonist and P-A stories. Specifically, four m parameters (in various combinations) were employed: One represented the primary theme (or the single protagonist schema), one represented the secondary theme (or the P-A schema), and two represented the elaboration of each of the two themes respectively (see

Bisanz & Voss, 1981). The value of the p parameter is based upon the number of cycles in which a proposition occurs. Equations representing the recall probability for each proposition were generated, and estimates of the parameter values for each hypothesized schema at each age were then obtained.

One result of these analyses was that the p parameter alone accounted for over 90% of the variance explained for all age groups and hypothesized schemata. Macrostructure parameters added to the variance explained, but the amount was small when compared to the p parameter. This result is understandable when one considers the implications of applying the Kintsch and van Dijk (1978) model to long passages. Many previous applications involved modeling the recall of relatively short passages (Kintsch & van Dijk, 1978; Miller & Kintsch, 1980), whereas our story has 281 propositions. Each of these propositions had a probability of recall associated with the p parameter. In contrast, only 11 to 97 of these propositions had a probability of recall associated with the various m parameters, depending upon which schema was assumed to control processing. Thus the p parameter is much more important than m in explaining the pattern of recall for longer passages simply because it is relevant to so many more propositions.

Since the p parameter in this analysis reflected knowledge of what determines the focal proposition in a sentence, one interesting issue is just what that knowledge may be. We suggest that knowledge about focal propositions is related to knowledge about human actions. This is not to say that story schemata are unimportant, but rather to point out that the features (propositions) in any reasonably long narrative that explicitly match the features of the controlling story schema will be relatively small compared to the total pattern of recall to be explained. As a consequence, explanations related to other types of knowledge must be considered. For narratives, knowledge of human actions is surely one important type.

Summary.   For all the fruitfulness of research focused on the role of story schemata, applications of such schemata are highly specialized strategies for processing text. Many of the interesting questions now surrounding story schemata cannot be answered without making reference to other types of knowledge, including knowledge of human actions. We now consider strategies related to the application of other types of knowledge.

Other Types of Knowledge

It is generally assumed that an individual who attempts to understand a given text brings to bear schemata relevant to the topic of the discourse (e.g., Just & Carpenter, 1980). This knowledge is thought to be applied in conjunction with or in lieu of a schema for text structure. While several content domains may be relevant to understanding narratives, most theories devoted to the study of knowledge other than that of story structure assume that stories are read primarily with an eye toward explaining the actions of main characters (cf. Omanson,

1982a). Given this emphasis, a considerable body of research has been accumulating that focuses upon knowledge about human actions (e.g., Black & Bower, 1980; Bruce & Newman, 1978; Graesser, Robertson, & Anderson, 1981; Lichtenstein & Brewer, 1980; Omanson, 1982a; Schank & Abelson, 1977; Warren, Nicholas, & Trabasso, 1979).

Knowledge of Human Actions. There have been several systems of passage representation developed to characterize the content of narratives in terms of knowledge of human actions (Black & Bower, 1980; Bruce & Newman, 1978; Graesser, Robertson, & Anderson, 1981; Omanson, 1982a; Schank & Abelson, 1977; Warren, Nicholas, & Trabasso, 1979). These approaches play down the importance of setting information as a separate constituent of stories and focus upon the units and relations that are thought to comprise action sequences. Central to most of these analyses is the assumption that human actions are understood by identifying goals and inferring characters' plans to achieve those goals. Analyses have differed in the nature of the units and relations identified and the degree to which specific knowledge about social actions rather than general knowledge about problem-solving procedures has been emphasized.

Bruce and Newman (1978) developed a representation of interacting plans in stories. This analysis uses sets of symbols within "belief spaces" to represent characters' models of a social situation. The symbols stand for basic entities (e.g., acts, intentions, beliefs, states) connected by labeled relations that are thought to be sufficient to characterize both plans mutually shared by characters and "virtual plans" designed to deceive. Omanson's (1982a) analysis is an attempt to develop a theory of centrality that predicts story recall. Central content is "that which is part of the purposeful-causal sequence of events that leads to the end of the narrative" (p. 22). It is hypothesized that individuals will judge it "more important" and recall it better than non-central content. Furthermore, the recall of central content can be enhanced by content defined as "supportive," but impaired by "distracting" content. The analysis assumes narrative understanding proceeds through the application of knowledge about social actions.

Schank and Abelson (1977) make a similar assumption concerning the importance of knowledge about social actions. In their theory, the meaning of narratives is characterized as a set of causal chains that link the representations of simple sentences (i.e., single thoughts or conceptualizations). Some causal chains lead to dead ends and others carry on the theme of the story. The latter are hypothesized to be remembered better. Since many of the causal relations that render a text understandable are not stated explicitly, Schank and Abelson (1977) discuss both general and specific types of knowledge that individuals use to infer such relations. Applications of these knowledge types have been referred to as "*plan-based*" and "*script-based*" *understanding*, respectively.

It is *Hierarchical-State-Transition theory* (Black & Bower, 1980) that proposes that the representation of stories is similar to the representation of problems used by problem solvers. In this analysis, the reader is "viewed as an interested observer-scientist trying to make sense of the story character's problem solving protocol'' (p. 244). Other analyses (e.g., Graesser, Robertson, & Anderson, 1981; Warren, Nicholas, & Trabasso, 1979) have drawn on insights provided by some of the previous theories, but have attempted to deal explicitly with the types of inferences a comprehender must make.

These systems of passage representation have contributed significantly to our understanding of narrative comprehension. For example, several approaches allude to what might be termed the *"primary causal path"* hypothesis. This is the hypothesis that narrative units comprising the sequence of goal-directed, causally related events that leads to the resolution of the plot will be better remembered. Black and Bower (1980) refer to such events as being on the "Critical Path," Omanson (1982a) calls this "Central Content," and Schank and Abelson refer to this "Causal Chain" as being special because of its multiple connections to other events in the story.[3] Indeed, studies designed to test this hypothesis have generally obtained positive findings (Black & Bower, 1980; Omanson, 1982b; Stein & Trabasso, 1982).

Another example of the contributions associated with these approaches is the research on knowledge of stereotypical action sequences, commonly referred to as "scripts" (Schank & Abelson, 1977). That individuals have and utilize such stereotypical knowledge in comprehending narrative text has been readily demonstrated (e.g., Bower, Black, & Turner, 1979; Graesser, Gordon, & Sawyer, 1979).

Specialized Knowledge.   Thus far in this section we have discussed the role knowledge of human actions in comprehending and remembering simple narratives. Another type of knowledge that has been shown to influence the processing of narratives is what we shall term "specialized knowledge." This refers to knowledge of a specific subject matter domain such as geography, history, sports, or religion. Typically, expertise in any of these fields is taken to require extensive training and/or experience.

The influence of specialized knowledge upon the comprehension of narrative text has been pursued via an extension of the novice-expert contrastive paradigm to text processing (Chase & Simon, 1973; de Groot, 1966). In an initial study, Spilich, Vesonder, Chiesi and Voss (1979) had individuals with high (HK) or low knowledge (LK) listen to a segment of a fictitious baseball game, the subjects being matched on reading ability. The text was analyzed in terms of its propositional structure. Macrostructure propositions were established based upon the goal structure of the game of baseball rather than linguistic rules. Thus, what was different about this analysis was that the controlling schema was assumed to be knowledge about the goals of baseball rather than a narrative schema. A major finding was that HK individuals recalled more information related to the goal-

---

[3]There are, of course, important differences among these analyses in the way the "primary causal path" is characterized.

structure of the game than did LK individuals. Moreover, HK individuals were especially superior in recalling the sequence of important events of the game. There was little difference in HK and LK performance in recalling information not related to the game's goal structure, e.g., the weather. Furthermore, application of the Kintsch and van Dijk (1978) model indicated that HK individuals showed a superior ability to carry over macrostructure propositions from one processing cycle to the next. Such an ability should both improve the connectivity of propositions in the memory representation and increase the chances that those macropropositions will serve as effective retrieval cues for related microstructure information.

A more recent study, using the same contrastive method, provided further insight into the role of specialized knowledge (Voss, Vesonder & Spilich, 1980). In this study HK and LK individuals generated a segment of a fictitious baseball game, with recall of the self-generated passage occurring 2 weeks later. A major difference in the texts generated was that HK individuals generated passages with more elaborated descriptions of game actions and related changes in the state of the game. In other words, while LK individuals generated state changes, the actions that enabled these state changes were omitted or stated with no elaboration; HK individuals, on the other hand, generated relatively elaborate descriptions of the actions.

In a second experiment HK- and LK-generated passages were presented and each type of passage was recalled by both HK and LK individuals. It was found that HK individuals recalled HK-generated passages better than LK individuals. However, for LK-generated passages, there was no difference in HK and LK recall.

These findings may be related to an earlier study by Black and Bower (1979) who showed that increasing the number of subordinate actions that elaborate the important actions of a story has the effect of increasing the recall probability of the latter. The stories in the Black and Bower study were about familiar situations like learning to play tennis, finding a book for a college class, or looking for a job. A general explanation of the Voss et al. data and the findings of Black and Bower data is that actions that elaborate the important events of a narrative keep the reader or listener at a central event longer, clarifying, amplifying, and embellishing its memory trace. This, in turn, increases the recall probability of the event (see Omanson, 1982b). Moreover, as argued by Voss, Vesonder, and Spilich (1980), such actions also provide additional retrieval cues that serve as a basis for remembering how the narrative moved from one state to the next. A general principle, then, is that *adding subordinate actions to a story should increase the probability that superordinate actions or related states will be recalled.* However, the elaborating information in Black and Bower's study is likely to have been highly familiar to the subjects. The study by Voss et al. (1980) adds a boundary condition to this principle, namely, *the principle holds only when it can be determined that the comprehender understands the domain-specific relations that make the added information subordinate and elaborative.*

The hypothesis behind this proposed boundary condition is as follows: The more elaborated descriptions generated by HK individuals in the Voss et al. study provided unique encodings of game actions for these individuals and these encodings served to facilitate subsequent retrieval. However, because the relationships of important game actions and state changes were less clear to LK individuals, these same descriptions were ineffective with respect to developing a representation that enabled the individual to retrieve the appropriate sequences of actions and state changes.

A Second Caveat. As with the discussion of research focused on story structure, our intent in this section has been to illustrate the benefits of approaches focused on knowledge about human actions and specilized knowledge. Again, there is little doubt that this perspective has been fruitful. However, two related problems emerge from this research whose resolution is critical to formulation of a general theory of knowledge and narrative processing. The first problem pertains to the explanatory status of story schemata and the second relates to the need for a theoretical framework that unifies our understanding of how the various types of knowledge influence story comprehension. We discuss each issue briefly, once again using examples from our own research to illustrate our points.

One issue that emerges from the perspective of research about human action is whether or not we really need models of schemata for story structure to account for narrative comprehension. As was mentioned earlier, researchers focusing largely on knowledge of story structure have acknowledged the importance of other types of knowledge. However, because the structure of planning behavior and narrative episodes are so similar, it is difficult to state categorically that researchers focusing on the role of other types of knowledge have always seen the importance of story schemata (e.g., Black & Bower. 1980). This is, in part, because of the simplicity of the stories examined empirically from a structural point of view: The "episode schema" can largely account for the understanding and recall of simple stories, and it is central to both story schema and "human action" accounts of narrative recall (see for example, Black & Bower, 1979). We would argue, however, that beyond very simple single protagonist stories, there are story genre where the expectations attributed to story schemata cannot as readily be attributed to other sources of knowledge. The data, described earlier, focused on individuals' expectations about P-A stories, is certainly preliminary evidence that supports this point. Moreover, the explanatory role of story schemata may be further clarified as developmental psychologists begin to formulate theories about the development of comprehension skills in children. For example, Means and Voss (1981) showed that the relative importance of knowledge of text structure and specialized knowledge may vary as a function of age.

Means and Voss (1981) employed what was termed an expanded narrative. In elementary schools, and especially in social studies, narratives arc occasionally presented that have subject matter information embedded in the narrative. For example, Jack and Jane take a trip to France with their parents and within this narrative context, information about France is presented in terms of what the family sees and does. In the Means and Voss study children of grades 2, 4, and 6 as well as college students were presented with a story about a vacation trip taken by a girl and her parents to the home of the girl's grandmother. The trip was taken from one Pennsylvania town to another by car. While the narrative describes episodes of the trip, during the ride the members of the family observe air pollution, and these observations produce discussion about the causes, effects, and solutions of air pollution. Prior to receiving the text, individuals were given a test of air pollution knowledge. Subsequent to the presentation of the text, individuals recalled the contents of the passage and were given a recognition test consisting of questions about air pollution and about the narrative portions of the text.

The results of concern pertain to the recall pattern. The second-grade subjects recalled more story information than air pollution information, but there was little organized recall with respect to either type of information. Fourth graders produced recall protocols that were highly "scripted," i.e., they recalled the narrative contents in the appropriate order and embedded air pollution information within the narrative. The modal response of the sixth graders and the college students was to recall narrative information up to the first embedding of air pollution information, from which point air pollution information followed. While sixth graders recalled some additional narrative information after recalling information about air pollution, college students recalled additional narrative information only rarely. Thus, while fourth graders stuck to the narrative format, sixth graders and especially college students tended to segment recall into the narrative and air pollution components. These findings suggest that knowledge of the story schema influenced the processing of the fourth graders, but the older subjects, while in part following the schema structure, departed significantly from that structure. Although these findings do not provide a direct test of the relative influence of text structure knowledge and specialized knowledge, they do indicate that older children and adults are able to and do depart from prototypical structures in recalling narratives under particular circumstances. Younger children either do not or are not able to depart from such structures.

One may ask whether these differences between recall protocols reflect a difference in the way in which the story was comprehended and/or whether the differences reflect a retrieval strategy. Means and Voss argue that the story is comprehended by developing an understanding of relations as the story unfolds. The second graders have difficulty in establishing any continuity in the story while the fourth graders are able to develop a representation of the story that is sequentially quite isomorphic with the story itself. However, sixth graders and especially college students have at their disposal alternative ways in which the story information can be organized, and the recall data primarily reflect an alternative organization of the story contents.

The developmental trend observed in this work is notable: There is a lack of application of text schema by younger children, evidence for the application of text schema by slightly older children, and evidence of alternative text processing strategies by still older children. Bisanz (Bisanz & Voss, 1981) found a similar trend with respect to Protagonist-Antagonist stories. An early set of studies by Mandler and her colleagues (Mandler, 1978; Mandler & De Forest, 1979) showed that for simple stories, children are more dependent upon story schemata for retrieval than adults. More recently, Goldman and Varnhagen (1981) provided evidence that young children overextend the use of story schema for multi-episode stories whereas older children and adults did not. All these studies suggest that at certain levels of knowledge acquisition, expectations about text structure play an important role in accounting for performance. However, it will take process explanations of such findings to clarify the theoretical status of such schemata.

The second issue that emerges in reviewing the literature on knowledge and the processing of narratives is that there is a clear need for a theoretical synthesis that encompasses the role that various types of knowledge play in narrative comprehension. Without a synthesis, the field lacks a comprehensive theory of narrative understanding. Furthermore, the adequacy of schema theory as a unifying conceptual framework remains uncertain. A major question then is, what form should this synthesis take? Two approaches are at least suggestive of directions for future theorizing.

One approach is the idea of "systems of schemata" discussed previously in connection with Rumelhart's work on summarization. The general strategy is to develop concrete models of schemata that play roles in comprehending a wide range of texts. Rumelhart (1977) specified an EPISODE schema, which indicates the relationships among the initiating event, goal, and attempt in problem-solving stories, and a TRY schema, which specifies the internal structure of the attempt. These schemata are represented as being hierarchically embedded, with the most abstract schemata at high levels in the structure. The EPISODE schema is the story schema that has come to be associated with story grammar theories. However, the TRY schema assigns a structure to events in a manner consistent with the theory of problem solving embedded in Newell and Simon's (1972) General Problem Solver. If the hierarchical structure were to be expanded to even lower levels, one could represent the utilization of specific kinds of social knowledge, like Schank and Abelson's (1977) "Persuade Package." Thus the approach represents one way to begin to specify how knowledge of story structure may relate to other types of knowledge in the understanding process.

A second approach may be derived from a discussion by Kintsch (1977) on the topic of how readers organize stories. Kintsch assumed that processing of standard narratives occurs under the guidance of a story schema. According to this view, the first task in the understanding process involves a chunking of the text into segments that correspond to schema categories. The second task is deriving a propositional label for each segment, which, together with the other labels, will constitute the macrostructure for the text. Kintsch's speculations about how segmenting occurs suggests another plausible link between knowledge of story structure and other types of knowledge.

Kintsch suggests that while there may be graphic and linguistic cues that help in segmentation, the most important cues are the "discontinuities in time, location, actors and the content of the story itself" (p. 42). For example, in one story, Kintsch speaks of a sequence of three frames, or schemata, as providing contexts for interpreting plot actions, beginning with a "Lovers" frame, then a "Poisoning" frame, a "Trial" frame, followed by a reinstatement of the "Lovers" frame. In this three-episode story, each place where the reader must change frames in order to interpret the action sequence signals both the beginning of a complication and a new episode. The proposal then is that *while processing under the control of a story schema, major changes in lower-level schemata that serve as contexts for interpreting actions, also serve as cues to text segmentation.* Previous work has focused on the coherence of action sequences in stories. Kintsch's speculations suggest that future work should also examine the coherence of the schemata that provide contexts for interpreting those actions.

The observation that the two approaches that we have considered have much in common suggests that a conceptual framework may be emerging that can encompass the various types of knowledge used in comprehending and remembering narrative text.

Summary.   Research focused on the role of knowledge of human actions and specialized knowledge has provided insights into general strategies of knowledge application and text processing. Whereas research focused on text structure is limited to explaining performance on clearly identifiable text genre, an approach focused on general knowlege is more likely to account for the wide variety of text that readers can comprehend. However, the possible explanatory role of story schemata for narratives of relatively simple and moderately complex structure should not be ignored, nor should their potentially important role in developmental theories of story comprehension. Progress depends upon the development of theoretical frameworks that unify our understanding of the roles that various types of knowledge play.

KNOWLEDGE AND THE PROCESSING
OF EXPOSITORY TEXT

The study of expository text has evolved in a manner somewhat different from that of narrative text. Specifically, research on expository text began with attempts to describe the structure of such text and determine how performance, usually recall of the text contents, was related to the proposed structure. With this orientation, the bulk of the research has consisted of proposing and evaluating models of text structure; little interest has been shown in postulating and investigating knowledge of the structure of expository text. Research on other types of knowledge relevant to the comprehension of expository passages is also scarce. Hence our treatment of expository text differs from our treatment of narratives. As a way of contrasting the two literatures, we begin by describing some of the research related to models of text structure and then describe the research that relates to knowledge.

Models of Text Structure

Beginning with the work of Dawes (1964, 1966), most attempts to analyze text structure have consisted of describing a particular passage in terms of a set of logical and/or linguistic relations. Subsequently, recall performance is compared to predictions yielded by the hypothesized structure. Crothers (1972) pursued this research strategy, although the recall performance he obtained did not map well onto the hypothesized text structure. Frederiksen (1972, 1975a; 1975b) developed a model of text structure that included the use of linguistic relations to describe within-sentence structure and logical relations to describe between-sentence structure. Meyer (1975) also developed a model of text structure and used linguistic relations to describe within-sentence structure. For between-sentence structure, she followed the model of Grimes (1975) using rhetorical predicates to describe the text relations. Meyer's work, as presented in this volume, describes higher-order relations via the use of five logical relations. While these systems of passage representation are undoubtedly intended to have wide applicability, virtually all of the systems have been applied primarily to analyze the structure of expository texts, with the exception of the *Circle Island* passage, which is a rather drab narrative.

While the previously described work utilizes linguistic and logical structure to analyze text, the role of text structure as it is conceived by Kintsch and his colleagues represents a somewhat different emphasis. Kintsch (1974) analyzed text into its propositional structure and, rather than hypothesizing some form of higher-order logical or linguistic structure, he distinguished levels of text structure in terms of argument repetition. This emphasis upon argument repetition thus provided a way to characterize passage coherence and at the same time derive a hierarchical structure. Support for the model was obtained (e.g., Kintsch, Kozminsky, Streby, McKoon, & Keenan, 1975). However, this initial model has since given way to a model that retains the notion of coherence but attributes many of the effects previously related to hierarchical structure to assumptions about how the individual processes the passage. (See Meyer's chapter in this volume for a discussion of the similarities and differences in the Meyer and Kintsch models.) Again, hypothetically it should make little difference whether the model is applied to expository, narrative or some other type of text, though many recent applications have involved expository texts (e.g., Kintsch & van Dijk, 1978; Miller & Kintsch, 1980).

With respect to determining how text structure and recall performance are related, it seems fair to assert that virtually all of the models discussed thus far have been concerned primarily with explaining a *levels effect*. That is, models typically yield passage descriptions that produce a hierarchy consisting of approximately four levels (cf. Meyer & McConkie, 1973). It is then demonstrated that information in the highest level is best recalled, information at the next highest level is recalled more frequently than at the third level, and so forth. How the levels are derived is, of course, what essentially distinguishes the models.

One of the issues pertaining to the levels effect is whether the text structure per se establishes the levels or whether the content of particular segments of text establishes the levels. Meyer (1977) presented identical segments of a text either as subordinate to a higher level of text or as superordinate to other text. It was found that recall of the contents of the text segment was better when the text segment was superordinate, thus indicating that recall is not simply a function of the text contents per se, but the context in which the text segment is presented. In another study, Britton, Meyer, Hodge, and Glynn (1980) found evidence supporting the view that the levels effect may be a retrieval rather than storage effect. The two studies thus point to the conclusion that the levels effect is not something that is produced by the characteristics of a given text segment per se, but that such an effect may vary with conditions, as for example context or recall strategy.

Knowledge of Text Structure

In the narrative literature, the influence of knowledge of text structure has been studied most frequently with children. The goal of the research has been to show the existence and operation of such knowledge in recall performance. In these studies, large differences in recall performance occur with age, which may be attributed to differences in knowledge—hence, the interest in characterizing the types of knowledge essential to understanding. In contrast, research on expository text has generally been conducted with college students who have had considerable reading experience and background knowledge relative to the passages they are reading. Furthermore, the texts used in almost all of the work cited thus far have quite a standard structure, i.e., a topic sentence and subtopics sequentially developed in the passage. Thus, given the experience of the individuals and the standardness of the texts, it would be expected that comprehension would largely reflect understanding of specific conceptual relations in the texts. Thus, it is the processing of these relations that most investigators have studied and not knowledge of some generalized text structure. Interestingly, in the one study that has been concerned with the relation between knowledge of narrative structure and knowledge of expository structure (Freedle & Hale, 1979), the performance of young children was examined.

It is important to note that the lack of studies concerning knowledge of expository text structure does not indicate that such knowledge does not exist. Certainly there is a consensus that an expository passage often involves a hierarchical organization consisting of a top-level statement, which in turn is considered in relation to a number of subtopics. However, there are other forms of expository text structure as well, with some structures being quite specific, e.g., knowledge of experimental reports. The notion that there does not appear to be a generalized expository text structure is similar to a problem found in studying narrative text, namely, that there also is no prototypical text structure for narratives except at perhaps the most general level. Thus, there may be a prototypical structure for single protagonist stories and protagonist-antagonist stories, but it is exceedingly difficult to indicate a prototypical narrative structure that includes all narratives, except perhaps for specifying SETTING-MIDDLE-END. However, unlike narratives, for expository texts there is no single knowledge domain, like knowledge of human actions, that can be expected to provide insights into the way most expository texts are understood when knowledge of structure is not guiding expectations. In theory, expository texts can focus on any knowledge domain. By comparison, the study of narratives looks highly constrained and the study of expository text stands as a major challenge to general theories of knowledge application and text processing.

While the major thrust of the research on expository prose has involved the development of models of text structure, there has been some recent research on expository schemata. The primary type of passage examined has been the scientific exposition. Carpenter and Just (1981) developed a grammar for technical passages, which they used in developing a process model based upon eye fixations. Also, a grammar of experimental reports was introduced by Kintsch and van Dijk (1978) and developed by Vesonder (1979). Vesonder postulated four major components of experimental reports and rewrite rules for decomposing each of the four parts into their respective constituents. Vesonder then presented two science passages to college students who were either science majors or non-science majors. He obtained results suggesting that science majors had a better knowledge of the prototypical structure of reports of experiments, as indicated by the pattern of performance. Thus, for this relatively specific type of text, evidence was found that supports the notion that knowledge of text structure may facilitate processing. However, some results of the study were not in agreement with the hypothesis, and the passages had scientific contents, a factor that provided a possible confounding of knowledge of prototypical text structure and domain knowledge. Nevertheless, the results are suggestive. In addition, Freedle and Hale (1979) have done research with children that suggests that narrative schemata may develop before expository schemata. The latter finding again suggests the importance of text schemata to developmental theories of comprehension skills.

Other Types of Knowledge

Specialized Knowledge.   Research on the role of knowledge of relevant content domains or specialized knowledge is virtually non-existent in the literature on expository texts. However, one would expect that such knowledge is quite important. Indeed, based upon the research on narrative text, one can hypothesize about the locus of the performance differences that should result from this knowledge in the domain of baseball. Specifically, with narrative text, HK individuals were better able to remember the sequence of information flow than were LK individuals. As mentioned previously, this difference was attributed primarily to the ability of high-knowledge individuals to use game actions to connect changes in game states and thus construct a representation that was sequentially coherent. LK individuals, however, were apparently not able to utilize the actions in this way. Expository text, however, does not have a State, Action, Change-of-State structure. Most often it has a hierarchical structure which has more general information at the top of the structure and more detailed, less important information at the bottom. However, there are usually a number of subtopics, and in some cases the sequence of subtopic development is important because the information is cumulative, whereas in other cases the order of presentation of the subtopics is unimportant. If we assume this general type of hierarchical structure, how should specialized knowledge about baseball influence performance?

The intuitive answer is that processing expository texts about baseball should be more difficult for LK individuals in at least two ways. First, because the contents of the lower levels of the hierarchical structure typically involve the detailed development of higher-level information, lower-level information should be more difficult to relate to the higher-level information for LK individuals. There are at least two possible reasons for this hypothesis. One is that LK individuals may be capable of carrying less information in a working memory buffer than HK individuals and thus have relatively more difficulty in relating the high-level to the low-level information. The other possibility is that the LK individual may not understand the conceptual links that relate higher-level information to low-level information. The second advantage that HK individuals should have is that if temporal order is of importance to subtopic development, HK individuals should be better able to understand the sequential flow of the subtopic contents. This hypothesis follows from the previously demonstrated specificity of high-knowledge individuals in recalling the sequential characteristics of narrative text.

Recently Post and Voss (1981) presented two expository passages to two groups of individuals with high or low baseball knowledge, respectively. One passage presented a description of how playing conditions had changed since the game of baseball was first played, while the second passage presented a description of strategies used in the game. The first passage contained primarily what Spilich et al. (1979) termed non-game information, which was expected to be readily recalled by both HK and LK individuals. The second passage described four strategies in terms of the play of the game and HK individuals were expected to recall more information from this passage than were LK individuals. The two passages were quite similar in structure, with a topic sentence beginning each passage and each passage having four subtopics, each of which was developed. Presentation of each passage was followed by recall, probe questions, and a recognition task.

The results indicated that recall of the "Playing Conditions" passage by HK and LK individuals was quite similar, both quantitatively and qualitatively, although recall was slightly superior for HK individuals. However, recall performance of the "Strategies" passage was considerably better for the HK than for LK individuals. The LK individuals recalled the major subtopics but, apart from the first subtopic, recall of subtopic subordinate information was poor.

A number of analyses were conducted in order to determine why HK recall was superior to that of the LK individuals. We applied the Kintsch and van Dijk (1978) model to the data, hypothesizing that in the "Strategies" passage HK performance was superior because the HK individuals could carry over more information in a short-term memory buffer than could LK individuals and thus enhance the likelihood that information just presented would be related to new information. In the Kintsch and van Dijk model, the amount of information, in terms of number of propositions carried over from one cycle to the next, is given by the s parameter and we applied the model with s values of 2, 3, and 4. Contrary to our hypothesis, for both HK and LK individuals and for both passages, the best fit of the model was always with $s = 2$, a result suggesting that HK individuals were not in fact carrying over more information in a short-term buffer than were LK individuals.

An examination of the contents of the passages suggested an alternative reason for the superiority of HK performance. In the "Strategies" passage subtopic development essentially consisted of defining a strategy, indicating when it is typically used, indicating desirable outcome it sometimes has as well as its major limitation. Thus, for "hit-and run," the passage would indicate that the strategy was used when runners were on base and they would run before the batter hits the ball, and so forth.

Specialized Knowledge and Cognitive Development.   Earlier in this chapter reference was made to the study by Means and Voss in which air pollution information was embedded in a narrative passage. As previously stated, a test of air pollution was given to the participants before the experiment, and a number of these questions pertained directly to the information contained in the passage. The results of the air pollution test indicated that as age increased, knowledge of air pollution increased. After the passage was presented and the contents recalled, the air pollution test was repeated. It was found that with a priori knowledge of air pollution covaried, there was no difference in performance with respect to amount of air pollution information recalled. The results thus indicate that while older individuals remembered more information from the passage about air pollution than younger individuals, this difference was eliminated when knowledge was covaried. While these results are only from one study, it is of more than passing interest that prior knowledge was quite important, as compared to age or the previously discussed differences in recall strategies of passage information. Similarly, in another study, it was found that second graders' knowledge about spiders was related to recall of information contained in a passage about spiders (Pearson, Hansen, & Gordon, 1979). However, the extent to which the children may have known any particular information in the passage was not reported.

Summary

The influence of various types of knowledge upon the comprehension and recall of expository text has received relatively little attention. The results that do exist suggest that the influence of various types of knowledge is similar to that found in the processing of narratives. Indeed, many of the conceptual problems that have arisen in studying knowledge in the processing of narratives should apply to expository text. One difference, however, is that there is no major content domain that researchers interested in expository text can examine as an alternative to knowledge of text structure. This difference poses a special challenge to general theories of knowledge application in text processing.

CONCLUDING REMARKS

In the study of narrative text, research has been stimulated by the assumption that individuals acquire knowledge of prototypical text structure and use this knowledge to understand and recall the text contents. More recently, models suggest that understanding the sequences of human action found in stories is a major contributor to the understanding of narrative text. Moreover, other work has indicated that specialized knowledge is of critical importance if the narrative content is in some special domain. Despite the differences in orientation found in this research, there is a common thread, namely, the need for a theoretical synthesis that specifies how various types of knowledge interact in the comprehension process.

With respect to expository text, there has been a greater emphasis upon the description of text structure. There has not been a concern analogous to the study of knowledge of prototypical text structure or human action as found in narrative text research. However, there has been a pronounced emphasis upon the nature of superordinate-subordinate structural relations, and much research has involved the study of levels of text and their relation to recall. The need now is for a better understanding of the role of knowledge in processing of expository text. Moreover, there is a need in the research on both expository and narrative text to gain a better understanding of the "on-line" process of text. Of course, the models, methods, and measures that may be employed for such research vary, but the recent work of Carpenter and Just (1982) serves as a good example. Using time spent looking at each word of a text as the basic measure, they have developed a model of text processing that takes into account processing at various levels of analysis, e.g., a word level, a syntactic level, and a schema level.

The understanding of how knowledge influences text processing will be advanced when conceptualizations are developed that provide for an improved description of knowledge and a better idea of how different types of knowledge interact during comprehension. While we are not in a position to offer such a conceptualization, we want to close this chapter by making three points that are germane to any integrative framework that may emerge.

First, text processing is generally viewed in terms of interaction of the language stimulus and the individual's knowledge. In fact, it involves the interaction of two individuals. As is frequently stated, language is a medium of communication. The linguistic influence in psychology, while having many positive ramifications, has perhaps produced too much of an emphasis upon language as a set of complex stimulus materials and not enough upon the fact that language is generated by individuals, and that comprehension involves not simply "language understanding" but language understanding in the context of the goals and particular modes of expression used by the individual generating the passage.

Second, a point that has not been emphasized enough is that comprehension is multifaceted with respect to semantic interpretation. It may happen, for example, that an individual understands the within clause and within sentence contents, but may have trouble integrating the information found in the clauses and sentences of an entire story. Thus, the individual may not be able to develop a representation of the plot, even though specific sentences are understood. Thus, text comprehension involves establishing inter-sentence coherence both locally and globally. Local coherence involves inter-sentence or inter-proposition links via the recognition that certain concepts are, for example, coreferents (Cirilo, 1981; Kintsch, 1974) or causally related (Black & Bern, 1981; Schank & Abelson, 1977). Global coherence is characterized by the relations identified in story grammar theories or analyses of text macrostructure. In this paper and in extent research, knowledge relevant to the latter processes has been emphasized. Indeed, recall is still probably the most prevalent dependent measure, and by its very nature it tends to assess the individual's ability to understand the more global aspects of a text. Future research must examine more closely the types of knowledge important to local coherence. Furthermore, any theoretical framework that purports to specify how various types of knowledge interact during comprehension must deal with knowledge relevant to both global and local coherence.

Finally, the work of Bartlett (1932) is widely cited in reference to research on knowledge and text processing yet Bartlett's primary concern was with formulating a particular model of memory. Indeed, he used not only stories but perceptual stimuli to develop his ideas about memory. It seems to us that much of the contemporary research on text comprehension and recall has, on occasion, lost sight of the fact that remembering information found in text is one facet of the study of memory. Similarly, learning from text is one facet of the general topic of learning. There has been little effort on the part of investigators interested in text comprehension and memory to relate the findings of text processing research to the more general issues of learning and memory. Only when this is done will the implications of research on text processing be fully realized.

ACKNOWLEDGMENTS

Research in this paper was supported by the Centre for the Study of Mental Retardation, University of Alberta, Edmonton, Alberta, Canada, and the Learning Research and Development Center (LRDC) at the University of Pittsburgh, Pittsburgh, Pennsylvania. The LRDC is supported, in part, as a research and development center by funds from the National Institute of Education, United States Department of Education.

REFERENCES

Adams, M., & Collins, A. A schema-theoretic view of reading. In R. Freedle (Ed.), *New directions in discourse processing* (Vol. 2). Norwood, N.J.: Ablex, 1979.

Bartlett, F. C. *Remembering.* London: Cambridge University Press, 1932.

Bisanz, G. L. Knowledge of persuasion and story comprehension: Developmental changes in expectations. *Discourse Processes,* in press.

Bisanz, G. L., & Voss, J. F. Sources of knowledge in reading comprehension: Cognitive development and expertise in a content domain. In A. M. Lesgold & C. A. Perfetti (Eds.), *Interactive processes in reading.* Hillsdale, N.J.: Lawrence Erlbaum Associates, 1981.

Bisanz, G. L., & Voss, J. F. Developmental changes in understanding story themes: Scaling and process analyses. Manuscript in preparation.

Black, J. B., & Bern, H. Causal coherence and memory for events in narratives. *Journal of Verbal Learning and Verbal Behavior,* 1981, *20,* 267–276.

Black, J. B., & Bower, G. H. Episodes as chunks in memory. *Journal of Verbal Learning and Verbal Behavior,* 1979, *18,* 309–318.

Black, J. B., & Bower, G. H. Story understanding as problem-solving. *Poetics,* 1980, *9,* 223–250.

Black, J. B., & Wilensky, R. An evaluation of story grammars. *Cognitive Science,* 1979, *3,* 213–230.

Botvin, G. J., & Sutton-Smith, B. The development of structural complexity in children's fantasy narratives. *Developmental Psychology,* 1977, *13,* 377–388.

Bower, G. H., Black, J. B., & Turner, T. J. Scripts in memory for text. *Cognitive Psychology,* 1979, *11,* 177–220.

Britton, B. K., Meyer, B. J., Hodge, M. H., & Glynn, S. M. Effects of the organization of text on memory: Tests of retrieval and response criterion hypotheses. *Journal of Experimental Psychology: Human Learning and Memory,* 1980, *6,* 620–629.

Brown, A. L. Recognition, reconstruction, and recall of narrative sequences by preoperational children. *Child Development,* 1975, *46,* 156–166.

Bruce, B., & Newman, D. Interacting plans. *Cognitive Science,* 1978, *2,* 195–233.

Carpenter, P. A., & Just, M. A. Cognitive processes in reading: Models based on readers' eye fixations. In A. M. Lesgold & C. A. Perfetti (Eds.), *Interactive processes in reading.* Hillsdale, N.J.: Lawrence Erlbaum Associates, 1981.

Carpenter, P. A., & Just, M. A. What your eyes do while your mind is reading. In K. Raynor (Ed.), *Eye movements in reading: Perceptual and language processes.* New York: Academic Press, 1982.

Chase, W., & Simon, H. Perception in chess. *Cognitive Psychology,* 1973, *4,* 55–81.

Cirilo, R. K. Referential coherence and text structure in story comprehension. *Journal of Verbal Learning and Verbal Behavior,* 1981, *20,* 350–367.

Crothers, E. J. Memory structure and the recall of discourse. In J. B. Carroll & R. O. Freedle (Eds.), *Language comprehension and the acquisition of knowledge.* Washington, D.C.: Winston, 1972.

Dawes, R. M. Cognitive distortion. *Psychological Reports,* 1964, *14,* 443–459.

Dawes, R. M. Memory and distortion of meaningful written material. *British Journal of Psychology,* 1966, *57,* 77–86.

de Groot, A. D. Perception and memory vs. thought: Some old ideas and recent findings. In B. Kleinmutz (Ed.), *Problem solving: Research, method and theory.* New York: Wiley, 1966.

Fraisse, P. *The psychology of time.* New York: Harper & Row, 1963.

Frederiksen, C. H. Task-induced cognitive operations. In J. B. Carroll & R. O. Freedle (Eds.), *Language comprehension and the acquisition of knowledge.* Washington, D.C.: Winston, 1972.

Frederiksen, C. H. Effects of context-induced processing operations on semantic information acquired from discourse. *Cognitive Psychology,* 1975, *7,* 139–166. (a)

Frederiksen, C. H. Representing logical and semantic structure of knowledge acquired from discourse. *Cognitive Psychology,* 1975, *7,* 371–458. (b)

Freedle, R. O., & Hale, G. Acquisition of new comprehension schemata for expository prose by transfer of a narrative schema. In R. O. Freedle (Ed.), *New directions in discourse processing* (Vol. 2). Norwood, N.J.: Ablex, 1979.

Glenn, C. G. The role of episodic structure and story length in children's recall of simple stories. *Journal of Verbal Learning and Verbal Behavior,* 1978, *17,* 229–247.

Goldman, S. R. & Varnhagen, C. K. *Comprehension of multi-episode stories: Memory for embedded vs. sequential episodes.* Paper presented at the Psychonomic Society Meetings, Philadelphia, November, 1981.

Graesser, A. C., Gordon, S. E., & Sawyer, J. D. Recognition memory for typical and atypical actions in scripted activities: Tests of a script pointer and tag hypothesis. *Journal of Verbal Learning and Verbal Behavior,* 1979, *18,* 319–332.

Graesser, A. C., Robertson, S. P., & Anderson, P. A. Incorporating inferences in narrative representations: A study of how and why. *Cognitive Psychology,* 1981, *13,* 1–26.

Grimes, J. E. *The thread of discourse.* The Hague: Mouton, 1975.

Just, M. A., & Carpenter, P. A. A theory of reading: From eye fixations to comprehension. *Psychological Review,* 1980, *87,* 329–354.

Kintsch. W. *The representation of meaning in memory.* Hillsdale, N.J.: Lawrence Erlbaum Associates, 1974.

Kintsch, W. On comprehending stories. In M. A. Just & P. A. Carpenter (Eds.), *Cognitive processes in comprehension.* Hillsdale, N.J.: Lawrence Erlbaum Associates, 1977.

Kintsch W., & Greene, E. The role of culture-specific schemata in the comprehension and recall of stories. *Discourse Processes,* 1978, *1,* 1-13.

Kintsch, W., Kozminsky, E., Streby, W., McKoon, G., & Kennan, J. M. Comprehension and recall of text as a function of content variables. *Journal of Verbal Learning and Verbal Behavior,* 1975, *14,* 196-214.

Kintsch, W., Mandel, T. S., & Kozminsky, E. Summarizing scrambled stories. *Memory and Cognition,* 1977, *5,* 547-552.

Kintsch, W., & van Dijk, T. A. Comment on sa rapelle et on resume des histories. *Languages,* 1975, *40,* 98-116.

Kintsch, W., & van Dijk, T. A. Toward a model of text comprehension and production. *Psychological Review,* 1978, *85,* 363-394.

Kintsch, W., & Vipond, D. Reading comprehension and readability in educational practice and psychological theory. In L. G. Nilsson (Ed.), *Perspectives on memory research.* Hillsdale, N.J.: Lawrence Erlbaum Associates, 1979.

Lichtenstein, E. H., & Brewer, W. F. Memory for goal-directed events. *Cognitive Psychology,* 1980, *12,* 412-445.

Mandler, J. M. A code in a node: The use of a story schema in retrieval. *Discourse Processes,* 1978, *1,* 14-35.

Mandler, J. M. Some uses and abuses of a story grammar. *Discourse Processes,* in press.

Mandler, J. M., & De Forest, M. Is there more than one way to recall a story? *Child Development,* 1979, *50,* 886-889.

Mandler, J. M., & Goodman, M. *On the psychological validity of story structure.* Paper presented at the Psychonomic Society Meetings, St. Louis, November, 1980.

Mandler, J. M., & Johnson, N. S. Remembrance of things parsed: Story structure and recall. *Cognitive Psychology,* 1977, *9,* 111-151.

Mandler, J. M., & Johnson, N. S. On throwing the baby out with the bathwater: A reply to Black and Wilensky's evaluation of story grammars. *Cognitive Science,* 1980, *4,* 305-312.

Mandler, J. M., Scribner, S., Cole, M., & De Forest, M. Cross-cultural invariance in story recall. *Child Development,* 1980, *51,* 19-26.

Means, M., & Voss, J. F. *Knowledge and development in the processing of expanded narrative text.* Unpublished manuscript, 1981.

Meyer, B. J. F. *The organization of prose and its effect upon memory.* Amsterdam: North Holland, 1975.

Meyer, B. J. F. The structure of prose: Effects on learning and memory and implications for educational practice. In R. C. Anderson, R. J. Spiro, & W. E. Montague (Eds.), *Schooling and the acquisition of knowledge.* Hillsdale, N.J.: Lawrence Erlbaum Associates, 1977.

Meyer, B. J. F., & McConkie, G. W. What is recalled after hearing a passage? *Journal of Educational Psychology,* 1973, *65,* 109-117.

Miller, J. R., & Kintsch, W. Readability and recall of short prose passages: A theoretical analysis. *Journal of Experimental Psychology: Human Learning and Memory,* 1980, *6,* 335-353.

Newell, A., & Simon, H. *Human problem solving.* Englewood Cliffs, N.J.: Prentice-Hall, 1972.

Omanson, R. C. An analysis of narratives: Identifying central, supportive and distracting content. *Discourse Processes,* 1982, *5,* 195-224. (a)

Omanson, R. C. The relation between centrality and story grammar categories. *Journal of Verbal Learning and Verbal Behavior,* 1982, *21,* 326-337. (b)

Pearson, P. D., Hansen, J., & Gordon, C. The effect of background knowledge on young children's comprehension of explicit and implicit behavior. *Journal of Reading Behavior,* 1979, *3,* 201-209.

Piaget, J. *The language and thought of the child.* London: Routledge & Kegan Paul, 1960. (Originally published, 1926).

Post, T. A., & Voss, J. F. *Knowledge and the processing of expository text.* Unpublished manuscript, 1981.

Poulsen, D., Kintsch, E., Kintsch, W., & Premack, D. Children's comprehension and memory for stories. *Journal of Experimental Child Psychology,* 1979, *28,* 379–403.

Rumelhart, D. E. Notes on a schema for stories. In D. G. Bobrow & A. Collins (Eds.), *Representation and understanding.* New York: Academic Press, 1975.

Rumelhart, D. E. Understanding and summarizing brief stories. In D. LaBerge & J. Samuels (Eds.), *Basic processes in reading: Perception and comprehension.* Hillsdale, N.J.: Lawrence Erlbaum Associates, 1977.

Rumelhart, D. E. On evaluating story grammars. *Cognitive Science,* 1980, *4,* 313–316. (a)

Rumelhart, D. E. Schemata: The building blocks of cognition. In R. Spiro, B. Bruce, & W. Brewer (Eds.), *Theoretical issues in reading comprehension.* Hillsdale, N.J.: Lawrence Erlbaum Associates, 1980. (b)

Rumelhart, D. E., & Ortony, A. The representation of knowledge in memory. In R. C. Anderson, R. J. Spiro, & W. E. Montague (Eds.), *Schooling and the acquisition of knowledge.* Hillsdale, N.J.: Lawrence Erlbaum Associates, 1977.

Schank, R., & Abelson, R. *Scripts, plans, goals, and understanding.* Hillsdale, N.J.: Lawrence Erlbaum Associates, 1977.

Spilich, G. J., Vesonder, G. T., Chiesi, H. L., & Voss, J. F. Text processing of domain-related information for individuals with high and low domain knowledge. *Journal of Verbal Learning and Verbal Behavior,* 1979, *18,* 275–290.

Stein, N. L., & Glenn, C. G. An analysis of story comprehension in elementary school children. In R. O. Freedle (Ed.), *New directions in discourse processing* (Vol. 2). Norwood, N.J.: Ablex, 1979.

Stein, N. L., & Nezworski, T. The effects of organization and instructional set on story memory. *Discourse Processes,* 1978, *1,* 177–193.

Stein, N. S., & Trabasso, T. What's in a story: An approach to comprehension and instruction. In R. Glaser (Ed.), *Advances in the psychology of instruction* (Vol. 2). Hillsdale, N.J.: Lawrence Erlbaum Associates, 1982.

Thorndyke, P. W. Cognitive structures in comprehension and memory of narrative discourse. *Cognitive Psychology,* 1977, *9,* 77–110.

Thorndyke, P. W., & Yekovich, F. R. A critique of schema-based theories of human story memory. *Poetics,* 1980, *9,* 23–47.

Vesonder, G. T. *The role of knowledge in processing experimental reports.* Unpublished doctoral dissertation, University of Pittsburgh, 1979.

Voss, J. F., Vesonder, G. T., & Spilich, G. J. Text generation and recall by high knowledge and low knowledge individuals. *Journal of Verbal Learning and Verbal Behavior,* 1980, *19,* 651–667.

Warren, W. H., Nicholas, D. W., & Trabasso, T. Event chains and inferences in understanding narratives. In R. O. Freedle (Ed.), *New directions in discourse processing* (Vol. 2). Norwood, N.J.: Ablex, 1979.

7

A Knowledge-Based Model of Prose Comprehension: Applications to Expository Texts

James R. Miller

Texas Instruments

INTRODUCTION

When, during the early 1970s, those cognitive scientists who were interested in language comprehension moved away from the study of single sentences in favor of connected discourse, there was a surprising consensus on the critical issues of this domain. Virtually everyone working on this question was concerned with the same three problems: how the meaning of a text is represented in memory, how this representation is derived from the text's natural language, and how the construction of this represention depends on a reader's general world knowledge. One further similarity was also apparent: Most of these researchers dealt with narrative texts, for a number of good reasons:

—There was already a substantial body of psychological, linguistic, and anthropological research on narrative texts (Bartlett, 1932; Colby, 1973; Propp, 1968).

—Research materials were readily available: Stories about restaurants (Schank & Abelson, 1977) and birthday parties (Charniak, 1977) were simple enough to get the research started, yet complex enough to identify many of the important properties of texts and of comprehension processes.

—Theories of story grammars (Mandler & Johnson, 1977; Rumelhart, 1975; Thorndyke, 1977) offered methods for formally describing the structure of narratives, and provided a link to the previous linguistic and psycholinguistic work on isolated sentences.

—Discussions of complex knowledge structures (Minsky, 1975; Rumelhart & Ortony, 1977; Schank & Abelson, 1977) suggested representational systems for the world knowledge implicit in these texts.

199

—Research in social psychology on plan and goal structures (cf. Abelson, 1975) provided a vocabulary for describing the actions of characters in goal-directed situations.

These factors worked together to form the general model of comprehension that has dominated cognitive science in recent years: that of a process in which a reader activates knowledge structures relevant to the text being read and interprets the text from the perspective of these structures. Since this process is complicated by the richness of language as an expressive medium and the extensive nature of a reader's knowledge about the world, much of the research in this area has tried to identify those strategies used by readers to facilitate their search for a text's meaning.

Some of these strategies evaluate sentence-level rhetorical and syntactical devices and suggest pieces of knowledge that might be useful in interpreting the text. These *text-driven* strategies have received rather little study, and will be discussed later. The members of a more prominent class of comprehension strategies are *knowledge-driven*. Two of the techniques cited earlier—the analyses of actors' plans and goals, and the analyses of the rhetorical structure of the text—are strategies of this type. Both use a reader's knowledge to guide the comprehension of the text, although in somewhat different ways, as can be seen by noting how such systems would process a text beginning with the sentence, *"John was very hungry."*

A system based on the analysis of human plans and goals (e.g., Schank & Abelson, 1977; Wilensky, 1978) would note that this sentence describes an undesirable internal state (hunger), and would predict that John will take some action to relieve this state. The reader's knowledge about hunger, food, restaurants, grocery stores, and other related topics could then be used to interpret the remainder of the text as an attempt by John to achieve the goal of no longer being hungry.

Alternatively, a system based on text grammars (e.g., Mandler & Johnson, 1977; Rumelhart, 1975; Thorndyke, 1977) would base its analysis of the text on a set of rewrite rules, one of which might be of the form:

STORY → PROBLEM + ATTEMPT + OUTCOME

This rule states that a story contains descriptions of three components: a problem, an attempt to solve the problem, and the outcome of that attempt.[1] Since this first sentence of the story corresponds to the first component of the rewrite rule—John's being hungry is a PROBLEM—the remainder of the text should describe an ATTEMPT and an OUTCOME.

---

[1]Fully developed text grammars offer more comprehensive descriptions of story structure than does this rule, which is intentionally simplistic for the purposes of this discussion.

These systems are not as different as they might seem; they differ primarily in which components of the comprehension process they choose to describe in detail. Those researchers working within the plan/goal framework have concentrated on the interaction between world knowledge, planning strategies and goal-subgoal structures. However, when a plan/goal system encounters a text describing a hungry person and predicts that the text will mention attempts by that person to get something to eat, this system is assuming that texts possess a certain rhetorical structure—exactly that structure that is characterized by the story grammar rule shown above. Story grammar researchers have developed descriptive systems of text structure in great detail, but, in contrast to the researchers working with plan/goal systems, they have assumed the presence of knowledge structures and knowledge-oriented processes that would permit inferences such as that John's being hungry is a problem and that getting something to eat is a reasonable way to solve this problem. A combination of strategies dealing with general world knowledge and with knowledge about text structure is then at the heart of both of these models of narrative comprehension.

The success of these strategies depends upon how well they match the structural properties of the text to which they are applied. Plan/goal strategies are most powerful when applied to a text that contains causal chains, in which one event establishes the preconditions for a second event, which establishes the preconditions for a third, and so on. Most narrative texts contain substantial causal chains, making the challenge in this research specifying methods that can locate and process the knowledge structures that underlie and explain these chains—in particular, to show how a particular chain instantiates a higher-order plan or goal structure.

In contrast, expository texts depend to a lesser extent upon causal plan/goal structures; this lesser constraint can be seen in many of the texts discussed in this volume. Consider the first sentence of Meyer's text (Table 7.1) about oil spills.

TABLE 7.1
Meyer's "Supertanker" Passage, Canonical Order (paragraph 1 only)

---

(1) A problem is prevention of oil spills from supertankers. (2) Attributes of a typical supertanker include carrying capacity of a half-million tons, size of five football fields, and cargo areas easily accomodating the Empire State Building. (3) The trouble is that a wrecked supertanker spills oil in the ocean. (4) As a result of spillage the environment is damaged. (5) An example took place in 1970 near Spain when an oil spill from a wrecked tanker exploded into fire. (6) The fire caused hurricane-force winds which whipped the oil into a mist and pulled all of it high into the air. (7) Several days later black rain resulting from this oil spill destroyed crops and livestock in the neighboring villages. (8) Another example of damage occurred in 1967 when the tanker, Torrey Canyon, crashed off the coast of Cornwall and resulted in the washing ashore of 200,000 dead seabirds. (9) Oil spills also kill microscopic plant life which provide food for sea life and produce 70 percent of the world's oxygen supply. (10) Most wrecks result from the lack of power and steering equipment to handle emergency situations, such as storms. (11) Supertankers have only one boiler to provide power and one propeller to drive the ship.

The text begins by describing a problem, which is the focus of the text: "A problem is prevention of oil spills from supertankers."

After this initial sentence (the statement of a problem in story grammar terms), there is a description of a supertanker, a further specification of the problem, the result of the problem, two examples, another result, and a cause. There is very little structure among these segments. Once the basic theme of the text is introduced, there is little reason for it to continue with the supertanker description instead of an example of an oil spill: either continuation could result in a perfectly comprehensible text. Nor could either ordering be expected to be "better" as measured by any quantitative measure of comprehension or memory. The flexibility of this text's structure can be observed by noting that the sentences of "Supertanker" can be scrambled (excluding the initial sentence that identifies the text's theme) without significantly impairing the text's comprehensibility (Table 7.2). In contrast, a similarly scrambled narrative—the "Old Farmer" text (Table 7.3)—is very difficult to comprehend and remember (Thorndyke, 1977, Experiments 1 and 2).

The use of causal chains is not restricted to narratives; the most significant problem in the randomized "Supertanker" text comes from the disruption of the causal chain found in sentences 5, 6, and 7: The oil spill caused a fire, which caused strong winds, which caused the oil to get sucked up into the air, which caused the "black rain" and the destruction of the crops. In addition, many expositions are causally richer than the "Supertanker" text: Mayer's "Radar" text uses causal chains to describe the operation of radar systems, and argumentive texts, such as newpaper editorials, similarly lead the reader through elaborate chains of inference.

However, narratives typically use causal chains in different ways than do these expositions. In most narratives, the reader already possesses the knowledge that

TABLE 7.2
Meyer's "Supertanker" Passage, Scrambled Order
(paragraph 1 only)

---

(1) A problem is prevention of oil spills from supertankers. (9) Oil spills also kill microscopic plant life which provide food for sea life and produce 70 percent of the world's oxygen supply. (5) An example took place in 1970 near Spain when an oil spill from a wrecked tanker exploded into fire. (11) Supertankers have only one boiler to provide power and one propeller to drive the ship. (3) The trouble is that a wrecked supertanker spills oil in the ocean. (7) Several days later black rain resulting from this oil spill destroyed crops and livestock in the neighboring villages. (10) Most wrecks result from the lack of power and steering equipment to handle emergency situations, such as storms. (4) As a result of spillage the environment is damaged. (6) The fire caused hurricane-force winds which whipped the oil into a mist and pulled all of it high into the air. (2) Attributes of a typical supertanker include carrying capacity of a half-million tons, size of five football fields, and cargo areas easily accomodating the Empire State Building. (8) Another example of damage occurred in 1967 when the tanker, Torrey Canyon, crashed off the coast of Cornwall and resulted in the washing ashore of 200,000 dead seabirds.

TABLE 7.3
Thorndyke's (1977) "Old Farmer" Text, Scrambled Order
(First sentence in proper position)

There once was an old farmer who owned a very stubborn donkey. Then the farmer asked the cat to scratch the dog. Then he pushed the donkey, but still the donkey didn't move. As soon as the cat got the milk it began to scratch the dog. The farmer pulled the donkey, but the donkey didn't move. Then the farmer went to the haystack and got some hay. Then the farmer saw his dog, and he asked him to bark loudly. One evening the farmer was taking a walk, when he saw his donkey. But the cat replied, "I am thirsty and would be happy if you would get me some milk." Then the farmer went to his cow and asked for some milk. The barking so frightened the donkey that it jumped immediately into its shed, which is precisely what the farmer had been trying to get the donkey to do from the beginning. But the cow replied, "I would rather have you give me some hay to eat." As soon as the cat scratched the dog, the dog began to bark loudly. When he gave the hay to the cow, the cow gave the farmer some milk. But the dog refused. So the farmer gave his milk to the cat.

will enable him to follow the links of the chain—the typical reader of the "Old Farmer" text knows that a cat's scratch hurts, and that if a dog is scratched, it will probably bark. In contrast, instructive and argumentive texts present carefully designed inferential chains that are intended to enable the reader to construct *new* knowledge structures: the descriptions and analogies in the "Radar" text are meant to build in the reader a coherent knowledge structure describing the operation of radar. A reader who knew nothing about radar and was reading the text in order to learn how radar works would apply a different set of knowledge structures and comprehension strategies to this text than would an expert radar technician who already possessed the knowledge structures that this text is intended to build. The study of such instructional texts should provide valuable insights on both basic comprehension processes and on how readers acquire information from text.

To the extent that the processes of comprehension and knowledge acquisition can be separated, this chapter is concerned with comprehension; in particular, with an attempt to define some of the structures and processes that comprise the human comprehension system. Simple expository texts are a useful testbed for studying these issues because they lack a complex causal structure: In such texts, a reader must use comprehension strategies whose effects are hard to observe in narratives because of the dominance of causal-oriented strategies. A discussion of two of these strategies follows.

Strategy 1: *Observe implicit and explicit signaling.* A reader can often derive constraints on the future content of a text from statements in the text that describe what will follow. For instance, the preceding paragraph of this chapter ended with

A discussion of two of these strategies follows.

This would suggest that the text will continue by discussing examples of non-causal comprehension strategies—as it has.

When the upcoming structure and content of a text is not explicitly signaled, it can often be inferred from the text's linguistic structure, especially from comparatives of various types. Consider, in Graesser's text (Table 7.4), the phrase:

However, until the Middle Ages, the wagons were no more than boxes.

The use of *however* and *until* to qualify the description of wagons suggests that the text will continue by describing how wagons were different *after* the Middle Ages. Similar constraints can also be derived from terms such as *despite:* consider the sentence:

Despite the precise planning of the Tournament of Roses, things still go wrong.

Miller & Kintsch (1981) found that subjects could use a combination of world and text knowledge to anticipate the conclusions of sentences and paragraphs; here, subjects were able to combine the first part of the sentence (i.e., up to "*the Tournament of Roses*") and their knowledge about the meanings of DESPITE and PLAN to determine that the sentence would conclude with a description of the failure of the precise planning to achieve its desired effect—that things still went wrong.

A weakness of this strategy is that signals like these can help the reader anticipate only relatively local parts of a text, such as the conclusion of a sentence. In the DESPITE example, it is possible to further hypothesize that the text will continue by discussing examples of mishaps, but hypotheses like this should be the concern of a discourse-level text grammar: If an event is mentioned (such as the occurrence of mishaps) then the text will continue by giving examples of this event).

Strategy 2: *Exploit surface structure constraints*. The sources of constraint thus far described are knowledge-driven; they use knowledge about the world or

TABLE 7.4
Graesser's "Wagon" Passage

The wheel and wagon developed at the same time, approximately 5,000 years ago. At that time, human beings found that they could pull their sledges more easily if they fitted them with wheels of solid wood. The Egyptians were among the earliest people to use wagons. The Scythians wandered over the plains of southeastern Europe as early as 700 B.C., carrying their possessions on two-wheeled carts covered with reeds. However, until the Middle Ages, the wagons were no more than boxes set upon axles between wheels. Then the four-wheeled coach was developed in Germany.

about the structure of texts to limit the search for an appropriate interpretation of the text. A second class of constraints is *text*-driven; these analyze aspects of the text's structure to limit the search for world knowledge structures that might be relevant to the forthcoming text.

One way in which text structure might influence the selection of relevant knowledge structures is by manipulating the conceptual focus of the text and its sentences. Typically, text focus is not very well behaved: A text may begin with a description of a trip to a restaurant, but focus on some other topic, such as the business discussion that took place in the restaurant, as it continues. A good comprehension system must track these shifts in focus in order to ensure that knowledge structures relevant to the text and to its comprehension are always available.

Most of the research on the question of sentence focus has studied the effects of sentence structure on the focus of the sentence itself (cf. Haviland & Clark, 1974). Some recent discussions of functional linguistics (Bates & MacWhinney, 1978; Givon, 1979) have outlined several factors that might influence this perception of focus:

—*Perspective taking:* At a nonlinguistic level, people are often interested in the agent of a sentence, due to the conceptual similarity between the reader and the sentence's typically animate agent. Black, Turner, and Bower (1979) have discussed how text comprehension and recall can be affected by the perspective adopted by a reader.

—*Subject position:* Most languages reserve the initial position of a sentence for central information: the sentence ''John kicked the cat'' seems to be mostly about John, while ''The cat was kicked by John'' seems to be mostly about the cat (see Clark, 1965; Johnson-Laird, 1968).

—*''Punchline'' position:* In contrast to the importance of subject position, the part of the sentence that appears in the final position can also be important. One might say

''John used a knife to slice the roast.''

to emphasize the fact that it was the roast, and not the bread, that was being sliced.

Some recent experiments (Miller, 1981) have examined the utility of these strategies in comprehension. Subjects read a number of texts of the form:

1. A big robbery had just taken place.
2. A detective and a reporter rushed to the scene of the crime.
3. The detective found the jewel in the basement.

These texts manipulated semantic focus, by describing multiple agents or objects for the text (in sentence 2, two possible agents are mentioned), and syntactic focus, by placing different components of the final sentence in subject and punchline position (in sentence 3, the agent from sentence 2 is in subject position).

In one experiment, after reading a text like that above, subjects wrote a sentence that described how they thought the text would continue. The focused topics of these continuations demonstrated the presence of several of the previously mentioned strategies—subjects tended to focus their continuations on:

—the agents of the final sentence of the text, indicating the presence of a perspective-taking strategy,
—the subjects of the final sentence, confirming the subject-position strategy. The interaction of these two factors was also significant: subjects were particularly likely to focus on the agent of an active sentence.
—the part of the final sentence receiving semantic focus from the second sentence, confirming the semantic focus strategy.

This experiment studied the effects of syntactic and semantic manipulations on generation; in a second experiment, these manipulations were also found to affect comprehension. Subjects read new versions of these texts in which an additional sentence was placed at the end; the subject of this sentence was either the agent or the object of the preceding sentence:

1. A big robbery had just take place.
2. A detective and a reporter rushed to the scene of the crime.
3. The detective found the jewel in the basement.
4a. The detective called his station for more information.
4b. The jewel was not damaged.

Subjects read these texts one line at a time under computer control, so that reading times could be collected for each sentence. The reading time for a text's final sentence was found to depend upon the agreement of that sentence's subject—its focus—with the focus created by the semantic and syntactic focus manipulations: the test sentence was read faster when there was agreement of either kind, and fastest of all when all three focus-manipulating sentences agreed in focus.

These experiments were meant to demonstrate that different syntactic structures can stress different parts of the idea expressed by that sentence. A comprehension system cannot rely only on the analysis of these syntactic structures—as these experiments demonstrated, perspective-taking and contextual strategies are very powerful—but syntactic analyses may provide a reader with clues to the forthcoming part of a text and allow him to limit his search for relevant world knowledge accordingly.

SOME BASIC PREMISES OF COMPREHENSION RESEARCH

A detailed model of the human comprehension system should include structures and processes that produce the text-structural and knowledge-based constraints illustrated in the experiments above. Walter Kintsch and I have been developing such a model, and, as this effort is the focus of the remainder of this chapter, I should identify some of the basic premises of this work, so that its methodological goals and strategies are clear.

Premise 1: *The goal of comprehension research should be to identify the psychological structures and processes at the heart of human prose comprehension.* This premise has a number of implications. First, what is already known about people as active processors of information should not be disregarded: Limitations in cognitive capacities should be an integral part of a psychological model. This distinguishes this work from research in artificial intelligence, which builds an interpretation of a sentence or a piece of text without regard for the psychological validity of the structures and processes that lead to this interpretation (Harris, 1977; Hendrix, 1979), and from research that describes texts as rhetorical or logical structures without also considering the nature of the cognitive processes that interpret these structures (Mandler & Johnson, 1977; Meyer, 1975).

These projects are relevant to the construction of process models of comprehension, despite their different orientations. Artificial intelligence research offers insights into the kinds of knowledge structures that are needed for complex information-processing tasks, and into efficient techniques for the manipulation of these structures. In addition, many AI systems have tried to control the effects of the ''combinatorial explosion'' by focusing their processing on limited parts of their problems, often through techniques that are comparable to a limited capacity working memory system (Hayes-Roth & Lesser, 1977). The text-structure research offers suggestions about potentially relevant text structures and representations, as well as performance measures that might be used to experimentally evaluate a comprehension model. In both cases, however, establishing and maintaining the psychological validity of a process model presupposes a different set of goals and requires a somewhat different set of methodological constraints than those which guide this work.

Premise 2: *Right now, nobody really knows how comprehension works.* Although there has been considerable progress in identifying the kinds of cognitive structures and processes that, at one level of abstraction or another, are responsible for comprehension, there are still gaps in our knowledge. Attempts to model comprehension will then contain ad hoc structures or processes that, in effect, allow these parts of the human system to be simulated through the intuitions of the researcher.

Premise 3: *The use of intuition in a complex theory is not necessarily bad:* It allows research to progress in those areas that are sufficiently understood to support detailed study, thereby forming a foundation for the study of the issues that have been finessed by intuition. Intuition, however, can be used only in exchange for "intellectual promissory notes" (cf. Dennett, 1978). It is the researcher's responsibility to identify which parts of a model are well defined and which are not, and to pay off these promissory notes by progressively specifying those parts of the model that rely upon intuition.

These methodological strategies have guided the work that Kintsch and I have carried out (Kintsch & Miller, 1980; Miller & Kintsch, 1980, 1981). This work can best be described by first summarizing a thoroughly specified but incomplete model of comprehension, commenting on the insufficiencies of this model, and then describing how a more recent model addresses these insufficiencies.

A MODEL OF MICROPROPOSITIONAL COHERENCE: MILLER & KINTSCH (1980)

Kintsch and van Dijk (1978) presented a model of prose comprehension that described an interactive set of processes that operate at two levels of abstraction. The information and relations present in the surface form of the text are represented at the *propositional* level, while the higher-order conceptual ideas present in and derived from the text are represented at the *macropropositional* level. Since this model was presented verbally, and since the model's performance was always dependent upon the intuitions of the researcher applying the model to a given text, a computer simulation of the propositional component of that model was developed (Miller & Kintsch, 1980).

The goal of this model was to describe how a text's propositional coherence is determined by a cognitive system whose processing and short-term storage capacities are limited. The first step in applying this model to a text is to derive the propositional representation of the text under analysis. A sample text (the SAINT text from Miller & Kintsch, 1980) and the propositions derived from its first sentence are presented in Fig. 7.1.

Given such a set of propositions (as well as the original text being studied), an initial component of the model isolates small groups of propositions that will be analyzed in each of the model's processing cycles. These groups of propositions typically correspond to either short complete sentences or major phrases within a sentence. The propositions that comprise the first of these "chunks" then enter working memory to begin the construction of the text's *coherence graph*. One proposition from this first chunk is selected (by the researcher, not the model) on the basis of its conceptual importance and semantic centrality in the text to stand at the top of the graph structure. Any other proposition in the chunk that shares arguments with this superordinate proposition is then con-

The "SAINT" text
(Miller & Kintsch, 1979)

In the request to canonize John Newman, the "frontier priest, bishop of Philadelphia in the 19th century, two miracles were attributed to him in this century. In 1923, Eva Benassi, dying of peritonitis, dramatically recovered after her nurse prayed to the bishop. In 1949, Kent Lenahan, hospitalized with two skull fractures, smashed bones, and a pierced lung after a traffic accident, rose from his deathbed and resumed a normal life after his mother had prayed ardently to Newman.

```
P1:  (REQUEST P2 P8)
P2:  (CANONIZE P3)
P3:  (ISA JOHN-NEWMAN FRONTIER-PRIEST)
P4:  (ISA JOHN-NEWMAN BISHOP)
P5:  (LOCATION P4 PHILADELPHIA)
P6:  (TIME-OF P4 19TH-CENTURY)
P7:  (TWO MIRACLES)
P8:  (ATTRIBUTE P7 JOHN-NEWMAN)
P9:  (TIME-OF P8 THIS-CENTURY)
```

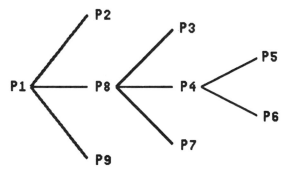

FIG. 7.1. The propositions from the first sentence of the "Saint" paragraph, and the resulting coherence graph.

nected to the superordinate; the remaining propositions are then compared to this structure and added to the graph, where possible, until all the propositions are included.

The set of propositions from the SAINT text results in the coherence graph shown in Fig. 7.1; this graph is constructed as follows:

—Proposition 1 is selected as the superordinate proposition and is placed at the top of the graph.

—The remaining propositions are then compared to Proposition 1; of these, Propositions 2, 8, and 9 either refer to or are referred to by Proposition 1, and so are connected to Proposition 1 and placed at level 2 of the coherence graph.

—The second-level propositions are then, in order of recency, compared to the remaining propositions; matches are sought between the remaining propositions and Propositions 9, 8, and 2—in that order—and connections are established where possible. Here, Propositions 3, 4, and 7 are connected to Proposition 8.

—Finally, the two remaining propositions are compared to the third-level propositions, again by recency; Propositions 5 and 6 are connected to Proposition 4.

While this graph, which corresponds to the first sentence of the text, contains nine propositions, only a few of these propositions can be retained in working memory for further processing, in view of the limited capacity of the working memory store where this structure resides. Hence, a version of Kintsch and van Dijk's ''leading edge'' strategy is applied to the working memory structure to select, on the basis of importance and recency, those propositions that should be retained for processing on the following cycle. The set of propositions selected for retention by this rule is determined by the proposed size of working memory—a parameter defined by the experimenter—and the way in which the propositions are connected—direct references by one proposition to another (as in Proposition 1's reference to Propositions 2 and 8) are preferred to connections established by argument overlap.

The next chunk of propositions is then passed to the coherence system, and the model's processing continues essentially as before. The only difference is that a new superordinate proposition is not chosen during this cycle. Rather, the propositions entering the model at this time are added to the structure left in working memory following the application of the leading edge strategy to the Cycle 1 coherence graph.

The above example is a somewhat idealized one, in which all the propositions entering working memory could be organized into a single graph. This is not always the case, since shifts in text topic or poor composition on the part of the author can result in a set of propositions that cannot be integrated only through direct propositional reference or argument repetition. In such cases, it is necessary to retrieve a proposition from long-term memory, or to generate a bridging inference that can integrate the disparate subsets of propositions. Note that, although the model reports when a bridging inference is necessary (i.e., when propositional coherence fails and when no proposition can be reinstated from long-term memory that will result in complete propositional coherence), its lack of appropriate knowledge structures and processes prevents the model from actually generating the required inference.

This model has several implications:

—Some propositions will be processed in working memory more often than others. These propositions should be better recalled than those propositions less frequently processed.

—Propositional coherence will be adequate to organize some texts, while other texts will require reinstatements or inferences for their organization. A text that can be organized purely on the grounds of propositional coherence should be easier to read than a text that requires frequent inferences and long-term memory retrievals.

—Differences in accessibility of the model's memory structures mean that it should be possible to access propositions in working memory more quickly than items in long-term memory.

These predictions have been empirically tested. Good fits were obtained for the propositional recall predictions for 16 of 20 short paragraphs, and the frequencies of variables drawn from the texts and from the model's processing of the texts produced multiple correlations of text reading time and readability with multiple r's between .8 and .9, with the frequencies of reinstatement searches and inference generation accounting for the largest proportion of the variance in these measures (Miller & Kintsch, 1980). More recently, Fletcher (1981) tested the model's predictions of working memory content. Subjects read the text studied by Miller and Kintsch and, at various points during their reading, were interrupted and asked to verify a sentence. These sentences corresponded to propositions that had been in the text and that were predicted by the model to either be or not be present in working memory at the time of the test, or to propositions that had not appeared in the current text. Those propositions predicted to be present in working memory were verified quickly, while the verification of true propositions that were no longer in working memory were verified more slowly, reflecting the additional time needed for the hypothesized search and retrieval of the propositions from long-term memory.

These results suggest that this model of propositional coherence provides a good description of how subjects process short, descriptive texts. However, these results must be qualified in a number of ways. The most important qualification is that this is a model of the *microprocessing* component of the comprehension system. Kintsch and van Dijk (1978) had suggested that a microprocessing model might be able to describe the processing of short texts in the absence of context, so the application of a propositional coherence model to short texts seemed plausible. However, even in these short, out-of-context texts, insufficiencies in the model's processing were present that could be traced to its lack of world knowledge and macrolevel strategies. Meyer's comments (this volume) on the limited ability of this model to describe high-level comprehension are thus well taken, and are similar to comments made at the time the model was first presented (Miller & Kintsch, 1980), and several times since (Kintsch & Miller, 1980; Miller & Kintsch, 1981).

Another shortcoming of this model is its lack of a parser. It is clear that reading is a word-by-word process, yet this model organizes an entire sentence's propositions at once. This is not just a theoretical shortcoming; rather, it creates practical verification problems. The power of post hoc verification techniques such as free recall or whole-text reading times are limited; more exact techniques are needed, especially ones that enable the examination of intermediate states of processing. Fletcher's (1981) experiments, which tested the model's predictions about individual sentences, are a step in that direction, but a more precise evaluation of the model requires predictions about smaller text units—phrases, or even individual words (cf. Just & Carpenter, 1980). Such fine-grained predictions are not possible with the coherence graph model, which works with groups of propositions corresponding to entire sentences.

Another problem, also related to the verification question, lies in the model's treatment of recall data. It is clear that a reader's preexisting knowledge structures play a large part in memory retrieval (Anderson & Ortony, 1975). Since this model did not describe such structures, the relations between these structures and text propositions could not be included in the model's treatment of recall. The model's recall predictions are based solely on a frequency theory of encoding; the absence of an explicit retrieval model prevents the evaluation of the model by cued recall, recall intrusion, or false recognition techniques.

In view of these insufficiencies, the development of this model has moved toward investigating and describing the knowledge-based, macrolevel structures and processes that are central to successful prose comprehension. The remainder of this chapter is then a description of a more powerful model that begins to describe the macroprocessing component of comprehension.

A KNOWLEDGE-BASED MODEL OF MACROPROCESSING[2]

The model to be described here has two concerns: the knowledge structures that are necessary to meaningfully interpret text, and the processes that derive a text's

---

[2]This section might best be read in conjunction with Chapter 15, which contains an example of the model's analysis of a text.

macrostructure from text propositions and knowledge structures. Although the procedural difficulties of defining and working with complex knowledge structures have led this work into the domain of artificial intelligence, the concerns of this work remain explicitly psychological. The structures and processes of the model have been designed with established pscyhological principles in mind, and with the goal of evaluating the model by comparing its predictions of various performance measures to experimental data.

The Model's Structure

The Knowledge Base.   The model's knowledge structures are instantiated in a schematic knowledge representation system (Stefik, 1979) of the sort described by Bobrow & Winograd (1977), Minsky (1975), and Rumelhart & Ortony (1977). This "knowledge base" consists of a large number of schematic units that are defined in ways that create a hierarchy among the units (Fig. 7.2). Starting from a "root" node, the hierarchy branches to concepts such as ACTIONS, OBJECTS, and EVENTS. Each of these concepts is then subdivided: OBJECTS into ANIMATE and INANIMATE objects, ANIMATE objects into PLANTS and ANIMALS, and so on. The units in the knowledge base may then be classified by this hierarchy—a PRIEST is a subclass of the class PEOPLE. This hierarchy controls the inheritance of properties: OBJECTS are defined as

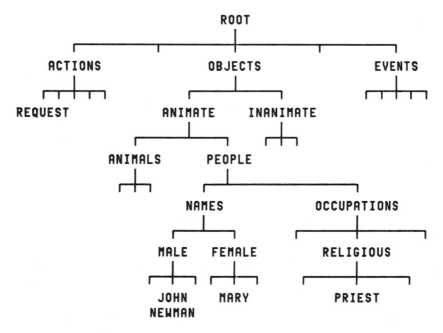

FIG. 7.2.   The hierarchy underlying the knowledge base.

TABLE 7.5
The Knowledge Base's
Representation of Request

REQUEST: an ACTION with
   agent: a PEOPLE
   recip: a PEOPLE
   object: an ACTION or an EVENT
   precond: a WANT with agent: (agent of REQUEST)
                      object: (object of REQUEST)
     and
     a POSSIBLE
          with agent: (recip of REQUEST)
               object: (object of REQUEST)
   result: a CAUSE with agent: (recip of REQUEST)
                    object: (object of REQUEST)

having properties such as SIZE and WEIGHT; by this definition, all units subordinate to OBJECTS also have SIZE and WEIGHT properties. The values of these inherited properties can also become increasingly restricted as they are passed down through the hierarchy: OBJECTS may have any size, but the size of ANIMATE objects is rather limited, and the size of PEOPLE is even more limited. New properties can be introduced at any level of the hierarchy, and all units below the unit to which the property is assigned will inherit that property.

A sample unit, REQUEST, is shown in Table 7.5. This concept is defined by specifying its "parent" unit in the tree structure (ACTION), and how the inherited contents of its slots differ from those of the parent unit. For instance, only PEOPLE may REQUEST things; this is represented by setting the contents of the *agent* slot to "a PEOPLE"—that is, any unit that is a hierarchical descendant of the knowledge base's PEOPLE unit. This structure is not simply a hierarchy. References like that between REQUEST and PEOPLE produce the interconnections of a network, and the representation is recursive—as seen in the PRECONDITION and RESULT slots, the content of a slot may intself be a unit structure, with additional units (and, conceivably, references to other units) embedded within the contents of that unit's slots.

Text Elements.   The development of this model has focused on the kinds and forms of knowledge that are necessary for comprehension, and on the construction of a text's macrostructure. Little has been done at the opposite end of the comprehension task, the parsing of natural language into propositions. This absence of a parser raises some of the problems discussed earlier—in particular, the desirability of some approximation to the word-by-word nature of reading.

As a temporary solution to this problem, the present model works with *text elements*—these structures are similar to propositions, but they specify the low-level semantic relations that a parser would derive from a text. For instance, the sentence:

John threw the ball to Mary.

would be represented by the text elements:

Element 1: (THROW AGENT JOHN)
Element 2: (THROW OBJECT BALL)
Element 3: (THROW RECIP MARY)

Each of these structures contains the concept to which the element refers (*THROW*), the case of the information that is represented in this element (e.g., in Element 1, who the *AGENT* is), and the information to which the stated case refers (that *JOHN* is the AGENT of the THROW). One of the primary tasks of the model is to combine these elements into a proposition:

(THROW (AGENT JOHN) (OBJECT BALL) (RECIP MARY))

In this way, the same set of propositions that were explicitly given to the coherence graph model are obtained, with the added feature that the arguments of the propositions are labeled with their case (*agent, object,* etc.). The text elements from the SAINT paragraph's first sentence are shown in Table 7.6.

What is gained by working with a text representation below the level of propositions is that the model can look at the comprehension process with a fine grain of analysis: the small groups of words that correspond to the text elements.

TABLE 7.6
Text Elements from the First
Sentence of "Saint"

In the request to canonize John Neumann, the "frontier priest," two miracles were attributed to him in this century.

Element 1: (REQUEST OBJECT CANONIZE)
Element 2: (CANONIZE RECIP JOHN-NEUMANN)
Element 3: (JOHN-NEUMANN PROPERTY PRIEST)
Element 4: (PRIEST PROPERTY FRONTIER)
Element 5: (MIRACLE PROPERTY TWO)
Element 6: (ATTRIBUTE OBJECT MIRACLE)
Element 7: (REQUEST PRECOND ATTRIBUTE)
Element 8: (ATTRIBUTE RECIP JOHN-NEUMANN)
Element 9: (ATTRIBUTE PROPERTY CENTURY)
Element 10: (CENTURY PROPERTY THIS)

In addition, it is not always the case that all the information contained in a proposition appears sequentially in a text: The REQUEST proposition in the SAINT text is built from text information found in both the beginning and the middle of the sentence. This distribution of propositional information rules out a model that would attempt to simulate "on line" comprehension by sequentially processing the propositions derived from the text (i.e., those shown in Fig. 7.1), since such a model would receive the text information in a different order than would aa human reading the same text. The text element system introduces this information to the model in the appropriate sequence.

Memory Structure.   The model is built around a hierarchically structured memory system like that used in the Hearsay-II speech understanding system (Newell, Barnett, Forgie, Green, Klatt, Licklider, Munson, Reddy, & Woods, 1973). The levels of this "hypothesis structure" represent the important levels of abstraction of the problem. For the speech understanding task, these levels included phonemes, syllabels, words, and phrases; the hypothesis structure for this model (Fig. 7.3) represents different levels of text information (PROPOSI-TION, ARGUMENT, and ELEMENT) and world knowledge (FRAME and SLOT), as well as the distinctions between long-term and working memory, and between text macrostructure and microstructure. The lines and points in this figure represent the levels at which these structures can be built.

The model processes a text by creating and interconnecting nodes at various levels of the hypothesis structure. For instance, a proposition is represented by a node at the PROPOSITION level, with links to the nodes at the ARGUMENT level that represent the proposition's arguments. In this way, the model still constructs propositional structures like those built by the coherence graph model, but this process can now be guided through the kinds of knowledge-driven processes that the coherence model's leading edge rule and dependence upon intuition were meant to approximate.

The Model's Processing Strategies

Knowledge Structure Organization.   The model's processes are organized into *knowledge sources;* these are packages of production rules with some common purpose, such as constructing propositions. The actions of a knowledge source can be represented as taking information from some part of the hypothesis structure, operating on it in some way, and adding new information to the hypothesis structure. The model's microprocessing component contains six knowledge sources:

—GET-ELEMENT: move the next text element into the ELEMENT level.
—BUILD-PROPOSITIONS: build a node at the PROPOSITION level from information found in a text element.

—FILL-PROPOSITIONS: create nodes at the ARGUMENT level to represent the propositions' predicates.

—LINK-PROPOSITIONS: build links between propositions that represent the same kinds of coherence relations as were studied in the coherence graph system.

—INSTANTIATE-FRAME: locate a knowledge structure in either the knowledge base or the long-term memory section of the hypothesis structure, and load this knowledge structure into the FRAME and SLOT levels of working memory.

—MATCH-PROPOSITIONS: match newly constructed or modified propositions against the instantiated knowledge structure.

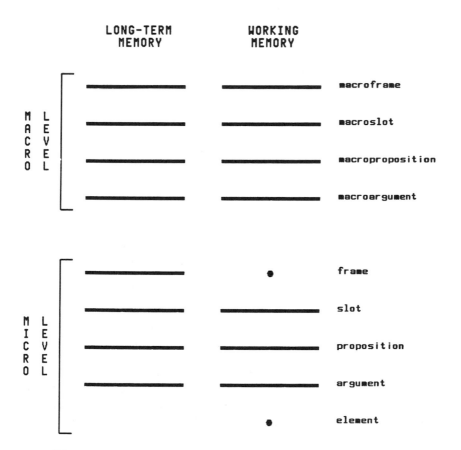

FIG. 7.3. The complete hypothesis structure of the model. Lines represent hypothesis levels at which more than one node can be built; only one node can be built at those levels represented by points.

The actions of these knowledge sources are shown in Fig. 7.4 as lines connecting hypothesis structure levels: the line from the ELEMENT level to the PROPOSITION level indicates BUILD-PROPOSITION's ability to construct a proposition from information found in a text element. The activation of these knowledge sources is controlled by the knowledge sources themselves: one of the actions taken when a knowledge source fires is to select the next knowledge source that should be executed. In this way, knowledge source execution is driven by the actions that take place during the analysis of a text.

Proposition Construction.   The GET-ELEMENT, BUILD-PROPOSITION, FILL-PROPOSITION, and LINK-PROPOSITION knowledge sources are responsible for building propositions from the information contained in the text elements. GET-ELEMENT retrieves the next text element to be processed from the list provided to the model, and enters it into the ELEMENT level of the hypothesis level. Since only one text element needs to be available at any time, the ELEMENT level is represented as a point in the hypothesis structure.

Once a text element has become available for processing, BUILD-PROPOSITIONS constructs a proposition around the initial concept in the element; these concepts are either actions (such as REQUEST in Element 1) or objects of whom properties are predicated (such as JOHN-NEUMANN in Element 3; see Table 7.6). FILL-PROPOSITIONS adds the text element's remaining information to the hypothesis structure, by constructing a node at the ARGUMENT level for this information and linking this argument to its proposition. For instance, the text element (REQUEST OBJECT CANONIZE) is transformed into a PROPOSITION node whose predicate is REQUEST and that is linked to an ARGUMENT node whose "case" and "contents" are OBJECT and CANONIZE, respectively. When a proposition is constructed in working memory, an identical proposition is also constructed in long-term memory; the contents of working memory can be thought of as pointers to those "active" portions of long-term memory.

Proposition Interpretation.   Once this construction phase is completed, the INSTANTIATE-FRAME and MATCH-PROPOSITIONS knowledge sources attempt to find a meaningful interpretation for this propositional structure. The most successful interpretation is typically offered by the knowledge structure corresponding to the proposition's predicate; hence, the interpretation process begins by instantiating the knowledge structure corresponding to the proposition's predicate at the FRAME level, with each of the slots of the knowledge structure instantiated as a separate node at the SLOT level. The limited capacity of working memory affects this process, in that only one knowledge structure can be active in working memory at any one time; for this reason, the FRAME hypothesis level is shown in Figs. 7.3 and 7.4 as a point. If a knowledge structure must be entered into working memory and there is already a structure

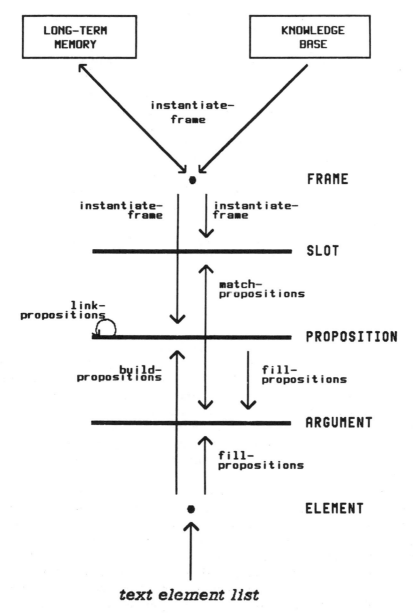

FIG. 7.4. The working memory microstructure portion of the hypothesis structure. Lines between hypothesis levels represent the actions of the model's knowledge sources.

219

present at the FRAME level (as there always will be except on the very first cycle of processing), the existing knowledge structure is saved in the model's long-term memory component from where it can be retrieved, if necessary, at a later time. It is then removed from working memory and is replaced by the new knowledge structure.

Once a knowledge structure has been instantiated in working memory, it is used to interpret the modifications made to the propositional component of the hypothesis structure in this processing cycle. This match exploits the similarity between frame-slot and proposition-argument structures. Just as a proposition and its arguments state the agents and objects of some action, so a frame and its slots state the permissible values of each of these roles in the case structure. The model's interpretation of propositions then becomes a matter of determining whether the concept identified in an argument meets the restrictions specified by the corresponding slot.

Consider the task of determining whether the REQUEST knowledge structure offers an appropriate interpretation of a proposition of the form:

(REQUEST (AGENT MARY . . .)

(i.e., MARY requested . . .). The model's task here is to determine whether the agent of this request, MARY, meets the restriction stated in the REQUEST knowledge structure's AGENT slot, "a PEOPLE" (see Table 7.5). This restriction requires that the AGENT of the REQUEST appear in the model's knowledge structure at a hierarchical level at or below PEOPLE. Since MARY does, the model concludes that REQUEST provides a suitable interpretation of this proposition, and this propositional structure can be integrated into the REQUEST knowledge structure: the contents of the AGENT slot are changed from "a PEOPLE" to "Mary." denoting that the agent of this particular request was Mary, and links are established between these frame-slot and proposition-argument structures.

The failure of this interpretational process does not necessarily mean that the propositional structure is nonsensical, but rather that some other knowledge structure needs to be found to provide an interpretation of the propositional structure. Such failures are common when the text needs to be interpreted at a higher level of abstraction than that provided by the proposition's predicate. Consider the representation of REQUEST: its preconditions state that (a) the person making the request wants the thing that is requested, and (b) it is possible for the recipient of the request to achieve the thing that is requested. Reasonable texts in which these preconditions are violated are not hard to find:

The corporal knew that the attack squad had already left on a dangerous mission, but he asked his sergeant for the assignment anyway.

The content of this sentence violates the second precondition of REQUEST: Since the mission is already in progress, it is not possible for the sergeant to grant the corporal's request. This failure suggests that a higher level of analysis is required than is provided by the REQUEST knowledge structure. Since the corporal is trying to impress his sergeant so that he might gain more favorable treatment later, an IMPRESS-THE-BOSS knowledge structure would provide a more appropriate interpretation; the challenge then becomes specifying how the model would locate this knowledge structure after the failure of the REQUEST interpretation. In any case, these same issues of knowledge structure selection and level of analysis are central to finding good interpretations of non-literal language, such as metaphor and simile (Clark, 1979; Ortony, 1979). In both cases, failed matches are just as important as successful matches, since these failures can help determine the appropriate level of analysis for a passage.

There is a final way in which these processes of proposition interpretation must be qualified. Consider the problem facing the model in finding an interpretation for the beginning of the SAINT text:

—the text states that John Neumann was canonized (cf. Proposition 2, (CANONIZE (RECIP JOHN-NEUMANN)))
—the CANONIZE knowledge structure requires that the recipient of canonization be a RELIGIOUS person (i.e., the unit representing the recipient must either be hierarchially below RELIGIOUS, or it must possess an OCCUPATION property that refers to some descendant of RELIGIOUS), and
—the information identifying Neumann as a priest has not been encountered when the CANONIZE proposition is to be verified (cf. Text element 3 and Proposition 3). Since the typical reader of the SAINT text would probably not know anything about John Neumann before reading the text, the model's knowledge about Neumann is limited to the fact that ''John Neumann'' is a male name. Without any knowledge about Neuman's religiousness, the model is logically unable to identify Neumann as an acceptable recipient of canonization.

This problem has arisen because the author of the text has used a rhetorical device in which a statement is made and then justified: the declaration of Neumann's canonization is followed by the evidence that supports his canonization. To accommodate these kinds of text structure, and to avoid wasting processing resources by rejecting and then reinstantiating an interpretation (as would happen if this initial failure caused the model to reject the canonization interpretation), the model will reject an interpretation only when information can be found that explicitly contradicts the proposed interpretation. By this rule, since no evidence is present that rules out Neumann's being canonized, the model assumes that the CANONIZE interpretation of Proposition 2 is correct. However, as the model continues its analysis, it will watch for information that will allow this interpretation to be conclusively confirmed or rejected. Brief assumptions of correctness, like that shown here, should permit the model's processing to proceed smoothly through a text. Alternatively, if the model were forced to maintain a number of assumptions like this for long periods of time without confirmation, either major insufficiencies in the knowledge structures or the reinterpretation of the text from the perspective of a different set of knowledge structures would be indicated.

Macroproposition Construction. The model views the macroproposition formation process as an attempt to find a proposition that can summarize the micropropositions in working memory at the time the macrolevel processes are initiated. As a beginning approximation to a well-defined set of knowledge-based macrolevel strategies, the model examines each of the propositions in working memory and selects the most "important" proposition for instantiation as a macroproposition. This selection is based on four evaluations of each proposition:

1. The number of propositions to which the proposition in question is connected. If a proposition has a large number of connections to other propositions in working memory, then that proposition is probably more central and relevant to the idea expressed by the propositions in working memory.

2. The a priori importance of the proposition's concepts: Following Schank (1978), some concepts are intrinsically interesting, and people are particularly likely to focus on these concepts during their processing of the text. In this example, miracles have been assumed to be intrinsically interesting because of their common relation to matters of life and death. Although the implementation of this is ad hoc, the inclusion of an interest-related factor is meant to reflect the importance of interest and reading goals on comprehension.

3. Whether the predicate of the proposition is or is not an action. Actions are perceived as being more central to a chain of events than are objects (Black, 1980); correspondingly, action-oriented propositions should be more likely for instantiation as macropropositions.

4. Whether the proposition received syntactic treatment characteristic of important concepts, such as placement in subject position.

The proposition selected by this evaluation process is then instantiated at the MACROPROPOSITION and MACROARGUMENT levels of the hypothesis structure,[3] and the information in the selected microproposition is moved into this structure. The techniques used to locate sound interpretations of text propositions are then applied here to tie the newly created macroproposition into the model's knowledge base and long-term memory.

Finally, working memory is reconfigured in response to these modifications. Since the newly created macroproposition is meant to summarize all the propositions in working memory, the PROPOSITION level of the working memory hypothesis structure is cleared of all propositions except the proposition which was instantiated as a macroproposition. The knowledge structure associated with this proposition (CANONIZE) is then reinstated from long-term memory into the

---

[3]Like micropropositions, macropropositions are built in both working and long-term memory.

FRAME and SLOT levels, so that the interpretation of this proposition is again represented in working memory. This processing cycle concludes with control being returned to the GET-ELEMENT knowledge source, and the processing of the next text element begins.

Summary

At this point, a comparison of this model to the coherence graph system is appropriate. First, note that the general goals of the coherence graph model are preserved: Working memory contains a set of propositions that is organized (in part) by the propositions' interrelations, and that is constrained by the limited capacity of working memory. Correspondingly, predictions can be derived about the course and results of the comprehension process from the model's operation: As in the coherence graph model, certain propositions spend more time in working memory, and so should be more likely to be recalled. In addition, the execution of the knowledge sources' rules provide a detailed description of the processes that are required for the comprehension of each text element. The numbers and types of rules that fire during each text element can then be used in multiple regression estimates of the reading times for the small parts of the text that correspond to the text elements, producing the desired finer-grained analysis of the comprehension process.

More importantly, this model emphasizes the interaction between knowledge structures and propositions: Propositions are organized by their relations to knowledge structures, rather than the simple techniques used by the coherence graph system. Similarly, the leading edge strategy has been replaced by macropropositional processes as the technique for selecting those propositions that will be retained in working memory on subsequent cycles. These connections between knowledge structures and propositions also permit a model of recall that includes retrieval processes based on an active search through an integrated representation of the text and the reader's prior knowledge about the topic. These relations should improve the model's free recall predictions, and will permit cued recall, recall intrusion, and false recognition tests.

SUMMARY AND COMMENTS ON RELATED RESEARCH

The research described in this chapter has focused on two components of the comprehension system: the interaction between text propositions and world knowledge structures, and the use and nature of text-driven comprehension strategies. These issues have also been the concern of the other projects discussed in this volume.

Of the work described here, Meyer's research on text analysis comments most directly upon the effects of the text on the comprehension process. The concern of Meyer's system is to determine the hierarchical nature of a text's rhetorical structure, with special interest in the linguistic devices used to signal this structure. Meyer assumes that readers will build this representation as a result of reading the text, and that the recall of a text segment will therefore be proportional to the position of the segment in the hierarchy; this is referred to as the "levels effect" (Meyer, 1975; Miller & Kintsch, 1980; Thorndyke, 1977).

Meyer's system is best viewed as a technique for defining important text elements and relations; it is not really a model of human prose comprehension. The system's sole prediction is that when the recall probabilities of the text segments are grouped according to the levels of its text representation, the levels effect will be observed. What this scoring system lacks—what keeps it from being a psychological theory—is a description of the reader's cognitive structures and processes that produce this representation and that retrieve information from it. Without a well-defined set of comprehension and retrieval strategies, knowledge structures, and working memory limitations, it is difficult to evaluate this work from the perspective of a process model of comprehension. Its most useful contribution perhaps lies in its description of the linguistic signaling of text structure and its proposal of expository structures—collection, comparison, description, and so on—that might serve as the foundation for developing a high-level description of expository structure, one comparable to plan/goal structures for narratives.

Mayer's "Radar" text illustrates the importance of comparing text and knowledge structures at several different levels of abstraction: The reader must understand not only the literal content of the text, but must also use his knowledge about waves traveling through water to understand the description of radar waves traveling through air. The challenge posed by texts such as this is to determine how comprehension at one level of abstraction facilitates comprehension at a higher (or lower) level, and how new knowledge structures are produced as a result of these processes. As was stated earlier, expositions offer an excellent testbed for studying learning of this sort, and experimental evidence on how knowledge acquisition takes place will be an essential part of developing a sound theoretical understanding of this process.

Although Voss's text is closer to a narrative than are the other texts studied in this volume, it also reveals the multileveled nature of comprehension: The immediate problems and goals of the characters in the text must be understood at the same time as the complex, metaphorical set of ideas about helpfulness and leadership. It also demonstrates that the reader must have metacognitive control over much of the comprehension process. In this text, it is necessary to relax, suspend, or alter certain processing strategies: it can be read and understood in spite of our knowledge that animals cannot really talk.

While the complexity of the texts discussed in this volume shows how many questions about comprehension remain to be answered, the model described in this chapter offers a starting place for the study of these questions. Further, they can be studied well with expository texts: The manipulation of old knowledge structures and the creation of new structures are essential parts of the comprehension of expositions, and the limited causal constraint of these texts allows the effects of text-driven strategies to be observed more clearly than in narratives, which rely upon more powerful plan/goal and causal chain structures. It is through a combination of methods like these that a complete picture of comprehension will emerge.

REFERENCES

Abelson, R. P. Concepts for representing mundane reality in plans. In D. G. Bobrow & A. M. Collins (Eds.), *Representation and understanding: Studies in cognitive science.* New York: Academic Press, 1975.

Anderson, R. C., & Ortony, A. On putting apples into bottles: A problem of polysemy. *Cognitive Psychology,* 1975, *2,* 167–180.

Bartlett, F. C. *Remembering: A study in experimental and social psychology.* Cambridge: Cambridge University Press, 1932.

Bates, E., & MacWhinney, B. The functionalist approach to the acquisition of grammar. In E. Kennan (Ed.), *Developmental pragmatics.* New York: Academic Press, 1978.

Black, J. B. *Memory for state and action information in narratives.* Paper presented at the annual meeting of the Psychonomics Society, November, 1980, St. Louis.

Black, J. B., Turner, T. J., & Bower, G. H. Point of view in narrative comprehension, memory, and production. *Journal of Verbal Learning and Verbal Behavior,* 1979, *18,* 187–198.

Bobrow, D. G., & Winograd, T. An overview of KRL, a Knowledge Representation Language. *Cognitive Science,* 1977, *1,* 3–46.

Charniak, E. A framed PAINTING: The representation of a common sense knowledge fragment. *Cognitive Science,* 1977, *1,* 355–394.

Clark, H. H. Some structural properties of simple active and passive sentences. *Journal of Verbal Learning and Verbal Behavior,* 1965, *4,* 365–370.

Clark, H. H. Responding to indirect speech acts. *Cognitive Psychology,* 1979, *11,* 430–477.

Colby, B. N. A partial grammar of Eskimo folktales. *American Anthropologist,* 1973, *75,* 645–662.

Dennett, D. C. *Brainstorms.* Montgomery, Vt.: Bradford, 1978.

Fletcher, C. R. Short-term memory processes in text comprehension. *Journal of Verbal Learning and Verbal Behavior,* 1981, *20,* 564–574.

Givon, T. *On understanding grammar.* New York: Academic Press, 1979.

Harris, L. R. User oriented data base query with the ROBOT natural language query system. *Proceedings of the Third International Conference on Very Large Data Bases,* October 1977.

Haviland, S. E., & Clark, H. H. What's new? Acquiring new information as a process in comprehension. *Journal of Verbal Learning and Verbal Behavior,* 1974, *13,* 515–521.

Hayes-Roth, F., & Lesser, V. R. *Focus of attention in the Hearsay-II speech understanding system.* Proceedings of the Fifth International Joint Conference on Artificial Intelligence, 1977.

Hendrix, G. G. *The LIFER manual: A guide to building practical natural language interfaces.* AI Center Technical Note 138, SRI International, Menlo Park, CA: 1979.

Johnson-Laird, P. The interpretation of the passive voice. *Quarterly Journal of Experimental Psychology,* 1968, *20,* 69–73.

Just, M. A., & Carpenter, P. A. A theory of reading: From eye fixations to comprehension. *Psychological Review,* 1980, *87,* 329–354.

Kintsch, W., & Miller, J. R. *Knowledge-based processes in prose comprehension.* Paper presented at the 21st annual meeting of the Psychonomic Society, St. Louis, 1980.

Kintsch, W., & van Dijk, T. A.   Toward a model of text comprehension and production. *Psychological Review*, 1978, *85*, 363–394.

Mandler, J. M., & Johnson, N. S.   Remembrance of things parsed: Story structure and recall. *Cognitive Psychology*, 1977, *9*, 111–151.

Meyer, B. J. F.   *The organization of prose and its effect upon memory*. Amsterdam: North-Holland, 1975.

Miller, J. R.   *Effects of semantic and syntactic focus on text production and comprehension*. Paper presented at the 22nd annual meeting of the Psychonomic Society, Philadelphia, November 1981.

Miller, J. R., & Kintsch, W.   *Recall and readability of short prose paragraphs*. Paper presented at the annual meeting of the Psychonomic Society, Phoenix, AZ, November 1979.

Miller, J. R., & Kintsch, W.   Readability and recall of short prose passages: A theoretical analysis. *Journal of Experimental Psychology: Human Learning and Memory*, 1980, *6*, 335–354.

Miller, J. R., & Kintsch, W.   Knowledge-based aspects of prose comprehension and readability. *Text*, 1981, *3*, 215–232.

Minsky, M.   A framework for representing knowledge. In P. Winston (Ed.), *The psychology of computer vision*. New York: McGraw-Hill, 1975.

Newell, A., Barnett, J., Forgie, J. W., Green, C. C., Klatt, D. H., Licklider, J. C. R., Munson, J. H., Reddy, D. R., & Woods, W. A.   *Final report of a study group on speech understanding systems*. Amsterdam: North-Holland, 1973.

Ortony, A.   *Metaphor and thought*. Cambridge: Cambridge University Press, 1979.

Propp, V.   *Morphology of the folktale*. Austin: University of Texas Press, 1968. (Originally published 1928.)

Rumelhart, D. E.   Notes on a schema for stories. In D. G. Bobrow & A. M. Collins (Eds.), *Representation and understanding: Studies in cognitive science*. New York: Academic Press, 1975.

Rumelhart, D. E., & Ortony, A.   The representation of knowledge in memory. In R. C. Atkinson, R. J. Spiro, & W. E. Montague (Eds.), *Schooling and the acquisition of knowledge*. Hillsdale, N.J.: Lawrence Erlbaum Associates, 1977.

Schank, R. C.   *Interestingness: Controlling inferences*. Yale University Department of Computer Science Technical Report 145, 1978.

Schank, R. C., & Abelson, R. P.   *Scripts, plans, goals, and understanding: An inquiry into human knowledge structures*. Hillsdale, N.J.: Lawrence Erlbaum Associates, 1977.

Stefik, M.   *An examination of a frame-structured representational system*. Proceedings of the Sixth International Joint Conference on Artificial Intelligence, 1979.

Thorndyke, P. W.   Cognitive structures in comprehension and memory of narrative discourse. *Cognitive Psychology*, 1977, *9*, 77–110.

Wilensky, R.   Why John married Mary: Understanding stories involving recurring goals. *Cognitive Science*, 1978, *3*, 235–266.

8 Cognitive Demands of Processing Expository Text: A Cognitive Workbench Model

Bruce K. Britton

*Department of Psychology and Institute for Behavioral Research
University of Georgia*

Shawn M. Glynn

*Department of Educational Psychology
University of Georgia*

Jeffrey W. Smith

*Department of Statistics and Computer Science
University of Georgia*

THEME AND OVERVIEW

The comprehension of scientific and technical expository text is a cognitively demanding task for several reasons. First, the reader must possess and be able to call upon large bodies of specialized knowledge. And second, the reader must be able to concurrently carry out a variety of *component reading processes* and *memory management processes*. The main claim of this chapter is that the comprehension of expository text can be facilitated by removing from the reader some of the cognitive load imposed by these processes.

The *component reading processes* that are discussed here include recognizing words, calling up the meaning of words, parsing sentences, and integrating text. The text integration process is the most important process because it produces the cognitive structures that are the desired end products of reading. For this reason, the text integration process is called the *higher-level* component process, while the other component processes are called *lower level*. The execution of each of

227

these component processes involves a series of mental operations, and these operations use the resources of the limited capacity cognitive system.

Because the short-term-working memory is so limited in its capacity (assuming conventional estimates of the capacity of short-term working memory are correct), it is often unable to hold at once all the component processes and prior knowledge used in reading. Consequently, extra cognitive processes are required to manage the short-term working memory store. These extra cognitive processes are called *memory management processes*. The management includes the moving of cognitive programs and prior knowledge rapidly in and out of the working memory as they are needed by the various processes that are being executed. These memory management processes themselves use cognitive resources and so make additional demands on the cognitive system.

In general, the controllable cognitive processes in reading are induced in the reader by the text features. The text features can be configured in many different ways; that is, there are many different ways of writing the same content. Each particular configuration of text features leads to a particular set of demands by lower-level component processes and by memory management processes. Some configurations of the text have relatively high costs in terms of the amount of cognitive resources they use, while others have relatively low costs. Other things being equal, the less costly configuration is best, because the resources saved on the lower level component cognitive processes and on the memory management processes can be reallocated to the text integration process, and this process, because it has more resources, can make better progress toward completion.

A cognitive workbench model for processing expository text is presented. The emphasis is on the cognitive demands of the memory management processes, because these have been investigated least in previous investigations of reading. Then the skill of reading expository text is analyzed using the cognitive workbench model, and ways to reduce the processing load of reading are identified.

COGNITIVE CAPACITY ALLOCATION TO PROCESSES

Unfortunately, the information-processing capacity of the human mind is limited. The more cognitive activities the reader must engage in concurrently, the less cognitive capacity is available for each. During the processing of text, there are at least two categories of cognitive activities that place concurrent demands on the reader's limited cognitive capacity: component reading processes and memory management operations. The component reading processes that are considered in this chapter are word recognition, word meaning retrieval, parsing, and text integration (Thibadeau, Just, & Carpenter, 1982). The memory management operations that are discussed are termed ''prefetching'' and ''demand fetching.'' The former refers to the activation of text relevant information and schema in advance of reading, while the latter refers to the activation that occurs during the course of reading.

It will be argued here that the comprehension of expository text can be improved in two ways. The first way is by reducing the load of the component reading processes, and the second way is by reducing the load of memory management processes. First, considering ways to reduce the load of component reading processes, if the load imposed by the lower-level component processes (word retrieval, meaning retrieval, and parsing) can be reduced, and if this additional capacity can be reallocated to the higher-level component process of text integration, then the text integration process can proceed more effectively, thus improving comprehension. (Following Thibadeau et al., 1982, the text integration process is considered to be the most important part of comprehension.) One means of reducing the cognitive load imposed by word retrieval, word meaning retrieval, and parsing sentences is to alter such features of the text as the familiarity of the vocabulary words and the complexity of the syntax used. In addition, it is possible to reduce some of the load of the process of text integration itself by employing preparatory devices such as text headings, advance organizers, and prequestions that will help the reader to activate appropriate schema. If the resources saved can be reallocated to other parts of the text integration process, then the process can proceed further.

Second, it is desirable to reduce the load of the memory management processes, if the saved resources can be reallocated to the text integration process. To explain how to do this, we need a model of the memory management processes, and this is presented below.

The entire argument presented above assumes that resources saved from lower-level or memory management processes can be reallocated to text integration processes. Experiments demonstrating that the cognitive resources saved in lower-level cognitive processes can be reallocated to other processes were reported in Britton, Glynn, Meyer and Penland (1982, Experiments 1 and 2) for the processes of word meaning retrieval, syntactic processing, and learning in two sets of expository texts. In these experiments, texts were rewritten in several different versions to decrease or increase the cognitive load of word meaning retrieval and syntactic processing. This was done by using more frequent or less frequent words, and by using less complex or more complex syntactic constructions. The results showed that the resources that were saved when the load of lower-level processes was reduced were reallocated to either an external task (as in Experiment 1) or to the higher-level process of learning (as in Experiment 2).

Also, in Experiment 3 of Britton et al., the aspect of text structure called signaling (e.g., Meyer, 1975) was manipulated in two other expository texts, and it was shown that when structural signals were present in text (signaling to the reader important aspects of the text structure and so aiding text integration), the load of inferring the text structure was reduced and the saved resources could be reallocated to an external task. Loman and Mayer (in press) have shown that resources saved from signaling can be reallocated to learning processes. These studies demonstrate the main point of this section, that reducing the cognitive demands of lower-level processes makes available additional cognitive resources that can be allocated to other processes.

The practical consequence of this idea is that the amount of resources that the reader has available to devote to text integration processes (which are the highest level component reading processes) can be increased by shifting some of the cognitive burden of component reading processes off the reader's cognitive system. If the load of some text integration processes can be reduced, it can be reallocated to other text integration processes. Also, if capacity can be saved from memory management processes, it too can be reallocated to text integration processes.

In order to understand the cognitive demands of memory management processes, it is necessary to have a model that provides a specification of these processes. This model, called the cognitive workbench model, is presented and applied to reading expository text in the next section of this chapter.

THE COGNITIVE WORKBENCH MODEL OF PROCESSING EXPOSITORY TEXT

Components of the Human Cognitive Processing System

The human cognitive processing system is limited in capacity. Figure 8.1 shows the conventional diagram of the cognitive processing system. Four of the five components are conventionally assumed to be very limited in their capacity, the exception being long-term memory, which is considered to have an essentially unlimited storage capacity. For the input and output devices the causes of the limited capacities are obvious, but the limits of these systems are not important for the present model and so they will not be considered further. It is assumed that the limitation on the capacity of the central processing unit is that it can do only one cognitive operation at a time. Also, the central processing unit can only perform operations on elements that are present on the cognitive workbench. The limited capacity component of primary interest here is the cognitive workbench.

The term 'cognitive workbench' is borrowed from Klatzky (1975), who used it in a somewhat different sense. It is used here to refer to those programs, data and working space that have been placed in an activated state so that the central processing unit can perform operations on them. This corresponds in part to the concepts of short-term and working memory, which is why those terms have been placed in parentheses in Fig. 8.1. The term "cognitive workbench" is introduced to help distinguish the properties of the entity described here from the entities described in the literature on short-term and working memory.

COGNITIVE SYSTEM

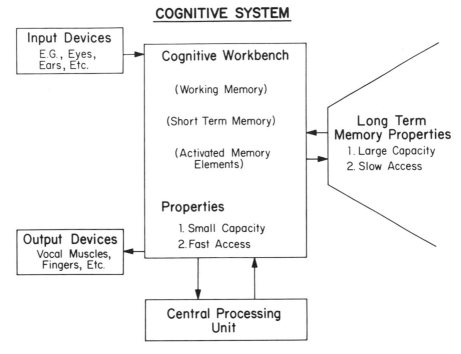

FIG. 8.1.   Schematic diagram of the standard multistore model of the cognitive system based on the computer analogy.

Processing Expository Text: Multiple Concurrent Tasks

Readers of expository text perform several cognitive processes concurrently. In general, the performance of any single cognitive process requires that three types of elements be present on the cognitive workbench:

1. *A Program:* a sequence of cognitive operations to be performed on the *data.*
2. *Data:* the input to be processed.
3. *Working Space:* a workbench memory region, empty at the beginning of the task, that can be used as the *program* proceeds to store the various intermediate results of the cognitive operations on the *data* as those results are obtained.

For example, in reading, one component process is word recognition. The *program* has a sequence of instructions: the first instruction takes as input the unanalyzed sensory pattern from the page (the *data*) and the last instruction produces as output the identity of the word. The products of all the instructions between the first and the last ones are stored temporarily in the *working space.*

TABLE 8.1
Some Component Processes in Complex Tasks

Reading Task	Flying Task
1. Word Recognition Process	1. Visual Information Processing
2. Word Meaning Look Up Process	2. Auditory Information Processing
3. Syntax Process	3. Kinaesthetic Information Processing
4. Literal Comprehension Process	4. Calculation of Desired Results
5. Inferential Comprehension Process	5. Motor Command Construction
6. Retrieval of Related Ideas Process	6. Feedback and Control Loops
ETC.	ETC.

In reading expository text, several such processes, each with program, data, and working space, are performed concurrently. Table 8.1 shows a list of a few component processes for the general case of reading on the left, and, for comparison, another set of processes for landing an aircraft on the right.

The cognitive workbench model of reading assumes that during complex reading tasks these multiple processes cannot all be present on the cognitive workbench simultaneously (at the same instant in time) because the capacity of the workbench is, in general, too small to hold them all. No estimate of the capacity of short term memory, working memory, or the activated memory system leaves anywhere near enough capacity in it to hold the programs, data, and working spaces for all the processes shown. Instead, the cognitive workbench model assumes that the component processes are moved back and forth from the very large capacity long-term memory to the workbench according to a higher order program. The program that manages these memories will be called the memory management program. With a memory management program, it is possible to perform several tasks concurrently (during the same interval of time). The memory management model presented here is based on computer memory management systems and is described in detail by Britton and Smith (1982).

Memory Management in Understanding Expository Text

The elements needed for performing any of the component processes of reading include a program, some data input, and a working space for the storage of intermediate results. As the reading task proceeds, the elements needed at each moment of time must be present on the workbench. There are two time periods when needed elements can be fetched from long-term memory and brought to the workbench, and it is useful to begin by considering each of them in turn.

The elements can be brought to the workbench before the task begins—called "prefetching"—or only at the time they are needed—called "demand fetching." Figure 8.2 shows the time relations. For example, in reading expository text, it would be possible to fetch a schema for the text structure in advance and activate it on the workbench: this would be prefetching. Alternatively, the schema for the text structure could be fetched only after the text had been partly read, and at a time when some executing task requested it: this would be an example of demand fetching.

Prefetching. Prefetching of all the elements needed for an expository reading task will rarely be possible, for two reasons. First, as pointed out earlier, the workbench is very unlikely to be large enough in capacity to hold all the elements needed for all the component processes. Second, and more important, only if the need for all the elements can be predicted in advance can they be prefetched. But it is evident that before the first reading of any unfamiliar expository text, it will not be possible to predict all the elements needed. This is partly because the content of the text is not yet known, and so prior knowledge relevant to the content cannot yet be identified; therefore, prior knowledge cannot be fetched. Also, the structure of an expository text is often not known in advance, because there is no single conventional expository text structure, so the schema for the structure cannot be fetched. So complete prefetching is probably rare but partial prefetching is possible in many reading situations. Prefetching could be encouraged by such devices as advance organizers, informative titles, outlines, headings, prequestions, and learning objectives (e.g., Mayer, 1979).

Prefetching has two substantial advantages over demand fetching. First, task performance need not be interrupted to fetch needed material. This is an advantage because interruptions are disruptive to the complex pattern of highly organized cognitive activity that is necessary for the understanding of complex expository texts. Second, prefetching can lead to faster response speed because the extra time needed for demand fetching can be avoided. Given the fallibility of

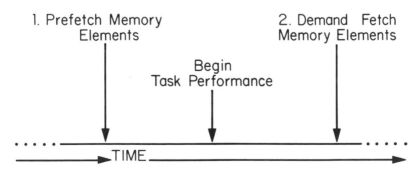

FIG. 8.2. Some time relations in fetching.

human memory, and the increase of forgetting with time, any practice that shortens the response time between related events is likely to reduce the probability of error, and so improve performance.

These advantages of prefetching must be balanced against the problems associated with prefetching. Two of these have already been mentioned: lack of predictability of needed elements, and lack of space on the workbench. A third problem of prefetching is that it places elements on the workbench that will not be needed for some time. These elements occupy *space* on the workbench for intervals of *time*. The amount of time over which they occupy their space can be referred to as a *space-time product,* or simply as space-time. The space-time product is the integral of the space the process occupies over the time it is present on the workbench. This is equivalent to the area under the curve in Fig. 8.3. Prefetching wastes space-time on the cognitive workbench. The amount of wasted space-time is equal to the total amount of space-time occupied by the prefetched elements minus the space-time during which the central processing unit is actually using them. Table 8.2 summarizes prefetching, its advantages and its problems.

Demand Fetching.   Demand fetching of the elements needed for understanding expository text is likely to occur more often than pure prefetching, particularly on the first reading of an unfamiliar expository text. Because the text is unfamiliar, its content, schemas, and structure are unknown in advance, so any relevant prior knowledge information that can be used for reducing the computational load will have to be fetched during the course of processing.

Two advantages of demand fetching are that it can be used for unpredictable tasks, and for tasks that are too large to be held on the workbench at once. The task of reading is, in general, unpredictable, and also has too many processes to

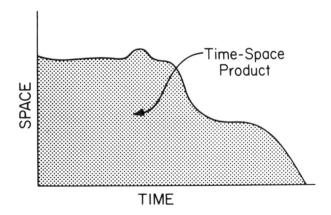

FIG. 8.3.   Schematic diagram of space-time product (based on Denning, 1978).

TABLE 8.2
Prefetching Advantages and
Problems

Prefetching

Only possible if
    1. Needed elements are predictable
    2. Workbench is large enough to hold them
Advantages of prefetching
    1. Performance is not interrupted to fetch
    2. Faster response speed
Problems of prefetching
    1. Wastes space-time on workbench
    2. Predictability is rare
    3. Capacity of workbench is often too small

---

be held on the workbench at once. This makes it evident that demand fetching is likely to be used extensively in reading tasks. Also, demand fetching wastes less space-time because elements do not occupy space-time before they are needed. The space-time saving of demand fetching over prefetching is the space-time between the time when the element would have been prefetched, and the time when the central processing unit starts executing it. The advantages of demand fetching are summarized in Table 8.3.

But demand fetching also has costs. The mental operations that are necessary to implement demand fetching themselves use processor time. Among these are the mental operations needed to detect when elements are needed, find them in long-term memory, fetch them, decide what element on the workbench is to be replaced with the new element (for the workbench is, in the general case, already full), update the addressing of the elements on the workbench so the system knows where to find the newly fetched element, and the proper transferring into long-term memory of any replaced elements that have been modified in their time on the workbench.

TABLE 8.3
Advantages of Demand Fetching

Demand Fetching

Fetch Elements only when needed
Advantages of demand fetching
    1. Works for unpredictable tasks
    2. Works for tasks too big to fit on workbench at once
    3. Wastes less space-time

TABLE 8.4
Overhead Costs of Demand Fetching

Overhead Cost in Space-time Due to Extra Mental Operations

A. Detect when elements are needed
B. Fetch them
C. Replacement decisions
D. Updating addressing in workbench
E. Transfer of modified elements to LTM
F. Memory management program is bigger for demand fetching

Not only do these mental operations use processor time, but a program to implement them must be resident on the workbench when they are being implemented, and the program itself occupies space-time. The overhead costs of demand fetching are summarized in Table 8.4.

Another cost of demand fetching, called *fragmentation,* is related to the unpredictable sizes of the elements fetched, along with the unpredictable sizes of the available empty spaces on the workbench, and the unpredictable times at which the elements are needed. Figure 8.4 shows the contents of the cognitive workbench over time as processes of different sizes are inserted and deleted. (This assumes a variable contiguous region model of memory allocation.) At Time 1, there are four processes, one large unused space and the memory management program. At Time 2, one process is added and one deleted, and there are two unused spaces; at Time 3, one process is added and one deleted and there are three unused spaces. The net result is that there are still four processes, but now there are three unused spaces. At Time 4, Process 7 cannot be read in as a whole, although it could have been read in at Time 1. Fragmentation, which is the development of larger and larger numbers of smaller and smaller unused spaces, will inevitably develop over time in demand fetching unless extra mental operations are used to prevent it. Since the unused spaces, as they become smaller, become less and less likely to be big enough to be able to hold any process, the unused spaces inevitably start to be wasted for longer and longer periods of time. The consequence is more and more wasted space-time as the task proceeds.

The process of fragmentation may be partially responsible for the widely reported decline in the effectiveness of reading complex expository text as the text is read continuously for longer and longer periods of time. In motor skills, such inhibitory effects can be attributed to muscular fatigue, but no such explanation is available for cognitive tasks.

Unless a demand-fetching system is perfect, errors will occur, as listed in Table 8.5, and the repair of such errors requires extra space-time. Finally, when the cognitive workbench is very full and very large numbers of lengthy fetches are needed, a critical condition may arise, called *thrashing.* In thrashing, every

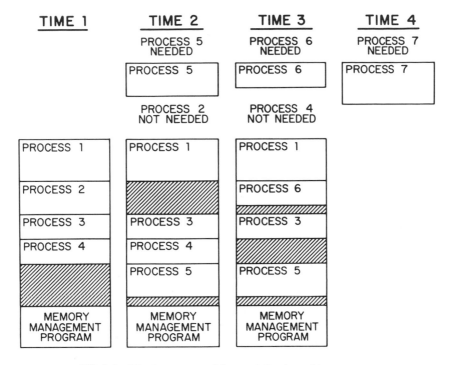

FIG. 8.4.   The time course of fragmentation in working memory.

fetched element displaces a needed element, which must then immediately be fetched, and this newly fetched element then displaces a needed element, which must be fetched, and so on. The consequence is that nearly all the processor time is devoted to fetching and none is available for progress on the task. Thrashing is summarized in Table 8.6.

Far from being an unusual event, performance near the margin of thrashing may actually be quite common when people first begin to perform a task that involves multiple concurrent processes with frequent transfer of information from long-term memory. For example, on a first reading of a complex expository

TABLE 8.5
Some Errors in Demand
Fetching

Errors due to

A. Overwriting
B. Failure to transfer changed elements to LTM
C. Addressing mistakes

TABLE 8.6
Thrashing

Thrashing Occurs When
A. Many fetches are needed
B. Workbench is very full
C. Every fetched element replaces a needed one immediately causing another fetch

Consequences
A. Nearly all processor time devoted to fetching
B. Little spare processor time to progress on the task
C. Progress slows drastically

text about an unfamiliar topic, the meanings of some words, phrases, or concepts frequently may have to be retrieved from long-term memory or even from external sources such as glossaries and dictionaries, and these retrievals take a long time. Since such reading involves multiple concurrent processes, relatively little cognitive workbench space may be available for each of the processes. With enough unfamiliar words and ideas, little central processing unit activity would be possible other than that required for fetching the meaning of the large number of needed but unfamiliar ideas.

Another example would be the task of reviewing an unfamiliar text. If the person was assigned the multiple tasks of concurrently comprehending the paper, proofreading it for style, and writing notes for the review, and if the relevant long-term memory retrievals associated with the comprehension process took long enough, thrashing might be the cognitive result, and breakdown on all the tasks the behavioral result.

Thrashing can be escaped from by *load control,* which in this case might involve reducing the load by deferring all processes except the process of comprehending the manuscript. Thrashing can be prevented if the words and concepts in the manuscript are made highly familiar to the reader, so that memory fetches do not take so long. On the second reading of the manuscript, the duration of long-term memory retrievals could be reduced, the first reading having primed the component meanings, making them more quickly available, so that on the second reading, more central processing unit time would be available for thinking about the ideas of the manuscript, and thrashing would be prevented.

This brief review of memory management has been intended to demonstrate that there is a large amount of computational load caused by memory management cognitive activities that are distinct from the understanding of the content of expository text. These memory management activities use processor time and workbench space-time that could have been more profitably allocated to the text integration processes. Processor time and workbench space-time are referred to collectively as cognitive *resources*. If the resource demands of these preparatory activities can be minimized, extra processing resources will be made available, and this will facilitate the understanding of the text.

PROCESSING LOAD DURING TWO READINGS
OF AN EXPOSITORY TEXT

Because expository texts are so cognitively demanding, they frequently have to be read twice (or more) to reach a satisfactory level of comprehension. This fact is given a position of central importance in the view of expository text comprehension adopted in this chapter and is viewed as the modal outcome of reading complex expository text. Reading a text twice has important effects on the cognitive processes that are induced in the reader. The processes that are affected include not only the component reading processes of word recognition, word meaning retrieval, parsing, and text integration, but also the memory management processes. From the standpoint of this chapter, the general effect of reading a text for the second time is to reduce certain cognitive demands. The saved resources can then be reallocated to other processes.

Processing Load on the First Reading
of an Expository Text

On the first reading of an unfamiliar expository text, the processing will have two properties that reduce the capacity available for the text integration processes. First, the lower level component processes will dominate the cognitive resources at the expense of the text integration processes. This is because the component processes involved in reading expository text have certain precedence relations among them. Precedence relations specify the order in which processes must be completed. The strongest theory of precedence relations in reading appears in the bottom-up models of reading (e.g., Gough, 1972). In Gough's model of reading, the precedence relations prescribe that some processes must be completed before others can be begun. For example, pattern recognition of letters must be complete before the lexicon can be consulted. Memory management activities also have precedence relations with other processes.

Bottom-up models apply most convincingly when the text is most unfamiliar and unpredictable. With very familiar and predictable texts, top-down processes (e.g., Goodman, 1967; Guthrie, 1973) play a larger role, and for texts of intermediate familiarity and predictability both types of processes interact (as in Thibadeau, Just, & Carpenter, 1982). We may consider a continuum of processing from bottom-up to top-down, and a parallel continuum from unpredictable and unfamiliar to predictable and familiar, as shown in Table 8.7.

Expository texts, particularly unfamiliar texts about scientific or technical topics, often contain novel, complex, multicomponent and difficult ideas, embodied in text structures that are not conventional. Such expository texts are likely to be unpredictable, so their processing is likely to be near the bottom-up end of the continuum. In bottom-up processing, the precedence relations are such that the lower level processes must be completed before the text integration processes can be begun. The more unfamiliar and unpredictable is the expository text, the more the lower level processes will dominate the workbench. The more resources are occupied by the lower level processes, the less are left for the text integration processes.

A second property of processing during the first reading of an expository text is that the contents of the workbench have two characteristics that are undesirable for the execution of the text integration processes. First, the workbench contains a large amount of material that is not needed for the text integration processes. This unneeded material includes the intermediate products of the programs of the lower level processes (such as unconfirmed word hypotheses, word meaning hypotheses, and syntactic hypotheses), unconfirmed predictions based on incomplete or incorrect ideas of the structure of the text, and irrelevant prior knowledge prematurely retrieved from memory as a result of incomplete or incorrect ideas about the content of the text. This material occupies workbench space-time but is unneeded for the text integration processes.

Second, the material on the workbench is fragmented and disorganized. Fragmentation increases as a function of the time spent in processing. The fragments of empty space occupy increasing amounts of unusable space-time, leaving less available for the execution of text integration processes. Disorganization is associated with increasingly complex addressing demands, and with interruptions that cause disruption. More complex workbench retrieval schemes are necessary

TABLE 8.7
Some Processing Continua

	Extremes of Continua	
Processing	bottom-up	top-down
Familiarity	unfamiliar text	familiar text
Predictability	unpredictable text	predictable text
Genre	expository text	narrative text
Subgenre	scientific and technical text	children's stories

when material is disorganized, and these use extra processor time and workbench space-time. Proper handling of interruptions requires cognitive operations to save the status of the interrupted process and then retrieve it later. These operations use processor time, and the stored status information occupies workbench space-time. If interruptions are not handled properly, the process has to be begun again, using extra resources, or errors will occur, necessitating error repair operations which use resources. The consequence of these two properties of the materials on the workbench is to reduce the resources that are free for the text integration processes.

There are also three types of content that the workbench does not contain on the first reading that would be very useful for executing the higher level processes. First, the workbench does not contain a correct and complete schema for the text organizational structure. The consequence in that correct predictions of future events cannot be made, leading to resource costs associated with consideration of large number of possibilities. Second, prior knowledge that is relevant to the text may not be present. The consequence is that the text content is more difficult to understand. Third, the content of the text itself is not present on the workbench at the beginning of the first reading. As the first reading proceeds. the content comes to be present on the workbench, but it is usually only present in incomplete form, and in any case it is only the *prior* content that is available (even in incomplete form), as reading proceeds, the later content becoming available only as it is encountered. These three types of materials would be useful for text integration processes if they were present, but to the extent that they are not present, the activity of text integration processes is reduced.

Ways to Reduce the Processing Load of the First Reading of an Expository Text

Increase Predictability.   If the text organizational structure is known to the reader, the reader can retrieve a schema to use to make predictions about what will happen next in the text. This will reduce computational load greatly because the reader can first test the predictions, one or more of which will usually be right, instead of having to consider all the possibilities, as he would if he couldn't predict at all. So knowing the schema will reduce resource waste. But of course holding the schema itself on the workbench will use space-time, and using it to make predictions will use processor time, so there is a trade-off between the resource cost of holding and using the schema, and the benefit of using the schema to predict. Obviously, schemas that predict more will have a better cost/benefit ratio. Commonly used text features that increase predictability by activating schemas include titles, abstracts, summaries, outlines, table of contents, and headings. Predictability can be improved further by explicit descriptions of the structure of the following text, foreshadowing, redundancy, and the use of cataphoric cohesive devices.

Minimize Resources Allocated to Fetches: Priming.   When a long-term memory element is activated onto the workbench, it remains in a slowly decreasing activated state for at least 48 hours (Scarborough, Cortese, & Scarborough, 1977). Psychologists say it has been "primed" (e.g., Ratcliff & McKoon, 1981). During those 48 hours, it can be fetched more quickly than if it had not been primed. Since every fetch takes time, and faster fetches take less time, priming reduces the resources used for fetches. Priming can be accomplished by activating needed elements in advance. This can be accomplished by many of the techniques suggested in the section on increasing predictability, the difference being that the predictability described there was increased by activating information about *structure,* while the priming is accomplished by activating information about *content.*

Minimize Resources Allocated to Fetches: Increase Locality of Reference.   If the program for a task *refers* to elements already present on the workbench, the elements need not be fetched, since they are already *locally* present. If the elements need not be fetched, resources used for fetching can be saved. The sequence of events in an expository text should be arranged so that the elements in use at any particular time have the maximum overlap with elements recently used, and with elements to be used soon. This will minimize fetches. In text, locality of reference is implemented at several levels: within the sentence, between sentences, within the paragraph, and between paragraphs.

Minimize Resources Allocated to Fetches: Replacement Policy.   If elements must be replaced to make way for new ones, it is obviously most economical to replace elements that will no longer be used. Readers have some control over their replacement decisions, and the author should help them by explicitly noting which concepts will no longer be needed, or will not be needed for some time. Since the author has a high degree of control over when concepts appear in the text, he can provide the reader with the materials to implement the optimal replacement policy. The optimal policy depends on knowing in advance what will and will not be needed, and the author has this knowledge. Appropriate communication of it to the reader will allow optimal replacement decisions.

Minimize Resources Allocated to Fetches: Signal Phase Transitions.   Phase transitions are regions where the set of needed elements undergoes a large change. For example, if the next sentence of this chapter was concerned with "Sailing in the Dalmatian Sea," a large phase transition would have occurred. Locality of reference may be high before a phase transition, but it goes to very low levels after a phase transition. That is, after a phase transition there is a new set of needed elements which has few elements in common with the set from before the phase transition. Since the set of needed elements changes at a phase transition, phase transitions are typically followed by periods of high fetch activity. But if the phase transition is not signaled, the reader may proceed into the next section of the text while retaining the old set of elements, which are now useless. The resulting memory management processing wastes processor time and workbench space-time resources, because the needed elements are not present and must be fetched, while unneeded ones occupy space to no effect. A signal of a phase transition can cause the reader to look for indications of what the new needed elements will be, and to undertake search, retrieval and addressing operations without delay. In expository text, phase transitions can be signaled by paragraph boundaries, headings, and explicit transitional statements. Ways to minimize space-time devoted to fetches are summarized in Table 8.8.

Prevent Thrashing.   Thrashing can be prevented or escaped by load control. Load control *prevents* too many tasks from entering the system (which prevents thrashing) or, if thrashing has already begun, it drops tasks from the system (which allows an *escape* from thrashing). Authors, because they have preknowledge of text events, can implement load control by prevention, and, insofar as they can predict the probable location of thrashing (for example, text locations where a very large number of concepts from prior knowledge must be integrated), they can warn the reader of it, provide tests for it, and provide load control instructions to permit escape.

This section has been concerned with techniques for facilitating comprehension during the first reading of an expository text. It should be noted that use of each of the techniques is likely to have costs as well as benefits. Some of the costs are borne by the reader, but others are incurred by the writer during the composition process. When the costs borne by the writer are removed from the reader, the cost/benefit ratio for the reader is improved.

TABLE 8.8
Ways to Minimize Resources
Devoted to Fetches

A. Prime needed items in advance
   1. Priming reduces fetch time
   2. Priming lasts 48 hours
B. Construct program to *refer* to elements
      already *locally* present on workbench i.e., increase locality
      of reference of program
C. Replacement policy
   1. Foreknowledge policy is optimal
   2. Best policy without foreknowledge is replace *least recently used* elements if locality of reference is present but this causes high overhead
   3. Random replacement policy has low overhead
D. Signal phase transitions

Irreducibility of Some Processing Loads on a First Reading.   It will be clear that some of the cognitive demands of the lower level processes and of the memory management processes can be reduced by careful cognitive design of the text. But some of the demands of scientific and technical text are irreducible on the first reading. We know that reviewers and readers of complex scientific reports very frequently have to read them two or more times before understanding them. This is because the processing situation on the second reading of an expository text is much more favorable for the execution of the text integration process.

Processing Load on the Second Reading of an Expository Text

Positive Effects from the First Reading.   If an expository text is read for the second time soon after it has been read for the first time, the output products of the first reading will still be highly available to the reader. If the second reading is immediate, the products may still be on the workbench. For example, this happens when a too-complex sentence is reread immediately. The presence on the workbench of the products of the previous reading guarantees high locality of reference, and fetching overhead is therefore avoided, leaving additional processor time and working space-time for higher-level comprehension processes, and the sentence can be comprehended more completely. If the second reading is delayed for some time, the products of the first reading may not still be present on the workbench, but they may still be primed, and so their fetching will be more rapid, reducing fetching overhead accordingly.

Among the products of the first reading may be a schema for the structure of the text. The schema, if it can be retrieved, can be used to make predictions about future text events, thereby reducing the computational load. Also, to the extent that the content of the text has been understood on the first reading, the structural schema has already been instantiated, and this can improve structural predictability almost to its limit.

Another product of the first reading may be the identification of relevant extra-text prior knowledge. If this knowledge is retrieved on the second reading, it can facilitate the understanding of the text. However, there is a danger that if too much prior knowledge is retrieved, it can overload the workbench, reducing the amount of free working space, increasing the number of fetches of other elements and increasing the probability of thrashing.

A third type of product of the first reading is some understood version of the content of the text itself. If this is retrieved at the second reading, it can reduce processing load by providing constraints on predictions about *content*. This is to be distinguished from the effect of the content in producing constraints on predictions about the *structure* of the text, mentioned earlier.

Negative Effects from the First Reading.   The first reading of an expository text also leaves certain undesirable products on the workbench and these can waste processor time and workbench space-time during the second reading. One undesirable product is a large amount of unneeded material, including the intermediate products of the lower-level processes (the contents of the working space), the unconfirmed predictions of future text events based on an incomplete conception of the text structure, and irrelevant prior knowledge which should not have been retrieved. If the second reading of the expository text occurs immediately, some of the unneeded material may still be present on the workbench, and will occupy space-time at the expense of higher-level processes.

There are various ways to avoid this problem. First, if the second reading is delayed long enough to cause the replacement of the unneeded material on the workbench, the material itself may only be in a primed state, and so will be fetched more quickly, but only if it is demanded during the second reading. If the delay between the first and second readings is long enough to allow the priming of the unneeded material to dissipate completely, the likelihood of its fetching will decrease to a level approaching the original level of activation before the first reading.

Second, it is clear that some of the material on the workbench will have been newly created during the first reading by the operations of programs upon the text and upon prior knowledge. Of this newly created material, some will be recognized (during the first reading) to be unneeded but some will be recognized to be useful. In the course of the first reading, it may be possible to select some of the useful material on the workbench for extra processing operations leading to learning of that material. If those learning operations are successful, then the material will be in long-term memory at the time of the second reading, and the activation of the learned material during the second reading will be more likely. But the newly created material that was recognized during the first reading as useless will not have been learned, will not be present in long-term memory, and so will not be activated. Similarly, it may be possible in the course of the first reading to distinguish the prior knowledge that is relevant from the irrelevant, and on the second reading to retrieve only the relevant knowledge.

The second undesirable product of the first reading is a fragmented and disorganized workbench, caused by the unpredictable insertion and deletion of memory elements of unpredictable sizes, and by the disrupting effects of interruptions caused by the blocking of higher-level processes by prerequisite lower-level ones. These interruptions are inevitable on a first reading of unfamiliar text, because prerequisite lower-level processes are always necessary to some extent.

The fragmentation and disorganization of the workbench during the first reading results in a workbench whose effective capacity is considerably reduced from the optimum. However, the fragmentation and disorganization can be eliminated before the second reading in a two-step process. The first step is to empty the workbench of the fragmented and disorganized contents, perhaps during recreation, rest, or sleep periods. The second step is to predict which material will be needed, and reload only it (and no unneeded material) at the start of the second reading. The predictability of the needed material is the result of the knowledge obtained during the first reading. Prefetching of the material avoids the large number of unpredictable insertions and deletions of elements of unpredictable size which is the cause of fragmentation. Also, to the extent that the material to be loaded on the second reading can be prefetched, the interruptions associated with demand fetching can be avoided, with consequent improvements in the organization of the workbench, and resource savings during the course of the second reading. Of course, probably not all of the material can be prefetched, but if the demand-fetching interruptions can be grouped, as far as possible, into regions of phase transitions, the number of separate interruption episodes will be reduced and the interruptions will be in regions where fetching interruptions are inevitable anyway. The grouping of demand-fetching interruptions into phase transitions is aided by the reader's knowledge of the location of topic focus changes in the text, and can also be aided by explicit marking of the topic focus changes by such techniques as paragraphing, headings, and explicit reference to them as in phases like "Now we turn to a different topic."

SUMMARY

The basic assumption of this chapter has been that the reader's understanding of expository text is determined by the on-line processing of the text surface form, organizational structure, and content. The effectiveness of the on-line processing is constrained by the limitations of the human information-processing system.

During reading, the resources of the information-processing system are allocated to many cognitive processes concurrently. It has been argued that reading is such a complex task that, in general, the space on the cognitive workbench is likely to be fully allocated at any one time. Therefore, in order to perform the different required reading processes concurrently, the processes must be moved onto and off the workbench, and memory management operations are required to organize this movement. These memory management operations use processor time and the program that controls them occupies space-time. The memory management operations also cause various side effects, including fragmentation, disorganization, and the presence of unneeded material on the workbench.

The cognitive load of the memory management operations, and of the lower-order reading processes, is by itself very large, so large, in fact, that it can dominate the workbench to the exclusion of the higher-order text integration processes. Such cases appear to be common in reading scientific and technical expository text, if anecdotal reports are any guide. One part of the solution is to remove some of the load from the lower-order processes of word recognition, word meaning retrieval, and parsing by simplifying features such as vocabulary level and the syntactic complexity of sentences. If these features are simplified, then the total amount of load imposed on the reader's cognitive system by the lower-order processes will be reduced, and the result will be that additional capacity will be available for pursuing the higher-order process of text integration. A second part of the solution is to reduce some of the load from the text integration process itself by employing preparatory devices such as text headings, advance organizers, and prequestions that will help the reader to activate appropriate schemas. The third part of the solution is to reduce the demands of the memory management processes. Some of these reallocations can be accomplished by changes in the form of the text. Other reallocations will only become possible as the text is read for a second time.

ACKNOWLEDGMENTS

This research was supported by NIMH grant 1-Ro3-MH-36579-01, by a University of Georgia Research Foundation Grant, and by funds administered by William Owens of the Institute for Behavioral Research of the University of Georgia. For intellectual assistance the authors are indebted to John Black, Bonnie J. F. Meyer, Abraham Tesser, Milton Hodge, David Rubin, and Ellen Gagne.

REFERENCES

Britton, B. K., Glynn, S. M., Meyer, B. J. F., & Penland, M. J. Effects of text structure on use of cognitive capacity during reading. *Journal of Educational Psychology*, 1982, *74*, 51–61.
Britton, B. K., & Smith, J. W. *A memory management framework for memory research.* Unpublished manuscript, 1982.
Britton, B. K., & Tesser, A. Effects of prior knowledge on use of cognitive capacity in three complex cognitive tasks. *Journal of Verbal Learning and Verbal Behavior*, 1982, *21*, 421–436.
Denning, P. J. The working set model for program behavior. *Communications of the Association for Computing Machinery*, 1968, *11*, 323–333.
Goodman, K. S. Reading: A psycholinguistic guessing game. *Journal of Reading Specialists*, May 1967, 126–135.
Gough, P. B. One second of reading. In J. F. Kavanaugh & I. G. Mattingly (Eds.), *Language by ear and by eye*. Cambridge: MIT Press, 1972.
Guthrie, J. T. Models of reading and reading disability. *Journal of Educational Psychology*, 1973, *65*, 9–18.
Klatzky, R. *Human memory: Structures and processes*. San Francisco: W. H. Freeman, 1975.
Loman, N. L., & Mayer, R. E. Signaling techniques that increase the understandability of expository prose. *Journal of Educational Psychology*, in press.
Mayer, R. E. Can advance organizers influence meaningful learning. *Review of Educational Research*. 1979, *49*, 371–383.

Meyer, B. J. F. *The organization of prose and its effects on memory.* Amsterdam: North-Holland, 1975.

Ratcliff, R., & McKoon, G. Does activation really spread? *Psychological Review,* 1981. *88,* 454–462.

Scarborough, D. L., Cortese, C., & Scarborough, H. S. Frequency and repetition effects in lexical memory. *Journal of Experimental Psychology: Human Perception and Performance,* 1977, *3,* 1–17.

Thibadeau, R., Just, M. A., Carpenter, P. A. A model of the time course and content of reading. *Cognitive Science,* 1982, *6,* 157–203.

9 An Exposition on Understanding Expository Text

John B. Black

Yale University

Expository texts are the meat and potatoes of the textual world, because expository texts are the ones that convey new information and explain new topics to people. In contrast, stories and other narrative texts mostly describe new variations on well-learned informational themes. Although such variations on familiar themes can be enjoyable, they are necessarily the dessert that comes after the main course provided by expository texts. Thus the recent increase in the amount of research devoted to investigating expository text means that after years of enjoying story desserts, text researchers are now seeking a more balanced diet.

The chapters in this book provide examples of the kinds of research on expository text that are being conducted and describe the findings emerging from that research. In this chapter, I try to integrate the other chapters by organizing their contents in a common framework to show that the various chapters make complementary contributions to a complete theory of how people understand expository text. The overall organization I use is the one that emerged in the introductory chapter—namely, that a complete theory of text understanding must account for the memory structures that people construct during comprehension, the world knowledge that enables readers to construct these memory structures from elliptical input, and the processes that construct the memory structures given world knowledge. Thus in the following three sections, I discuss first memory structures, then world knowledge, and finally the processes that use these structures and knowledge.

This chapter is an example of an expository text, so in addition to discussing the expository texts from the other chapters in this book, I also apply these results to analyze the exposition on expository text that is this chapter. For example, as I discuss later, although expository texts focus on new information, they frequently use old information to introduce new by using an analogy between the new domain and a familiar domain. Note that the first paragraph of this chapter does this by using an analogy between different kinds of food in a meal and different kinds of texts. Some readers may find the analogy strained, but such an introduction catches the attention and interest of even the doubters better than would a dry, factual presentation of the same information in literal form. The reason analogies are interest-arousing is that they immediately provide a framework for understanding and organizing the new information, so the reader is able to respond to the new material by applying knowledge from the analogous domain. Such an active response is better than passively processing the new information, even if the response is to disagree with the analogy.

MEMORY STRUCTURES

In a recent survey of research concerning how people understand and remember stories (Black, in press), I found that the memory structures related to stories fell into three classes—namely, coherence relations linking pairs of propositions, higher-level cognitive units integrating groups of propositions, and memory retrieval structures that provide an overall indexing scheme for organizing these propositions and higher-level cognitive units. The same three categories of memory structures seem appropriate for expository text, so I also use them here. These three categories are roughly equivalent to Kintsch and van Dijk's (1978) distinction between microstructure (propositions linked by coherence relations), macropropositions (propositions that summarize higher-level cognitive units) and macrostructures (memory retrieval structures). This Kintsch and van Dijk distinction has been used in most of the chapters in this book.

Coherence Relations

In my previous survey, I found that the important coherence relations for stories are referential, causal, motivational, and setting relations. From my own examination of expository texts and drawing upon the discussions in the chapters in this book, referential, causal, and motivational coherence relations are also important in expository text, but one must add that property and support coherence relations are also important in expository text. Property relations are actually a more general form of setting relations (i.e., setting relations are particular kinds of properties typically found in narratives), so the support relations are the only completely new ones. I now discuss the role of each of these coherence relations in expository text and use examples from the texts given in Tables 9.1-9.5. These are the same expository texts that are used as examples throughout this book.

Referential.   The minimal criterion for coherence in a text is that the statements in it refer to common concepts (Kintsch, 1974). Thus referential coherence is the most basic kind of coherence relation because it is present in all meaningful texts. For example, the text given in Table 9.1 is referentially coherent because the concepts of *wheel* and *wagon* are repeated throughout the text. Similarly, the concept *radar* is a common thread throughout the text in Table 9.2, *supertanker* in Table 9.3, and *bishop* in Table 9.4.

Frequently, the referential coherence relations are not explicitly stated but must be inferred from knowledge about the world in general or specialized knowledge about the topic at hand. For example, the text in Table 9.5 also seems quite coherent, even though there is not much explicit repetition of the same concepts from sentence to sentence. This text is coherent because the reader can easily infer that *bronze, copper, gold,* and so forth, are all instances of the general concept *metal,* and thus it is *metal* that implicitly provides the referential coherence here.

In this book, the chapters by Miller and Kieras provide the most detailed discussions of referential coherence.

Causal.   Causal relations are another prevalent kind of coherence relation (Schank, 1975). In fact, causal relations between propositions provide a particularly strong linkage (Black & Bern, 1981). Causal relations can be used to relate actions in historical sequence as in the texts in Table 9.1 (e.g., fitting sledges with wheels allows them to be pulled more easily), Table 9.4 (e.g., two skull fractures, smashed bones, and a pierced lung were the result of a traffic accident), and Table 9.3 (e.g., the tanker Torrey Canyon breaking up resulted in 200,000 dead seabirds). As with referential relations, these causal relations frequently have to be inferred. For example, when reading the *Metals* text in Table 9.5, people infer that the Hellenes using bronze swords against the Greeks' softer copper shields resulted in the Hellenes winning a war with the Greeks.

Causal relations are also used in expository texts to explain how mechanisms function: i.e., how changing one part of a mechanism will result in or allow a change in another part of the mechanism. For example, the *Radar* text in Table

TABLE 9.1
Graesser's *Wagon* Text

The wheel and the wagon developed at the same time, approximately 5000 years ago. At that time, human beings found that they could pull their sledges more easily if they fitted them with wheels of solid wood. The Egyptians were among the earliest people to use wagons. The Scythians wandered over the plains of Southeastern Europe as early as 700 BC, carrying their possessions on two-wheeled carts covered with reeds. However, until the middle ages, the wagons were no more than boxes set upon axles between wheels. Then the four-wheeled coach was developed in Germany.

9.2 explains that the fact that radio waves reflect from objects allows radar to measure the distance between the radio source and the object. Similarly, the *Supertanker* text in Table 9.3 states that supertanker crashes result from lack of power and steering equipment to handle emergencies.

The chapter by Graesser and Goodman, and Graesser (1981) provide the most detailed treatment of causal coherence relations.

TABLE 9.2
Mayer's *Radar* Text

Radar means the detection and location of remote objects by the reflection of radio waves. The phenomena of acoustic echoes is familiar: sound waves reflected from a building or a cliff are received back at the observer after a lapse of a short interval. The effect is similar to you shouting in a canyon and seconds later hearing a nearly exact replication of your voice. Radar uses exactly the same principle except that the waves involved are radio waves, not sound waves. These travel very much faster than sound waves, 186,000 miles per second, and can cover much longer distances. Thus radar involves simply measuring the time between transmission of the waves and their subsequent return or echo and then converting that to a distance measure. To send out the radio waves a radio transmitter is connected to a directional antenna which sends out a stream of short pulses of radio waves. This radio pulse that is first transmitted looks very much like the effect of tossing a pebble into a quiet lake. It creates concentric circles of small waves that continue to grow outward. Usually both a transmitter and a receiver are employed separately but it is possible to use only one antenna in which pulse transmission is momentarily suppressed in order to receive echo pulses. One thing to remember though is that radar waves travel in fundamentally straight lines and that the curvature of the earth eventually interferes with long range transmission. When you think about the reception of the returning pulses or echoes you should remember that any object in the path of the transmitted beam reflects some of the energy back to the radio receiver. The problem then becomes transmitting the pulses picked up by the receiver to a display mechanism for visual readout. One mechanism in large use is the cathode-ray tube. A familiar item in airport control towers which looks somewhat like a television screen. It is easiest to understand how radar is displayed if you begin with one of the earliest models used around the 1930's. These types of display systems were able to focus the broad radar pulse into a single beam of light which proceeded from the left of the screen to the right. When no object impedes the traveling radar pulse it continues its travel until lost from the screen on the right. When there is an object present the pulse would strike it and begin to travel back to the receiver. When the object is struck by the radar pulse it creates a bright spot on the face of the screen and the distance of the object can be measured by the length of the trace coming from the object back to the receiver. With this model, however, you are only able to measure the distance of an object and not its absolute location since the beam of light on the screen actually represents the entire width of the broader radar pulse. Models employed today use two simple techniques which make location of objects much easier. First, the transmitter now operates much like the search light used in airports. It emits a single beam of radar pulses that make continuous circular sweeps around the area under surveillance. Secondly, the display screen is adjusted so that its center corresponds to the point where the radar pulses begin. The radar pulse seen on the screen operates like the second hand of a clock which continually moves. When an object is present it leaves a bright spot on the face of the screen. An additional feature is that the face of the screen actually shows a map-like picture of the area around the radar giving distance and, of course, location. Thus it is very easy now to determine the location of the objects by noting their location on the screen's map.

TABLE 9.3
Meyer's *Supertanker* Text

A problem is prevention of oil-spills from supertankers. Attributes of a typical supertanker include carrying capacity of a half-million tons of oil, a size of five football fields and cargo areas easily accommodating the Empire State Building. The trouble is that a wrecked supertanker spills oil in the ocean. As a result of spillage the environment is damaged. An example took place in 1970 near Spain when an oil spill from a wrecked tanker exploded into fire. The fire caused hurricane-force winds which chipped the oil into a mist and pulled all of it high into the air. Several days later, black rain resulting from this oil spill destroyed crops and livestock in the neighboring villages. Another example of damage, occurred in 1967 when the tanker, Torrey Canyon, crashed off the coast of Cornwall and resulted in the washing ashore of 200,000 dead seabirds. Oil spills also kill microscopic plant life which provide food for sea life and produce 70 percent of the world's oxygen supply. Most wrecks result from lack of power and steering equipment to handle emergency situations, such as storms. Supertankers have only one boiler to provide power and one propeller to drive the ship. The solution to the problem is not to halt the use of tankers on the ocean since 80 percent of the world's supply is carried by supertankers. Instead, the solution lies in the following three tactics. First, officers of the supertankers must get top training in how to run and maneuver their ships such as provided by the tanker simulator at the Maritime Research Center. Second, tankers should be built with several propellers for extra control and backup boilers for emergencies. Third, ground control stations should be installed at places where supertankers come close to shore because they would act like airplane control towers guiding tankers along busy shipping lanes and through dangerous channels.

Motivational.   Whether reading an account of actions performed by historical figures or actions to be performed to operate a piece of equipment, it is important to know why the actions are performed. Thus one important contribution to coherence in texts is made by the motivational relations that link actions that form a plan and the goals they are trying to attain, in addition to linking these goals and the reasons for the goals being desired (Abbott & Black, 1982; Schank & Abelson, 1977). For example, in the *Saint* text given in Table 9.4, the nurse prayed to the bishop in order to save Eva Bernassi from dying; and in the Table 9.5 *Metals* text, the Spaniards conquered the Incas in order to get the Incas' gold. These two examples are both motivational relations that give reasons for the actions of historical characters.

Examples of motivational relations as the reasons for actions in operating instructions are provided by the texts in Tables 9.2 and 9.3. For example, in

TABLE 9.4
Miller's *Saint* Text

In the request to canonize the "frontier priest," John Neumann, bishop of Philadelphia in the 19th century, two miracles were attributed to him in this century. In 1923, Eva Bernassi, dying from peritonitis, dramatically recovered after her nurse prayed to the bishop. In 1949, Kent Lenahan, hospitalized with two skull fractures, smashed bones and a pierced lung after a traffic accident, rose from his deathbed and resumed a normal life after his mother had prayed ardently to Neumann.

TABLE 9.5
Kieras's *Metals* Text

Different cultures have used metals for different purposes. The ancient Hellenes used bronze swords. The ancient Greeks used copper shields. The Hellenes invaded ancient Greece before the Trojan War. The bronze weapons that were used by the Hellenes could cut through the copper shields that were used by the Greeks. Because the color of gold is beautiful, the Incas used gold in religious ceremonies. The Incas lived in South America. However, the Spaniards craved the monetary value of gold. Therefore, the Spainards conquered the Incas. Because aluminum does not rust and is light, modern Western culture values aluminum. Aluminum is used in camping equipment. Titanium is used in warplanes and is essential for spacecraft. Warplanes are extremely expensive. Titanium is the brilliant white pigment in oil paints that are used by artists.

Table 9.2 *Radar* text radio waves are bounced off objects, the time is measured for them to return to their source, and the time in seconds is multiplied by 186,000 miles per second to yield the distance between the radar source and the object. The goal here is to find the distance to the object and whenever such a goal exists the steps in this routine can be performed to accomplish it (presuming there is a radar set handy). The Table 9.3 *Supertanker* text recommends that to accomplish the goal of reducing the number of supertanker wrecks, a backup boiler powerplant and several propellers should be installed on each tanker. Here these actions provide a plan for the goal of avoiding an undesirable state of affairs—namely, the extensive environmental damage caused by the wreck of a supertanker.

The most extensive treatment of motivational coherence relations is provided by the Graesser and Goodman chapter and Graesser (1981).

Property.   Property coherence relations are descriptive relations that link propositions providing information about how something looks (e.g., a large red knob), how it relates to other things (e.g., next to a green knob in the center of the control panel), and its components (e.g., the knob has a grasping area and a shaft that connects it to the control panel). Setting relations in stories are a special case of property relations. Specifically, they are property relations that describe the fictional story world in which the story actions occur. Examples of an appearance type of property relation are provided by the Table 9.2 *Radar* text statement that a cathode-ray tube looks like a television screen, and by the Table 9.5 *Metals* text statements that aluminum is light and does not rust. Examples of the relational type of property relation are provided by the Table 9.2 *Radar* text statements that a radar set is composed of a sender, a receiver, and a display screen; and by the Table 9.3 *Supertanker* text statements that a supertanker has one propeller and one boiler.

The most detailed treatment of property relations is provided by Meyer's chapter.

Support.   Support relations are the kind of coherence relations that are found in most expository texts but few narrative texts (unless a small expository text is embedded in a larger narrative). Support relations link general propositions that make assertions (e.g., History is not a science) with other propositions that support or attack the truthfulness of those assertions. This support can be provided either by logical argument (e.g., History focuses on specific cases, while science focuses on general principles), by citing examples as evidence or counterexamples (e.g., The historical research conducted by Toynbee certainly did not follow scientific procedures), or by citing an expert or authority (e.g., Bertrand Russell argued that history is not a science).

The *Supertanker* text in Table 9.3 provides some examples of support coherence relations. The text first asserts that "as a result of spillage the environment is damaged" then cites examples of a tanker exploding and catching fire near Spain in 1970 and of 200,000 seabirds being killed off the coast of Cornwall in 1967. The assertion that "the solution to the problem is not to halt the use of tankers on the ocean" is supported by implicit logical argument from the statement "80 percent of the world's oil supply is carried by supertankers." The argument is implicit because for the support link to be established, the reader has to infer that oil must continue to be carried and that there is no other transport vehicle available capable of handling such a large percentage.

Other examples of support coherence relations are provided by the *Metals* text in Table 9.5. Specifically, the text first asserts that "Different cultures have used metals for different purposes" then proceeds to cite specific examples of this general statement. The specific examples consisted of Greeks using copper for shields, Hellenes using bronze for weapons, Incas using gold for religious ceremonies and modern Western cultures using aluminum for camping equipment.

The chapter by Meyer provides the most complete treatment of support relations.

Cognitive Units

While the coherence relations described in the previous section are important, they are not the whole story because the propositions linked by coherence relations do not form a uniform network but instead cluster together into higher-level cognitive units in memory. These higher-level memory units allow people to overcome the problems inherent in learning and remembering the enormous amount of information that is necessary for intelligent behavior. The more unrelated facts one learns about a topic the longer it takes later to remember any given fact about the topic (Anderson, 1974). However, if learners can integrate this information into a higher-level cognitive unit using their knowledge of the world (Smith, Adams, & Schorr, 1978), then they can later evaluate the plausibility of facts about the topic without going through the laborious and time-consuming fact-retrieval process (Reder & Anderson, 1980b).

Thus it is important to determine what are the higher-level cognitive units in various domains. In my own examination of expository text and in the discussions found in the other chapters in this book, four kinds of higher-level cognitive units have emerged as important in expository text—namely, episodes, mechanisms, descriptions, and arguments. I now discuss each of these using the example texts given in Tables 9.1–9.5.

Episodes.   Episodes are the main cognitive units in stories (Black & Bower, 1979), but they also play a major role in expository text. An episode is a goal linked by motivational coherence relations to the actions that constitute a plan for accomplishing it. The actions in the plan are also linked to each other by causal coherence relations. The example stories in Tables 9.1, 9.4 and 9.5 illustrate the kinds of expository texts that contain episodes—namely, expository texts that contain historical development. However, these particular examples are so brief that they only exhibit episodes in barest outline, but they will serve as illustrations.

In the Table 9.1 *Wagons* text, the initial episode is composed of the goal "pull the sledges more easily" and the sketchy plan is "fitted them with wheels of solid wood." A fuller version of this episode would relate the detailed series of actions required to get the wood, make wheels from it, fit the wheels to the sledge and then discover that the sledge now could be pulled more easily. In the Table 9.4 *Saint* text, the first episode is composed of the goal of curing Eva Bernassi from peritonitis and the sketchy plan is the nurse praying to the bishop. Again a fuller version of this elliptical episode would describe the various actions that led up to the nurse praying to the bishop, the details of her praying to him over a period of time, and then everybody's reaction as Eva Benassi began to recover. In the Table 9.5 *Metals* text, one episode is composed of the Spaniards goal of getting gold and their successful plan of conquering the Incas to get it. Again the episode would be better formed if it contained more of the details of this historical incident.

The most complete treatment of episodes in this book is contained in the chapter by Voss and Bisanz.

Mechanisms.   Mechanism cognitive units are very similar to episode units because they are also composed of a goal linked by motivational coherence relations with a plan of causally linked actions. However, mechanism units differ from episodes in that they describe the causal contingencies between actions that can be used to accomplish a goal with a piece of equipment (e.g., operating instructions) or in a social organization (e.g., office procedures), while episodes describe a series of actions that were performed in the past to accomplish a goal. The *Radar* text in Table 9.2 contains examples of mechanisms units for radar equipment. One example is provided by the goal of obtaining a measure of the distance to an object by sending out a broad radar pulse that continues if no object is in the way, but bounces back otherwise and makes a bright spot on the radar screen. The radar operator then determines the distance by measuring the length of the trace on the display screen. Other examples of mechanism units in the *Radar* text are provided by the goal of obtaining the specific location of an object (not just the distance to it) and the series of actions that comprise the "search light" technique for determining the object location.

The chapter by Mayer contains a discussion of what I am calling mechanism units, although Mayer calls them "explanatory units."

Descriptions.   A description cognitive unit is a cluster of stative propositions linked together by property coherence relations. Probably the most widespread use of description units in expository texts is in texts that present classifications or taxonomies: For example, in the chapter you are currently reading, each section is a description unit. However, our example texts also have descriptions mixed in with the other cognitive units. For example, the Table 9.1 *Radar* text contains the description unit that until the middle ages wagons "were no more than boxes set upon axles between wheels." The Table 9.2 *Radar* text contains the description that radar sets are composed of a transmitter, a receiver, and a display. The Table 9.3 *Supertanker* text contains a detailed, but fragmented, description unit that describes a supertanker as having a capacity of a half-million tons of oil, being the size of five football fields, having a storage area that can accomodate the Empire State Building, having only one propeller, and having only one boiler.

The chapter by Meyer gives the most detailed treatment of description cognitive units.

Arguments.   An argument cognitive unit is composed of propositions giving a general assertion and related propositions linked to them by support coherence relations. For example, in the Table 9.3 *Supertanker* text one argument unit is provided by the assertion that a supertanker wreck results in damage to the environment and the two supporting examples of wrecks in 1970 near Spain and 1967 off the coast of Cornwall. The whole Table 9.5 *Metals* text is actually an example of an argument unit. It first asserts that "Different cultures have used metals for different purposes," then the rest of the text provides examples supporting that general statement.

The chapter by Meyer provides a discussion of argument units.

Memory Retrieval Structures

A skilled reader must not only construct coherence relations and higher-level cognitive units when comprehending a text, but must also organize all of this information using an effective indexing system so that it can be accessed when needed later. The memory retrieval structures provide these indexing systems.

There are two kinds of memory retrieval structures: The first kind are structures that are networks linking the whole higher-level cognitive units that I have discussed, while the second kind are more complicated structures that not only link cognitive units but also have complex interactions between the units. I call the simple linked-unit structures cognitive unit networks and the more complicated structures rhetorical networks. In the next two sections I discuss these two kinds of memory retrieval structures.

Cognitive Unit Networks.   These networks involve simple linkages of higher-level cognitive units. The *Wagon* text in Table 9.1 provides an example of a linear chain of episodes: First, we have an episode about sledges (and Egyptians) 5,000 years ago, which established the preconditions needed (namely, the existence of rudimentary sledge-wagons) for an episode about Scythians wandering over Europe around 700 BC, followed by an episode about wagons in the middle ages and an episode about four-wheeled coaches in Germany. Because the *Wagon* text is abnormally short, these episodes are only stated in summary form, but in a more natural text each would be elaborated. In fact, a longer version of the *Wagon* text would probably have a hierarchical episode network where more detailed episode units would be subordinated to the current ones in the top-level chain. For example, the 5000-year-old episode might have one subepisode about the Egyptians discovering rudimentary wagons and another subepisode about the Chinese independently discovering primitive wagons.

Similarly, mechanism, description and argument cognitive units can be linked together at the same level of abstraction (like the linear chain of episodes in the *Wagon* text) or hierarchically at different levels of abstraction. In fact, the chapter you are reading is an example of a hierarchical network of description units. None of the other chapters in this book explicitly discuss cognitive unit networks, but Meyer's chapter comes the closest.

Rhetorical Networks

Rhetorical networks involve more interaction between the component cognitive units than are involved in the simple linkages of the cognitive unit networks. So far I have found three kinds of rhetorical networks in my own research, in the chapters in this book by Meyer and Mayer, and in other work by Mayer (summarized in Mayer, 1981). The three kinds of rhetorical networks are comparison networks, response networks, and mental models.

In a comparison network two or more episodes, mechanisms, descriptions or arguments are compared and contrasted by highlighting similarities and differences. Analogies are a frequently encountered kind of comparison network and the *Radar* text in Table 9.2 provides two examples of analogies. Specifically, the first analogy compares the mechanism of radar with the mechanism of a sound echo from a shout bouncing off a building, while the second analogy compares the mechanism of radar waves with the mechanism of tossing a pebble into a quiet lake. The memory structure for a historical essay comparing the history of the two island nations Britain and Japan would contain a comparison network involving episodes. Similarly, the memory structure for a cultural essay comparing the architecture of the new IBM and ATT buildings in New York City would contain a comparison network involving descriptions; and the memory structure for an editorial comparing the arguments for a national industrial policy to the arguments for an unfettered free market would contain a comparison network involving arguments. Meyer discusses comparison networks in her chapter and in Meyer (1975).

In a response network, one set of episodes, mechanisms, descriptions or arguments calls forth another as a response to it (which may in turn call for other units in response). The Table 9.3 *Supertanker* text provides an example of an argument response network. Here the first half of the text presents arguments that spills from supertanker wrecks are a problem, then the second half argues for certain solutions to this problem. This problem-solution pattern is one kind of argument response network, but there are others (e.g., argument-counterargument).

One kind of episode response network is the protagonist-antagonist network that Voss and Bisanz discuss briefly in their chapter. For example, a history of the space race might give one episode describing the Russian Sputnik satellite then give other episodes in response to that describing the American struggles to launch a satellite.

Similarly, one example of a mechanism response network would be a technical essay that relates the mechanism of the Russian satellite-killer system (e.g., launched in advance by a big rocket, kept in orbit until needed, then directed to target satellite and blown up), then relates the mechanism of the American anti-satellite weapon (e.g., small missile carried by a jet fighter, launched directly at the target satellite when needed) that is a response to the Russian one.

One example of a description response text would be an art appreciation essay that describes somewhat overwrought Beaux Arts architecture, then describes clean-lined Modernist architecture that is a response to it and goes on to describe Post-Modernist architecture that is a response to the somewhat sterile Modernist architecture. Meyer discusses responses in her chapter and in Meyer (1975).

The final kind of memory retrieval network that I have found so far in expository text is the mental model. A mental model is a metamechanism that closely links other mechanism cognitive units into a higher-level mechanism. For example, Mayer (1981) used a mental model in an instruction manual to teach the BASIC computer programming language to computer-naive people. His mental model combined four mechanisms: a memory scoreboard mechanism, an input window mechanism, a program list and pointer mechanism, and an output pad mechanism. What makes this a mental model and not simply a multi-mechanism text is that explaining the various commands of BASIC involves interactions of these four component mechanisms. Although the primary cognitive units used in mental models are mechanisms, the other cognitive units (episodes, descriptions and arguments) can also be part of mental models, but in subsidiary roles. For example, episodes can provide a "walkthrough" of how to program in BASIC guided by the model, descriptions can explain how to visualize the model, and arguments can try to convince the reader that the mental model is an appropriate way to think about BASIC.

WORLD KNOWLEDGE

Texts rarely explicitly state all of the information needed to construct memories containing the coherence relations, cognitive units, and retrieval structures that I have discussed. However, skilled readers are able to construct such memories because the tests contain just enough information to cue the appropriate pieces of knowledge about the world needed to make the requisite inferences. Thus an essential part of a complete theory of understanding expository text is an account of the knowledge needed to make the inferences necessary to construct coherence relations, cognitive units, and retrieval networks. The chapters in this book by Voss and Bisanz, Graesser and Goodman, and Miller explicitly discuss the kinds of knowledge needed. From their chapters and my own investigations, I have found four essential kinds of knowledge for expository text: namely, knowledge about human actions, knowledge about physical events, knowledge about objects and locations, and knowledge about human reasoning. I now discuss these kinds of knowledge and what we know about them.

Knowledge about Human Actions

Knowledge about human actions is required to understand texts involving causal and motivational coherence relations, episode and some mechanism (particularly, mechanisms involving human organizations) cognitive units, and memory retrieval structures involving these cognitive units. This knowledge about human actions forms a folk or naive psychology of human behavior that is correct in many ways, but also wrong in systematic ways (Heider, 1958; Schneider, Hastorf, & Ellsworth, 1979). Whether right or wrong, however, this knowledge about human actions forms the basis for our ability to understand texts involving human actions. This knowledge includes characteristics of people and social roles that serve as the sources of goals (e.g., shy people, corporate executives, people in love, each have certain kinds of goals), characteristics of different kinds of goals (e.g., achievement goals, satisfaction goals, preservation goals), the packages of plans that provide possible ways of accomplishing various kinds of goals (e.g., if you want to use something then you must know its location, go to that location, gain control over it, perform any preparations needed, then you can do what you want with it; or if you want to know something then alternative ways of finding out are asking someone, bargaining for the information, threatening someone if they don't tell you), and the packages of actions that comprise the plans—including the standard sequences of actions that form scripts for conventional situations (e.g., the standard sequence of actions that occur when going to a doctor's office or restaurant). Schank and Abelson (1977), Miller and Kintsch (1981) and Wilensky (1983) describe in detail various kinds of knowledge about human actions.

As Voss and Bisanz discuss in their chapter, knowledge about actions includes not only information about topics known to everyone, but also specialized knowledge about actions in particular situations. For example, people who are knowledgeable about baseball can understand the actions of the players better and therefore make appropriate inferences and remember the important parts of games much better than people who have little knowledge about baseball (Spilich, Vesonder, Chiesi, & Voss, 1979). This specialized knowledge about actions appears to come in the same forms I described in the previous paragraph (goal sources, kinds of goals, plan packages, and plan actions), but the content of each form is specialized for the specific domain (e.g., plans for winning baseball games instead of general plans).

One example of using knowledge about human actions to make inferences is provided by the Table 9.4 *Saint* text statements about Eva Bernassi recovering from dying after her nurse prayed to Bishop Neumann. The connection between these statements makes sense because the bishop appears to be a saint (and saints can cure people), so making a request by praying to him for a cure is a reasonable plan for accomplishing the goal of curing the patient. Another example is provided by the Table 9.5 *Metals* text statements that Spaniards craved gold so they conquered the Incas who had it. The connection between these statements makes sense because overpowering (by conquering) someone who owns something you want is a reasonable plan for gaining ownership of that thing.

Knowledge about Physical Events

Knowledge about physical events is required to understand texts involving causal coherence relations, episode and mechanism cognitive units, and memory retrieval structures containing these cognitive units. This knowledge about physical events forms a folk or naive physics that has much in common with Newtonian mechanics, but also deviates in significant ways (Caramazza, McCloskey, & Green, 1981; DiSessa, 1982). Whether right or wrong, however, such knowledge serves as the basis for understanding texts involving physical events.

Unlike human actions, the details of how people represent in memory their knowledge about physical events have not been investigated. However, like human actions, knowledge of physical events seems to exist at different levels of abstraction. For example, people's knowledge of what happens during a hurricane or an earthquake is a concrete sequence of physical events analogous to scripts of human actions. Also, there is more abstract knowledge about force, distance, mass, and so on that seems analogous to the more abstract, goal-oriented knowledge about human actions.

One example of using knowledge about physical events to make inferences are the statements in the Table 9.2 *Radar* text about tossing a pebble in a lake and therefore creating concentric circles of small waves moving away from where the pebble hit the water. Here either our specific knowledge about having tossed rocks in lakes ourselves or our abstract knowledge about what happens when a comparatively heavy solid object enters a pool of liquid allows us to meaningfully connect these two statements with a causal inference. Another example is provided by the Table 9.3 *Supertanker* text statements that the fire caused hurricane-force winds, which then led to "black rain" several days later. Here our general knowledge about what happens to gasses when they are heated and our specific knowledge about how rain occurs allow us to connect the statements with causal coherence relations.

Knowledge about Objects and Locations

Knowledge about objects and locations is required to understand texts involving referential and property coherence relations, all four kinds of cognitive units (episodes, mechanisms, descriptions, and arguments), and memory retrieval structures containing these cognitive units. This knowledge about objects forms a folk or naive taxonomy of the world that has been intensively studied in cognitive psychology under the rubric of "semantic memory" (Mervis & Rosch, 1981; Smith, 1978). Recently, these investigations have also been extended to the study of people's knowledge about locations (Tversky & Hemenway, 1983). Whether right or wrong, however, such knowledge serves as the basis for understanding texts involving objects and locations.

The Table 9.5 *Metals* text contains several examples of using knowledge about objects to make inferences needed to construct a memory representation of the text content. For example, knowledge that copper, bronze, gold, aluminum, and titanium are all metals establishes referential coherence links between the first sentence and the rest. Similarly, knowledge that Greeks, Hellenes, Incas, and Spaniards are kinds of cultures also connects the first sentence with the others. The Table 9.2 *Radar* text provides an example of a location inference. Specifically, knowledge that airports have search lights and knowledge about what these search lights look like allow one aspect of radar to be explained in terms of an analogy to airport search lights.

Knowledge about Human Reasoning

Knowledge about human reasoning is required to understand texts involving support coherence relations, argument cognitive units, and memory retrieval structures containing this type of cognitive unit. This knowledge about human reasoning forms a folk or naive logic that has much in common with formal logic, but is frequently different (Erickson, 1974; Johnson-Laird & Steedman, 1978). Whether right or wrong, however, such knowledge serves as the basis for understanding texts involving human reasoning.

One rule of human reasoning that conflicts with formal logic is that two examples suffice to prove a generalization (Anderson, Kline, & Beasley, 1979). In fact, an informal survey I have made indicates that most arguments in expository texts contain exactly two examples in support of the general point. When reading these texts, one example does not seem sufficient to prove the point and three seems to belabor the point, but two examples seems just right. Two (naturally) of our example texts contain instances of this phenomenon. In the Table 9.3 *Supertanker* text, the generalization "As a result of spillage, the environment is damaged" is asserted, then two examples (a 1970 oil spill in Spain and a 1967 one off Cornwall) are provided to prove the point. Similarly, in the Table 9.4 *Saint* text, the request that John Neumann be canonized is backed up by citing two example miracles.

PROCESSES

I have discussed the memory structures constructed when reading expository text and the knowledge structures that provide the information needed to construct them but to provide a complete account of how people understand expository text I also need to specify the processes that act on these structures. Comprehension processes perform three kinds of functions: They use cues from the text to access the knowledge needed to understand the text, they manage both the text and knowledge information in limited working memory while processing the text, and they construct the memory representation of the text that becomes part of long-term memory.

Accessing Relevant Knowledge

When comprehending a text, readers must process the first few propositions in a bottom-up fashion with little assistance from higher-level pieces of knowledge. However, if the text is well written, the readers will soon encounter a distinctive piece of information that accesses one or a small number of pieces of knowledge that integrate the information (Black, Galambos, & Read, in press) and aid in the comprehension of the next few propositions—particularly if those propositions are related to central parts of the knowledge accessed (Galambos & Rips, 1982). Thus comprehension is an interaction of bottom-up processes that access relevant knowledge based on low-level analyses of incoming information and top-down processes in which accessed knowledge aids in understanding and integrating low-level information. As Kieras points out in his chapter, this process proceeds most smoothly if the key topic information that accesses the knowledge needed to provide the top-level organization of the text is near the beginning of the text, so the readers are biased toward thinking one of the first two sentences contains this topic information. As Miller and Britton, Glynn and Smith describe in their chapters, this interaction between top-down and bottom-up processes takes place at several levels: Words and other text elements on the bottom are integrated into propositions, which are linked by coherence relations (into a microstructure) and integrated into higher-level cognitive units (macropropositions), which are in turn linked by memory retrieval networks (macrostructures).

For example, in the Table 9.4 *Saint* text, the distinctive words *request* and *miracles* access the knowledge that is the key to understanding the rest of the text and constructing an integrated memory representation of the text content. Of course, accessing relevant knowledge is problematic when the information being conveyed is completely new, so analogies between the new information and known information are used in such cases. For example, before getting too far into the possibly new topic of radar, the Table 9.2 *Radar* text provides an analogy between radar and the familiar topic of sound echoes from shouting in a canyon.

Managing Working Memory

As Britton, Glynn and Smith discuss in their chapter, all of these top-down and bottom-up processes must take place in real-time within the confines of a limited working memory, so effective management of mental resources in working memory is an important part of skilled reading. Unfortunately, memory management is also a topic that has received little study so far, but a few observations can be made. Specifically, comprehension of a text proceeds most effectively when the reader can utilize just-in-time processing: that is, when knowledge can be pre-fetched so as to arrive in working memory at precisely the same time as the input information to which it is relevant. With such processing, working memory is not cluttered with input information awaiting the knowledge to process it nor is working memory cluttered with knowledge accessed too early. Also important is knowing when the processing of a certain chunk of information is complete (e.g., when an episode or description cognitive unit is completed), so the finished product can come off the working memory assembly line and be shipped off to long-term memory.

One implication of this line of argument is that if a text interrupts a cognitive unit and returns to it later, then that text will be comparatively hard to understand and the interrupted cognitive unit will be harder to remember later. For example in the Table 9.2 *Supertanker* text, the information that makes up the description unit of the supertanker is scattered discontinuously throughout the text. In the beginning of the text, we are given the carrying capacity of a supertanker, but it is only much later that we get more properties (e.g., they have only one propeller and one boiler). Thus we would expect readers to have a comparatively hard time integrating and remembering this information.

Constructing the Memory Representation

It is also important not to ship off just anything from working memory to long-term memory, but to make sure the product is a quality one. Just as shoddy products come back to haunt manufacturers, so shoddy or poorly designed memories will penalize readers when they later try to use the information they have learned. In their chapter, Graesser and Goodman discuss how the enormous amount of potential information is narrowed down from what could be included in the memory representation based on the mixture of the input information and the inferences that could be made from the knowledge used to understand it. This pruning is one of the reasons for having knowledge at many levels of abstraction, because the higher-level knowledge can be used to constrain the inferences made from lower-level knowledge during comprehension, and narrow down even the inferences that are made during comprehension to the most important ones for inclusion in the long-term memory representation.

For example, frequently when reading new material in an expository text, readers construct a memory representation that is so cluttered with details and ill-structured that they would have been better off just reading a summary of the text (Reder & Anderson, 1980a). In such cases, the reader should probably re-read the text as Britton, Glynn and Smith suggest so that they can construct a better memory representation. However, as Mayer points out in his chapter, the memory representation must be constructed with the tasks in mind that the information will later be used to perform. Thus, for example, if the information is to be used for problem solving, then Mayer has found that explanations of the mechanisms behind the general statements are essential. If the explanatory details in the mechanism cognitive units in the Table 9.2 *Radar* text and the Table 9.3 *Supertanker* text were removed, then we would expect people who read these nonexplanative versions not to be able to use the general statements in problem-solving tasks (e.g., devising how to use radar for a task not described in the text like weather forecasting, or proposing solutions not described in the text to the supertanker spillage problem) as effectively as people who read the current explanative versions.

CONCLUDING REMARKS

I have described what I see as the framework for studying how people understand expository text that has emerged from the other chapters in this book and related research. Furthermore, I have filled in this framework with what now appears to me to be the memory structures, world knowledge and comprehension processes involved in understanding expository text. I hope this framework and these results and guesses will inspire or enrage others to pursue this important topic further.

ACKNOWLEDGMENT

The writing of this paper was supported by contract N00014-82-C-0424 from the Office of Naval Research and the Army Research Institute.

REFERENCES

Abbott, V., & Black, J. B. *A comparison of the memory strength of alternative text relations.* Paper presented at the 1982 Meeting of the American Educational Research Association, 1982.

Anderson, J. R. Retrieval of propositional information from long-term memory. *Cognitive Psychology,* 1974, *5,* 451–474.

Anderson, J. R., Kline, P. J., & Beasley, C. M. A general learning theory and its application to schema abstraction. In G. H. Bower (Ed.), *The psychology of learning and motivation* (Vol. 13). New York: Academic Press, 1979.

Black, J. B. Understanding and remembering stories. In J. R. Anderson & S. M. Kosslyn (Eds.), *Tutorial essays in learning and memory.* San Francisco, Calif.: Freeman, in press.

Black, J. B., & Bern, H. Causal coherence and memory for events in narratives. *Journal of Verbal Learning and Verbal Behavior,* 1981, *20,* 267–275.

Black, J. B., & Bower, G. H. Episodes as chunks in narrative memory. *Journal of Verbal Learning and Verbal Behavior,* 1979, *18,* 309–318.

Black, J. B., Galambos, J. A., & Read, S. J. Comprehending stories and social situations. In R. Wyer & T. Srull (Eds.), *Handbook of social cognition* (Vol. 3). Hillsdale, N.J.: Lawrence Erlbaum associates, in press.

Caramazza, A., McCloskey, M., & Green, B. Naive beliefs in "sophisticated" subjects: Misconceptions about trajectories of objects. *Cognition,* 1981, *9,* 117–123.

DiSessa, A. Unlearning Aristotelian physics: A study of knowledge-based learning. *Cognitive Science,* 1982, *6,* 37–75.

Erickson, J. R. A set analysis theory of behavior in formal syllogistic reasoning tasks. In R. Solso (Ed.), *Theories in cognitive psychology.* Hillsdale, N.J.: Lawrence Erlbaum Associates, 1974.

Galambos, J. A., & Rips, L. J. Memory for routines. *Journal of Verbal Learning and Verbal Behavior.* 1982, *21,* 260–281.

Graesser, A. C. *Prose comprehension beyond the word.* New York: Springer-Verlag, 1981.

Heider, F. *The psychology of interpersonal relations.* New York: Wiley, 1958.

Johnson-Laird, P. N., & Steedman, M. The psychology of syllogisms. *Cognitive Psychology,* 1978, *10,* 64–99.

Kintsch, W. *The representation of meaning in memory.* Hillsdale, N.J.: Lawrence Erlbaum Associates, 1974.

Kintsch, W., & van Dijk, T. A. Toward a model of text comprehension and production. *Psychological Review,* 1978, *85,* 363–394.

Mayer, R. E. The psychology of how novices learn computer programming. *Computing Surveys,* 1981, *13,* 121–141.

Mervis, C. B., & Rosch, E. Categorization of natural objects. *Annual Review of Psychology,* 1981, *32,* 89–115.

Meyer, B. J. F. *The organization of prose and its effects on memory.* Amsterdam: North-Holland, 1975.

Miller, J. R., & Kintsch, W. Knowledge-based aspects of prose comprehension and readability. *Text,* 1981, *1,* 215–232.

Reder, L. M., & Anderson, J. R. A comparison of texts and their summaries: Memorial consequences. *Journal of Verbal Learning and Verbal Behavior,* 1980, *19,* 121–134. (a)

Reder, L. M., & Anderson, J. R. A partial resolution of the paradox of interference: The role of integrating knowledge. *Cognitive Psychology,* 1980, *12,* 447–472. (b)

Schank, R. C. The structure of episodes in memory. In D. G. Bobrow & A. M. Collins (Eds.), *Representation and understanding; Studies in cognitive science.* New York: Academic Press, 1975.

Schank, R. C., & Abelson, R. P. *Scripts, plans, goals and understanding.* Hillsdale, N.J.: Lawrence Erlbaum Associates, 1977.

Schneider, D. J., Hastorf, A. H., & Ellsworth, P. C. *Person perception.* Reading, Mass.: Addison-Wesley, 1979.

Smith, E. E., Adams, N., & Schorr, D. Fact retrieval and the paradox of interference. *Cognitive Psychology,* 1978, *10,* 438–464.

Smith, E. E. Theories of semantic memory. In W. K. Estes (Ed.), *Handbook of learning and cognitive processes: Vol. 6, Linguistic functions in cognitive theory.* Hillsdale, N.J.: Lawrence Erlbaum Associates, 1978.

Spilich, G. J., Vesonder, G. T., Chiesi, H. L., & Voss, J. F. Text processing of domain-related information for individuals with high and low domain knowledge. *Journal of Verbal Learning and Verbal Behavior,* 1979, *18,* 275–290.

Tversky, B., & Hemenway, K. Categories of environmental scenes. *Cognitive Psychology,* 1983, *15,* 121–149.

Wilensky, R. *Planning and understanding.* Reading, Mass.: Addison-Wesley, 1983.

A RESEARCH HANDBOOK FOR TEXT AND WORLD KNOWLEDGE ANALYSIS

10

Prose Analysis: Purposes, Procedures, and Problems

Bonnie J. F. Meyer

Arizona State University

This section of my contribution to this book is meant to augment the two procedures discussed in Part 1: (1) analysis of text and (2) scoring recall protocols. These issues were discussed in Part 1 under the subtopics of "Meyer's Approach to Prose Analysis" and "Detailed Comparison of Kintsch and Meyer Approaches." In Part 2, I give definitions and examples of rhetorical and role or case labels for the content structure. The analysis of the supertanker passage is discussed. Other texts, including the various versions of the railroad text, are examined for top-level structures. In addition, rules for scoring free recall protocols are provided with examples from the supertanker passage.

CONSTRUCTING THE CONTENT STRUCTURE

The content structure is best formed by following a top-down procedure. The passage is first examined for its top-level structure. The top-level structure will be the rhetorical relationship that can interrelate the greatest amount of text. The content structure is formed by unpeeling layers of rhetorical relationships in a top-down fashion. Once the top-level structure is identified, then the next most inclusive relations are identified until the case grammar level of analysis is reached. First, we look at the rhetorical relationships and then the role or case relationships. Finally, in this section, we go through the analysis of the supertanker passage.

Rhetorical or Logical Relationships

As mentioned in Part 1, the 18 rhetorical relationships discussed in Meyer (1975; also Grimes, 1975) can be chunked into five distinct groups: *collection, causa-*

tion, response, comparison, and *description.* Discourse can be classified according to which of these relationships serve as the top-level structure or overall plan for writing the text. These basic types of top-level structures or plans are familiar in various contexts. The collection relationship is exemplified in the time-order plan of history texts. Scientific treatises often adhere to the response type, first raising a question or problem and then seeking to give an answer or solution. Political speeches are often of the comparison type, and in particular, its adversative subtype. Newspaper articles are often of the description type, telling us who, where, how, and when. Of course, many texts will reflect more than one of these basic five structures. Folktales contain much description and collection: time-order within a response plan, where the protagonist confronts and resolves a problem. Finally, folktales may carry an overall comparison plan, such as demonstrating the contrast between good and evil, selfishness and altruism, industry and slothfulness, and much more.

We will begin our look at finer distinctions among these five types of structures by making one more chunking of these relationships into three groups. The first group of relationships includes *collection, causation,* and *response* and varies along the continuum shown in Fig. 2.3 (Part 1). That is, in order for content to be related by a *collection,* the only requirement is that the arguments are grouped together. Going up the scale to *collection: time-order,* the interrelated content must be grouped together and also must be before and after in time. The arguments or content interrelated by a *causation* relationship must be (1) group together, (2) before and after in time, and (3) logically or quasi-logically related. The propositions or content interrelated by a *response* relationship must satisfy all of the above constraints, but also must have some overlap between content of the topic of the problem and that of the solution as shown in Fig. 2.4 (Part 1). Thus, the first grouping of rhetorical relationships has similarities and differences that can be arranged on this continuum of argument constraints. However, the second major category *comparison* varies on different dimensions as does the third major category *description.* Each is defined and distinctions between their subtypes are explained.

Collection, Causation, Response.   Collection interrelates a list of elements related in some unspecified manner. The basis for the collection ranges from a group of attributes of the same character, event or idea, to a group related by association, to a group related by simultaneity, to a group related by time sequence (see railroad texts and Fig. 2.17, Part 1).

Examples:

Parakeets are small, soft, colorful, beady-eyed.

The explosion demolished the car, film, and TV.

Jennifer eats at 3, bathes at 4, dances at 5.

Loss of body water is required of wrestlers, boxers, judo contestants, karate contestants, weight lifters, and members of 150-pound football teams.

A loss of 5% results in heat exhaustion, faintness, and nausea.

The following depicts the format of a collection in a left-rooted tree (most practical format for long texts). For scoring a time sequence, Litteral's (1972) time typology can be used and each time index can be placed on a separate line and scored (see Fig. 2.17 in Part 1; also see Meyer, 1975; Meyer, Haring, Brandt, & Walker, 1980).

```
┌ collection
├ WRESTLERS
├ BOXERS
├ JUDO CONTESTANTS
└ etc.
```

Causation shows a causal relationship between ideas where one idea is the antecedent or cause and the other is the consequent or effect. The relation is often referred to as the condition, result, or purpose with one argument serving as the antecedent and the other as the consequent. The arguments are before and after in time and causally related. There are two types: the *covariance* with equally weighted arguments and the *explanation* where the antecedent conditions or principles are subordinate to the consequent, the event or idea explained.

Examples of *Causation: Covariance:*

Most wrecks result from a lack of power and steering equipment to handle emergency situations.

Our bright and brawny construction trucks run on child power, not batteries. So there's never an energy shortage.

A wrecked supertanker spills oil in the ocean. As a result of spillage the environment is damaged.

If not treated, death will result.

The loss of body water is frequently required of athletes by coaches so that athletes will attain specified body weights.

```
┌ causation: covariance, antecedent
├ NOT TREATED
├ causation: covariance, consequent
└ DEATH
```

Causation: explanation is found when previously stated information is explained in a more abstract manner (related to broader context, premises widely accepted in society of which the writer and reader are apart), or explained through more concrete background events.

Examples:

You cannot stand 3 feet out from the 3rd floor window because of the law of gravity.

The solution is not to halt the use of tankers on the ocean since 80% of the world's oil supply is carried by tankers.

The AMA condemns dehydration. Dehydration impairs cardiovascular functioning.

In the following example both types of causation can be found (refer to idea units 108, 134-156 of the content structure of the supertanker passage for a complete analysis):

Guardsmen found chemical clues which led to the arrest on November 7, 1975 of a Greek tanker captain, Vasilios K. Psarroulis, because of failure to report the loss of an estimated 40,000 gallons of oil.

> ┌ *causation: covariance, antecedent* (LED TO)
> ├ GUARDSMEN FOUND CHEMICAL CLUES
> ├ *causation: covariance, consequent* (LED TO)
> └ ARREST (etc.)
>   ├ *causation: explanation* (BECAUSE)
>   └ FAILURE TO REPORT (etc.)

Response: problem/solution (also remark and reply, question and answer variations) is similar to the causation in that the problem is before in time and an antecedent for the solution. However, in addition, there must be some overlap in topic content between the problem and solution; that is, at least part of the solution must match one cause of the problem. The arguments (e.g., problem and solution) are equally weighted and occur at the same level in the content structure.

Examples:

Where will you be on George Washington's birthday? I will be watching the elephants at the zoo.

We have several daffodils in bloom. I'd better dig for worms and get out the boat.

Prevention is needed of oil spills from supertankers. A wrecked supertanker spills oil into the ocean. As a result of spillage, the environment is damaged. Transport of oil across the ocean should be forbidden.

We need to stop annoying noises and wasting water. We can either get the water master or call Max, the plumber.

Format:

> ┌ *response*
> ├ *problem*
> ├ PREVENTION IS NEEDED OF OIL SPILLS FROM SUPERTANKERS
>   ├ *causation: covariance, antecedent* (AS A RESULT)
>   ├ A WRECKED SUPERTANKER SPILLS OIL INTO THE OCEAN
>   ├ *causation: covariance, consequent* (AS A RESULT)
>   └ THE ENVIRONMENT IS DAMAGED
> ├ *solution*
> └ TRANSPORT OF OIL ACROSS THE OCEAN SHOULD BE FORBID-DEN

Response is listed and scored separately from *problem* and *solution* because it is possible to identify something as a problem and not give a solution. However, *causation: covariance* is not listed nor scored independently of *antecedent* and *consequent* because identification of an antecedent is not possible without a consequent.

Comparison.   The comparison relation points out differences and similarities between two or more topics. There are three subtypes of comparison: *alternative, adversative,* and *analogy.*

The *alternative* interrelates equally weighted alternative options or equally weighted opposing views.

Examples:

Alveretta, you may have a nutty buddy, or an ice cream cone, or an ice cream sandwich. Or you may have some cotton candy.

Heavy Duty Reynolds Wrap gives you 2 juicy options: wrapped or tented.

Pillsbury's new basic bundt cake is made to be baked in a 13 by 9-inch pan or in a Bundt fluted tube pan.

Opinions on body water loss differ between coaches and doctors.

Format:

> ⌐ *comparison: alternative*
> ├ WRAPPED
> └ TENTED

The *adversative* relates a favored view to less desirable opposing view or relates what did happen to what did not happen.

Examples:

In contrast to the stupid action taken by coaches, doctors forbid dehydration.

Our bright and brawny construction trucks run on child power, not batteries.

An immediate halt of the use of tankers is not possible. Instead, we must train drivers carefully, build better tankers, and install ground control towers.

Format:

> ⌐DOCTORS FORBID DEHYDRATION
> ⌐*comparison: adversative* (IN CONTRAST TO THE STUPID)
> └ACTIONS TAKEN BY COACHES

Comparison: analogy gives an analogy (parallel idea with different content) to support an idea or event. The format of the analogy is the same as the comparison: adversative.

Example:

Ground control stations should be installed at places where supertankers come close to the shore. They would function like airplane control towers.

Format:

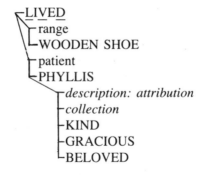

┌ GROUND CONTROL STATIONS SHOULD BE INSTALLED AT
│   PLACES WHERE SUPERTANKERS COME CLOSE TO THE
│   SHORE
├ *comparison: analogy* (FUNCTION LIKE)
└ AIRPLANE CONTROL TOWERS

Description.   The description relates a topic to more information about it. A greater number of distinctions are made among descriptive relations. All descriptive relations have the same format in the content structure. The descriptive argument and descriptive relation are subordinate to the topic described.

Description: attribution describes qualities of a proposition; it adds colors, qualities, attributes; we often find collections of attributes describing a person, event, or idea.

Examples:

Kind, gracious, beloved Phyllis lived in a wooden shoe.

Oil spills kill microscopic plant life which provide food for sea life and produce 70% of the world's oxygen supply.

Format:

┌ LIVED
│ ┌ range
│ └ WOODEN SHOE
├ patient
└ PHYLLIS
    ┌ *description: attribution*
    ├ *collection*
    ├ KIND
    ├ GRACIOUS
    └ BELOVED

Description: specific gives more specific information about something that was stated in a general way; abstract to concrete; statement to examples. The superordinate is less precise/more inclusive, while subordinate is more precise/less inclusive; cues are "namely," "that is," "for example."

Examples:

At 5 a.m. I heard birds squawking. They were my neighbor's parakeets.

The bright construction trucks run on child power.

Most wrecks result from the lack of power and steering equipment to handle emergency situations, such as storms.

Oil spills damage the environment. In 1967, an oil spill killed 200,000 seabirds. Oil spills also kill microscopic plant life.

Loss of body water can impair cardiovascular functioning. A loss of 5% results in heat exhaustion, faintness, and nausea.
Format:

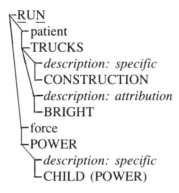

```
┌RUN
│ ├patient
│ ├TRUCKS
│ │ ├description: specific
│ │ └CONSTRUCTION
│ │ ├description: attribution
│ │ └BRIGHT
│ ├force
│ └POWER
│   ├description: specific
│   └CHILD (POWER)
```

Description: equivalent restates the same information in a different way. The dominate argument is staged in the foreground by more frequent usage in the text.
Example:
The tanker, Torrey Canyon, crashed off the Coast of Cornwall.
Format:

```
┌TANKER
 ├description: equivalent
 └TORREY CANYON
```

Distinctions between *attribution, specific,* and *equivalent* can be seen in their different relationships to the superordinate topic or referent that they describe. Attribution gives a quality of a referent. Specific is more specialized than the referent. Equivalent refers to the same referent.
Description: manner describes the way an event or event complex is performed. Manners describe how much, how often, how difficult, and so forth.
Examples:
The corn shells easily.
The boss fired the scientist. He screamed obscenities and shoved him and his rats out of the research center.
Specified body weights are considerably below usual weights.
Loss of body water is frequently required.
The AMA strongly condemns dehydration.
Format:

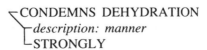

```
┌CONDEMNS DEHYDRATION
 ├description: manner
 └STRONGLY
```

Description: evidence gives evidence through perception of a situation to support some idea.

Examples:

The supertanker crashed on a rock; I heard it.

Parakeets are ideal pets for people with limited time. In 2 minutes I give my parakeet food and water each day.

Format:

```
┌THE SUPERTANKER CRASHED ON A ROCK
├─description: evidence
└I HEARD IT
```

There are three *description: setting* relationships: *time, location,* and *trajectory. Description: setting time* gives the time in which the event or idea occurred. *Description: setting location* gives the location in which it occurred. *Description: setting trajectory* gives a list of different times or locations that match a time index and reflect changing background of characters or ideas.

Examples:

In the year of 1970 near Spain an oil spill from a wrecked tanker exploded into fire.

In July 1975, the Coast Guard of the United States mopped up acres of oil from the beach at Geiger Key, Florida.

The story of Abraham's faithfulness to God as told in his travel from Ur to Haran to the Promised Land.

Format:

```
┌THE COAST GUARD OF THE UNITED STATES MOPPED UP
│   ACRES OF OIL FROM THE BEACH
├─description: setting time
└JULY 1975
├─description: setting location
└GEIGER KEY, FLORIDA
```

(For complete analysis, see the content structure of the supertanker passage units 109–133).

There are also three *description: identification* relationships. *Description: representative identification* is found when one element of the group stands for the group as a whole.

Example:

A typical supertanker carries a half-million tons of oil. (For format in the content of the supertanker text, see 7, 8, 9 in the supertanker's content structure.)

The average consumer finds it hard to make up his mind. He listens to TV commercials, etc.

Format:

⌐SUPERTANKER
├─*description: representative identification* (TYPICAL)
└─SUPERTANKERS

Description: replacement identification is found when one element stands for a group but isn't a group member; this assignment is arbitrary. Mathematics texts have a large number of these relationships (e.g., let x stand for the number of subjects in the experiment).

Example:

Suppose we let the banana stand for the supertanker and the nuts for the rocky channel. When the storm hits I move the banana so and you see how, etc.

Format:

⌐BANANA
├─*description: replacement identification*
└─SUPERTANKER

Description: constituency identification identifies a part in relation to its whole.

Example:

Geiger Key, Florida

Format:

⌐GEIGER KEY
├─*description: constituency identification*
└─FLORIDA

Progress Check: Identifying Top-Level Structures in Text

Following this section, five passages are presented that were taken directly from ninth-grade textbooks (Bartlett, 1978). See if you can identify the most superordinate rhetorical relationships in these texts. Answers can be found in the appendix. For extra practice examine advertisements for their top-level structure; I have found this practice to entertain as well as instruct students. For example, examine the captions from these ads:

1. "Most wraps just wrap. Reynolds Wrap wraps, molds and seals tightly."
2. "Cover Girl Oil Control Make-Up: No shining, no streaking, no yellowing, no fading, no blotching, no caking."
3. "Want a tough stain out? SHOUT it out!"

4. "This is where a wrinkle could start (around eye of lovely model). This is what could stop it (picture of Maybelline Moisture Whip)."
5. "EVEREADY DOUBLE GUARANTEE. Guarantee #1 The Eveready Skipper Flashlight. We give it a 10-year guarantee. Guarantee #2 Eveready Flashlight Batteries. They're guaranteed against damaging your flashlight in any way."

Did you find a *comparison: adversative* for 1, a *collection* of *description: attributions* for 2, a *response* for 3 (question/answer) and 4 (problem/solution), and *description: specific* for 5? If not, try again.

Find the top-level structures of the following ninth-grade materials. Check the top-level structures that you identify with those listed for the texts in the appendix.

Miracle Rice

There is a miracle rice that grows well in places in the Phillipines. And in West Africa, too. It is a miracle rice because it grows well where it is hard to grow anything at all. It grows fast. It produces big crops. It has the right color and taste. It contains large quantities of vitamins, particularly of the vitamin B family. These vitamins help people fight disease so that the rice is a good food. It is an easy crop to harvest and store. The rice is larger than other varieties and is bulkier. It can produce food for many, many people. So, it is a miracle rice. (From *Biology: Patterns in the Environment,* p. 391)

Anthrax

Scientists had puzzled for a long time about how animals got disease called anthrax. It was a disease that was killing many cattle and other farm animals. It was also killing many wild animals, but it was the loss of stock that worried farmers, scientists and the general public most of all. Sick animals had rod-like organisms in their blood. The animals gradually lost weight and strength and finally died. No one could understand why or how it happened. Finally, Robert Koch discovered the cause of anthrax. The disease was caused by a bacteria. Koch's discovery lead to a treatment for anthrax. (From *Biology: Patterns in the Environment,* pp. 202–203)

Chicken-Hawks

In one district, farmers began to kill the chicken-hawks. Large parties of men would go on bird-shoots. They not only shot adult birds, but also destroyed nests and breeding areas used by the hawks. Any young found in the nests were killed immediately. As a result of these hunts the farmers' chickens were not eaten. But, the farmers found something else wrong. Their store of grain in the barns was eaten by rats. Soon the rats were overrunning the farms. There was nothing to stop the spread of the rats. The farmers had removed a natural enemy of the rats—the chicken-hawk. (From *Biology: Patterns in the Environment,* p. 184)

How Historians View History

Different views exist among historians on how history might be studied. These differences may be grouped into the view of history as a game, and the view of history as a stream. Some historians view history as a game with players, rules, and clever plans. The players are people of all civilizations. The rules are the many sciences, such as biology, geology, archaeology, and geography. By studying people of the past and their planned "moves," we discover which moves lead to success or bring destruction. However, each person must first decide whether to be an active player in the game of history or a "pawn." As players, we try to improve the world in which we live. As pawns, we ignore the moves and decisions that others make which affect our lives.

Other historians see history as a stream. On the surface it appears to flow steadily onward, moving at will. Actually, however, it is slowed down, changed, and forced onward by strong undercurrents. This view is not as prominent as the other, but, no matter what their viewpoint, historians agree that history does repeat itself. Human nature and life today are not much different from the way they were in the days of Noah, Caesar, or Kennedy. Decisions facing us today are much the same as ones that had to be made in the past. History is the study of things that are past. It also helps us to understand what is happening in the world today, and it is a guide to what might be happening tomorrow. (From *Streams of Civilization,* topic area *Views of History,* p. 7)

The Early Railroads

Two contrasting views on the usefulness of railroads existed for early Americans. American men of business were quick to recognize the promise of railroads, and by 1830 several companies had been formed to construct railroad lines in the United States. Both the South Carolina Railroad and the Baltimore and Ohio Railroads, America's earliest lines, commenced operations in 1830. The first American locomotive engines were built and delivered in the same year. Most of the early railroads were short lines—the longest in the United States was also the longest in the world, 136 miles. Railway development proceeded rapidly. In the first six years, more than a thousand miles of track were laid, and railroads began to run trains in eleven states.

In the 1850's, rail service was extended to the Mississippi River. Except for the bulkiest of goods, railroads became the most economical form of transportation within the United States. Traveling by water between New York City and Detroit in the 1850's took ten days; by rail, the same trip required only four days.

Railroads were not popular with everybody. Farmers complained that the noise frightened their cattle, and that sparks from the engines set their fields afire. Some physicians feared that the human body could not endure travel at speeds so high as 30 miles an hour. Canal companies tried to keep railroads from building lines that might compete with canals. (From *The American Adventure: Expansion, Conflict, & Reconstruction* (1825–1880), p. C-50)

Depicting Patterns of Organization in Text

In the semantic grammar of propositions (Grimes, 1975), the rhetorical relationships are predicates that show the relationships among their arguments, other rhetorical propositions, lexical propositions, or referential indices (the word/concept to which one is referring). A rhetorical proposition is a proposition with a *rhetorical* relationship that interrelates its arguments, while a lexical proposition has a *word* relationship (a verb and its adjuncts) that interrelates its arguments. The case or role relationships in the lexical proposition label the type of arguments that the particular lexical predicate can take and does take in a particular sentence.

Logical relationships, such as causation, are shown between simple sentences, complex sentences, paragraphs, and so forth, with the rhetorical relationships. However, these logical relationships within simple sentences are shown with verbs and role-related arguments in case grammar (Fillmore, 1968; Grimes, 1975). For example, an *agent* is shown to instigate an action, such as PRODUCE, and the *patient* (or object) is the thing that results from the action, this production. Here is a causal chain with something producing something else. An example from the supertanker text is MICROSCOPIC PLANT LIFE (agent) PRODUCE OXYGEN (patient). If we were considering larger text segments, we would show this causal relationship with causation: covariance: antecedent/ consequent. For example, there could be a paragraph on the biological system of microscopic plant life which could be linked as the antecedent to a paragraph describing 70% of the world's oxygen supply which results from these tiny plants.

I view the rhetorical relationships of collection, causation, response, comparison, and description in text as evidence for use of these general schemata by writers. Their various subtypes are more specified schemata. These rhetorical relationships in text match up with patterns or ways of thinking in the mind of the writer and the mind of the reader. When in the mind (rather than formalized in a text), these logical relations satisfy the four properties of schemata outlined by Rumelhart and Ortony (1977). Lexical predicates (primarily verbs) also satisfy these properties and were used as examples of schemata in the Rumelhart and Ortony paper. The rhetorical (logical) and lexical (verb) relationships (1) have variables; (2) can embed, one within the other; (3) vary in abstractness, and (4) represent knowledge rather than definitions (see Rumelhart & Ortony, 1977).

When analyzing text, I attempt to identify the schemata or organizational patterns used by the writer to understand and communicate the information on a topic to a reader. The lexical predicates describe the patterns within simple sentences and the rhetorical predicates describe the organizational patterns not described by verbs and their case-related arguments.

Lexical Relationships

For this analysis procedure, the lexical predicates are identified and placed one level above their role-related arguments in the content structure. This format procedure plus the format procedures for the rhetorical propositions produce the levels in the hierarchical content structure. This section presents the definitions of the role (case) labels along with some examples.

Causal Roles.   *Agent, instrument, force,* and *vehicle* are all causal roles. If you are not interested in the distinctions among some of these roles, you may want to simply call them all agents.

The *agent* is instigator of an action; it is the person or thing responsible for an action. It is signaled with ''by'' in a passive sentence. In the examples below the lexical predicate will be identified with dashes beneath it.

My husband (agent) made the cage (patient).

The ball (patient) was thrown by the toddler (agent).

The shoe (agent) crushed the hornet (patient).

The *instrument* is something used inanimately by agent to perform an action (to have an instrument there must be an agent). The instrument is signaled by ''with'' as can be seen in the examples below.

The tractor (agent) seeded the field (patient) with a drill (instrument).

The Hulk (agent) broke the window (patient) with the villain (instrument).

The *force* is the cause of a process but devoid of responsibility. It is not found in the same lexical proposition as agents, instruments, or vehicles and is not with lexical predicates that show change of orientation of an object. Forces are signaled by ''of, from, on, and in'' in passive sentences.

Examples:

Meningitis (force) damaged her intelligence (patient).

The fire (force) burnt the house (patient).

The hail storm (force) ruined the crop.

The girl (patient) died of malaria (force).

The *vehicle* is something that conveys a patient or moves along with it. Force is used with process lexical predicates, while vehicle is used with lexical predicates which show a change in orientation. Thus, vehicles are not confused with forces. Vehicles can be in the same sentence with agents and instruments.

Examples:

The tanker (vehicle) carried the oil (patient).

The peasant (agent) carried the water (patient) on her head (vehicle) with a jar (instrument).

The following list of rules helps to differentiate among the four causal roles.

1. If there is only one causal element in chain of action, regardless of whether it is animate or inanimate and regardless of whether there is a paraphrase that refers to the same entity as the instrument, label as agent.

2. If there are two causal elements, the one cast as more responsible is the agent; the other is the instrument.

3. Agents, instruments, and vehicles are never in the same lexical proposition as a force. Agent, instrument, and force have priority over other roles to be mapped as the subject of the sentence.

These three rules should be helpful in labeling arguments of lexical predicates as agents, instruments, forces, or vehicles.

The *patient* is the role seen, but not defined, in the above examples. It is the thing that is affected by the action of the agentive role. The patient is the thing moving, the thing in a particular position, the thing directly affected, or the thing in particular state.

Examples:

The lava (patient) rolled down the mountain (range).

The parakeet (patient) sits on a perch (range).

The shell (patient) split.

The daffodil (patient) is yellow.

I (patient) am glad.

I (patient) feel lonely.

The *benefactive* is someone or something on whom an action has a secondary effect, good or bad. Thus, the action has the primary effect on the patient and a secondary effect on the benefactive; the benefactive is not found without a patient.

Example:

We (agent) carried the groceries (patient) for Mother (benefactive).

The *former* is where the motion begins or the source. For process verbs the former is the state prior to the occurrence of the process. In contrast, the *latter* is where a motion ends or the goal; it is the resultant state after the process. The patient often combines with former as well as latter; then both roles are given as seen in the examples listed below.

Examples:

The letter (patient) fell from her hand (former) to the floor (latter).

Susan (agent) made the picture frames (patient, latter) out of driftwood (former).

She (agent) turned the pumpkin (patient, former) into a pie (latter).

The Hulk (agent) carried Sally (patient) from the zoo (former) to the hospital (former) for Grandma (benefactive).

The coed (agent) carried her books patient) with a bag (instrument) on her back (vehicle) from the dorm (former) to the classroom (latter).

The final role, the *range,* limits the extent of verb. As are other roles, the range is a component of the meaning of the verb as opposed to the *description: setting location* which can be put in a separate clause or sentence from the verb. The *range* is the path or area covered, or the static location of an object. For process verbs the range limits the process to a specified field or object.

Examples:

Zona (patient) fell off the ladder (range).

Tempe (range) was hot.

It (nothing) was hot it Tempe (range).

The cabin (patient) is situated near the lake (range).

She (agent) knitted the booties (patient) on the patio (*description: setting location*).

While she was on the patio (*description: setting location*), she (agent) knitted the booties (patient).

We (agent) talked about language acquisition (range).

This book (patient) cost 20 dollars (range).

The following examples can be used to check your understanding of the definitions of the role relations. Answers can be found in the appendix.

1. We carried the gear from camp all the way up the mountain for the scouts on our backs with twine.
2. Robert hit Zona with the daffodil.
3. The new house burnt in the fire.
4. The wind blew the ball from the beach into the sea.
5. Susan fed Percy Parrot for Grace.
6. Percy was alive in December.
7. Guardsmen found chemical clues.
8. Microscopic plant life provide food for sea life.
9. Ground control stations guide tankers along busy shipping lanes and through dangerous channels.
10. The American Medical Association condemns dehydration in athletes.
11. Whales are friendly.
12. Whales dive to depths of 1000 feet.

Analysis of the Supertanker Text

Some Solutions for the Supertanker Problem

A problem is prevention of oil spills from supertankers. Attributes of a typical supertanker include the following: it carries a half-million tons of oil; it is the size of five football fields; it could accommodate easily the Empire State Building in its cargo area. The trouble is that a wrecked supertanker spills oil in the ocean. As a result of this spillage, the environment is damaged. An example took place in 1970 near Spain when an oil spill from a wrecked tanker exploded into fire. The fire caused hurricane-force winds which whipped the oil into a mist and pulled all of it high into the air. Several days later black rain resulting from this oil spill destroyed crops and livestock in the neighboring villages. Another example of damage occurred in 1967 when the tanker, Torrey Canyon, crashed off the coast of Cornwall and resulted in the washing ashore of 200,000 dead seabirds. An example which happened nearer to home came to pass in July 1975 when the United States Coast Guard mopped up acres of oil from the beach at Geiger Key, Florida, north of Key West. Guardsmen found chemical clues which led to the arrest on November 7, 1975 of a Greek tanker captain, Vasilios K. Psarroulis, because of failure to report the loss of an estimated 40,000 gallons of oil. Oil spills also kill microscopic plant life which provide food for sea life and produce 70% of the world's oxygen supply.

Oil spills result from the lack of power and steering equipment to handle emergency situations, such as storms. Supertankers have one boiler to provide power and one propeller to steer the ship.

The solution to the problem is not to halt the use of tankers on the ocean since about 80% of the world's oil supply is carried by supertankers. Instead, the solution lies in the following three tactics. First, officers of the supertankers must be trained in how to run and maneuver their ships; this training must be top training, such as that provided by the tanker simulator at the Maritime Research Center. Second, tankers should be built with several propellers for extra control and backup boilers for emergency power. Third, ground control stations should be installed at places where supertankers come close to shore because they would act like airplane control towers, guiding tankers along busy shipping lanes and through dangerous channels. (Elaboration of the supertanker passage (Meyer, Brandt, & Bluth, 1980, originally adapted from *Read* magazine (1975)).

Response: problem/solution interrelates all of the propositions in the text. Thus. the top-level structure for this text is response. The propositions composing the problem can be divided into a description of supertankers and an explanation of the problem, why we need to prevent oil spills from supertankers. The propositions in the solution are organized with a collection relationship and a comparison relationship. A collection of three favored solutions is contrasted to an unfavored solution.

To analyze the supertanker text, these major rhetorical relationships in the text should be sketched out in a form similar to that seen in Fig. 2.2 (Part 1). Then, start with the superordinate response node and begin a detailed analysis as seen in the content structure for this text (Fig. 10.1). In the content structure, the rhetorical predicates are found in lowercase letters and underlined. Any explicit signaling of these predicates in the text is indicated on the right-hand column of the page. The lexical predicates are capitalized with dashes beneath them. The role relationships are printed in lowercase letters without underlining. To understand how all the propositions are interrelated, careful attention needs to be given to the lines that interconnect the units. The numbers in parentheses by the causation: covariance relationships indicate which antecedents and consequences go together.

Units 1 and 2 in this figure are response and problem. The argument of the problem is the lexical proposition PREVENT (or some paraphrase) OIL SPILLS FROM SUPERTANKERS. Thus, this lexical proposition is analyzed and becomes units 3–7 in the content structure. The first and second sentences in the text are related by a description of a referent in the first sentence. SUPERTANKERS, the former in the lexical proposition comprising the problem, is described in terms of attributes of a typical supertanker. (Usually the group is a level lower than the element that stands for the group in *representation identification,* but in the context of this entire passage the group of supertankers is emphasized more than the average supertanker.) The second sentence in the

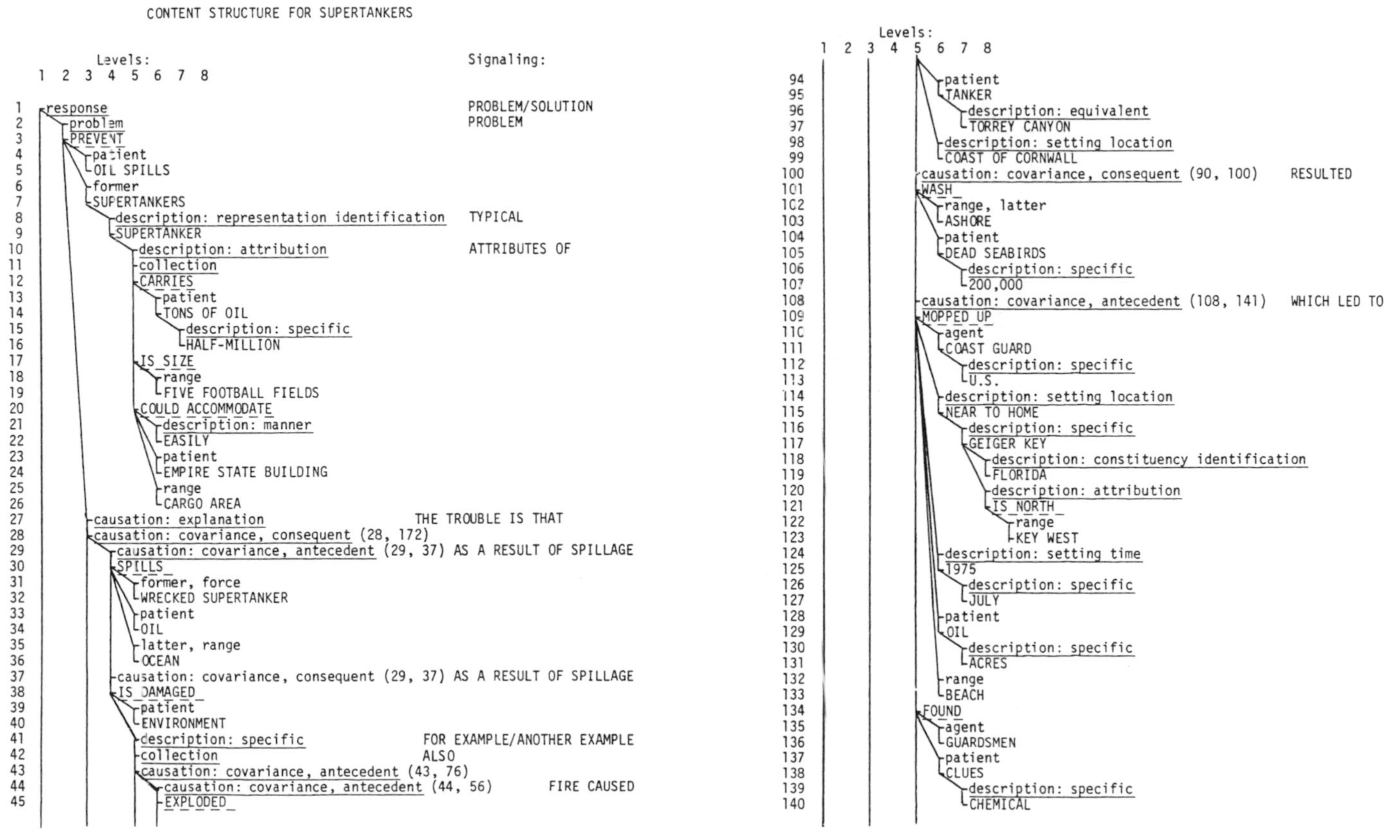

FIG. 10.1. Content structure for supertankers.

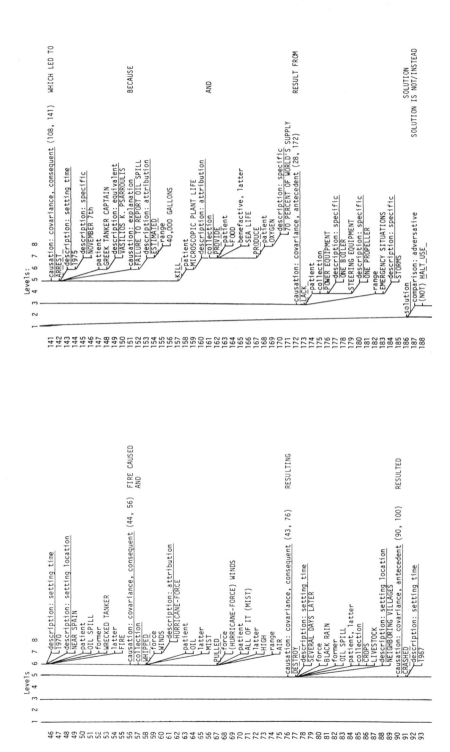

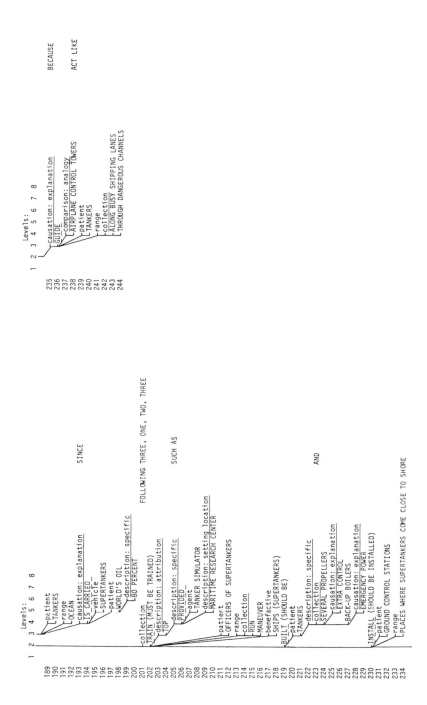

FIG. 10.1. (Continued)

287

supertanker passage lists three attributes of the typical supertanker. Thus, in the content structure these attributes are interrelated by *collection* (unit 11) and placed at a subordinate level to SUPERTANKER by *description: attribution* (unit 10). For each of these three descriptive propositions, SUPERTANKER could be repeated and shown in the lexical proposition. However, as pointed out in Part 1, the repeated referent is deleted, since it is already represented at a higher level in the text. A simplified content structure and scoring task result from this deletion of repeated higher-order nodes in their descriptive lower-level propositions. Units 12 through 26 in the content structure show the three lexical propositions that describe attributes of supertankers. From examining these units, we are again faced with the issue (see Part 1) of how minutely to analyze the referents. There is a trade-off between specificity and scoring time.

The remaining propositions in the first two paragraphs in the supertanker text are related to the problem by a causation: explanation relationship; these propositions explain why we have a problem of preventing oil spills from supertankers. The antecedent conditions that led to recognition of this problem are presented in a subordinate role to the problem itself. Embedded causation: covariance relationships are found within this causation: explanation. LACK OF POWER AND STEERING EQUIPMENT IN EMERGENCY SITUATIONS (Units 172–195) causes the two causally related events, OIL SPILLS (28–36) and DAMAGE TO THE ENVIRONMENT (28, 37–40). The embedded causal relation (see units 29, 37) is put on level lower than the more inclusive causal relation (Units 28, 172).

The remaining propositions in the first paragraph are related to ENVIRONMENT IS DAMAGED by description: specific (unit 41). Four examples of damaged environment are given and related by collection (unit 42). In the first example, there are two causation: covariance relationships (units 43 and 76 and units 44 and 56); the explosion caused the whipping and pulling from the winds; the ultimate consequence was the destruction from the black rain. The second example is also interrelated by causation: covariance (90, 100). The third example has two antecedents (108, 109, 134) of the consequent (142), ARREST OF THE GREEK TANKER CAPTAIN. The final example of environmental damage concerns the KILLING OF MICROSCOPIC PLANT LIFE (157).

Units 172–185 in the content structure diagram the second paragraph of the supertanker text. These propositions are the antecedent of the superordinate covariance relationship under the problem. The referent SUPERTANKER is not repeated in these units since these propositions are modifying PREVENTION OF OIL SPILLS FROM SUPERTANKERS. The second sentence in the text presents more specific descriptions of the power equipment and steering equipment. The only new information in this sentence is ONE BOILER and ONE PROPELLER; these referents appear as subordinate arguments to the general concepts they specify (see units 176–181 in the content structure).

The solution in the third paragraph of the text is organized with collection and comparison relationships; a collection of three favored solutions is contrasted (comparison: adversative) to an unfavored solution. Further unpeeling of the relationships in the solution requires examining each of the three posited solutions. The first solution (TRAIN OFFICERS) and the second (BUILD TANK-ERS) are described by giving more specific information about them. For the third solution (INSTALLATION OF GROUND CONTROL STATIONS), the rationale (antecedent reasoning) for this solution is given; within this rationale or explanation for the solution is an analogy: a similarly operating and successful plan for guiding airplanes. This causation relation gives the explanation for GROUND CONTROL STATIONS which is staged at a more superordinate level in this text.

Scoring the Supertanker Text

The content structure derived in the preceding section is used as the scoring key for scoring recall protocols. The following lists the rules to follow in scoring recall protocols.

Purpose for Scoring: ascertain subject's recall of the *meaning* the text is attempting to get across: (a) recall of topic content, and (b) recall of relationships (text-based: explicit or implicit) among aspects of the topic content

Score as present in protocol the following:

1. Verbatim recall of topic content: referential indices and lexical predicates.
2. Substantive recall of topic content: referential indices and lexical predicates. Judgment is required here—any reasonable paraphrase in terms of general meaning should be counted in scoring. Scorers may have to come to joint agreement on limits for acceptable paraphrases—particularly for referential indices that could be analyzed more minutely but haven't, such as microscopic plant life (could be further analyzed to life—*specific* plant—*specific* microscopic). (We opted in our study to require some indication of small plant life for credit.)

text	*Scored as substantive recall*
TOP (TRAINING)	any positive quality given to describe training
BLACK RAIN (black due to oil)	rain of oil
SEA LIFE	fish
FAILURE TO REPORT OIL SPILL	illegal spillage
HALF-MILLION TONS	hundreds of thousands of tons

3. Role relationships are scored only when the lexical predicate dominating it is also scored; however the topic content (referent) it relates to the lexical predicate need not be scored if it does not meet requirements in either 1 or 2 above.

4. Lexical predicates are scored *much* more loosely than other content words due to rule 3 above and their purpose of showing correct interrelationships rather than representing referents of topic content. Lexical predicates can be scored present in a protocol on the basis of rules 1 and 2 and also rule 4 below. Score present if (a) at least *two* referential indices (topic content) are correctly scored in the particular lexical proposition in the content structure, (b) these referential indices are related by the lexical predicate in question in exactly the same manner as they are related by the lexical predicate in the content structure (one argument may be superordinate due to building the hierarchy, but it would take the same role if the sentence were analyzed in isolation); that is, they are interrelated on basis of the same role relationships—or more rarely rhetorical relationships, such as manner and settings.

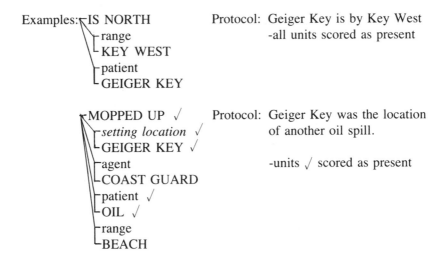

Examples: IS NORTH   Protocol: Geiger Key is by Key West
            ┬ range   -all units scored as present
            └ KEY WEST
            ┬ patient
            └ GEIGER KEY

            MOPPED UP √   Protocol: Geiger Key was the location
            ┬ *setting location* √   of another oil spill.
            └ GEIGER KEY √
            ┬ agent   -units √ scored as present
            └ COAST GUARD
            ┬ patient √
            └ OIL √
            ┬ range
            └ BEACH

5. Rhetorical predicates are scored as present only if (a) the *correct* rhetorical relationship is signaled or implied in the protocol *and* (b) at least one of its arguments is scored as present in the protocol

Examples: *text structure*   *Protocol*
           LACK OF POWER EQUIP-   size *causes spills*
           MENT CAUSES SPILLS

                                         scored as correct (causation)

           APPLES, ORANGES, AND
           PEARS   *apples and* grapes

                                         scored correct (collection)

6. Circle in protocol, count, and record content units in the protocol that were not in the text; i.e., New England in "Birds washed ashore when oil tanker crashed off a New England shore."—compare with units 91–107 in content structure.

7. Circle in protocol, count, label (collection, causation, response, comparison, or description) logical relationship units in the protocol that were not in the text; i.e., causal relation not in original text: "Spills are in part due to the large size of tankers—5 football lengths." Compare with units 3–19, 28–36, 172–185 in content structure.

8. Note on protocol and count the number of intratext confusions; intratext confusions are where content unit (referential index) from one lexical proposition is transposed and substituted for the correct content unit in another lexical proposition; i.e., "microscopic plant life produce 80% of the world's oxygen supply." Score as correct units 159, 160, 167, 168, 169, 170, and 200; they took the 80% from world's oil supply and confused it with the 70% oxygen supply.

9. Score top-level structure of protocol.

Scored as use of Response Top-Level Structure

1. Signaled Problem and Solution and organized in problem/ solution format
2. Signaled only Solution and organized in problem/solution format
3. Signaled only Problem and organized in problem/solution format
4. No Signaling of Problem nor Solution, but response structure is implicit and the protocol is organized in problem/solution format
5. Organized with other structure (comparison, causal), but state problem and solution in one or two sentences
6. Overall organization is a collection (list) of descriptions, but mentions problem/solution in one or two sentences
7. Other structure (comparison, causal) organized protocol and no mention of problem/solution
8. Overall organization is a collection (list) of descriptions and no mention of problem/solution
9. Random list with no association for grouping

The following two recall protocols were written by adults immediately after reading the supertanker passage. The subjects read the text at their own pace and recorded their reading and writing times with a digital timer. Prior to reading the supertanker passage, they read and recalled a practice text; they were informed that the task consisted of reading the text and writing down all they could remember from it in their own words or in words from the passage. They were asked to write in paragraphs rather than just listing ideas.

Immediate Recall of the Supertanker Text *S1*

Minutes: 5   Seconds: 11
Reading Time

The problem is oil spillage from tankers and how to reduce their number or avoid them. A spill from a tanker off Spain in 1970 caused a fire which in turn caused a gale force wind. This whipped the oil into a black mist which rained down several days later on coastal villages. In 1967 the Torrey Canyon spill off England caused the death of 200,000 sea birds which washed up on the beaches. Another spill from a Greek tanker off Florida left clues that were traced to the ship and captain with resultant heavy fines on both.

The average tanker carries one half million gallons of oil, is big enough to hold the Empire State building and covers an area of several football fields. To cope with the spillage problem we should not abandon the use of tankers but adopt three procedures: (1) Train the tanker captains better as at the Maritime Institute, (2) Equip tankers with several propellers and fuel tanks (they only have one of each now) to make them more maneuverable in a storm or other emergency, (3) build control towers on shorelines to guide tankers when they are in coastal waters the way air control towers control planes.

Minutes: 11   Seconds: 14
Writing Time for
this Passage

Immediate Free Recall of the Supertanker Text *S2*

Minutes: 1   Seconds: 18
Reading Time

This passage contained information on supertankers which transport 80% of the worlds oil. There was 3 different example of leakage which caused considerable damage. The first was off the coast of Spain when it caught fire and the hurricane gale winds took the black smoke up into the air. Several days later it rained black and resulted in the death of livestock and vegetation. One ship leaked off the Coast of Cornwell and resulted in the death of over 200,000 sea birds. The last example was at the Florida Keys where a Greek captain was fined for not reporting an oil spill (40,000 gals). Most of the accidents occurs during stormy seas. The captains of these tankers need more training in maneuvering there ships, someplace in Cal has a simulator for this training, also most ships have 1 boiler and 1 rudder, an increase in boilers and rudder should be available during time of an emergency. The tankers are large as 3 football fields and the Empire State Bldg can fit inside. The use of controllers (like air traffic controllers) should be used at points near land.

Minutes: 8   Seconds: 35
Writing Time for
this Passage

Prior to scoring, scorers must be thoroughly familiar with the content structure. They must know the location of the information in the structure for quick

CONTENT STRUCTURE FOR SUPERTANKERS

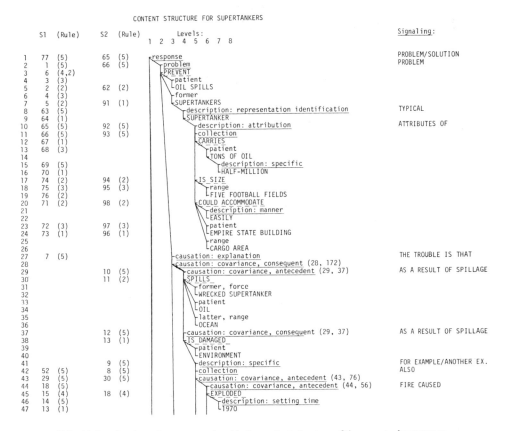

	S1	(Rule)	S2	(Rule)	Levels: 1 2 3 4 5 6 7 8	Signaling:
1	77	(5)	65	(5)	response	PROBLEM/SOLUTION
2	1	(5)	66	(5)	problem	PROBLEM
3	6	(4,2)			PREVENT	
4	3	(3)			patient	
5	2	(2)	62	(2)	OIL SPILLS	
6	4	(3)			former	
7	5	(2)	91	(1)	SUPERTANKERS	
8	63	(5)			description: representation identification	TYPICAL
9	64	(1)			SUPERTANKER	
10	65	(5)	92	(5)	description: attribution	ATTRIBUTES OF
11	66	(5)	93	(5)	collection	
12	67	(1)			CARRIES	
13	68	(3)			patient	
14					TONS OF OIL	
15	69	(5)			description: specific	
16	70	(1)			HALF-MILLION	
17	74	(2)	94	(2)	IS SIZE	
18	75	(3)	95	(3)	range	
19	76	(2)			FIVE FOOTBALL FIELDS	
20	71	(2)	98	(2)	COULD ACCOMMODATE	
21					description: manner	
22					EASILY	
23	72	(3)	97	(3)	patient	
24	73	(1)	96	(1)	EMPIRE STATE BUILDING	
25					range	
26					CARGO AREA	
27	7	(5)			causation: explanation	THE TROUBLE IS THAT
28					causation: covariance, consequent (28, 172)	
29			10	(5)	causation: covariance, antecedent (29, 37)	AS A RESULT OF SPILLAGE
30			11	(2)	SPILLS	
31					former, force	
32					WRECKED SUPERTANKER	
33					patient	
34					OIL	
35					latter, range	
36					OCEAN	
37			12	(5)	causation: covariance, consequent (29, 37)	AS A RESULT OF SPILLAGE
38			13	(1)	IS DAMAGED	
39					patient	
40					ENVIRONMENT	
41			9	(5)	description: specific	FOR EXAMPLE/ANOTHER EX.
42	52	(5)	8	(5)	collection	ALSO
43	29	(5)	30	(5)	causation: covariance, antecedent (43, 76)	
44	18	(5)			causation: covariance, antecedent (44, 56)	FIRE CAUSED
45	15	(4)	18	(4)	EXPLODED	
46	14	(5)			description: setting time	
47	13	(1)			1970	

FIG. 10.2. Scoring of two protocols with the content structure of the supertanker passage.

access; and more important, they must know the function of each relationship in the structure. For example, unit 27, causation: explanation, is scored if a problem (or need to change something) is explained. For this structure, 27 is scored if unit 2 *or* 3 is scored and if 38, 77, 100, 157, 109, 132, 133 *or* some of negative consequence of oil spills is recorded.

Also, prior to scoring, read a recall protocol from beginning to end. Write the content structure on ¼-inch graph paper and label each unit in the content structure with a number. Then, line up a correspondingly numbered sheet of graph paper, allot one column for each subject's recall protocol, and paper clip the sheets of paper together. Next, start with the first words in the recall protocol and determine whether or not they appear in the content structure. If they or their paraphrase (scoring rules 1 and 2) appear in the content structure, place a number in the box on the scoring sheet that corresponds to idea unit (content or relation) recalled. The number corresponds to the order in which the idea was recalled in the recall protocol. In Fig. 10.2, the recall protocol from Subject 1 is scored; in parentheses are the scoring rules that led to scoring a particular idea unit. One

	S1	(Rule)	S2	(Rule)	Levels:	
					1 2 3 4 5 6 7 8	

```
48   11  (5)    15  (5)              ┌description: setting location
49   12  (2)    14  (2)              └NEAR SPAIN
50                                 ┌patient
51    8  (2)                       └OIL SPILL
52    9  (3)                       ┌former
53   10  (2)                       └WRECKED TANKER
54   16  (3)    16  (3)            ┌latter
55   17  (1)    17  (1)            └FIRE
56   19  (5)                    causation: covariance, consequent (44, 56)      FIRE CAUSED
57                              collection                                       AND
58   24  (1)                   WHIPPED
59   23  (3)                    ┌force
60   22  (1)                    └WINDS
61   21  (5)    19  (5)              ┌description: attribution
62   20  (2)    20  (1)              └HURRICANE-FORCE
63   25  (3)                    ┌patient
64   26  (1)                    └OIL
65   27  (3)                    ┌latter
66   28  (1)                    └MIST
67              23  (2)         PULLED
68              22  (3)          ┌force
69              21  (1)          └(HURRICANE-FORCE) WINDS
70              24  (3)          ┌patient
71              25  (2)          └ALL OF IT (MIST)
72              26  (3)          ┌latter
73              27  (2)          └HIGH
74              28  (3)          ┌range
75              29  (1)          └AIR
76   30  (5)    31  (5)         causation: covariance, consequent (43, 76)       RESULTING
77                              DESTROY
78   32  (5)    32  (5)          ┌description: setting time
79   33  (1)    33  (1)          └SEVERAL DAYS LATER
80              34  (3)          ┌force
81   31  (2)    35  (2)          └BLACK RAIN
82                              ┌former
83                              └OIL SPILL
84              36  (3)          ┌patient, latter
85              37  (5)          └collection
86              39  (2)          ┌CROPS
87              38  (1)          └LIVESTOCK
88   34  (5)                     ┌description: setting location
89   35  (2)                     └NEIGHBORING VILLAGES
90   43  (5)    40  (5)         causation: covariance, antecedent (90, 100)      RESULTED
91   42  (4)    43  (2)         CRASHED
92   37  (5)                     ┌description: setting time
93   36  (1)                     └1967
94   38  (3)    41  (3)          ┌patient
95              42  (2)          └TANKER
96                                   ┌description: equivalent
97   39  (1)                         └TORREY CANYON
98   40  (5)    44  (5)          ┌description: setting location
99   41  (2)    45  (1)          └COAST OF CORNWALL
100  44  (5)    46  (5)         causation: covariance, consequent (90, 100)      RESULTED
101  48  (1)    50  (4)         WASH
102. 49  (3)                     ┌range, latter
103  50  (2)                     └ASHORE
104  51  (3)    51  (3)          ┌patient
105  45  (1)    47  (1)          └DEAD SEABIRDS
106  46  (5)    48  (5)              ┌description: specific
107  47  (2)    49  (1)              └200,000
108  60  (5)                    causation: covariance, antecedent (108, 141)     WHICH LED TO
109                             MOPPED UP
110                              ┌agent
111                              └COAST GUARD
112                                  ┌description: specific
113                                  └U.S.
114  55  (5)    54  (5)          ┌description: setting location
115                              └NEAR TO HOME
116                                  ┌description: specific
117                                  └GEIGER KEY
118            52  (5)                  ┌description: constituency identification
119  56  (1)  53  (1)                   └FLORIDA
120                                         ┌description: attribution
121                                         └IS NORTH
122                                            ┌range
123                                            └KEY WEST
124                              ┌description: setting time
125                              └1975
126                                  ┌description: specific
127                                  └JULY
128                              ┌patient
129  53  (2)                     └OIL
130                                  ┌description: specific
131                                  └ACRES
132                              ┌range
133                              └BEACH
134  58  (2)                    FOUND
135                              ┌agent
136                              └GUARDSMEN
137  59  (3)                     ┌patient
138  57  (1)                     └CLUES
139                                  ┌description: specific
140                                  └CHEMICAL
141  61  (5)                    causation: covariance, consequent (108, 141)     WHICH LED TO
142  62  (2)    56  (2)         ARREST
143                              ┌description: setting time
144                              └1975
145                                  ┌description: specific
146                                  └NOVEMBER 7th
```

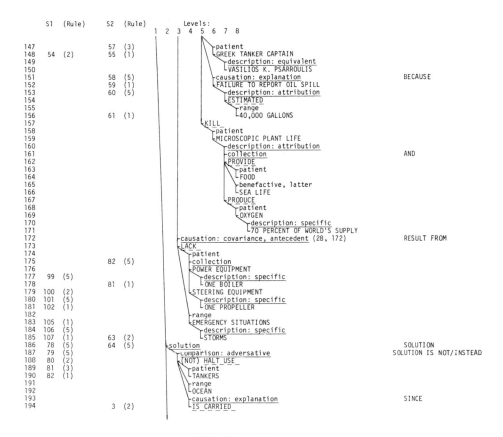

FIG. 10.2.   (*Continued*)

hundred nineteen units were scored; no content nor relationship units were added, but there was one intratext confusion: gallons (156) was confused with tons (14). The top-level structure is scored 1; this reader used the response top-level structure. The problem was signaled with "THE PROBLEM IS" and the solution was signaled with "TO COPE WITH THE SPILLAGE PROBLEM." The protocol is organized into a description and explanation of a problem and a solution to that problem. As seen in the scoring rules for top-level structure, scores 1–4 are classified as using the same top-level structure as that found in this text with its response structure; it is the organization of the protocol that is essential, although we record any explicit signaling of the structure.

The recall protocol for subject 2 is scored in Fig. 10.2 along with scoring rules in parentheses. The total number of idea units recalled was 105 with three content intrusions (Cal., rudder, and 3), no relation intrusions, and no intratext confusions. The top-level structure used to organize this recall protocol was scored 6. A collection of descriptions about supertankers was presented in a list-

```
      S1  (Rule)    S2  (Rule)        Levels:
                                  1  2  3  4  5  6  7  8
195                  2   (3)               ┌vehicle
196                  1   (1)               └SUPERTANKERS
197                  7   (3)             ┌patient
198                  6   (1)             └WORLD'S OIL
199                  5   (5)                ┌description: specific
200                  4   (1)                └80 PERCENT
201   83  (5)       80   (5)    ┌collection                        FOLLOWING THREE, ONE, TWO, THREE
202   84  (1)       70   (1)    TRAIN (MUST BE TRAINED)
203   87  (5)       69   (5)    ┌description: attribution
204   88  (2)                   └TOP
205   89  (5)       75   (5)        ┌description: specific         SUCH AS
206   90  (2)       75   (2)        └PROVIDED
207                 78   (3)        ┌agent
208                 79   (1)        └TANKER SIMULATOR
209   91  (5)       77   (5)        ┌description: setting location
210   92  (2)                       └MARITIME RESEARCH CENTER
211   85  (3)       68   (3)     ┌patient
212   86  (2)       67   (2)     └OFFICERS OF SUPERTANKERS
213                 71   (3)     ┌range
214                              ┌collection
215                              ┌RUN
216                 72   (1)     ┌MANEUVER
217                 72   (3)     ┌benefactive
218                 74   (1)     └SHIPS (SUPERTANKERS)
219   93  (2)       83   (2)   BUILT (SHOULD BE)
220   94  (3)       84   (3)     ┌patient
221   95  (1)       85   (2)     └TANKERS
222   96  (5)       86   (5)        ┌description: specific
223   97  (5)       87   (5)        ┌collection                    AND
224   98  (1)                       └SEVERAL PROPELLERS
225  103  (5)                         ┌causation: explanation
226  104  (2)                         └EXTRA CONTROL
227                 88   (1)        └BACK-UP BOILERS
228                 89   (5)           ┌causation: explanation
229                 90   (2)           └EMERGENCY POWER
230  108  (2)      101   (2)   INSTALL (SHOULD BE INSTALLED)
231  109  (3)      100   (3)     ┌patient
232  110  (2)       99   (2)     └GROUND CONTROL STATIONS
233  111  (3)      104   (3)     ┌range
234  112  (2)      105   (2)     └PLACES WHERE SUPERTANKERS COME CLOSE TO SHORE
235  113  (5)                    ┌causation: explanation           BECAUSE
236  114  (1)                    └GUIDE
237  118  (5)      102   (5)        ┌comparison: analogy
238  119  (1)      103   (1)        └AIRPLANE CONTROL TOWERS        ACT LIKE
239  115  (3)                      ┌patient
240  116  (1)                      └TANKERS
241  117  (3)                    ┌range
242                              ┌collection
243                              ┌ALONG BUSY SHIPPING LANES
244                              └THROUGH DANGEROUS CHANNELS
Total 119          105
TLS    1             6
```

FIG. 10.2.   (*Continued*)

like order. However, in this list structure a response: problem/solution was suggested (e.g., NEED MORE TRAINING), but it was not used to organize what the learner remembered from the text.

Reliability among trained scorers using this scoring system is high. It has been found to range from .90 to .99 in various studies (e.g., Meyer, 1975; Meyer, Brandt, & Bluth, 1980; Meyer & Rice, 1981).

REFERENCES

Bartlett, B. J. *Top-level structure as an organizational strategy for recall of classroom text.* Unpublished doctoral dissertation, Arizona State University, 1978.

Fillmore, C. The case for case. In E. Bach & R. Harms (Eds.), *Universals in linguistic theory.* New York: Holt, Rinehart, & Winston, 1968.

Grimes, J. E. *The thread of discourse.* The Hague: Mouton, 1975.

Hyma, A., & Stanton, M. *Streams of civilization.* San Diego: Creation-Life Publishers, 1976.

Litteral, R. Rhetorical predicates and time topology in Anggor. *Foundations of Language, 1972, 8,* 391–410.

Meyer, B. J. F. *The organization of prose and its effects on memory.* Amsterdam: North-Holland, 1975.

Meyer, B. J. F., Brandt, D. M., & Bluth, G. J. Use of the top-level structure in text: Key for reading comprehension of ninth-grade students. *Reading Research Quarterly, 1980, 16,* 72–103.

Meyer, B. J. F., Haring, M. J., Brandt, D. M., & Walker, C. H. Comprehension of stories and expository text. *Poetics: International review for the theory of literature, 1980, 9,* 203–211.

Meyer, B. J. F., & Rice, G. E. Information recalled from prose by young, middle, and old adults. *Experimental Aging Research, 1981, 7,* 253–268.

Morholt, E., Brandwein, P. F., & Ward, L. S. *Biology: Patterns in the environment.* New York: Harcourt, Brace, Jovanovich, 1972.

Rumelhart, D., & Ortony, A. The representation of knowledge in memory. In R. C. Anderson, R. Spiro, & W. Montague (Eds.), *Schooling and the acquisition of knowledge.* Hillsdale, N.J.: Lawrence Erlbaum Associates, 1977.

Social Science Staff of the Educational Research Council of America. *The American adventure: Expansion, conflict and reconstruction (1825–1880).* Boston: Allyn & Bacon, 1975.

Supertankers. In J. A. Ball (Ed.), *Read: The magazine for reading and english,* 1975, *24* (12), 2–4.

APPENDIX

Contents

1. The Five Versions of the Railroad Passage
2. Rhetorical Structures for Practice Passages
3. Lexical Predicates and Role Related Arguments for Practice Sentences

WITH-SIGNALING LOGICAL STRUCTURE + GENERAL DETAILS

Disagreement Over Early American Railroad Development

When railroads were first developing in America, not everyone approved of them. Businessmen were in favor of early railroad development because they believed that the railroads had great economic potential. As a result of this conviction, businessmen worked to improve rail travel. For example, they refined the locomotive engine. They experienced numerous problems with the first locomotive, which was the one they had shipped from overseas early last century. To solve these problems, American businessmen chartered companies for the purpose of manufacturing their own locomotives. An example was the first American-built locomotive, a steam engine, which made its trial run one fine day. This particular locomotive was designed by an engineer, pulled dozens of people in several cars, and attained a speed faster than other contemporaneous vehicles. Another example of American-made locomotives were those built by a company in Philadelphia. These became most widely used; the first was built soon after that first trial run.

Another improvement which businessmen instigated was to make railroad travel more efficient. For instance, they consolidated numerous short lines. As a result, direct railroad service extended from the East to the Midwest by the middle of the century. These direct lines made it possible for people and goods to travel hundreds of miles within a few days. For example, traveling by rail on one of the early sleeping cars between two eastern cities took only a few days in those days; in contrast, by water the same trip took more than twice as long. Another result of consolidation was that the railroads became the least expensive form of transportation in the United States for all but very bulky items.

As stated earlier, however, railroad development was not favored by everyone. It was opposed by various groups of people. Specifically, many short-sighted people refused to believe railroads would ever be more than just a supplement for waterways. Canal companies made efforts to prevent railroads from building any lines that might compete with the canals. Some farmers complained that the noise frightened their livestock, and that sparks from the engine would set their fields afire. A number of physicians were afraid that the human body could not survive travel at speeds as high as the trains went. In addition, many northeastern townspeople didn't want their quiet disturbed by steam engines and strangers.

WITH-SIGNALING LOGICAL STRUCTURE + SPECIFIC DETAILS

Disagreement Over Early American Railroad Development

When railroads were first developing in America, not everyone approved of them. Businessmen were in favor of early railroad development because they believed that the railroads had great economic potential. As a result of this conviction, businessmen worked to improve rail travel. For example, they refined the locomotive engine. They experienced a number of problems with the first locomotive, which was the one they had shipped from England in 1829. To solve these problems, American businessmen chartered companies for the purpose of manufacturing their own locomotives. An example was the first American-built locomotive, Best Friend, which made its trial run in 1830. This particular locomotive was designed by Horatio Allen, pulled 40 people in four cars, and it attained the speed of 21 miles an hour. Another example of American-made locomotives were those that were built by Mathias Baldwin, which became most widely used. His first locomotive was built in 1832.

Another improvement which businessmen instigated was to make railroad travel more efficient. For instance, they consolidated numerous short lines. As a result, direct railroad service extended from the Eastern seaboard to the Mississippi River by the middle of the century. These direct lines made it possible for people and goods to travel hundreds of miles within a few days. For example, traveling by rail on one of G. M. Pullman's sleeping cars between New York City and Detroit took only 4 days in 1863; in contrast, by water the same trip required 10 days. Another result of consolidation was that railroads became the least expensive form of transportation in the United States for all but very bulky items.

As stated earlier, however, railroad development was not favored by everyone. It was opposed by various groups of people. Specifically, many short-sighted people refused to believe that railroads would ever be more than just a supplement for waterways. Canal companies made efforts to prevent railroads from building any lines that might compete with the canals. Some farmers complained that the noise frightened their livestock, and that sparks which came from the engines would set their fields afire. A number of physicians were afraid that the human body could not survive travel at speeds as high as 30 miles an hour. In addition, many New England townspeople didn't want their quiet disturbed by steam engines and strangers.

WITHOUT-SIGNALING LOGICAL STRUCTURE + GENERAL DETAILS

Early Development of Railroads in America

When the railroads were first starting in America, businessmen wanted to see them developed. They were of the conviction that the railroads had great economic potential. Businessmen made efforts to improve the quality of travel on the railways. They made improvements in the locomotive engine. They experienced a number of difficulties with the first locomotive. They had shipped it from overseas early last century. American businessmen chartered companies that could manufacture their own locomotives. The first American-built locomotive was a steam engine and it made its trial run one fine day. This locomotive was designed by an engineer. It pulled dozens of people in several cars. It attained a speed faster than other contemporaneous vehicles. The American-made locomotives that were built by a company in Philadelphia were ones which became most widely used. The first of these locomotives was built soon after that first trial run.

Businessmen were responsible for making travel on the railroad more efficient than it had been. They instigated the consolidation of a large number of short lines. Direct railroad service extended from the East to the Midwest by the time of the middle of the century. It was possible for people and goods to travel hundreds of miles within a few days. Traveling by rail on one of the early sleeping cars, to go between two eastern cities took a few days at that time. Traveling by water it took more than twice as many days to make the same trip. Railroads became the form of transportation which was the least expensive in the United States for all items except those that were very bulky.

Various groups of people had other ideas about the development of railroads when they first began. Many short-sighted people refused to believe that the railroads would ever be more than just a supplement for waterways. Canal companies made efforts to prevent the railroads from building any lines that might compete with the canals. Some farmers made the complaint that the noise frightened their livestock, and that sparks which came from the engines would set their fields on fire. A number of physicians were afraid that the human body could not survive travel at speeds as high as the trains went. Many townspeople in the northeast didn't want their quiet disturbed by steam engines and strangers.

WITHOUT-SIGNALING LOGICAL STRUCTURE +
SPECIFIC DETAILS

Early Development of Railroads in America

When the railroads were first starting in America, businessmen wanted to see them developed. They were of the conviction that the railroads had great economic potential. Businessmen made efforts to improve the quality of travel on the railways. They made improvements in the locomotive engine. They experienced a number of difficulties with the first locomotive. They had shipped it from England in the year of 1829. American businessmen chartered companies that could manufacture their own locomotives. The first American-built locomotive was named the Best Friend and it made its trial run in 1830. This locomotive was designed by Horatio Allen. It pulled 40 people in four cars. It attained the speed of 21 miles an hour. The American-made locomotives that were built by Mathias Baldwin were ones which became most widely used. His first locomotive was built in 1832.

Businessmen were responsible for making travel on the railroad more efficient than it had been. They instigated the consolidation of large numbers of short lines. Direct railroad service extended from the Eastern seaboard to the Mississippi River by the time of the middle of the century. It was possible for people and goods to travel hundreds of miles in the space of a few days. Traveling by rail on one of the sleeping cars of G. M. Pullman, to go from New York City to Detroit took a total of four days in 1863. Traveling by water it took 10 days to make the same trip. Railroads became the form of transportation which was the least expensive in the United States for all items except those that were very bulky.

Various groups of people had other ideas about the development of railroads when they first began. Many short-sighted people refused to believe that the railroads would ever be more than just a supplement for waterways. Canal companies made efforts to prevent the railroads from building any lines that might compete with the canals. Some farmers made the complaint that the noise frightened their livestock, and that sparks which came from the engines would set their fields on fire. A number of physicians were afraid that the human body could not survive travel at speeds as high as 30 miles an hour. Many townspeople in New England didn't want their quiet disturbed by steam engines and strangers.

WITHOUT-SIGNALING LOGICAL STRUCTURE +
EMPHASIZED SPECIFIC DETAILS

Early Development of Railroads in America

When the railroads were first starting in America, businessmen wanted to see them developed. They were of the conviction that the railroads had great economic potential. Businessmen worked to improve the quality of rail travel. They made improvements in the locomotive engine. They experienced a number of difficulties with the first locomotive. They had shipped it from England in the notable year of 1829. American businessmen chartered companies that could manufacture their own locomotives. The first American-built locomotive was the mighty Best Friend which made its trial run in the landmark year of 1830. The locomotive was designed by the gifted Horatio Allen. It pulled 40 people in four cars. It attained the speed of 21 miles an hour. The American-made locomotives that were built by the great Mathias Baldwin were ones which became most widely used. His first locomotive was built in the significant year 1832.

Businessmen were responsible for making travel on the railroad more efficient than it had been. They instigated the consolidation of large numbers of short lines. Direct railroad service extended from the Eastern seaboard to the Mississippi River by the middle of the century. It was possible for people and goods to travel hundreds of miles in the space of a few days. Traveling by rail on one of the sleeping cars of the renowned G. M. Pullman, to go from New York City to Detroit took 4 days in progressive 1863. Traveling by water it took 10 days to make the same trip. Railroads became the least expensive form of transportation in the United States for all items except those that were very bulky.

Various groups of people had other ideas about the development of railroads when they first began. Many short-sighted people refused to believe that the railroads would ever be more than just a supplement for waterways. Canal companies made efforts to prevent the railroads from building any lines that might compete with the canals. Some farmers made the complaint that the noise frightened their livestock, and that sparks which came from the engines would set their fields on fire. A number of physicians were afraid that the human body could not survive travel at speeds as high as 30 miles an hour. Many townspeople in New England didn't want their quiet disturbed by steam engines and strangers.

RHETORICAL STRUCTURES FOR PRACTICE PASSAGES

Miracle Rice appears to be a *causation,* an explanation of the antecedents that led to the labeling of this variety of rice as a miracle. However, most of the text is a *description: attribution* which gives a *collection* of descriptions about the rice. This collection of wonderful attributes about the rice led to its name, "miracle" rice. Since so much space is given to the antecedents, I would not use a *causation: explanation* format, but rather the more equally weighted causation: covariance format. The top-level structure is depicted in the following:

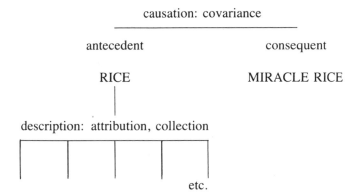

Anthrax is organized with a response: problem/solution top-level structure.

Chicken-Hawks is organized with a causation: covariance: antecedent/ consequent top-level structure.

Most of the history passage is organized with comparison: adversative top-level structure. However, in the middle of the last paragraph, there is information (about historians' agreement that history does repeat itself) that does not fit into the first comparison. Now we can find two related comparisons. The top-level structure might be seen as follows:

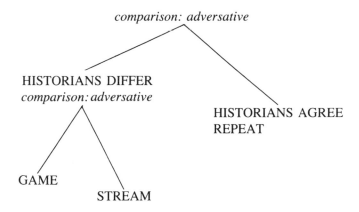

The railroad text is organized with a comparison: adversative top-level structure. This structure is signaled in this text. As we saw with the Meyer and Rice (see Part 1) study when the signaling is removed an alternative structure emerges that competes with the structure built on the comparison and embedded causal relationships in this text. Without signaling the hierarchy changes as seen in Figs. 2.17 and 2.18 in Part 1. The comparison structure and a collection: time order structure share the top-level structure spot.

LEXICAL PREDICATES AND ROLE RELATED
ARGUMENTS FOR PRACTICE SENTENCES

1. We (agent) carried the gear (patient) from camp (former) all the way up (latter) the mountain (range) for the scouts (benefactive) on our backs (vehicle) with twine (instrument).
2. Robert (agent) hit Zona (patient) with the daffodil (instrument).
3. The new house (patient) burnt in the fire (force).
4. The wind (vehicle) blew the ball (patient) from the beach (former) into the sea (latter).
5. Susan (agent) fed Percy Parrot (patient) for Grace (benefactive).
6. Percy (patient) was alive in December (range).
7. Guardsmen (agent) found chemical clues (patient).
8. Microscopic plant life (agent) provide food (patient) for sea life (benefactive, latter).
9. Ground control stations (agent) guide tankers (patient) along busy shipping lanes and through dangerous channels (collection of ranges).
10. The American Medical Association (agent) condemns dehydration (patient) in athletes (range, benefactive).
11. Whales (patient) are friendly.
12. Whales (agent) dive to 1,000 feet (range, latter).

11 How to Analyze Science Prose

Richard E. Mayer

University of California, Santa Barbara

The purpose of this section is to summarize the procedure for analyzing science prose, and to provide examples of analyzed passages.

PROCEDURE FOR ANALYZING PROSE

The first section of my paper in Part 1 of this volume provides a detailed description of the procedure for analyzing expository prose, so only a summary is presented here.

1. The first step is to choose a passage that fits into cell D or F of Table 3.1, i.e., an expository passage that explains some event, state, action, or relationship.

2. The next step is to break the passage down into idea units, where each idea unit conveys one major event, state, or action.

3. The major step is to identify the "explanative" idea units, by using any of the three techniques described earlier. The structural method involves identifying a mental model that explains the underlying mechanism, and noting which idea units map directly onto the model. The logical method involves identifying creative transfer questions, and noting which idea units are necessary for making the required inferences. The empirical method involves giving readers a test on creative problem solving and recall, and noting which idea units that good problem solvers recall that poor problem solvers do not recall.

4. The final step is to validate the analysis by determining the relation between recall of explanative information and performance on tests of creative problem solving.

EXAMPLES OF ANALYZED PASSAGES

This section contains four appendices. Appendix A gives the analyzed breakdown for the Radar passage used by Mayer & Cook (1981). Each line corresponds to an idea unit, with key words italicized. Explanative idea units are indicated by an "E" in the margin. Appendix B provides the analyzed breakdown for the Supertanker passage used by Meyer (1975). Appendix C gives the analyzed breakdown for the Lion passage (Voss & Bisanz, 1981). Appendix D gives a revised version of the Radar passage, following many recommendations for making the explanative information more obvious.

REFERENCES

Mayer, R. E., & Cook, L. K. Effects of shadowing on prose comprehension and problem solving. *Memory & Cognition*, 1981, *9*, 101–109.

Meyer, B. J. F. *The organization of prose and its effects on memory.* Amsterdam: North-Holland, 1975.

Voss, J. F. & Bisanz, G. L. *Models and methods used in the study of prose comprehension and learning.* Paper presented at the Symposium on Expository Text, American Educational Research Association, Los Angeles, April 14, 1981.

APPENDIX A
THE RADAR PASSAGE

1. Radar means the *detection* and *location* of remote *objects*
2. by the *reflection* of radio *waves.*
3. The phenomena of acoustic *echoes* is familiar:
4. *sound* waves *reflected* from a *building* or a *cliff*
5. are *received* back at the *observer*
6. after a *lapse* of a short *interval.*
7. The effect is similar to you *shouting* in a *canyon*
8. and seconds *later*
9. *hearing* a nearly exact *replication* of your voice.
10. Radar uses exactly the *same* principle
11. except that the waves involved are *radio waves,* not sound waves.
12. These *travel* very much *faster* than sound waves,
13. 186,000 miles per second,
14. and can *cover* much *longer distances.*
E 15. Thus radar involves simply *measuring* the *time*
E 16. between *transmission* of the waves
E 17. and their subsequent *return* or *echo*
E 18. and then *converting* that to a *distance* measure.
19. To *send out* the radio *waves*

20. a radio *transmitter* is *connected* to a directional *antenna*
21. which *sends out* a stream of short *pulses* of radio *waves.*
22. This radio pulse that is first transmitted *looks* very much *like* the effect
23. of *tossing* a *pebble* into a quiet *lake.*
24. It *creates* concentric *circles* of small waves
25. that continue to *grow* outward.
26. Usually both a *transmitter* and a *receiver* are employed *separately*
27. but it is possible to *use* only *one antenna*
28. in which pulse *transmission* is momentarily *suppressed*
29. in order to *receive* echo *pulses.*
30. (One thing to remember though)
31. is that radar waves *travel* in fundamentally *straight lines*
32. and that the *curvature of the earth* eventually *interferes* with *long range transmission.*
33. (When you think about)
34. the *reception* of the returning *pulses* or echoes
35. (you should remember)
E 36. that any *object* in the path of the transmitted beam *reflects* some of the *energy* back to the radio receiver.
37. (The problem then becomes) *transmitting* the *pulses*
38. *picked up* by the *receiver*
39. to a *display* mechanism for visual readout.
40. One mechanism in large use is the *cathode-ray tube*
41. A familiar item in *airport* control towers
42. which *looks* somewhat *like* a *television screen.*
43. (It is easiest to understand how radar is displayed)
44. if you begin with one of the *earliest models*
45. used around the *1930's.*
46. These types of display systems were able to *focus* the broad radar pulse into a *single beam* of light
47. which *proceeded* from the *left* of the screen *to the right.*
E 48. When *no object impedes* the traveling radar pulse
E 49. it *continues* its travel
50. until *lost* from the screen on the *right.*
E 51. When there is an *object present*
E 52. the *pulse* would *strike* it
E 53. and begin to *travel back* to the receiver.
54. When the *object* is *struck* by the radar pulse
55. it *creates* a *bright spot* on the face of the screen
E 56. and the *distance* of the object can be *measured* by the *length* of the trace
E 57. *coming from* the *object* back *to the receiver.*
58. (With this model however)
59. you are only able to *measure* the *distance* of an object
60. and *not* its absolute *location*

61. since the beam of light on the screen actually *represents* the entire width of the *broader* radar pulse.
62. *Models employed today* use two simple techniques
63. which *make location* of objects much *easier.*
64. (First), the *transmitter* now *operates* much *like* the *search light* used in airports.
65. It *emits* a *single beam* of radar pulses
66. that *make continuous circular sweeps* around the area under surveillance.
67. (Secondly), the *display screen is adjusted*
68. so that its *center corresponds* to the point where the radar *pulses begin.*
69. The radar *pulse seen* on the *screen*
70. *operates like* the *second hand of a clock*
71. which *continually moves.*
72. When an *object* is *present*
73. it *leaves a bright spot* on the face of the screen.
74. (An additional feature is)
75. that the face of the *screen* actually *shows a map*-like picture of the area around the radar
76. *giving distance* and of course *location.*
77. Thus it is very easy now to *determine* the *location* of objects
78. by *noting* their *location* on the screen's *map.*

APPENDIX B
THE SUPERTANKER PASSAGE

1. (A problem is)
2. *prevention* of *oil spills* from *supertankers.*
3. (Attributes of a typical *supertanker* include)
4. carrying *capacity* of a *half-million* tons of oil
5. size of *five football fields*
6. and cargo areas easily *accommodating* the *Empire State Building.*
7. (The trouble is that)
E   8. a *wrecked* supertanker *spills oil* in the ocean.
9. (As a *result* of spillage)
E 10. the *environment* is *damaged.*
11. (An example)
12. took place in *1970* near *Spain*
13. when an *oil spill* from a wrecked tanker *exploded* into *fire.*
14. the fire *caused hurricane*-force winds
15. which *whipped* the *oil* into a *mist*
16. and *pulled* all of it high *into* the *air.*
17. (Several days *later*)

18. *black rain result*ing from this oil spill
19. *destroyed crops* and *livestock* in the neighboring villages.
20. (Another example of damage),
21. occurred in *1967*
22. when the *tanker*, Torrey Canyon, *crashed off* the *coast* of Cornwall
23. and resulted in the washing ashore of *200,000* dead sea*birds*.
E 24. Oil spills also *kill* microscopic *plant* life
E 25. which *provide food* for sea life
E 26. and *produce 70 percent* of the world's *oxygen* supply.
E 27. Most *wrecks result* from lack of *power*
E 28. and *steering* equipment
E 29. to handle *emergency* situations, such as *storms*.
E 30. *Supertankers* have only *one boiler*
E 31. to *provide power*
E 32. and *one propeller*
E 33. to *drive* the ship.
34. (The solution to the problem)
35. is *not* to *halt* the use of *tankers* on the ocean
36. since *80 percent* of the world's *oil* supply is carried by *supertankers*.
37. (Instead, the solution lies in the following three tactics.)
38. (First)
39. *officers* of the supertankers must *get* top *training*
40. in how to run and *maneuver* their ships
41. such as *provided* by the tanker simulator at the *Maritime Research Center.*
42. (Second),
E 43. *tankers* should be built with *several propellers*
E 44. for extra *control*
E 45. and *backup boilers*
E 46. for emergency *power*.
47. (Third),
48. *ground control stations* should be installed
49. at places where supertankers come close to *shore*
50. because they would act *like airplane control towers*
51. *guiding tankers* along busy shipping lanes and through dangerous channels.

APPENDIX C
THE LION PASSAGE (SELECTED PORTIONS)

1. (*Once upon a time*)
2. *Lion, King of the animals*

3. was *walking* through the *forest*
4. when he became *caught* in a hunter's *trap*.
5. The trap *pulled Lion up,* up,
6. until he was *hanging upside-down* high in a tree.
7. The other *animals, hearing* the *noise,*
8. rushed to *see what* had *happened.*
9. *Lion looked down* at the animals
10. and *said*:
11. "Friends, *I have been* a good *leader* for many years.
12. Now *you* must *help me.*"
E 13. The *tiger, who wanted to be King of the animals* himself,
14. shouted up:
15. "*Why* should we risk our lives *helping you*?
16. Each animal should *look out for himself* in times of danger.
17. Any animal who *cannot help himself* is *not fit to live.*
18. This is the *way of* our *animal kingdom.*"
19. Then the *tiger turned* to the other animals and *said*:
20. "*What do you say* my friends?"

. . .

E 21. The *horse,* who was too *proud of his good looks* to care about anyone but himself
22. *said* to the animals:
23. "The *tiger is right.*
24. If *Lion can't help himself,*
25. *Lion* should *stay* in the trap."

. . .

26. Only the *mouse hadn't spoken.*
E 27. The *mouse* was terribly *afraid of* the *tiger*
28. so when it was *his turn*
E 29. just to *make the tiger happy*
30. he *said* very quickly:
31. "*I agree with tiger.*
32. *Lion* should *not* be *helped.*"

. . .

APPENDIX D
A REVISED VERSION OF THE RADAR PASSAGE

Definition

Radar involves five basic steps. Once you understand these five steps, you will have a basic knowledge of how radar works. The five steps are:

1. Transmission—A radio pulse is sent out.
2. Reflection—The pulse strikes and bounces off a remote object.
3. Reception—The reflected pulse returns to the source.
4. Measurement—The amount of time between transmission and reception is measured.
5. Conversion—This information can be translated into a measure of distance, if we assume the pulse travels at a constant speed.

Thus, radar involves the detection and location of remote objects by reflection of radio waves.

Echo Example

In order to see how these five steps of radar relate to one another, let's consider an example. The example is a familiar phenomenon, an acoustic echo.

1. First, you shout in a canyon. This is like transmission of a pulse.
2. Second, the sound waves are reflected from a cliff. This is like reflection of a pulse off a remote object.
3. Third, a nearly exact replication of your voice is received back at the observer. This is like reception of a radar pulse.
4. Fourth, there is a short lapse between shouting and hearing an echo. This corresponds to measurement of time.
5. Fifth, you notice that the further away a cliff is, the longer it takes to receive back an echo. This corresponds to conversion of time to a measure of distance of remote objects.

The same principle is used in radar, except that the waves involved are radio waves, not sound waves. These travel very much faster than sound waves, 186,000 miles per second, and can cover much longer distances.

Devices

Let's consider the actual devices that are used for the five steps of radar.

Transmission.   To send out the radio waves, a radio transmitter is connected to a directional antenna which sends out a stream of short pulses of radio waves. As an example of how the antenna sends out radio waves, think of tossing a pebble into a quiet lake. The pebble creates concentric circles of small waves that continue to grow outward.

Reflection.   Any object in the path of the transmitted beam reflects some of the energy back to the radio receiver.

Reception.   Usually a transmitter and a receiver are employed separately, but it is possible to use only one antenna. In this case, pulse transmission is momentarily suppressed in order to receive echo pulses. One thing to remember about the reception of returning pulses or echoes is that radar waves travel in fundamentally straight lines, and that the curvature of the earth eventually interferes with long-range transmission.

Measurement and Conversion.   The problem then becomes transmitting the pulses picked up by the receiver to a display for visual readout. One mechanism in large use is the cathode-ray tube, a familiar item in airport control towers which looks somewhat like a television screen.

Early Display System

The earliest display system, used around the 1930s, dealt with the five steps of radar as follows:

To represent transmission, the display system focused the broad radar pulse into a single beam of light, which proceeded from left of the screen to right. When no object impedes the traveling radar pulse, it continues to travel until lost from the screen on the right.

To represent reflection, a bright spot is created on the face of the screen when an object is struck. Thus, when an object is present, the pulse would strike it and begin to travel back to the receiver.

To represent reception, there is a trace on the screen coming from the object back to the receiver.

To represent measurement and conversion, the distance of the object can be measured by the length of the trace. With this system, however, you are only able to measure the distance of object and not its absolute location.

Modern Display Systems

Display models employed today use different techniques for representing the five steps of radar, and thus make location of objects much easier.

For transmission, the transmitter emits a single beam of radar pulses that make continuous circular sweeps around the area under surveillance. Thus, an example is to think of the transmitter as being like the search light used at airports. In addition, the display screen is adjusted so that its center corresponds to the point where the radar pulse begins. As an example, the radar pulse seen on the screen operates like the second hand of a clock which continually moves.

For reflection, when an object is present it leaves a bright spot on the face of the screen.

For reception, there is a trace coming back from the bright spot to the center of the screen.

For measurement and conversion, the face of the screen actually shows a map-like picture of the area around the radar, giving distance and of course location. Thus, it is very easy now to determine the location of objects by noting their location on the screen's map.

12

A Guide to Propositional Analysis for Research on Technical Prose

Susan Bovair
David E. Kieras

University of Arizona

1.0 INTRODUCTION

Recently, many researchers on prose comprehension have used propositional analysis for representing the content of prose materials. This method involves preparing a relatively formal representation of the semantic content of the material, expressed in the form of a list of propositions. This representation can then be used as a relatively rigorous characterization of the material, and so serves as a basis for evaluating and analyzing readers' performance in comprehension experiments.

This is a practical manual, distributed originally as a Technical Report (Bovair & Kieras, 1981), for the use of the propositional method of analyzing text, and scoring subject response protocols. The texts dealt with can be described as *technical prose,* rather than stories, and the response protocols dealt with are (1) gist recall protocols from prose memory experiments in which reproductive recall only is scored, and (2) responses produced in a "main idea" task, where after reading a passage the subject must produce a one-sentence statement of the "main idea." For recall protocols, the material to be "propositionalized" is normally a passage and the propositions form a scoring key. For comparing main idea responses, the responses are first propositionalized and then closely synonymous arguments and propositions are grouped together. This enables similarity in responses to be determined in a reasonably systematic and objective way.

The method described here was developed from Kintsch (1974), based mostly on the practical manual written by Turner and Greene (1977). However, our work led us to develop an approach that we felt was simpler and more oriented to

315

experimental purposes than Turner and Greene's treatment. Their propositional analysis approach tended to focus on theoretical issues of semantics, and emphasized literary texts; but in our experience these matters have little relevance in the scoring of responses made in our experiments on memory and summarization of technical prose. This report is thus a summary of the rules and approaches that we developed from experience with the problems encountered dealing with actual text and subject responses. Therefore, apart from a few introductory examples, all the examples used are from actual texts and subject responses. It is hoped that other researchers will find this report useful in applying and further developing these methods.

2.0   REPRESENTATION OF PROPOSITIONS

2.1 Format of Propositional Representation

Although this method of constructing propositions from a text is not intended to be used by a computer simulation, the actual representation is intended to be readable by the LISP programming language. We have used a LISP program to read the proposition lists for subjects' main idea responses and then count similar propositions and arguments as an aid in the comparison process. Thus, there are some features of the format of the representation that are done purely because they enable LISP to use it.

An example will best illustrate the general method and format of this representation:

Ex 1: The fat cat ate the gray mouse.
    P1 (EAT CAT MOUSE)
    P2 (MOD CAT FAT)
    P3 (MOD MOUSE GRAY)

The proposition P1 is a simple verb frame consisting of the predicate EAT and two arguments: the logical subject, the word concept CAT, and the logical object, the word concept MOUSE. P2 consists of the predicate MOD (modify) followed by two arguments, the word concepts CAT and FAT. The predicate of a proposition is always written first, followed by its arguments. Word concepts are capitalized to distinguish them from words and they are normally singular. Because, in Example 1, the cat that is fat is the same cat that eats the mouse, the same word concept is used. If there were two cats in the sentence, they would have to be distinguished:

Ex 2: The black cat and the gray cat . . .
    P1 (MOD CAT1 BLACK)
    P2 (MOD CAT2 GRAY)

Predicates and arguments are separated by spaces and the whole proposition enclosed in parentheses. Each proposition is labeled with a number to make individual propositions easy to refer to. Since LISP handles numbers in different ways from alphanumeric symbols, all numbers, including proposition labels, are preceded by a letter character to force LISP to treat them as symbols. For numbering propositions this is done with the letter *P*, as shown in the examples. For numerical arguments, the prefix is *N* so that 150,000 would be represented as N150000 (the comma should not appear if LISP is used). Alternatively the number can be written out so that 2 would be represented as TWO.

Arguments for a predicate can be either word concepts or other propositions.

Ex 3: The cat quickly ate the mouse.
　　　　P1 (EAT CAT MOUSE)
　　　　P2 (MOD P1 QUICK)
OR
　　　　P1 (EAT CAT MOUSE)
　　　　P2 (MOD (EAT CAT MOUSE) QUICK)

Here the first argument to the predicate MOD is the P1 proposition. It is, of course, far more convenient to refer to a proposition by its label than to write it out in its entirety each time it is used.

Finally, because LISP treats spaces as string separators, when two words are used together as a single argument, they must be joined by a hyphen.

Ex 4: ice cream parlor.
　　　　P1 (MOD PARLOR ICE-CREAM)

2.2 Normal Order of Arguments

As we have seen, the predicate of a proposition is represented first and the arguments to the predicator follow. The order in which the arguments are shown is important: (EAT CAT MOUSE) and (EAT MOUSE CAT) should represent different things.

The rule that we have used is that the predicate should be interpreted as being after the first argument. For most propositions, which have two arguments, this means that the predicate can be thought of as operating between the arguments.

Some examples will illustrate this:

Ex 1: (EAT CAT MOUSE)
Interpreted as: cat eats mouse.

Ex 2: (EAT MOUSE CAT)
Interpreted as: mouse eats cat.

Ex 3: (MOD CAT BLACK)
Interpreted as: cat modified by black.

The correct ordering of arguments is particularly important when the predicate is a word like *because*. This is because it must be clear in the proposition which argument is cause and which effect.

Ex 4: Because B is true, A is true.
   P1 (BECAUSE A-TRUE B-TRUE)
Interpreted: A-true because B-true.

2.3 Practical Considerations of Representation

Some general rules can be stated for constructing propositional representations of prose material. These rules are justified by their practical effect on using propositional scoring. Specific cases of these rules show up in the detailed treatment below. Our practice is that, where helpful, we sacrifice technical accuracy of representation for simplicity and ease of construction and use of the representation.

1. When there are several reasonable ways to represent the text, choose the simplest.

2. Try to avoid embedding; non-embedded representations are simpler to work with, and simplify scoring.

3. Avoid unnecessary propositions by representing compound nouns as a single term. For example, terms such as *X-ray star* can often be represented as a single term, X-RAY-STAR, rather than by multiple modification of STAR. In the case of *black hole*, it is clear why this is useful: a black hole in the astronomical sense is not simply a hole that is black. Hence:

Ex 1: X-ray stars are black holes.
   P1 (ISA X-RAY-STAR BLACK-HOLE)

4. Try to avoid unnecessary variants of terms; for example, use QUICK instead of both QUICK and QUICKLY.

5. Invent predicate terms freely where they result in a simpler representation and correspond to a common structure. For example, don't attempt to analyze complex common verb forms into their constituent propositions. Instead form a single term, so that *know how to* would be represented simply as KNOW-HOW-TO. We also invented the predicate EXTENT-OF to represent a confusing variety of expressions about size, length, and so forth.

6. Where possible, fully propositionalize experimental text material before it is used, so that it can be modified to produce simpler representations that will be easier to score.

7. For recall experiments, choose representations that will reflect partial or paraphrased recall most easily.

Ex 1: Radio galaxies emit radio waves.
P1 (EMIT GALAXY WAVE)
P2 (MOD GALAXY RADIO)
P3 (MOD WAVE RADIO)
not
P1 (EMIT RADIO-GALAXY RADIO-WAVE)

The first representation shown allows one to distinguish recall that preserves the "radio" modification from those that don't.

However, for comparing summarization responses, minimizing the number of propositions and embedding them will eliminate many unimportant differences between responses and so facilitate determining the similarities and important differences.

3.0   CONSTRUCTION OF PROPOSITIONS

3.1 Verb-based Propositions

3.1.1 Representation of Ordinary Verbs.   These propositions are normally formed from the main verb of a clause, but they are also formed from participles and infinitives.

Our representation system, like the original Kintsch (1974) proposal, is based on a case grammar representation for verb-based propositions. However, we have found that almost all of the detailed analysis of case assignments presented in Kintsch (1974) and Turner and Greene (1977) is not really necessary for the practical purposes of scoring recall or comparing responses. As a result, our methods emphasize representing the propositional content in as simple a way as possible.

In this system, verb predicates are represented by the infinitive form of the verb. Tenses are disregarded, and auxiliaries are not represented.

Verbs have a case structure that can be, in some instances, fairly complex. For example, the verb *call* has cases for the person or thing that assigns the name, the person or thing that is named, and the name given.

Ex 1: Scientists call the radio galaxy DA240.
P1 (CALL SCIENTIST RADIO-GALAXY DA240)

Ex 2: The radio galaxy is called DA240 by scientists.
P1 (CALL SCIENTIST RADIO-GALAXY DA240)

In both examples, the scientists are performing the act of calling (or naming) on the radio galaxy, while DA240 is the name used in the action. The passive construction, shown in Example 2, does not change the case grammar of the verb: the same things are happening to the same people and things. Thus, when propositionalizing, passive constructions are represented in the same way as their equivalent active construction.

In this method, a fairly simple case structure is used for verbs and they preferably take two cases, although some take one, and a few take three. Whenever possible only two cases are used: the logical subject and the logical object.

Ex 3: Devices have existed . . .
      P1 (EXIST DEVICE)

Ex 4: Asteroids have affected the evolution of planets.
      P1 (AFFECT ASTEROID EVOLUTION)
      etc.

Sometimes, although the verb naturally takes two cases, no argument is supplied in the text. This missing argument is denoted by the placeholder $.

Ex 5: Metals are used.
      P1 (USE $ METAL)

Finally, unlike many other case grammar approaches, we do not complicate the representation by insisting on distinguishing animate actors from inanimate ones.

3.1.2 *Verbs with Prepositions.*   The common use in English of verbs that take prepositions tends to be confusing in a case grammar approach. The preposition itself is variable; it can be one of several alternatives, or it could be absent entirely. The simplest way to deal with such forms is to consider the preposition as a part of the verb itself: for example, DIFFER-IN, ADVANCE-WITH. This representation avoids unnecessary embedding of propositions and is also clear and unambiguous. Examples 1 and 2 illustrate the great difference in meaning that a preposition can cause, and how easily this difference can be represented.

Ex 1: Metal technology has advanced civilization.
      P1 (ADVANCE TECHNOLOGY CIVILIZATION)
      etc.

Ex 2: Metal technology has advanced with civilization.
      P1 (ADVANCE-WITH TECHNOLOGY CIVILIZATION)
      etc.

The presence or absence of a preposition does not always change the meaning, and this can lead to a problem in representation. Consider these examples:

Ex 3: Clocks differ in accuracy.

Ex 4: Cars differ and so . . .

In Example 3, the verb predicate would be DIFFER-IN. The preposition is represented as an explicit part of the verb because this is clearer. In Example 4, either DIFFER-IN or DIFFER could be used as the predicate.

Ex 3: Clocks differ in accuracy.
      P1 (DIFFER-IN CLOCK ACCURACY)

Ex 4: Cars differ and so . . .
      P1 (DIFFER CAR)
      etc.
OR
      P1 (DIFFER-IN CAR $)
      etc.

3.1.3 *Verbs that Take Verbs.*   Verbs often have a double structure, where the first verb takes a second verb. For example, the verbs *to tend to* and *to continue to* both take a second verb. This is most simply represented with two propositions:

Ex 5: People tend to use cars frequently.
      P1 (TEND-TO PEOPLE P2)
      P2 (USE PEOPLE CAR)
      etc.

Ex 6: Cars continue to be used by most people.
      P1 (CONTINUE-TO PEOPLE P2)
      P2 (USE PEOPLE CAR)
      etc.

In both these examples the prepositional part of the verb is explicitly represented. This explicit representation will avoid possible confusion like that between *to tend to* and *to tend* in the sense of *to look after*.

Other two-verb constructions can be handled in the same way:

Ex 7: Metals can be used in many ways.
      P1 (ABLE-TO $ P2)
      P2 (USE $ METAL)

Ex 8: Scientists know how to classify X-ray stars.
    P1 (KNOW-HOW-TO SCIENTIST P2)
    P2 (CLASSIFY SCIENTIST X-RAY-STAR)

Here *can* is treated as part of the verb *to be able* and *to know how to* is treated as a single verb analogous to the French *savoir*.

3.1.4 *Propositions as Arguments.*   Some verbs take propositions as arguments, although they do not have the double structure described above. This is often expressed in English by a *that* clause.

Ex 1: Astronomers think that X-ray stars are black holes.
    P1 (THINK ASTRONOMER P2)
    P2 (ISA X-RAY-STAR BLACK-HOLE)

3.1.5 *Verbs as Participles.*   Verb participles are often found that are not part of the main verb of a clause. They are propositionalized using the infinitive form of the verb.

Ex 1: Humans have detected flashes containing five quanta of light.
    P1 (DETECT HUMAN FLASH)
    P2 (CONTAIN FLASH QUANTUM)
    etc.

3.1.6 *May.*   The verb *may* could be propositionalized in two ways: by analogy with *can* as above (see Sec. 3.1.3, Ex 7), or as equivalent to the adverb *possible*. The second method is the one that we prefer.

Ex 1: Asteroids may affect planets.
    P1 (AFFECT ASTEROID PLANET)
    P2 (MOD P1 POSSIBLE)

3.1.7 *Have.*   *Have* in a sentence needs care because it has several possible uses and is propositionalized differently, depending on the use. Thus, we never use HAVE as a predicate. Sometimes it is merely an auxiliary and can be disregarded:

Ex 1: Metals have been used by many cultures.
    P1 (USE CULTURE METAL)
    etc.

Have can also be part of a compound, such as *to have to*. *Have to* means *must* or *necessary,* and is better propositionalized as one of these forms:

Ex 2: Nixon had to resign.
P1 (MUST NIXON P2)
P2 (RESIGN NIXON)
OR
P1 (MOD P2 NECESSARY)
P2 (RESIGN NIXON)

Have can also indicate possession:

Ex 3: Metals have many uses.
P1 (POSSESS METAL USE)
etc.

3.1.8 *To Be.*   When the main verb is a form of the verb *to be,* then there are three possible propositionalizations, depending on the structure.
If the structure is

NOUN1 is a NOUN2
OR
NOUN1 is the NOUN2

an ISA or REF proposition, respectively, is formed (see Examples 1 and 2 below).
If the structure is

NOUN is ADJECTIVE

then a MOD proposition is formed (see Sec. 3.2.1 below).
REF can be thought of as meaning *is the* and is used to indicate that one thing is the same as another (has the same REFerent). SAME-AS would be an alternative predicate.

Ex 1: The corona is the outer atmosphere of the sun.
P1 (REF CORONA ATMOSPHERE)
etc.
OR
P1 (SAME-AS CORONA ATMOSPHERE)
etc.

ISA is used to denote membership of the first argument in the set defined by the second:

Ex 2: A piano is a keyboard instrument.
    P1 (ISA PIANO INSTRUMENT)
    etc.

3.1.9 *Become.*   This verb can cause a few problems in propositionalization. The case grammar of *become* is such that it demands two arguments, the first of which is normally a noun. The second can also be a noun, in which case the propositionalization is simple:

Ex 1: Microprocessors have become the workhorses of industry.
    P1 (BECOME MICROPROCESSOR WORKHORSE)
    etc.

Occurrences where the second argument is adjectival have two possibilities for propositionalization:

Ex 2: Clocks have become very accurate.
Method 1:
    P1 (BECOME CLOCK ACCURATE)
    etc.
Method 2:
    P1 (BECOME CLOCK P2)
    P2 (MOD CLOCK ACCURATE)
    etc.

There seems to be no advantage of method 2 over method 1. Method 2 is clumsier, uses unnecessary embedding and, compared with method 1, is not particularly clear.

3.2. Representation of Modifiers

3.2.1 *Modification.*   Modifiers, in the limited definition used here, are normally adjectives and adverbs that modify nouns or verbs. Some examples of modifier propositions have already been used in this report:

Ex 1: Fat cat . . .
    P1 (MOD CAT FAT)

The object of modification can be a noun (adjectival modification) or a proposition (adverbial modification).

Ex 2: Keyboard instrument.
    P1 (MOD INSTRUMENT KEYBOARD)

Here KEYBOARD is an adjectival modification of INSTRUMENT. Although *keyboard* is a noun, English permits this type of construction.

In English, adjectival modification is often expressed with the verb *to be*:

Ex 3: Cars are popular.
    P1 (MOD CAR POPULAR)

In adverbial modification, the adverb modifies the verb. For convenience, but at the sacrifice of technical accuracy, this is represented as modification of the whole verb proposition.

Ex 4: The control was greatly improved.
    P1 (IMPROVE $ CONTROL)
    P2 (MOD P1 GREAT)

3.2.2 *Multiple Modification.*   Multiple modification is represented without embedding of propositions. Thus, in Example 1, *sophisticated* is not a modification of *modern clock* but of *clock*.

Ex 1: Sophisticated modern clocks . . .
    P1 (MOD CLOCK MODERN)
    P2 (MOD CLOCK SOPHISTICATED)

Sometimes multiple modifications are made up of modifiers that are actually single concepts:

Ex 2: Quartz crystal watches . . .

Based on Example 1 above, one might think that this should be propositionalized as:

    P1 (MOD WATCH CRYSTAL)
    P2 (MOD WATCH QUARTZ)

However, the watches are not quartz watches that are also crystal watches. A better representation might be:

    P1 (MOD WATCH CRYSTAL)
    P2 (MOD CRYSTAL QUARTZ)

But since we prefer simple structures, we prefer not to divide up modifications too finely. The actual modification is that the watch is of a certain type, a *quartz-crystal* type. Thus, the preferred propositionalization is:

P1 (MOD WATCH QUARTZ-CRYSTAL)

3.2.3 *Negation.*   Propositions are negated by means of the NEGATE predicate. NEGATE has one argument and this argument is always a proposition.

Ex 1: The speed is not constant.
P1 (MOD SPEED CONSTANT)
P2 (NEGATE P1)

Sometimes, there can be a question as to exactly which proposition is being negated. This can only be decided by careful consideration of the meaning.

Ex 2: The players did not play chess carelessly.
P1 (PLAY PLAYER CHESS)
P2 (MOD P1 CARELESS)
P3 (NEGATE P?)

The question here is whether the negation should be of P1 or P2. The meaning of this sentence is not that the players did not play chess, rather that they did play but not carelessly. Therefore the negation is of P2, not P1.

3.2.4 *Time.*   Some propositions place their first argument into a time frame. These are time propositions and are commonly represented in one of two ways. The first uses the predicate TIME and the second DURATION-OF. TIME is used when a proposition or word concept is given a reference to a particular point in time. DURATION-OF is used when an action is described as being over some period of time.

Ex 1: A natural nuclear reactor was active in the Precambrian era for many years.
P1 (MOD REACTOR ACTIVE)
P2 (TIME P1 PRECAMBRIAN-ERA)
P3 (DURATION-OF P1 YEAR)
etc.

The Precambrian era is the point in time when the reactor was active and so a TIME proposition is used. The reactor was also active over the period of many years and so a DURATION-OF proposition should be used.

Example 2 shows that not only propositions can be put into a time frame. Here there are two types of chess player, from two different times.

Ex 2: Today's chess players are better than players of the 19th century.
    . . . .
    P2 (TIME PLAYER1 TODAY)
    P3 (TIME PLAYER2 N19TH-CENTURY)

3.2.5 *Label.* Compound proper names present difficulties in propositionalization. Simple proper names can be used as arguments with no problem:

Ex 1: John hit Mary.
    P1 (HIT JOHN MARY)

But consider:

Ex 2: The British won the Battle of Jutland.

Ex 3: Hydrogen maser clocks are used by the National Bureau of Standards.

In these two examples it is senseless to attempt to propositionalize the names: *the Battle of Jutland* is the name of a particular battle and the relationship between *battle* and *Jutland* is not a modification or possession relationship. Similarly *the National Bureau of Standards* is the name of a particular bureau. In these circumstances, the LABEL predicate is useful. It assigns to an ordinary noun a particular name.

Ex 2: The British won the Battle of Jutland.
    P1 (WIN BRITISH BATTLE)
    P2 (LABEL BATTLE BATTLE-OF-JUTLAND)

Ex 3: Hydrogen maser clocks are used by the National Bureau of Standards.
    P1 (USE BUREAU CLOCK)
    P2 (LABEL BUREAU NATIONAL-BUREAU-OF-STANDARDS)
    P3 (MOD CLOCK HYDROGEN-MASER)

P3 in Example 3 is not represented with a LABEL predicate because *hydrogen maser clock* is a type of clock rather than a proper name for a particular clock.

3.3 Representation of Prepositions

3.3.1 *Prepositions as Predicates.* Prepositions take two arguments: the second is almost always a noun while the first can be a noun or a proposition.

Ex 1: Metals have been used for many purposes.
    P1 (USE $ METAL)
    P2 (FOR P1 PURPOSE)
    etc.

Ex 2: People in the United States like cars.
    P1 (LIKE PEOPLE CAR)
    P2 (IN PEOPLE UNITED-STATES)

In Ex 2, P2 was not propositionalized as:

    (IN P1 UNITED-STATES)

because the people are what is in the United States, not the act of liking cars.

Some propositions, such as *between,* can take three arguments, instead of the normal two for prepositions. For *between,* this is because one thing is usually between two other things.

Ex 3: The Battle of Jutland was between the Germans and the British.
    P1 (BETWEEN BATTLE GERMAN BRITISH)
    etc.

3.3.2 *Prepositions That are Part of Connectives.*   When an apparent preposition has propositions for both arguments, it is probably a connective: for example, *to* for IN-ORDER-TO, *for* for IN-ORDER-FOR (see Sec. 3.9.3 below).

Ex 1: Microprocessors are used to improve many devices.

The *to* in this example means *in order to* and is propositionalized as a connective.

3.3.3 *Prepositions that should disappear.*   Sometimes, a structure that uses a preposition is more conveniently considered as a verb. Thus, the preposition may not appear in the representation.

Ex 1: The Battle of Jutland was a surprise to the British.

Possible propositionalization:

    P1 (REF BATTLE SURPRISE)
    P2 (TO SURPRISE BRITISH)
    P3 (LABEL BATTLE BATTLE-OF-JUTLAND)

Better propositionalization:

> P1 (SURPRISE BATTLE BRITISH)
> P2 (LABEL BATTLE BATTLE-OF-JUTLAND)

The actual word use is changed in the better version in that *surprise* is used as a verb rather than as a noun, but the "better" version is neater, simpler, and more easily worked with.

3.4. Propositions that express Quantity

3.4.1 *Number-of.*   Number can be definite or indefinite. A definite quantity is expressed by an actual number, while an indefinite quantity is expressed by words such as *several, all,* or *most.* Many number propositions use the predicate NUMBER-OF:

Ex 1: There are three prototypes.
> P1 (EXIST PROTOTYPE)
> P2 (NUMBER-OF PROTOTYPE THREE)

Ex 2: Most people . . .
> P1 (NUMBER-OF PEOPLE MOST)

Ex 3: Hundreds of people . . .
> P1 (NUMBER-OF PEOPLE HUNDREDS)

OR

> P1 (NUMBER-OF PEOPLE HUNDRED)
> P2 (NUMBER-OF HUNDRED SOME)

The first method shown in Example 3 is clearest.

3.4.2 *Amount-of.*   Another predicate used for number is AMOUNT-OF. This is used similarly to NUMBER-OF when NUMBER-OF or MOD are inappropriate. This representation is very useful for quantities such as *all of* or *half of.*

Ex 1: The portal vein carries all the blood from the intestines.
> P1 (CARRY VEIN BLOOD)
> P2 (AMOUNT-OF BLOOD ALL)
> etc.

3.4.3 *Rate-of.*   In technical prose, various measurements are often expressed as rates of one kind or another. Such rates are very difficult to propositionalize using NUMBER-OF or AMOUNT-OF. In this sort of case, the RATE-OF predicate is useful:

Ex 1: The car is traveling at sixty miles per hour.
     P1 (TRAVEL CAR)
     P2 (RATE-OF P1 MILES-PER-HOUR)
     P3 (NUMBER-OF MILES-PER-HOUR SIXTY)

3.4.4 *Degree-of.* The use of DEGREE-OF for measurement is illustrated by:

Ex 1: Clocks today are accurate to one second in a million years.
     P1 (MOD CLOCK ACCURATE)
     P2 (TIME CLOCK TODAY)
     P3 (DEGREE-OF P1 ONE-SECOND-PER-MILLION-YEAR)

This would be the simplest method, but an alternative representation would be:

     P3 (DEGREE-OF P1 SECOND-PER-YEAR)
     P4 (NUMBER-OF SECOND ONE)
     P5 (NUMBER-OF YEAR MILLION)

Both methods have their advantages; the first would be most useful for comparing subject responses, while the second would be better for a recall scoring key.

DEGREE-OF can also represent indefinite values:

Ex 2: Modern clocks have incredible accuracy.
     P1 (POSSESS CLOCK ACCURACY)
     P2 (MOD CLOCK MODERN)
     P3 (DEGREE-OF ACCURACY INCREDIBLE)

Of course, P3 could also be represented using a MOD proposition. For recall scoring, MOD would be adequate but for comparing subject responses DE-GREE-OF would be better as it helps make the similarity of Examples 1 and 2 more obvious.

3.5 Part-Whole Relations and Possession

This section illustrates our approach of ignoring niceties of the semantics in favor of simple straightforward representations. Our treatment of part-whole and possession relations is easy to apply, but ignores some of the difficulties grappled with by Turner and Greene (1977).

The predicate PART-OF can be used to represent the part-whole relation. In general terms:

PART-OF PART WHOLE

This is most useful when the part-whole relationship is explicit in the text:

Ex 1: The corona is part of the sun.
    P1 (PART-OF CORONA SUN)

Possessive forms in English can be confusing because of the looseness of the concept of possession. Our system uses POSSESS very loosely to simplify the representation.

Ex 2: The sun has a corona.

This is not very different in meaning from Example 1 but would be propositionalized:

    P1 (POSSESS SUN CORONA)

Many times *of* can be interpreted as meaning possession.

Ex 3: The properties of metals have been valued by many cultures.
    P1 (VALUE CULTURE PROPERTY)
    P2 (POSSESS METAL PROPERTY)
    etc.

This would be the same propositionalization as for:

Ex 4: Many cultures have valued metals' properties.
or
Ex 5: Metals have properties that have been valued by many cultures.

Thus *of* can frequently be considered as an alternative construction to *have* and can be propositionalized using POSSESS. However, *of* can be used for many different purposes, and care needs to be taken in defining these (see below in section 4.5).

3.6 Superlatives

Superlative forms are considered simply as adverbs and adjectives and thus they use a MOD construction. Superlatives that are constructed using *most* are represented with *most* as an adverb. Superlatives with special forms like *best* are treated as simple adjectives:

Ex 1: The car is the most popular form of transportation.

. . . .

P2 (MOD FORM POPULAR)
P3 (MOD P2 MOST)

. . . .

Ex 2: The car is the best form of transportation for most people.

. . . .

P2 (MOD FORM BEST)
P3 (FOR FORM PEOPLE)
P4 (NUMBER-OF PEOPLE MOST)

Example 2 shows that *most* can be either the superlative, propositionalized using MOD, or a quantity, propositionalized using NUMBER-OF (Sec. 3.4.1).

3.7 Comparatives

There are a large number of comparative constructions. These include *more something than, better than, different from* and *as something as*. Most compare two things along some dimension; sometimes the dimension is explicit, as in *more accurate than,* and sometimes not, as in *compare to*. Rather than attempting to represent the subtle semantic structure of a comparative, we use a rather simple form:

Ex 1: The piano is better than the harpsichord.
P1 (BETTER-THAN PIANO HARPSICHORD)

Ex 2: The piano is different from the harpsichord.
P1 (DIFFERENT-FROM PIANO HARPSICHORD)

Some comparatives could be propositionalized in two ways:

Ex 3: The piano is more expressive than the harpsichord.
Method 1:
P1 (MORE-THAN P2 P3)
P2 (MOD PIANO EXPRESSIVE)
P3 (MOD HARPSICHORD EXPRESSIVE)

Method 2:
P1 (MORE-EXPRESSIVE-THAN PIANO HARPSICHORD)

Method 2 treats *more expressive than* as a single relation between the two arguments. It is most useful when comparing subject responses with each other. Method 1, on the other hand, is most useful when scoring recall protocols because a subject could get credit for recalling only that the piano is expressive even though the other parts of the relationship are not recalled. If method 2 was used, that subject would not get any credit at all.

3.8 Questions

Questions do not usually appear in the descriptive prose which has been the material in our work. However, subjects will sometimes respond using questions. Question predicates have one argument which is always a proposition.

Ex 1: How did a nuclear reactor occur naturally?
P1 (HOW P2)
P2 (OCCUR REACTOR)
etc.

Ex 2: The passage described how people have used metals.
P1 (DESCRIBE PASSAGE P2)
P2 (HOW P3)
P3 (USE PEOPLE METAL)

What tends to be clumsy to propositionalize in whatever way it is done. One way is to treat it exactly like other question words:

Ex 3: What is an X-ray star?
P1 (WHAT P2)
P2 (ISA X-RAY-STAR $)

Ex 4: Scientists do not know what X-ray stars are.
P1 (KNOW SCIENTIST P3)
P2 (NEGATE P1)
P3 (WHAT P4)
P4 (ISA X-RAY-STAR $)

3.9 Connectives

3.9.1 *Logical Connectives.* There are two main logical connectives. They are AND and OR. Both express a logical relationship between two propositions.

Frequently in text, *and* (and sometimes *or*) is used to string together a list. In such cases, the *and* is a purely linguistic device and has no logical content. We propositionalize such sentences just as if they consisted of several separate sentences, with the *and* not even appearing in the representation:

Ex 1: Different metals have various strengths, uses and values.
P1 (POSSESS METAL STRENGTH)
P2 (POSSESS METAL USE)
P3 (POSSESS METAL VALUE)
etc.

Ex 2: The piano is more expressive than the clavichord or the harpsichord.
P1 (MORE-EXPRESSIVE-THAN PIANO CLAVICHORD)
P2 (MORE-EXPRESSIVE-THAN PIANO HARPSICHORD)

Ex 3: The piano is more expressive than the clavichord and the harpsichord.
P1 (MORE-EXPRESSIVE-THAN PIANO CLAVICHORD)
P2 (MORE-EXPRESSIVE-THAN PIANO HARPSICHORD)

In cases such as these examples, one is tempted to further simplify the representation by defining a set of terms, and then apply a proposition to the set. For example, Example 1 above could be represented as:

P1 (SET-MEMBERS STRENGTH USE VALUE)
P2 (POSSESS METAL P1)

However, the simplicity of this representation is deceptive. In attempting to score recall protocols there is no obvious criterion for when to score P1 as recalled if only some of the terms are recalled. The method used in Example 1, however, always produces well-defined scoring if only some of the terms appear in recall.

Occasionally, *and* and *or* are used not just as grammatical devices but in ways corresponding to the actual logical content. For example, in Example 4, both the propositions connected by *and* must be true in order for the last to be true. This is a logical AND and must be propositionalized. Synonyms for *and* include *both* and *as well as*. An exclusive *or* should be propositionalized, while inclusive *or* would not need to be. The *either . . . or* in Example 5 is an exclusive OR. *Or* alone can be inclusive or exclusive and care should be taken to decide which it is.

Ex 4: If a woman is RhD negative and her fetus is RhD positive, she may
develop RhD antibodies.

. . .
P2 (MOD WOMAN RHD-NEGATIVE)
P3 (MOD FETUS RHD-POSITIVE)
P4 (AND P2 P3)
etc.

Ex 5: X-ray stars are either black holes or neutron stars.
P1 (OR P2 P3)
P2 (ISA X-RAY-STAR BLACK-HOLE)
P3 (ISA X-RAY-STAR NEUTRON-STAR)

3.9.2 *Propositional Connectives.* One group of connectives is usually found in a sentence linking together two main clauses. They include: *although, because, if,* and *in order to.* The propositions linked by these connectives are the verb propositions of the clauses.

Ex 1: The Battle of Jutland was a strategic victory for the British, although the Germans won tactically.
P1 (ALTHOUGH P2 P4)
P2 (REF BATTLE VICTORY)
P3 (LABEL BATTLE BATTLE-OF-JUTLAND)
P4 (WIN GERMAN BATTLE)
P5 (MOD P4 TACTICAL)

Ex 2: Because keyboard instruments vary, the performer can control the sound.
P1 (BECAUSE P4 P2)
P2 (VARY INSTRUMENT)
P3 (MOD INSTRUMENT KEYBOARD)
P4 (ABLE PERFORMER P5)
P5 (CONTROL PERFORMER SOUND)

Ex 3: If a quartz crystal watch is adjusted properly, it is extremely accurate.
P1 (IF P5 P2)
P2 (ADJUST $ WATCH)
P3 (MOD P2 PROPER)
P4 (MOD WATCH QUARTZ-CRYSTAL)
P5 (MOD WATCH ACCURATE)
P6 (MOD P5 EXTREME)

Ex 4: Different cars have been developed in order to meet different needs.
P1 (IN-ORDER-TO P2 P4)
P2 (DEVELOP $ CAR)
P3 (MOD CAR DIFFERENT)
P4 (MEET CAR NEED)
P5 (MOD NEED DIFFERENT)

A second group of connectives is those that link clauses and whole sentences with material that was presented earlier. This group includes *thus, therefore,* and *however.* Sometimes the earlier material referred to will be simply earlier in the same sentence, but more frequently, it will be in a previous sentence. The arguments to these predicates are connective propositions or, if there are no connectives, verb-based propositions.

Ex 1: The Incas valued gold because they used it in religious ceremonies. However, the Spaniards wanted it for monetary reasons.
P1 (BECAUSE P2 P3)
P2 (VALUE INCA GOLD)
P3 (USE INCA GOLD)
P4 (IN P3 CEREMONY)
P5 (MOD CEREMONY RELIGIOUS)
P6 (HOWEVER P1 P7)
P7 (WANT SPANIARD GOLD)
P8 (FOR P7 REASON)
P9 (MOD REASON MONETARY)

It may be found useful, when propositionalizing a long text, to preserve the original sentence boundaries. This can be represented with an extra label on the propositions.

S1:P1 (BECAUSE P2 P3)
  P2 (VALUE INCA GOLD)
  P3 (USE INCA GOLD)
  . . . .
S2:P1 (HOWEVER S1:P1 S2:P2)
  P2 (WANT SPANIARD GOLD)

There is another group of connectives that is like the second group described above in that these connectives link current material to that in previous sentences. However, they use a short phrase like *This means that* . . . rather than a single word. These phrases are represented using the single predicate that is the closest in meaning to the phrase: for example, *this means that* can be represented by IMPLY, and *this results in* can be represented by CAUSE.

Ex 1: Travel by airplane is very expensive. This means that people tend to use airplanes only for occasional long trips.
S1:P1 (MOD TRAVEL EXPENSIVE)
  P2 (MOD P1 VERY)
  P3 (BY TRAVEL AIRPLANE)

S2:P1 (IMPLY S1:P1 P2)
  P2 (TEND-TO PEOPLE P3)
  P3 (USE PEOPLE AIRPLANE)
  P4 (FOR P3 TRIP)
  P5 (MOD P4 ONLY)

P6 (MOD TRIP OCCASIONAL)
P7 (MOD TRIP LONG)

A final group of predicates can be considered connectives because they are often ordinary connectives used in this particular way. *Because* can be just an ordinary connective linking two propositions:

Ex 1: Because the mechanisms of keyboard instruments differ, the player has varying control over the sound.
P1 (BECAUSE P3 P2)
P2 (DIFFER MECHANISM)
P3 (POSSESS PLAYER CONTROL)
etc.

For the sake of simplicity, we sometimes use *because* to connect a proposition with a single argument. Usually, we distinguish this from BECAUSE by using BECAUSE-OF:

Ex 2: The player can control sound differently on different instruments because of their different mechanisms.
P1 (BECAUSE-OF P2 MECHANISM)
P2 (ABLE PLAYER P3)
P3 (CONTROL PLAYER SOUND)
etc.

3.9.3 *Contracted Connectives.*   Because our method of propositionalization does not attempt to classify connectives, problems can arise in the representation of words like *to* and *for*. When these words have propositions as arguments, they are acting as connectives and it is useful to distinguish such use from a prepositional use. For example, consider *to* in the following:

Ex 1: Microprocessors are used to improve many devices.

The meaning of *to* here is the same as if the sentence were:

Ex 2: Microprocessors are used in order to improve many devices.

Thus the *to* in Example 1 may be considered a contraction of *in-order-to* and the propositionalization of both examples would be:

P1 (IN-ORDER-TO P2 P3)
P2 (USE $ MICROPROCESSOR)
P3 (IMPROVE MICROPROCESSOR DEVICE)
etc.

3.10 Miscellaneous Constructions

3.10.1 *Pronouns.*   When propositionalizing pronouns the actual word concept referred to must be inferred. This is, of course, what normally happens in reading.

Ex 1: Cultures have many uses for their metals.
       P1 (POSSESS CULTURE USE)
       P2 (FOR P1 METAL)
       P3 (POSSESS CULTURE METAL)

It is inferred that the possessive pronoun refers to *cultures.*

3.10.2 *Exist.*   The EXIST predicate can be used in two ways: the first is to represent the verb *exist,* and the second is to represent the *there is a . . .* construction. Example 1 below shows the use of EXIST to represent *exist.* In Example 3, note that *there are . . .* can be ignored so that the propositionalization is the same as for Example 2. Alternatively the EXIST predicate can be used.

Ex 1: Clocks have existed for centuries.
       P1 (EXIST CLOCK)
       P2 (DURATION-OF P1 CENTURIES)

Ex 2: Many clocks are used today.
       P1 (USE $ CLOCK)
       P2 (NUMBER-OF CLOCK MANY)
       P3 (TIME P1 TODAY)

Ex 3: There are many clocks that are used today.
       P1 (USE $ CLOCK)
       P2 (NUMBER-OF CLOCK MANY)
       P3 (TIME P1 TODAY)

OR

       P1 (EXIST CLOCK)
       P2 (NUMBER-OF CLOCK MANY)
       P3 (USE $ CLOCK)
       P4 (TIME P3 TODAY)

3.10.3 *Example-of.*   In technical prose, examples are frequently used. They can be represented using the predicate EXAMPLE-OF, whose first argument is an example of the second. As with many predicates already described, there are alternative ways to propositionalize text than to use EXAMPLE-OF, but such a use is recommended by its clarity and ease.

Ex 1: Hydrogen maser clocks are examples of modern timepieces.
      P1 (EXAMPLE-OF CLOCK TIMEPIECE)
      P2 (MOD CLOCK HYDROGEN-MASER)
      P3 (MOD TIMEPIECE MODERN)

3.10.4 *Appositional Phrases.*   Appositional phrases are represented by REF or ISA.

Ex 1: One isomer, the 11-cis form, is converted to another isomer, the all-trans form.
      P1 (CONVERT-TO $ ISOMER1 ISOMER2)
      P2 (REF ISOMER1 FORM1)
      P3 (MOD FORM1 N11-CIS)
      P4 (REF ISOMER2 FORM2)
      P5 (MOD FORM2 ALL-TRANS)

Ex 2: Cowpox, a mild disease, can prevent smallpox.
      P1 (PREVENT COWPOX SMALLPOX)
      P2 (ISA COWPOX DISEASE)
      etc.

3.10.5 *Idioms.*   Idiomatic expressions are not used very often in the technical prose that we have studied, but they are fairly common in literary prose or in subject responses. It is often pointless to try to propositionalize an idiom as it stands and therefore the representation should normally be based on the meaning of the idiom.

Ex 1: Mary blew up.
      P1 (BECOME MARY ANGRY)
      P2 (MOD P1 SUDDEN)

Ex 2: It is hot today.
      P1 (MOD WEATHER HOT)
      P2 (TIME P1 TODAY)

Many expressions use an "It is . . ." construction, as in Example 2. The meaning of the expression should be determined and then propositionalized.

Ex 3: It is possible that asteroids have affected the evolution of planets.
      P1 (MOD P2 POSSIBLE)
      P2 (AFFECT ASTEROID EVOLUTION)
      etc.

Sometimes, an idiomatic phrase is best propositionalized exactly as it stands. This happens when the idiom has an unambiguous meaning and no simple non-idiomatic synonym. In Example 4, *all the way* is an idiom that is best left as it stands.

Ex 4: Black moved his King's Bishop all the way across the board to capture material.
P1 (IN-ORDER-TO P2 P7)
P2 (MOVE BLACK BISHOP)
P3 (ACROSS P2 BOARD)
P4 (MOD P3 ALL-THE-WAY)
P5 (POSSESS'BLACK BISHOP)
P6 (LABEL BISHOP KINGS-BISHOP)
P7 (CAPTURE BLACK MATERIAL)

4.0 SOME DIFFICULT PROBLEMS IN PROPOSITIONALIZATION

4.1 Ambiguity

There are two types of ambiguity found when propositionalizing a text. One type occurs when one word can have different functions. *To* as discussed in connectives (Sec. 3.9.3) is an example of this. *When* is another example, since it can function both as a question and as a temporal connective. In both these cases, it is obvious how to propositionalize once the usage is determined.

The other kind of ambiguity is more difficult to resolve. It occurs when the text itself is ambiguous in meaning and thus the exact function of a word is hard to determine. One would hope that this kind of ambiguity would not exist in text used as an experimental material except by design. Thus when constructing a recall scoring key this should not be a problem. Propositionalizing a text before it is used is a good way to discover unintended ambiguity before presenting the text to subjects.

It is in subject responses that ambiguity is most likely to occur. Ambiguity can often be caused by subjects' careless use of English. If a subject wrote the classic:

Ex 1: If the baby does not thrive on raw milk, boil it.

It would be pedantic to insist that *it* is ambiguous here. However, consider this subject's response:

Ex 2: X-ray stars have energy and gravity though it affects its partner more.

The meaning here is not obvious whichever way one decides to consider the two appearances of *it*. The context supplies important clues. The passage for which this was a response talked about the fact that X-ray stars have partner stars and so the possessive pronoun almost certainly represents *X-ray star*. *Its partner* could therefore be propositionalized:

P? (POSSESS X-RAY-STAR PARTNER)

However, the first *it* is still incomprehensible. One possible referent is *X-ray star* and this seems the most likely. If this were being scored for recall and there was a proposition about X-ray stars affecting their partners, one could safely assume that this was what the subject was trying to say. Otherwise one could do either of two things: represent the most likely meaning, or represent all possible meanings.

4.2 So Great That

Ex 1: The thermal energy of the gas is so great that the sun cannot retain the corona.

For comparing subject responses to each other, a very surface-oriented propositionalization is sufficient:

P1 (SO-GREAT-THAT ENERGY P2)
P2 (RETAIN SUN CORONA)
P3 (NEGATE P2)
etc.

For a recall scoring key, it is easier if P1 is broken down into smaller units that are less surface-oriented. One proposition that can be easily extracted is:

P1 (MOD ENERGY GREAT)

The energy being great implies that the sun will not retain the corona

P2 (IMPLY P1 P3)
P3 (RETAIN SUN CORONA)

The emphatic quality of *so* could be represented by a DEGREE-OF proposition so the final propositionalization:

P1 (MOD ENERGY GREAT)
P2 (MOD ENERGY THERMAl)
P3 (DEGREE-OF P1 GREAT)
P4 (IMPLY P3 P5)
P5 (RETAIN SUN CORONA)

4.3 Some-other

Ex 1: Some clocks are more accurate than others.

This very common construction is difficult to accurately propositionalize. A simple, but not entirely satisfactory method is:

P1 (MORE-ACCURATE-THAN CLOCK1 CLOCK2)
P2 (MOD CLOCK1 SOME)
P3 (MOD CLOCK2 OTHER)

4.4 Complex Set Constructions

4.4.1 *They both have the same number* . . .   Consider the following sentence:

Ex 1: Maleic acid and fumaric acid both have the same number of carbon, hydrogen and oxygen atoms.

This example is from a text that was to be used for a recall experiment. There is no obvious good way to represent it with propositions. Use of set constructions, mentioned above (see Sec. 3.9.1), might be useful here, but the result is extremely complex, and impractical to use for scoring. After struggling for some time, in this one case a special analysis of the sentence was used, based on idea units:

Idea unit	Propositions
A. Maleic acid and fumaric acid have atoms such that:	3
B. they have the same number of each type of atoms	3
C. A type of atom is carbon	1
D. A type of atom is hydrogen.	1
E. A type of atom is oxygen.	1

Thus, a subject scored 3 propositions for recalling A, 3 more for recalling B and one each for C, D and E. This is not an ideal solution by any means but it served its purpose and was easy to use in practice. Our recommendation is to avoid using material that has these characteristics.

4.4.2 *One of the* . . .   This very common construction has no really satisfactory method for propositionalization. Here are some of the ways we have done it:

Ex 1: An asteroid could destroy one of a planet's moons.
P1 (ABLE ASTEROID P2)
P2 (DESTROY ASTEROID MOON1)
P3 (ISA MOON1 MOON2)
P4 (NUMBER-OF MOON1 ONE)
P5 (POSSESS PLANET MOON2)
P6 (NUMBER-OF MOON2 SOME)

Ex 2: Five men were arrested for illegally entering the Watergate building,
and one of them was James McCord Jr. who was head of security for
the Committee to Re-Elect the President.
P1 (ARREST $ MAN1)
P2 (FOR P1 P3)
P3 (ENTER MAN1 BUILDING)
P4 (MOD P3 ILLEGAL)
P5 (NUMBER-OF MAN1 FIVE)
P6 (MOD BUILDING WATERGATE)
P7 (ISA MAN2 MAN1)
P8 (NUMBER-OF MAN2 ONE)
P9 (LABEL MAN2 JAMES-MCCORD-JR)
P10 (REF MAN2 HEAD-OF-SECURITY)
P11 (FOR HEAD-OF-SECURITY COMMITTEE)
P12 (LABEL COMMITTEE COMMITTEE-TO-RE-ELECT-THE-
PRESIDENT)

4.4.3 *The Strange Case of the Hypothetical Planet.* Here is another complex construction that demands a somewhat unusual representation.

Ex 1: If planets had evolved only by the accretion of particles, they would be
more uniform than they are.
P1 (If P6 P2)
P2 (EVOLVE PLANET2)
P3 (BY P2 ACCRETION)
P4 (MOD P3 ONLY)
P5 (OF ACCRETION PARTICLE)
P6 (MORE-UNIFORM-THAN PLANET2 PLANET1)
P7 (MOD PLANET2 HYPOTHETICAL)
P8 (EXIST PLANET1)

4.4.4 *Growing Together.* Here there is another difficult-to-represent construction.

Ex 1: The fleets grew together in the mists of the North Sea, until finally the
main battleship groups encountered each other.

P1 (UNTIL P2 P8)
P2 (GROW-TOGETHER FLEET)
P3 (NUMBER-OF FLEET TWO)
P4 (MOD P2 CLOSER)
P5 (IN P2 MIST)
P6 (POSSESS SEA MIST)
P7 (LABEL SEA NORTH-SEA)
P8 (ENCOUNTER-EACH-OTHER GROUP1 GROUP2)
P9 (ISA GROUP1 GROUP)
P10 (ISA GROUP2 GROUP)
P11 (MOD GROUP BATTLESHIP)
P12 (MOD GROUP MAIN)
P13 (MOD P8 FINALLY)

4.5 Of

The simple word *of* is a very sophisticated word that has more than one role. The possession role was mentioned above (see Sec. 3.5). But consider:

Ex. 1: Biotransformation causes the inactivation of drugs.

In this example, *biotransformation* is obviously the subject of the verb *cause* but the phrase *the inactivation of drugs* is somewhat difficult to represent. *Of* can be considered a meaning of POSSESS and so this sentence could be propositionalized:

P1 (CAUSE BIOTRANSFORMATION INACTIVATION)
P2 (POSSESS DRUG INACTIVATION)

POSSESS seems peculiar here because *inactivation* has a strong verb "flavor," although it is actually a noun. Another representation would be:

P1 (CAUSE BIOTRANSFORMATION P2)
P2 (INACTIVATE $ DRUG)

However, embedded propositions are always difficult to work with. In addition, this representation is clearly very different in meaning from the original. When the meaning of *of* is difficult to determine, the simple solution is to use it as a predicate itself and not worry about its exact meaning.

P1 (CAUSE BIOTRANSFORMATION INACTIVATION)
P2 (OF INACTIVATION DRUG)

5.0 EXAMPLE ANALYSIS OF A TEXT

5.1 Procedure for Propositional Analysis of a Text

The procedure for propositionalization can be shown as an algorithm:

I. Read the text through carefully.
II. For each sentence:
   (1) Loosely parse into clauses.
   (2) Pick out any connectives.
   (3) For main clause (or first main clause):
      (a) Represent main verb.
      (b) Represent modifiers of predicate proposition.
      (c) Represent modifiers to arguments of predicate proposition.
      (d) Represent modifiers to other propositions or other arguments.
   (4) Repeat a–d for any other clauses.

5.2 Example Analysis of a Text

The example text, shown in Table 12.1, was used in a recall experiment. For psychological reasons the passage could not be modified to produce a simple representation, as we advised above (see Sec. 4.1). This extended example illustrates in detail how the above rules and principles are applied to an extended piece of technical prose. The propositions for this example are listed by sentence.

After reading through the text and ensuring that it is fully understood, examine the first sentence:

S1:Biotransformation is the chemical transformation that causes the inactivation of drugs, the detoxification of environmental pollutants, and the deactivation of chemicals that can cause cancer.

TABLE 12.1
Text to be Used for Recall Experiment

Biotransformation is the chemical transformation that causes the inactivation of drugs, the detoxification of environmental pollutants and the deactivation of chemicals that can cause cancer. Biotransformation of harmful agents involves an oxidation reaction which is mediated by complex enzymes, and if this process does not take place, a drug entering the body may act indefinitely. Biotransformation defends the body against the effects of toxins and is carried out in the liver. The liver, weighing three pounds in the human adult, is the largest organ in the body and performs diverse functions. Through the large portal vein of the liver passes all the blood that has absorbed digested food and other substances from the intestines.

There is a main clause and a compound subordinate clause. In the main clause, the verb is *is*. In this case, the *is* is part of a *NOUN is the NOUN* construction and should be represented with a REF predicate. The first argument is *biotransformation* and the second is *transformation*. Thus:

S1: P1 (REF BIOTRANSFORMATION TRANSFORMATION)

There are no modifiers to this P1 proposition but one of the arguments is modified: the noun *transformation* is described as *chemical transformation* and so:

P2 (MOD TRANSFORMATION CHEMICAL)

Now the main clause is fully represented:

S1: P1 (REF BIOTRANSFORMATION TRANSFORMATION)
     P2 (MOD TRANSFORMATION CHEMICAL)

The subordinate clause can be broken down into a list of sub-clauses, all of whose verb is *cause*. The first sub-clause is "that causes the inactivation of drugs." The subject of the verb is the relative pronoun *that* which represents *transformation*. *Inactivation* is the object of the verb and the simplest way to represent the phrase *inactivation of drugs* is to use OF as the predicate (see Sec. 4.5).

P3 (CAUSE TRANSFORMATION INACTIVATION)
P4 (OF INACTIVATION DRUG)

The second sub-clause is "that causes . . . the detoxification of environmental pollutants." This is represented in a similar way to the first sub-clause except that an extra proposition must be added to represent the modification of *pollutant*.

P5 (CAUSE TRANSFORMATION DETOXIFICATION)
P6 (OF DETOXIFICATION POLLUTANT)
P7 (MOD POLLUTANT ENVIRONMENTAL)

The last sub-clause is itself a compound, containing a main and a relative clause. The main clause "that causes the deactivation of chemicals" is similar to the sub-clauses already propositionalized:

P8 (CAUSE TRANSFORMATION DEACTIVATION)
P9 (OF DEACTIVATION CHEMICAL)

In the relative clause, "that can cause cancer," the subject, *that*, refers to *chemicals* and so CHEMICAL will be the first argument of any verb propositions. The first verb is *can* which is represented by ABLE-TO with another proposition as second argument:

P10 (ABLE-TO CHEMICAL P11)

The second verb is *cause* and what the chemicals are able to do is to cause cancer. Thus:

P11 (CAUSE CHEMICAL CANCER)

So the final propositionalization of this sentence:

S1: P1 (REF BIOTRANSFORMATION TRANSFORMATION)
     P2 (MOD TRANSFORMATION CHEMICAL)
     P3 (CAUSE TRANSFORMATION INACTIVATION)
     P4 (OF INACTIVATION DRUG)
     P5 (CAUSE TRANSFORMATION DETOXIFICATION)
     P6 (OF DETOXIFICATION POLLUTANT)
     P7 (MOD POLLUTANT ENVIRONMENTAL)
     P8 (CAUSE TRANSFORMATION DEACTIVATION)
     P9 (OF DEACTIVATION CHEMICAL)
     P10 (ABLE-TO CHEMICAL P11)
     P11 (CAUSE CHEMICAL CANCER)

The second sentence is:

S2:Biotransformation of harmful agents involves an oxidation reaction which is mediated by complex enzymes, and if this process does not take place, a drug entering the body may act indefinitely.

Reading through this sentence it becomes clear that this is a compound sentence where two sentences have been combined into one by use of the *and*. This is not a logical *and* and so is not propositionalized as a connective. It seems easiest to treat the sub-sentences separately and the first is:

S2A:Biotransformation of harmful agents involves an oxidation reaction which is mediated by complex enzymes.

Here we have a main and a subordinate clause. In the main clause, the verb is *involve* whose subject is *biotransformation* and whose object is *reaction*. Thus:

S2:P1 (INVOLVE BIOTRANSFORMATION REACTION)

There are no modifiers to this proposition but both of the arguments are modified. The first argument is modified by *of harmful agents*. As in the first sentence this *of* phrase is a little unusual and the predicate used here is OF.

P2 (OF BIOTRANSFORMATION AGENT)

The second argument of P2 is modified and is most neatly represented next, to keep it separate from modifications to the second argument of P1.

P3 (MOD AGENT HARMFUL)

The second argument of P1, REACTION, is modified by an adjectival clause, "which is mediated by complex enzymes," and by the noun *oxidation* used as an adjective. The modification by *oxidation* comes first in the text and so:

P4 (MOD REACTION OXIDATION)

In the adjectival clause, the pronoun *which* represents *reaction* and the verb here is *mediate*. The verb is in passive form and the logical subject is *enzyme* since it is enzymes that are doing the mediating. What they are mediating is the reaction:

P5 (MEDIATE ENZYME REACTION)

ENZYME is modified by *complex*:

P6 (MOD ENZYME COMPLEX)

The second sub-sentence of the second sentence is:

S2B:If this process does not take place, a drug entering the body may act indefinitely.

Here there are two clauses joined by the conditional connective IF. The IF proposition is the highest level proposition and so is represented first. The appropriate arguments can be filled in later.

P7 (IF P? P?)

The first clause is "this process does not take place." The verb here is *take place* and can most simply be represented by the predicate TAKE-PLACE. The subject of this verb is *process* and the verb does not take a second argument.

P8 (TAKE-PLACE PROCESS)

This proposition is negated:

P9 (NEGATE P8)

The argument of P8, PROCESS, is modified by *this*. What is *this process*? Looking at the first sub-sentence, it seems that *this process* refers to *biotransformation* and therefore means *the process is biotransformation* which is a "NOUN is NOUN" construction. *Process* is not a member of the set of things called *biotransformation,* so ISA is not correct here. *The process is biotransformation* does seem to say that *process* is the same thing, the same referent, as *biotransformation* and so REF should be used.

P10 (REF PROCESS BIOTRANSFORMATION)

The second clause is "a drug entering the body may act indefinitely." The main verb is a double construction *may act* whose subject is *drug*. *May* is represented using POSSIBLE:

P11 (MOD P12 POSSIBLE)

What is possible is that drugs act:

P12 (ACT DRUG)

This proposition is modified by *indefinitely*. *Indefinitely* here expresses some period of time and so MOD is not used. Since *indefinitely* is not a particular point in time, TIME is inappropriate and DURATION-OF should be used.

P13 (DURATION-OF P12 INDEFINITE)

The argument DRUG of P12 is modified by a phrase, *entering the body,* which uses the participle *entering*. Participles can be represented by the predicate of the verb of which they are a part, in this case ENTER. What is doing the entering is a drug, and what is being entered is the body, so:

P14 (ENTER DRUG BODY)

Now we can return to P7 and fill in the correct arguments to the IF connective. Interpreting the connective as between the arguments, the representation will be of *drugs may act IF the process does not take place.*

P7 (IF P11 P9)

S2: P1 (INVOLVE BIOTRANSFORMATION REACTION)
     P2 (OF BIOTRANSFORMATION AGENT)
     P3 (MOD AGENT HARMFUL)
     P4 (MOD REACTION OXIDATION)
     P5 (MEDIATE ENZYME REACTION)
     P6 (MOD ENZYME COMPLEX)
     P7 (IF P11 P9)
     P8 (TAKE-PLACE PROCESS)
     P9 (NEGATE P8)
     P10 (REF PROCESS BIOTRANSFORMATION)
     P11 (MOD P12 POSSIBLE)
     P12 (ACT DRUG)
     P13 (DURATION-OF P12 INDEFINITE)
     P14 (ENTER DRUG BODY)

The third sentence is:

S3: Biotransformation defends the body against the effects of toxins and is
carried out in the liver.

Here there are two clauses linked by *and,* but once again this is not a logical
connective and the *and* is not represented. The clauses should be considered
separately, and the first is:

S3A: Biotransformation defends the body against the effects of toxins.

The verb is *defends* and its subject is *biotransformation,* its object *body.*
Defend normally takes the preposition *against* but this will not be included as
part of the verb here, in order to avoid a three-argument verb.

S3: P1 (DEFEND BIOTRANSFORMATION BODY)
     P2 (AGAINST P1 EFFECT)

The effect of toxins is a straightforward POSSESS:

    P3 (POSSESS TOXIN EFFECT)

The second clause is:

S3B: (biotransformation) is carried out in the liver.

Here the verb is *carry-out* in passive form, where the surface subject *biotransformation* is the logical object, and there is no logical subject supplied to fill the first argument of the verb.

P4 (CARRY-OUT $ BIOTRANSFORMATION)

This proposition is modified by a prepositional phrase of location:

P5 (IN P4 LIVER)

S3: P1 (DEFEND BIOTRANSFORMATION BODY)
     P2 (AGAINST P1 EFFECT)
     P3 (POSSESS TOXIN EFFECT)
     P4 (CARRY-OUT $ BIOTRANSFORMATION)
     P5 (IN P4 LIVER)

The fourth sentence:

S4: The liver, weighing three pounds in the human adult, is the largest organ in the body and performs diverse functions.

Here, once again, there is a non-logical *and* connecting two separate clauses. The first clause is:

S4A: The liver, weighing three pounds in the human adult, is the largest organ in the body.

The main verb is *is*. The relationship between *liver* and *organ* is clearly an ISA relationship: *liver* is a member of the class *organ*.

S4: P1 (ISA LIVER ORGAN)

Both arguments to this proposition are modified, the first, *liver,* by *weighing three pounds in the human adult. Weighing* is a participle represented by the predicate WEIGH. WEIGH can be used in two quite different ways: for example, "I weighed the cat. The cat weighs six pounds." The first sentence here shows *weigh* with a simple structure: (WEIGH I CAT). In the second, the cat is not doing the weighing although *cat* is the surface subject. This is the same use of *weigh* as in *the liver weighs three pounds*. One way to represent this is to use AMOUNT-OF:

P2 (WEIGH $ LIVER)
P3 (AMOUNT-OF P2 POUND)
P4 (NUMBER-OF POUND THREE)

Another way to represent this is to consider WEIGH as a two-argument verb that as two possible structures: WEIGH SUBJECT OBJECT or WEIGH SUBJECT AMOUNT. Inspection of the proposition would be needed to determine which structure was being used. Thus:

P2 (WEIGH LIVER POUND)
P3 (NUMBER-OF POUND THREE)

For scoring recall protocols, this second method is simpler and, in some ways, it seems more natural to consider the liver weighing some pounds as being a single proposition.

In the human adult is straightforward enough:

P4 (IN P2 ADULT)
P5 (MOD ADULT HUMAN)

Note that P4 here assumes that the second method of propositionalizing *weighing three pounds* was used. If it had been the first, then the two propositions would be labeled P5 and P6, and P5 would be (IN LIVER ADULT).

The modification of *organ* is the superlative *largest* represented by a MOD proposition:

P6 (MOD ORGAN LARGEST)

This is modified by a prepositional phrase of location: *in the body*.

P7 (IN P6 BODY)

The second clause in this sentence is very simple:

S4B: (the liver) performs diverse functions.

P8 (PERFORM LIVER FUNCTION)
P9 (MOD FUNCTION DIVERSE)

S4:   P1 (ISA LIVER ORGAN)
P2 (WEIGH LIVER POUND)
P3 (NUMBER-OF POUND THREE)
P4 (IN P2 ADULT)
P5 (MOD ADULT HUMAN)
P6 (MOD ORGAN LARGEST)
P7 (IN P6 BODY)
P8 (PERFORM LIVER FUNCTION)
P9 (MOD FUNCTION DIVERSE)

The fifth sentence is:

S5: Through the large portal vein of the liver passes all the blood that has absorbed digested food and other substances from the intestines.

Here there is a main clause and a compound subordinate clause. In the main clause, "Through the large portal vein of the liver passes all the blood," the main verb, at first glance, is *pass* whose subject is *blood*. However, what the blood is doing is passing through a vein and so the predicate is PASS-THROUGH:

S5:   P1 (PASS-THROUGH BLOOD VEIN)
       P2 (AMOUNT-OF BLOOD ALL)

Vein is modified by both *large* and *portal* and by *of the liver*.

       P3 (MOD VEIN PORTAL)
       P4 (MOD VEIN LARGE)
       P5 (POSSESS LIVER VEIN)

The subordinate clause, "that has absorbed digested food and other substances from the intestines," once again has a non-logical *and*. *That* represents *blood* and is the logical subject of the verb *absorb*.

       P6 (ABSORB BLOOD FOOD)

From the intestines modifies this proposition and so:

       P7 (FROM P6 INTESTINE)

Food is modified by *digested*:

       P8 (MOD FOOD DIGESTED)

The second predicate proposition is:

       P9 (ABSORB BLOOD SUBSTANCE)

The prepositional phrase also applies to this proposition:

       P10 (FROM P9 INTESTINE)

Substance is modified by *other* and this can be represented by a MOD proposition:

P11 (MOD SUBSTANCE OTHER)

When the meaning of *other* in this context is examined, it seems that *other* is being used as a disguised comparative and that what is really being said here is *substances other than food*;

P11 (OTHER-THAN SUBSTANCE FOOD)

Either way the meaning is clear.

S5:   P1 (PASS-THROUGH BLOOD VEIN)
       P2 (AMOUNT-OF BLOOD ALL)
       P3 (MOD VEIN PORTAL)
       P4 (MOD VEIN LARGE)
       P5 (POSSESS LIVER VEIN)
       P6 (ABSORB BLOOD FOOD)
       P7 (FROM P6 INTESTINE)
       P8 (MOD FOOD DIGESTED)
       P9 (ABSORB BLOOD SUBSTANCE)
       P10 (FROM P9 INTESTINE)
       P11 (MOD SUBSTANCE OTHER)

6.0   USE OF PROPOSITIONAL ANALYSIS IN EXPERIMENTS

6.1 Scoring Recall Protocols

The scoring methods usually used in the propositional framework involve all-or-none scoring; a proposition is counted either as recalled, or as not recalled. No partial credit is given.

Consistency in scoring is the most important aspect of scoring from the experimenter's point of view. Hence, scoring of subject recall protocols demands that criteria be established so that scoring is consistent. Criteria can be strict, allowing only close reproductions of propositions, or they can be liberal, or "gist," scoring. Our experience is that strict scoring is much easier to perform and results in more consistency than liberal scoring. Most of the time, we have seen little difference in the patterns of effects appearing under the two criteria, so strict scoring appears to be the best approach. However, it is important to keep in mind that strict scoring is very sensitive to similarities in the surface form between the recall protocol and the to-be-recalled text. Scorings of intermediate degrees of strictness and liberality can also be done, although there seems to be no advantage in doing so.

Strict scoring can be defined as giving credit for a proposition only when it is closely reproduced in the protocol. Because subjects rarely produce protocols that are word for word exactly like the original text, some degree of latitude in interpretation is necessary. However, such latitude must be defined and limited or the scoring will no longer be strict. Thus, what we mean by ''close reproduction'' is that the proposition must be reproduced in the protocol exactly or by a close synonym, but care must be taken to ensure that the synonyms accepted really are close. One way to define a close synonym would be to use dictionary definitions. Thus, *hepatic portal vein* would be a strict reproduction of *portal vein of the liver* since, by definition, *hepatic* means *of the liver*.

Guidelines must also be established for dealing with embedded propositions. In strict scoring credit is given only for propositions that have other propositions as arguments if the proposition in the argument position is also present in the protocol.

Liberal scoring can be of several degrees of liberality. We have found a very liberal set of criteria to be the most useful form of liberal scoring. Our criterion is to give credit for those propositions either explicitly present, or directly implied by the protocol. By directly implied, we mean ''what propositions must the subject have had in memory in order to say what was said in the protocol?'' This obviously will result in an extremely subjective scoring, although this is a problem with all liberal scorings. If the scorings are done blind to any experimental manipulations, and efforts are made by scorers to be consistent across subjects and passages, then this subjective quality should not be a problem. However, clearly there will be more ''noise'' in a liberal scoring than in a strict, and so effects will not be as clean and clear-cut. If the level of recall is so low that there is a floor effect with strict scoring, the liberal scoring may be useful.

6.2 Example Protocols and Scoring

The actual recall protocols shown in Table 12.2 are from the passage propositionalized earlier (see Sec. 5.2, Table 12.1). A scoring of these protocols for both strict and liberal criteria is shown in Table 12.3. Some points of scoring policy can be illustrated using these examples.

For Subject 1 on the strict scoring, credit was given for only two propositions, S1:P11 and S2:P10. The protocol is not very close to the original, unlike Subject 2 for instance, so this low score is not surprising. The proposition S2:P10 is obviously credited for *Biotransformation is the process.* S1:P11 was credited because *carcinogenic* was judged to mean *cancer causing* and *substance* was acceptable as a synonym for *chemical.* A case could be made that *carcinogenic* means *able to cause cancer* and that P10 should therefore have been given credit for as well. However, the strict decision not to do so was applied consistently to all subjects, and so this problem is not important.

TABLE 12.2
Example Recall Protocols

Subject 1:
Biotransformation is the process by which your body rids itself from various unneeded foods, toxins and carcinogenic substances. The food, toxin, or whatever, goes through your liver from your large intestine where it is further cleaned and then expelled or utilized. The liver is your largest . . .

Subject 2:
The liver (at about three pounds in the adult human) is the largest organ in the human body. The portal vein carries all the blood that contains digested food from the intestines to the liver. Biotransformation is the enzymatic process by which toxins and environmental pollutants are detoxified in the body. Without this process, many toxins would remain in their toxic state.

Subject 3:
The liver processes all the blood in the body. It serves many purposes, one of which is to break down the chemical form of toxic materials. This is done through an oxidation reaction known as biotransformation. If biotransformation did not occur many noxious substances would remain in the bloodstream indefinitely.

Notice that S5:P7 and P11 were not given credit for Subject 1 in the strict scoring. This is because the embedded proposition could not be given credit for on the strict scoring.

A point that is not fully illustrated in these examples is the treatment of arguments of REF and ISA propositions. REF means SAME-AS and the two arguments are therefore equivalent. Thus, any propositions using one argument are synonymous with similar propositions using the other. It was decided to give credit for these on the strict scoring only if the REF proposition was explicit in

TABLE 12.3
Scoring of Example Recall Protocols

			Criterion					
			Strict			*Liberal*		
Proposition		*Subject*	*1*	*2*	*3*	*1*	*2*	*3*
S1:	P1	(REF BIOTRANSFORMATION TRANSFORMATION)						
	P2	(MOD TRANSFORMATION CHEMICAL)						
	P3	(CAUSE TRANSFORMATION INACTIVATION)						
	P4	(OF INACTIVATION DRUG)						
	P5	(CAUSE TRANSFORMATION DETOXIFICATION)		X			X	
	P6	(OF DETOXIFICATION POLLUTANT)		X			X	
	P7	(MOD POLLUTANT ENVIRONMENTAL)		X			X	
	P8	(CAUSE TRANSFORMATION DEACTIVATION)				X		
	P9	(OF DEACTIVATION CHEMICAL)				X		

(continued)

TABLE 12.3 *(Continued)*

Proposition	Subject	Strict			Liberal		
		1	*2*	*3*	*1*	*2*	*3*
P10	(ABLE-TO CHEMICAL P11)						
P11	(CAUSE CHEMICAL CANCER)	X			X		
S2: P1	(INVOLVE BIOTRANSFORMATION REACTION)					X	
P2	(OF BIOTRANSFORMATION AGENT)						
P3	(MOD AGENT HARMFUL)						
P4	(MOD REACTION OXIDATION)			X			X
P5	(MEDIATE ENZYME REACTION)					X	
P6	(MOD ENZYME COMPLEX)						
P7	(IF P11 P9)					X	X
P8	(TAKE-PLACE PROCESS)		X			X	X
P9	(NEGATE P8)		X			X	X
P10	(REF PROCESS BIOTRANSFORMATION)	X	X		X	X	X
P11	(MOD P12 POSSIBLE)					X	
P12	(ACT DRUG)						X
P13	(DURATION-OF P12 INDEFINITE)					X	X
P14	(ENTER DRUG BODY)						X
S3: P1	(DEFEND BIOTRANSFORMATION BODY)						
P2	(AGAINST P1 EFFECT)						
P3	(POSSESS TOXIN EFFECT)						
P4	(CARRY-OUT $ BIOTRANSFORMATION)						
P5	(IN P4 LIVER)						
S4: P1	(IS A LIVER ORGAN)		X			X	
P2	(WEIGH LIVER POUND)		X			X	
P3	(NUMBER-OF POUND THREE)		X			X	
P4	(IN P2 ADULT)		X			X	
P5	(MOD ADULT HUMAN)		X			X	
P6	(MOD ORGAN LARGEST)		X		X	X	
P7	(IN P6 BODY)		X			X	
P8	(PERFORM LIVER FUNCTION)			X			X
P9	(MOD FUNCTION DIVERSE)			X			X
S5: P1	(PASS-THROUGH BLOOD VEIN)		X		X	X	X
P2	(AMOUNT-OF BLOOD ALL)		X	X		X	X
P3	(MOD VEIN PORTAL)		X			X	
P4	(MOD VEIN LARGE)						
P5	(POSSESS LIVER VEIN)					X	X
P6	(ABSORB BLOOD FOOD)		X		X	X	
P7	(FROM P6 INTESTINE)		X		X	X	
P8	(MOD FOOD DIGESTED)		X			X	
P9	(ABSORB BLOOD SUBSTANCE)				X		
P10	(FROM P9 INTESTINE)				X		
P11	(MOD SUBSTANCE OTHER)				X		
	Total:	2	19	4	11	25	13

TABLE 12.4
ISA Propositions in Recall
Scoring

Text:
The corona, a hot gas, produces the solar wind.
P1 (PRODUCE CORONA SOLAR-WIND)
P2 (ISA CORONA GAS)
P3 (MOD GAS HOT)
Protocols:
Subject 1:   The hot corona, which is a gas, produces
               the solar wind.
Subject 2:   The corona is a hot gas and the gas
               produces the solar wind.

the protocol. Thus, Subject 3 did not get credit for *biotransformation did not occur* because the text has *the process did not take place,* and the (REF PROCESS BIOTRANSFORMATION) proposition is not in the protocol. Of course, in the liberal scoring credit could be given for this.

ISA is treated differently from REF. Here the first argument is a member of the class defined by the second. If the ISA relationship is explicit in the protocol, it seems reasonable to decide that propositions about the second argument are also about the first: that is, propositions about a class apply to individual members of that class. The reverse is not, however, true: propositions that apply to a member of a class may not apply to the class itself.

This passage, as already shown, provides a good illustration of the treatment of REF but not, as it happens, of ISA. But an example can be given from another text and is shown in Table 12.4. Subject 1 would get credit for all three propositions, while Subject 2 would only get credit for P2 and P3.

6.3 Propositional Analysis for "Main Idea" Experiments

In our "main idea" experiments, subjects were asked to summarize a paragraph-length passage as a single, brief (80 characters), complete sentence stating the main idea of the passage. We then studied how the content of these responses varied with manipulations of the presented passages, which typically involved two versions of the same body of material. The method basically consists of propositionalizing the responses, making them as similar as possible, and then separating the responses according to the original version and comparing the two resulting sets of response propositions. Since the process is done blind to which version the subject saw, the method results in a rigorous comparison of the response content.

6.3.1 *Subject Response Propositionalization.*   Because the goal of this propositionalizing of responses is different from propositionalizing texts for use in recall experiments, the method is also somewhat different. We analyze responses in two steps. The first step consists of propositionalizing the responses, and the second of reducing the number of unique or idiosyncratic response representations by finding synonymous propositions and arguments, grouping them together and replacing each member of the group with a group label. Because propositionalizing subject responses is the first of the two steps, the propositionalization can be much more surface oriented and so much easier to perform than recall text propositionalization. Several examples of this surface-oriented response propositionalization have already been given in this report. Experience shows that it is much faster and more effective to propositionalize in this way, leaving differences in expression to be ironed out by the ''synonymization'' process. Sometimes, too, it is almost impossible to decide what a subject meant, and a noncommittal surface propositionalization is the safest method of dealing with this.

For example, consider:

Ex 1: The Battle of Jutland was slight and worthy only of retreat.

The first clause of this response is easy to propositionalize but in the second, *worthy of retreat* presents a difficult problem to unravel. The simple surface oriented representation is adequate for this type of analysis.

P3 (WORTHY-OF BATTLE RETREAT)
P4 (MOD P3 ONLY)

Another example is:

Ex 2: The superb practice force of any item may fail.

This response, surprisingly enough, was made to the same passage as the first example, a passage about the Battle of Jutland in World War I. One can guess at what the subject might have had in mind; the passage talks about how the Germans had practiced certain maneuvers that enabled them to extricate themselves from the danger posed by a greatly inferior tactical position during the battle. The passage also states that despite some success for the Germans in the battle, their fleet never again left harbor and so the battle must be considered a defeat for them. Knowing this background information certainly helps to understand the sort of lines the subject might have been thinking along. But it does not provide enough information to know what *item* is supposed to represent, for people. We simply propositionalized this response in a literal, surface fashion.

Ex 2: P1 (MOD P2 POSSIBLE)
       P2 (FAIL FORCE)
       P3 (MOD FORCE SUPERB)
       P4 (MOD FORCE PRACTICE)
       P5 (POSSESS ITEM FORCE)
       P6 (MOD ITEM ANY)

One very useful procedure to follow during the propositionalization step is to observe and keep in mind obvious synonyms. When there are several ways to propositionalize a particular phrase, one should be chosen that will make the structure of similar phrases easily comparable. Then the second step of finding synonyms will be greatly simplified. For example:

Ex 1: A variety of purposes.
       P1 (MOD PURPOSE VARIETY-OF)

Ex 2: Various purposes.
       P1 (MOD PURPOSE VARIOUS)

There are several ways to propositionalize Example 1, but the best would be one similar to that used for Example 2, as shown. The second step would then consist simply of noting that *variety-of* and *various* were synonyms and replacing them with a single term.

Another example is:

Ex 3: Many cultures.
       P1 (NUMBER-OF CULTURE MANY)

Ex 4: A lot of civilizations.
       P1 (NUMBER-OF CIVILIZATION A-LOT)

Another good example of propositionalizing in order to make similarities and synonyms more obvious is to be found earlier in this report. (See Sec. 3.4.4).

6.3.2 *"Synonymizing" Subject Main Idea Responses.*   In our method, after subject main idea responses are propositionalized, the proposition lists for the subjects are entered onto a computer. A program written in the LISP programming language processes these lits and produces a list showing predicates, arguments and propositions listed in order of frequency of occurrence for the whole set of data. These predicates, arguments and propositions are then compared and when synonyms are found all members of a synonym group are replaced by a group label. Copies of the LISP program can be obtained by writing to David E. Kieras, Department of Psychology, University of Arizona, Tucson, AZ 85721.

For example, one passage we used was about a performer's ability to control tone and pitch on different keyboard instruments. In the argument list, four subjects used the argument PERFORMER, five used PLAYER and one used PERSON. It was judged that all three of these arguments were synonymous. Because the passage itself used *performer,* every occurrence of PERFORMER, PLAYER and PERSON in the proposition lists was replaced by &PERFORMER. The ''&'' shows that this is a group label and a record was kept of which original arguments belonged to this group.

A similar process is used for predicates and also for propositions. Particularly for propositions, and to a lesser extent for predicates, reference to the subject's original proposition list may have to be made. This is because it is not always clear exactly what a subject means, or whether two propositions are synonyms, just by examining an isolated proposition.

For example, the predicates ON and POSSESS do not seem to be likely synonyms but when the subject's proposition list contained (ON EXPRESSIVENESS PIANO) it seemed reasonable to consider this a synonym of (POSSESS PIANO EXPRESSIVENESS). Similarly, (AS-REFINED-AS CLAVICHORD PIANO) and (MORE-SOPHISTICATED-THAN PIANO CLAVICHORD) are not obviously synonymous but the original responses from which they were derived seemed to be:

Ex 1: The clavichord is not as refined as the piano.

Ex 2: The piano is more sophisticated than the clavichord.

These responses really seemed to say the same thing in different ways, and so (MORE-SOPHISTICATED-THAN PIANO CLAVICHORD) was used for both subjects.

Now that the principles for our synonymizing process have been described, a procedure will be outlined.

Step 1: List all predicates, arguments, and propositions with LISP program.

Step 2: Synonymize predicates and arguments.

Step 3: List all predicates, arguments, and propositions in synonymized list with LISP program.

Step 4: Correct oversights in predicates and arguments.

Step 5: Synonymize propositions.

Step 6: Produce final version of list with LISP program.

Synonymizing the propositions is done only after step 4 because working with the propositions can be difficult enough, especially if there is a large number of subjects. This difficulty is reduced by not having to waste time working on a proposition only to discover that a change in predicates would have changed it anyway. This is an important consideration when there can be 400 different original propositions to be examined.

To further simplify the data, steps 1 through 5 can be done twice; the first time using strict criteria for synonymity and the second time using liberal ones. The number of different terms will be considerably reduced after using the liberal criterion, which makes the data much simpler to work with.

After the synonymization is complete, the same LISP program is used to produce lists broken out by different experimental conditions. The lists can then be compared and differences between conditions noted.

ACKNOWLEDGMENT

The work summarized in this paper was supported by the Office of Naval Research, Personnel and Training Research Programs, under Contract Number N00014-78-C-0509, NR 157-423.

REFERENCES

Bovair, S., & Kieras, D. E. *A guide to propositional analysis for research on technical prose.* Technical Report No. 8, University of Arizona, July, 1981.

Kintsch, W. *The representation of meaning in memory.* Hillsdale, N.J.: Lawrence Erlbaum Associates, 1974.

Turner, A., & Greene, E. *The construction and use of a propositional text base.* Institute for the Study of Intellectual Behavior, Technical Report No. 63, University of Colorado, April, 1977.

13 How to Construct Conceptual Graph Structures

Arthur C. Graesser
Sharon M. Goodman

California State University, Fullerton

The purpose of this chapter is to describe how to construct conceptual graph structures using Graesser's representational system. In Part 1 of this book, we provided an overview of the representational system and how the system has been integrated with research and theory. The present chapter should be helpful to researchers who want a more detailed understanding of the representational system.

What is a conceptual graph structure? In our representational theory, a conceptual graph structure consists of a set of labeled statement nodes that are interrelated by a network of labeled, directed arcs. Conceptual graph structures may be used to represent specific passages and also schemas that embody generic knowledge about the physical world and social world. A conceptual graph structure for a passage includes implicit knowledge in addition to explicit information. Thus, the information in a graph structure for a passage includes n explicit statement nodes plus m distinct inferences. As described in Part 1, the inferences may be extracted empirically by using a question-answering method (see also Graesser, 1981; Graesser, Robertson, & Anderson, 1981).

In the studies that have been conducted so far, conceptual graph structures have been useful for representing knowledge at a meaningful, conceptual level. Conceptual graph structures capture conceptual connectivity, but not sequential connectivity for statements in text, i.e., the order in which statements are mentioned and certain surface structure regularities. The graph structures also do not capture pragmatic knowledge that exists between the writer and reader or between the speaker and listener. It is presently an open question whether the proposed representational framework can be expanded to incorporate regularities in sequential coherence and pragmatic coherence.

The construction of a conceptual graph structure includes three major steps, which are summarized below.

1. Segment information into statement nodes
2. Assign each statement node to a node category
3. Interrelate nodes by labeled, directed arcs.

Generally speaking, step 1 is completed before step 2 and step 2 is completed before step 3. However, it is good practice to have some idea of how information will be categorized (step 2) and structured (step 3) during the segmentation phase (step 1). Similarly, it is a good practice to have some idea of how statements will be structured (step 3) during the categorization phase (step 2). It is hoped that this chapter will clarify how each of the three steps is completed.

SEGMENTING INFORMATION INTO STATEMENT NODES

A statement node is a conceptual unit rather than a linguistic unit. A statement node represents a single idea that corresponds to a state, an event, a process, or an action. A statement node is quite similar to van Dijk's notion of a FACT node (van Dijk, 1980).

It is informative to compare statement nodes with propositions. Propositions denote states, events, and facts about other propositions. A proposition contains a predicate, one or more arguments, and a modality. Arguments are specific entities, concepts, and indices that are relevant to a passage or knowledge domain. Arguments include persons, objects, parts of objects, locations, points in time, ideas, and embedded propositions. Predicates operate as functions that ascribe properties to arguments or that interrelate arguments. Predicates include verbs, adverbs, adjectives, prepositions, nouns, and certain combinations of these lexical items. The modality of a proposition includes a variety of indices, such as truth value and topicalization.

The number and types of arguments in a proposition depend on what the predicate is. Case structure grammars in linguistics (Fillmore, 1968; Stockwell, Schachter, & Partee, 1973) have provided many critical insights about the categorization of verb predicates. Verb predicates may be categorized according to their arguments' *case roles,* i.e., agent, object, patient, instrument, location, time, source, goal, and also according to which arguments are obligatory versus optional. Obligatory arguments must be specified whereas optional arguments need not be. The examples below include the obligatory arguments for different verb predicates.

X *cries*
X *sleeps*
X *hits* Y

X *finds* Y
X *put* Y *on* Z
X *gives* Y *to* Z
Prepositions have two or three obligatory arguments.

X is *in* Y
X is *by* Y
X is *between* Y and Z
Adjectives have one obligatory argument.

X is *red*
X is *funny*
Comparative adjectives have two obligatory arguments.

X is *greater than* Y
X is *equal to* Y
X is *sloppier than* Y
In most propositional analyses, the arguments are usually enclosed in parentheses to the right of the predicate, as shown below.

cry (X)
find (X, Y)
put on (X, Y, Z)
red (X)
greater than (X, Y)
soldier (X)
toy (X)

In addition to the obligatory arguments, there are a number of optional arguments and indices that are part of virtually any proposition. For example, propositions are bounded by time and location indices; a proposition is true for a specific time span and in a specific world and location. Actions and events may occur in a specific manner, e.g., *X occurs quickly*. The indices of time, location, manner, and the optional arguments are specified when there is another proposition that serves as a modifier of the proposition.

Sometimes an argument may be an embedded proposition. For example, the *people knew that wagons were sturdy* involves an embedded proposition, *wagon is sturdy,* plus a proposition that has the embedded proposition as an argument, *people know PROP.*

Some example propositional analyses are provided below. There are a number of references available for further discussions of propositional analyses (Anderson, 1976; Clark & Clark, 1977; Graesser, 1981; van Dijk, 1980).

People developed the wagon.

  Proposition 1: develop (A1,X1)
  Proposition 2: people (A1)
  Proposition 3: wagon (X1)
Wheels rolled on the surface.

  Proposition 1: roll (X1,L1)
   (Note: L1 is a specific location)

Proposition 2: wheel (X1)
Proposition 3: is on (L1,X2)
Proposition 4: surface (X2)
The base of the tree is round.
Proposition 1: is round (X1)
Proposition 2: base (X1)
Proposition 3: HAS (X2, X1)
Proposition 4: tree (X2)
People wanted to transport possessions.
Proposition 1: want (A1, Proposition 2)
Proposition 2: transport (A1,X1)
Proposition 3: people (A1)
Proposition 4: possessions (X1)

A statement node refers to a state, event, process, or action and consists of one or more proposition nodes. Thus, there are usually more propositions than statement nodes. The reader may wonder why we are adopting statement nodes as our basic unit of analysis rather than propositions. The primary reason is that statement nodes seem to be more natural units for text analysis than propositions. Some other researchers have arrived at similar conclusions (Chafe, 1980; Van Dijk, 1980). The conceptualizations conveyed in statement nodes are usually self-contained, complete thoughts; most propositions are fragmentary ideas that cannot be interpreted without other propositions. Statement nodes have proven to be quite functional in our research that has analyzed the symbolic mechanisms in comprehension and question answering. It would have been difficult to discover the symbolic procedures involved in question answering if we had selected propositions as our unit of analysis. Thus, we found it easier to detect systematic patterns in symbolic structures and procedures when adopting statement nodes. Propositional structures are usually too cluttered to detect these patterns. We have also found that moderately trained judges can segment protocols into statement nodes more readily and reliably than they segment protocols into propositions. In order to segment protocols into propositions, the judges must be aware of many esoteric issues; many of these issues are circumvented when statement nodes are adopted as a unit of analysis.

How do propositions map onto statement nodes? We have identified most of the mapping rules but not all of the rules. Listed below are some critical rules and guidelines for combining propositions into statement nodes.

1. *Nouns as Referring Expressions.*   Some propositions have nouns as predicates. Such propositions refer to persons, objects, locations, concepts, and classes of entities or concepts. For example, consider the propositional analysis below.

People put boxes on axles.
Proposition 1: put on (X1,X2,X3)
Proposition 2: people (X1)

Proposition 3: boxes (X2)
Proposition 4: axles (X3)

Propositions 2, 3, and 4 are referential propositions with nouns as predicates. The nouns ascribe properties to the specific entities, X1, X2, and X3. Propositions 2, 3, and 4 would not be counted as separate statement nodes. Thus, *People put boxes on axles* is only one statement node. This rule has also been adopted by several researchers who adopt propositions as a unit of analysis (Kieras, 1981; Kintsch, 1974; Miller & Kintsch, 1980).

2. *Quantifiers.*   Quantifiers are not counted as separate statement nodes unless the quantifiers are specific numbers. For example, each of the following sentences has only one statement node.

Many people put boxes between wheels.
Some wheels are round.
All wagons had wheels.

Separate statement nodes are not created from quantifiers such as *some, many, all*. Similarly, separate statement nodes are not created to distinguish singular (*box*) from plural (*boxes*), or to distinguish single entities from classes or collections (*crowd*). In principle, however, the proposed representational system could accommodate such distinctions.

Quantification may involve a specific number, e.g., *three, 87, 4.7*. In these instances, an additional statement node is normally created. For example, the sentence *the sledges had two wheels* would have the following statement nodes.

Statement Node 1: Sledges had wheels
Statement Node 2: There were two wheels

The fact that separate statement nodes are created from numerical quantifiers but not linguistic quantifiers is admittedly arbitrary. The rule is based upon practical considerations. Specifically, the conceptual graph structure would quickly appear cluttered and congested if each argument of each statement node was quantified with an additional statement node. Moreover, these additional nodes would not functionally improve our conceptual graph structures and symbolic procedures that operate on the graph structures. For those investigators who are not interested in simplicity, non-numerical quantifiers could be represented by creating additional statement nodes.

3. *Adjectives and Prepositional Phrases.*   When an argument is modified by an adjective or a prepositional phrase, an additional statement node is created. For example, there are three statement nodes in the following sentence.

Large wagons with covers hold grain.

Statement Node 1: Wagons hold grain
Statement Node 2: Wagons are large
Statement Node 3: Wagons have covers

However, sometimes there are familiar adjective-noun combinations and expressions with prepositional phrases which operate as a unit. The following expressions are regarded as words.

Middle Ages
once upon a time

4. *Auxiliary Verbs and Tenses.*   Additional nodes are *not* created in order to denote the tense of a state, event, process, or action. Modal verbs denoting necessity, obligation, norms, and negation do not create new propositions. Each sentence below contains only one statement node.

The wheels would not turn.
Sledges could carry more weight.
People needed to carry possessions.
Mothers should protect their children.
Soldiers rarely stay home.

5. *Verbs with Propositional Arguments.*   Some verbs co-occur with an argument that is an embedded proposition. Such verbs involve cognition (*know, believe*), perception (*see, hear*), communication (*tell, ask*), and desire (*want, hope*). The embedded proposition is incorporated with the main proposition in statement nodes referring to a cognition, perception, communication, or desire. For example, each of the following sentences has an embedded proposition, but there is only one statement node.

People wanted to carry the possessions.
The Egyptians knew that wheels were round.
The King told the people to return home.

The embedded propositions may form separate statement nodes if they refer to an existing state, event, process or action, i.e., *the wheels were round* and *the people returned home. The Egyptians knew that the wheel was round* is a different node than *the wheels were round.*

6. *Statement Nodes as Arguments.*   Statement nodes often embellish other statement nodes. When a specific statement node has been created, other nodes

may have an argument that refers to the statement node as a compiled, unit-like idea. For example, suppose that a structure contains the following node.

Wood is solid

Another node may refer to *solid wood* as a unit that satisfies an argument slot, as shown below.

Solid wood rolls best.

The following pair of statement nodes also illustrates how a statement node may be referenced as an argument in another statement.

People pulled sledges.
Pulling sledges was difficult.

The above rules should provide a more detailed impression of how propositions get mapped onto statement nodes. The above rules and guidelines account for over 90% of the statement nodes that we have analyzed. Of course, there are more esoteric rules that we have not described. Sometimes, we rely on our implicit intuitions when segmenting information into statement nodes. Our analytical system can handle many or most passage protocols. However, some excerpts are difficult to segment and the outcomes depend on the intuitions of trained judges. Of course, all available theories of representation are incomplete and therefore blessed with this problem.

NODE CATEGORIES

Each statement node is assigned to one of the following six node categories.

Physical State
Physical Event
Internal State
Internal Event

Goal $\Longleftarrow$
$\begin{array}{l} + \text{ (action)} \\ - \\ ? \end{array}$

Style

A brief description of each node category is presented in Table 5.1 in Part 1 of this book. In the present section we define each node category in more detail.

Physical State Nodes (*PS*).   Physical State nodes refer to ongoing states in the physical or social world. The physical world includes objects, properties of objects, people, properties of people, spatial information, and relationships among objects, people, and locations. The statements below are physical states.

> Wheels were round.
> Egyptians were strong.
> Axles have one wheel on each side.
> Tools were electric.

These states would remain constant throughout the passage. Physical States also include static facts about the social world, as shown below.

> The man was the father of the boy.
> Scythians were nomads.
> The psychologist was married.

It would perhaps be appropriate to segregate the physical states from social states. However, such a distinction was not critical in the passages analyzed so far.

Physical State nodes include statements referring to physical abilities or necessities and to social obligations or norms. The following statements are Physical States.

> Sledges could carry more weight than people.
> Balance required several wheels.
> Psychologists are supposed to help people.
> Children should not swim.

Points in time are categorized as Physical States.

> The time was during the Middle Ages.
> The time was 5000 years ago.

Physical States include definitions, classifications, and semantic properties, as shown below.

> Man is an animal.
> A cart is a wagon.
> Carts are made out of wood.

Biological states are Physical State nodes.

The Scythians were hungry.
The disease was chronic.

Physical State nodes include statements referring to the existence of entities and the locations of entities.

There were tools for shaping.
The trees were in the forest.

Physical Event Nodes (PE).   These statement nodes refer to state changes in the physical and social world. Physical Events involve state changes that are not intended by an agent. As a result of some occurrence described in a passage, a state may change. An entity or property of an entity may change from existing to not existing, or from not existing to existing. Physical Events may involve a change in the intensity of a process. The following statements are Physical Events.

Sledges became more mobile.
Sledges came to be off the ground.
Wheels rolled on surfaces.
Scythians became powerful.
The person died.

It is important to point out that context is sometimes needed in order to decide whether a node is a state or event.

Internal State Nodes (IS).   These statements refer to ongoing mental states, emotional states, beliefs, attitudes, and sentiments of a person. The statements below are Internal States.

The Egyptians were intelligent.
The people knew that wheels were round.
The Scythians didn't like boats.

These states reside in the minds of animate beings.

Internal Events (IE).   These statements refer to changes in mental states, emotional states, beliefs, attitudes, and sentiments of animate beings. The statements below are Internal States.

The boy became frustrated.
The man no longer believed in God.
An Egyptian discovered the wagon.

Sometimes changes in knowledge states are accomplished through sense organs.

> The man heard the rumor.
> The child saw the murder.

The sensory organs provide the vehicle for knowledge to be added to the minds of animate beings. Internal Events may include *forgetting, remembering, choosing,* and so on.

Goal Nodes.   Goal statements convey achieved or unachieved desired states. If the Goal is achieved, then the Goal node is coded as a Goal+. If the Goal is not achieved then the Goal is marked as a Goal−. The node is marked a Goal? if it is unknown whether or not a goal is achieved. Intentional actions are categorized as Goal+. The following statement nodes convey intentional actions and are categorized as Goal+.

> People put boxes between wheels.
> People made wheels.
> The Scythians carried possessions.

The following statements reflect Goals that are not achieved and are categorized as Goal−.

> The girl wished she were a princess.
> The boy wanted to become president.

Unachieved Goals often have verbs such as want, desire, wish, hope for.

Actions (Goal+) have both an intentional aspect and a behavioral (Physical Event) aspect. To achieve the goal the agent invokes a plan. The plan involves behavior of some sort. Some verbs specify the behavioral aspect to some extent whereas other verbs do not specify the behavior. Consider the following statement nodes.

> The people moved the possessions.
> The people dragged the possessions.

Dragging specifies the behavior more them *moving* does, even though dragging does not completely specify the behavior.

Style Nodes (S).   Style nodes modify actions (Goal+) or Events, but not States. Style nodes include specification of speed, intensity, quality, and instrumentality.

X occurred quickly.
X did something quickly.
X occurred forcefully.
X did something forcefully.
X moved one foot at a time.
X occurred in circles.
X did something with a knife.

The direction in which something moves is a Style node.

The wheel rolled *toward a cave.*
The ball blew *upward.*

When Style nodes are articulated linguistically, the modified action or event is expressed as an embedded proposition or a gerund, as shown below.

People pulled sledges quickly.
Pulling the sledges was quick.

Temporal constraints may be categorized as Style nodes when two or more actions and events are temporally related.

Event 1 and Event 2 occurred *at the same time.*

ARC CATEGORIES

Listed below are the five categories of labeled, directed arcs.

Reason (R)
Initiate (I)
Manner (M)
Consequence (C)
Property (P)

In Table 5.2 of our chapter in Part 1 we presented a brief definition of these arc categories, along with some examples. In this section we define the arcs and arc constraints in more detail.

Reason Arcs.   Goal nodes may be interrelated by Reason arcs. One goal node is the reason for invoking another Goal. Goal nodes and reason arcs form the heart of goal-oriented conceptualizations. We believe that organized action sequences are mediated by a hierarchical structure of Goal nodes which are interrelated by Reason arcs. Goal 1 is invoked in order to achieve Goal 2; Goal 2 is invoked in order to achieve Goal 3. Instrumental activity and means-end analyses are captured by Goal hierarchies. Consider the three Goal statements below.

Goal 1: Scythians stay alive.
Goal 2: Scythians get food.
Goal 3: Scythians wander over plains.

These Goals are hierarchically ordered with Goal 1 as most superordinate and Goal 3 as most subordinate. The three Goals would be interrelated as follows:

$$R \qquad\qquad R$$
$$<G3> \ ----> \ <G2> \ ----> \ <G1>$$

Thus, it is appropriate to make the following statements.

The Scythians wandered over the plains *in order to* get food.
The Scythians got food *in order to* stay alive.

It is inappropriate to say

The Scythians stayed alive *in order to* get food.
The Scythians got food *in order to* wander over the plains.

The connective *in order to* reveals the direction of the arc. Suppose the following relation exists:

$$R$$
$$<Goal\ n> \ ----> \ <Goal\ m>$$

Then the following derivations would be correct.

Goal n is subordinate to Goal m.
Goal m is superordinate to Goal n.
Goal n *in order to* Goal m.
Goal m *by* Goal n.

In this sense the connective *by* is the inverse of the connective *in order to*.

The Scythians stayed alive by getting food.
The Scythians got food by wandering over the plains.

It would be incorrect to say the following:

The Scythians wandered over the plains by getting food.
The Scythians got food by staying alive.

Reason arcs can only relate Goal nodes. This constraint is captured by rule 1.

$$R$$
Rule 1: $<Goal>$ -----> $<Goal>$

In a strictly hierarchical system, any given Goal node n has at most one superordinate node, i.e., one Reason arc emanating from it in the forward direction. Most of the goal structures that we have analyzed have been strictly hierarchical. However, a few structures have deviated from a strict hierarchy; such deviations occur when a particular Goal node is invoked for two or more independent reasons.

Initiate Arcs.   The Goals of an agent are initiated by states, events, and actions. Initiate arcs link these states, events, and actions to the Goal nodes. Thus, the second rule is shown below.

$$I$$
Rule 2: $<\quad>$ -----> $<Goal>$

Virtually any node can initiate a Goal, except for another Goal node that has as a common agent the Goal that is initiated. At a purely metaphysical level, the states, events, and actions that initiate goals must be internal events and states; information must be in the mind of the agent before the agent can create a goal. Unfortunately, the question-answering protocols often do not elicit these internal states because these internal states are so obvious. Therefore, Physical States, Physical Events, and actions are often directly linked to Goals by Initiate arcs.

In order to provide an example of Initiate arcs, consider the statement nodes below:

PS1: Solid wheels are easy to pull.
PS2: Wood is solid.
G+3: People made wheels out of wood.
G+4: People cut down trees.
PS5: Trees are made out of wood.

These five nodes would be interrelated as follows:

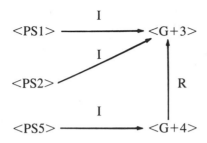

The creation of any given Goal node, G, is based on (1) a Goal that is superordinate to Goal G and (2) a set of initiating statement nodes, which capture the situational context.

Consequence Arcs.   States, events, and actions may lead to other states and events by cause-driven mechanisms. States are needed to enable or disable events. Causal links and enabling links are captured by Consequence arcs. The following rule captures the constraints. (The brackets mean that either of the elements is possible).

$$\text{Rule 3:} \quad < \qquad \overset{C}{\qquad} > \ \text{-----}> \ <\{\text{Event/State}\}>$$

Rule 3 is a general rule permitting any node to lead to a state or event via the Consequence arc. Rule 3 does not capture certain restrictions on causality. For example, internal states and events cannot cause physical states and events because telekinesis is a violation of causality. Also, a set of states cannot alone cause an event; a prior event must occur to initiate the process leading to the event in question. These additional restrictions are not captured in Rule 3 for two reasons. First, the Consequence arc does not mean cause in the strict sense. The comprehender does not always know about the causal mechanisms that actually connect events and states. However, some form of conceptual connectivity is established. Second, subjects do not always articulate all of the knowledge that is part of the functional conceptualization. Sometimes there are conceptual gaps even when the Q/A task is used to tap implicit knowledge.

The Consequence arc is also used to handle logical implication. Sometimes a state can be logically derived from another set of states.

PS1: Wood is solid.
PS2: Wheels are made out of wood.
PS3: Wheels are solid.

PS3 is a logical implication of PS1 and PS2. The three statement nodes would be structured as follows.

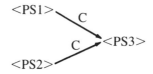

Manner Arcs.   Style nodes modify Goal nodes and event nodes by virtue of the manner arc, as shown in Rule 4 below.

$$\text{Rule 4:} \quad < \left\{ \begin{array}{l} \text{Goal} \\ \text{Event} \end{array} \right\} > \underset{\text{-----}}{\overset{M}{<}} \ <\text{Style}>$$

Consider the statement below.

Goal 1: People pulled sledges.
Style 2: Pulling was by hand.

These two nodes would be related as follows.

$$\overset{M}{<\text{G1}> -----> \ <\text{S2}>}$$

Sometimes two Goal nodes are connected by Manner arcs rather than Reason arcs as shown by Rule 5.

$$\overset{M}{\text{Rule 5:} \ <\text{Goal}> -----> \ <\text{Goal}>}$$

When a subgoal specifies the style of some action but is not necessary for or pertinent to the achievement of the primary Goal, the two Goals (Goal+) are related by a Manner arc rather than a Reason arc. Consider the following statements.

G+: People cut down trees.
G+2: People cut the base of trees.
PS3: The base of a tree is round.

These nodes would be related as follows:

$$\begin{array}{c} <\text{G+1}> \\ \Big| \ \ M \\ \overset{I}{<\text{PS3}> -----> \ <\text{G+2}>} \end{array}$$

Cutting at the base of the tree is not necessary when one cuts down a tree; one might cut at the middle.

The question often arises whether Goal nodes are related by Manner arcs or Reason arcs. If a Reason arc is appropriate, then it makes sense to say "G1 in order to G2" but not "G2 in order to G1." If a manner arc is appropriate, it does not make sense to say "G1 in order to G2" and it does not make sense to say "G2 in order to G1." There is one other criteria for distinguishing Manner from Reason arcs. A subgoal G1 is achieved before the Goal G2 when there is a Reason arc. However, when there is a Manner arc, Goal G1 is achieved during the achievement of Goal G2.

Property Arcs.   An argument of a statement node may be modified by a State node that ascribes an attribute to the argument. This is accomplished by the Property arc as shown by Rule 6 below.

$$P$$
Rule 6: <Argument of node> -----> <State>

Consider the three nodes below.

PS1: Wagons were boxes at that time.
PS2: Boxes were made out of wood.
PS3: The time was before the Middle Ages.

These three nodes would be related as follows.

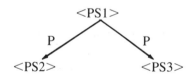

It should be noted that Kintsch's (1974) argument repetition rule applies to Property arcs. If node 1 and node 2 are linked by a Property arc, then the two nodes must have an equivalent argument. For example, PS1 and PS2 share the *boxes* argument. PS1 and PS3 share the *time* argument.

The nodes and arcs have now been specified. In addition we have introduced six rules that summarize the constraints on how nodes can be related by arcs. These rules are summarized in Table 5.3 of our chapter in Part 1.

AN EXAMPLE CONCEPTUAL GRAPH STRUCTURE

A conceptual graph structure has been prepared for the expository passage entitled *The Development of the Wagon*. This passage is shown in Table 13.1. A

TABLE 13.1
Development of the Wagon

The wheel and the wagon developed at the same time, approximately 5000 years ago. At that time, human beings found that they could pull their sledges more easily if they fitted them with wheels of solid wood. The Egyptians were among the earliest people to use wagons. The Scythians wandered over the plains of southeastern Europe as early as 700 B.C., carrying their possessions on two-wheeled carts covered with reeds. However, until the middle ages, the wagons were no more than boxes set upon axles between wheels. Then the four-wheeled coach was developed in Germany.

listing of the nodes and arcs is shown in Table 13.2. The structure is depicted in a list format because there are a large number of them. The conceptual graph structure has 93 nodes altogether. Twenty-five nodes were explicitly stated in the passage. These explicit nodes are flagged with asterisks in Table 13.2. The other 68 nodes were derived empirically from the question-answering protocols. A conceptual graph structure can be composed from the node and arc list in Table 13.2.

We should mention that the order in which nodes are listed in Table 13.2 does not correspond to the order in which information was presented in the passage. As we pointed out in Part 1, the conceptual graph structures were developed to explain conceptual connectivity but not sequential connectivity. The order of nodes in Table 13.2 roughly follows the chronological order of occurrences when the wagon and wheel were developed. The order in which statements are presented in expository passages often deviates from an underlying chronological order.

TABLE 13.2
List of Labeled Nodes and Labeled, Directed Arcs in *The
Development of the Wagon*
(Nodes with asterisks were explicitly stated in the passage)

Nodes	Arcs
(1) G+ : People transport possessions	R <G+2> -----> <G+1>
(2) G+ : People carry possessions	M <G+2> -----> <S3>
(3) S : Carrying was by hand	C <G+2> -----> <PS4>
(4) PS : Carrying possessions was difficult	I <PS4> -----> <G+5>
(5) G+ : People make carrying possesions easier	R <G+6> -----> <G+5>
* (6) G+ : People pull sledges	R <G+10> -----> <G+5>

(*continued*)

TABLE 13.2   *(Continued)*

Nodes	Arcs
	R
(7) G+ : People tie rope to sledge	\<G+7\> -----\> \<G+6\>
	M
(8) S : Pulling was by hand	\<G+6\> -----\> \<S7\>
	C
(9) PS : Pulling sledges was difficult	\<G+6\> -----\> \<PS9\>
	I
* (10) G+ : People make pulling sledges easier	\<PS9\> -----\> \<G+10\>
	C
(11) IE : Someone thought of wheel	\<G+10\> -----\> \<IE11\>
	C
(12) IS : People were intelligent	\<IS12\> -----\> \<IE11\>
	I
* (13) G+ : People put wheels on sledges	\<IE11\> -----\> \<G+14\>
	R
* (14) G+ : People developed wheel	\<G+14\> -----\> \<G+13\>
	R
(15) G+ : People attached wheels to axle	\<G+13\> -----\> \<G+10\>
	R
(16) G+ : People attached axle to sledge	\<G+17\> -----\> \<G+13\>
	R
(17) G+ : People make wheels	\<G+15\> -----\> \<G+13\>
	R
	\<G+16\> -----\> \<G+13\>
	M
(18) G+ : People make wheels out of wood	\<G+17\> -----\> \<G+18\>
	I
(19) PS : Solid wheels are easier to pull	\<PS19\> -----\> \<G+18\>
	I
* (20) PS : Wood is solid	\<PS20\> -----\> \<G+18\>
	I
(21) PS : Wood is only solid material around	\<PS21\> -----\> \<G+18\>
	R
(22) G+ : People cut down trees	\<G+22\> -----\> \<G+18\>
	I
(23) G+ : People shape wood	\<PS24\> -----\> \<G+22\>
	P
(24) PS : Trees are made of wood	\<PS24\> -----\> \<PS25\>
	M
(25) PS : Wood is green	\<G+22\> -----\> \<G+26\>
	I
(26) G+ : People cut at base of trees	\<PS30\> -----\> \<G+26\>
	C
	\<G+26\> -----\> \<PS29\>

(continued)

380

TABLE 13.2 (*Continued*)

Nodes	Arcs
(27) PS : There were tools for shaping wood	C <PS29> ----> <PE31>
(28) PS : Wheels were smooth	M <G+18> ----> <G+23>
(29) PS : Wheels were round	I <PS27> ----> <G+23>
(30) PS : Base of tree is round	C <G+23> ----> <PS28>
(31) PE : Wheels rolled on surface	C <PS28> ----> <PE31> C <G+6> ----> <PE31>
(32) PE : There was less friction	C <G+13> ----> <PE33>
(33) PE : Sledges came to be off ground	C <PE31> ----> <PE32>
(34) PE : Sledges became more mobile	C <PE33> ----> <PE32>
(35) PS : Sledges could carry more weight	C <PE33> ----> <PE34>
(36) PE : Pulling sledges required less exertion	C <PE34> ----> <PE35>
(37) PE : Load became easier to pull	C <PE34> ----> <PE36> C <PE36> ----> <PE37>
(38) IS : Egyptians were intelligent	C <G+5> ----> <IE39>
(39) IE : Egyptians invented the wagon	R <G+41> ----> <G+5>
* (40) PS : Egyptians were first people to use wagon	C <IE39> ----> <PS40>
* (41) G+ : People use wagon	C <IS38> ----> <IE39>
(42) G+ : People work	P <G+41> ----> <PS40>
(43) G+ : People transport people	I <IE39> ----> <G+44>
* (44) G+ : People develop wagon	R <G+44> ----> <G+41> R <G+41> ----> <G+42>
* (45) S : Wheel and wagon developed at the same time	R <G+41> ----> <G+43>
* (46) PS : Time was 5000 years ago	M <G+44> ----> <S45>

(*continued*)

TABLE 13.2 *(Continued)*

Nodes	Arcs
(47) PS : Wagons require wheels	M <G+14> -----> >S45> P <S45> -----> <PS46> C <PS47> -----> <S45>
*(48) PS : Wagons were boxes at the time	P <G+44> -----> <PS48>
(49) PS : Wagon had two wheels at the time	P <PS48> -----> <PS50>
(50) PS : Boxes were wood	P <PS48> -----> <PS51>
(51) PS : Boxes had sides	P <PS48> -----> <PS53>
(52) PS : There were four sides	P <PS48> -----> <PS54>
*(53) PS : Time was before Middle Ages	P <PS51> -----> <PS52>
(54) PS : Boxes had shape	P <PS54> -----> <PS55> P <PS49> -----> <PS53>
(55) PS : Shape was geometrical	P <G+44> -----> <PS49>
(56) PS : More than one wheel was needed for balance	C <PS57> -----> <PS56>
(57) PS : Weight is distributed better over several wheels than one wheel	C <PS56> -----> <PS49> M <G+44> -----> <G+58>
*(58) G+ People put box on axle	I <PS59> -----> <G+58>
(59) PS : Axles allow wheels to carry boxes	I <PS60> -----> <G+58>
(60) PS : If box was on wheel, wheel wouldn't turn	M <G+44> -----> <G+62>
(61) PS : Axle has one wheel on each side	C <G+62> -----> <PS61>
*(62) G+ : People put box between wheels	M <G+44> -----> <G+63>
(63) G+ : People attach wheels to axle	C <G+58> -----> <PE64>
(64) PE : Box became easier to pull	C <G+62> -----> <PE64>

(continued)

TABLE 13.2 *(Continued)*

Nodes	Arcs
(65) PS : Carts were wagons	P \<PS49\> -----> \<PS65\>
* (66) PS : Carts had two wheels	P \<PS66\> -----> \<PS65\>
	P \<G+68\> -----> \<PS66\>
(67) G+ : Scythians pulled carts	M \<G+68\> -----> \<G+67\>
* (68) G+ : Scythians used carts	R \<G+69\> -----> \<G+68\>
(69) G+ : Scythians made carts	M \<G+69\> -----> \<G+70\>
* (70) G+ : Scythians covered carts with reeds	M \<G+70\> -----> \<S71\>
(71) S : Scythians covered carts completely	I \<PS72\> -----> \<G+70\>
(72) PS : Reeds protected possessions from weather	I \<PS73\> -----> \<G+70\>
(73) PS : Reeds prevented things from falling out of cart	M \<G+70\> -----> \<G+74\>
(74) G+ : Scythians put reeds over things that needed covering	R \<G+68\> -----> \<G+80\>
	R \<G+81\> -----> \<G+80\>
	M \<G+78\> -----> \<G+80\>
(75) G+ : Scythians stay alive	M \<G+78\> -----> \<S79\>
(76) G+ : Scythians find home	R \<G+78\> -----> \<G+77\>
(77) G+ : Scythians get food	R \<G+78\> -----> \<G+76\>
* (78) G+ : Scythians wander over plains	R \<G+77\> -----> \<G+75\>
(79) S : Wandering is on foot	R \<G+76\> -----> \<G+75\>
* (80) G+ : Scythians transported possessions	I \<PS82\> -----> \<G+78\>
(81) G+ : Scythians pull things on sledges	P \<G+78\> -----> \<PS83\>
(82) PS : Scythians were nomads	P \<G+78\> -----> \<PS85\>
* (83) PS : Plains were in Europe	P \<PS83\> -----> \<PS84\>

(continued)

TABLE 13.2 *(Continued)*

Nodes	Arcs
*(84) PS : Plains were in the southeast	I <PS86> -----> <G+68>
*(85) PS : The time was 700 B.C.	I <PS87> -----> <G+68>
(86) PS : Carts are easy for travel	R <G+88> -----> <G+43>
(87) PS : Scythians had too many possessions to carry	R <G+89> -----> <G+88>
	P <G+88> -----> <PS90>
	C <PS91> -----> <PS90>
(88) G+ : Wagon be more stable	M <G+89> -----> <G+92>
*(89) G+ : People developed coach	P <G+92> -----> <PS93>
*(90) PS : Germans were first to develop coach	
(91) PS : German technology was advanced	
(92) G+ : People added on another set of wheels	
*(93) PS : There were four wheels	

REFERENCES

Anderson, J. R. *Language, memory, and thought.* Hillsdale, N.J.: Lawrence Erlbaum Associates, 1976.

Chafe, W. L. *The pear stories: Advances in discourse processes.* Norwood, N.J.: Ablex, 1980.

Clark, H. H., & Clark, E. V. *Psychology and language.* New York: Harcourt Brace Jovanovich, 1977.

Fillmore, C. J. The case for case. In E. Bach & R. T. Harms (Eds.), *Universals in linguistic theory.* New York: Holt, Rinehart & Winston, 1968.

Graesser, A. C. *Prose comprehension beyond the word.* New York: Springer-Verlag, 1981.

Graesser, A. C., Robertson, S. P., & Anderson, P. A. Incorporating inferences in narrative representations: A study of how and why. *Cognitive Psychology,* 1981, *13,* 1–26.

Kieras, D. E. Component processes in the comprehension of simple prose. *Journal of Verbal Learning and Verbal Behavior,* 1981, *20,* 1–23.

Kintsch, W. *The representation of meaning in memory.* Hillsdale, N.J.: Lawrence Erlbaum Associates, 1974.

Miller, J. R., & Kintsch, W. Readability and recall of short prose passages: A theoretical analysis. *Journal of Experimental Psychology: Human Learning and Memory,* 1980, *6,* 335–354.

Stockwell, R. P., Schacter, P., & Partee, H. *The major syntactic structures of English.* New York: Holt, Rinehart & Winston, 1973.

van Dijk, T. A. *Macrostructures: An interdisciplinary study of global structures in discourse, interaction, and cognition.* Hillsdale, N.J.: Lawrence Erlbaum Associates, 1980.

14

Knowledge and the Processing of Narrative and Expository Text: Some Methodological Issues

James F. Voss
University of Pittsburgh

Gay L. Bisanz
University of Alberta

As we indicated in Part 1 of this volume, the investigation of knowledge as a factor in text processing has not relied upon any formal system for characterizing knowledge analogous to those systems developed for characterizing passage structure. Thus, this section draws no comparison between our work and that of others. Instead, we discuss some problems that occur when one attempts to study the role of knowledge and text processing. These problems include (a) difficulties in assessing knowledge, (b) problems associated with use of the contrastive method, (c) issues related to scoring recall protocols, and (d) the need to determine the interaction between text structure and the effects of knowledge. The first three problems involve pragmatics of research, and the last a problem that is at once both conceptual and methodological.

ASSESSMENT OF KNOWLEDGE

We generally have used two devices to assess knowledge; one is a questionnaire and the other, perhaps surprisingly, consists of the data of the study in question.

Knowledge Questionnaires

In the baseball research (e.g., Spilich, Vesonder, Chiesi, & Voss, 1979; Voss, Vesonder, & Spilich, 1980), we constructed a completion test consisting of 45 questions, and to this we added 30 "trivia" questions, although we did not use the trivia questions in establishing high- and low-knowledge individuals. The questions on the test were aimed at terminology, rules, and principles of the game of baseball. The test did not include explicit questions about strategy. Typically, subjects that we designated as "high knowledge" got 40–45 items correct. On a few occasions we needed to judge whether a particular answer was appropriate, although scoring was certainly not a problem.

Because their scores on the test were highly similar, one should not get the impression that high-knowledge individuals were quite similar in what they knew. In a number of research settings, we have been impressed with how much the experts varied in their knowledge. Obviously, the test we developed did not completely differentiate the experts with respect to what they knew. However, given a highly refined theory about reasoning in a given domain, one should, in principle, be able to design such a test. The fact that our experts differed in their knowledge and interpretation of information should not be surprising, given the differences or controversies that exist among experts in almost all knowledge domains.

The scoring categories that designated low-knowledge individuals varied somewhat with the study and with our ability to obtain individuals who would score in the lower range. We would note that we never told individuals beforehand that we wanted high- or low-knowledge individuals because of the probability that individuals would respond in a manner simply so that they could serve in the experiment (for pay). Also, we found it quite difficult to find males with low baseball knowledge and females with high baseball knowledge.

The question of what constitutes "low knowledge" is, of course, a relative matter. However, there are practical issues to consider. If the low-knowledge individuals are completely ignorant of the subject matter, the individual will have difficulty understanding the simplest domain-related terminology. On the other hand, the low-knowledge person cannot be so knowledgeable that the high- versus low-knowledge distinction becomes meaningless. We were fortunate in that we found few individuals with really poor knowledge, as for example, having 0 to 5 correct on the test. In general, our low-knowledge individuals ranged from 10 to 25 correct, with these scores indicating that they had some knowledge of the game especially with respect to general terminology.

Another issue that requires consideration is the extent to which a questionnaire designed to assess prior knowledge should be related to target task information. Two contrasting examples can be considered. At one extreme is a study (Means & Voss, 1981) in which we examined text processing in children with a passage that contained air pollution information. In this study there were three requirements in designing the questionnaire. First, we wanted the questionnaire to discriminate between high-knowledge and low-knowledge individuals with respect to knowledge about air pollution. Second, the questionnaire had to contain items that could be understood and answered by young children. Similarly, the questionnaire could not be too long because of its use with young children. Third, the questionnaire was to serve as a pretest for the experimental conditions, and subsequently as a posttest to determine improvement as a function of the experimental condition. These three requirements, when considered together, essentially meant that we needed to construct a questionnaire that could cover the air pollution material that was contained in the text. To include more questions would have made the questionnaire too long. Thus, constraints on the questionnaire played a role in determining the contents of the passage that we employed.

One aspect of the air pollution study is worth special comment, namely, how the contents of the questionnaire interact with the purpose of the experiment. Assume that a general questionnaire about topic "x" is given and high- and low-knowledge groups are established. Then a passage is given to the two groups and the high-knowledge group recalls more of the passage contents than the low-knowledge group. This finding may be of considerable interest, but it also may be misleading. Let us assume that the purpose of the experiment was to determine if high-knowledge individuals acquire new information more readily than low-knowledge individuals, and the results are taken to support this idea. The results are of interest if general knowledge about pollution lead to a faster acquisition of specific new material. The problem arises if the high-knowledge individuals (or low, but more likely high) knew the information in the text prior to coming into the study and thus were not acquiring new information. Such results could be deceptive because the low-knowledge individuals could conceivably have learned more new information. In the air pollution study, the pretest-posttest difference was used to take into account such a priori knowledge.

In contrast to the air pollution study, in the baseball research, we made no effort toward relating the pretest and task information; we were interested in identifying two groups and were not interested in relating the pretest knowledge to the text we used in the study in any specific way. The material used in the experimental task was new to both high-knowledge and low-knowledge individuals, and the goal of the study was to determine how differences in a priori knowledge influenced recall and other performance characteristics. Assuming that high knowledge individuals developed a model or representation of passages that was not present in low-knowledge individuals, the question was how the fictitious account of the game could map onto their knowledge structure. The two examples cited thus indicate that the contents of a questionnaire designed to measure knowledge should be considered in relation to the purpose of the study.

Experimental Data

Yet another attempt to "measure" or infer knowledge differences comes from the data itself. In the studies we cited in Part 1 of this volume by Bisanz and Voss (1981, in preparation), and that of Bisanz (in press), as well as most empirical work involving story grammars (e.g., Mandler & Johnson, 1977; Stein & Glenn,

1979), and script research (e.g., Bower, Black, & Turner, 1979; Graesser, Gordon, & Sawyer, 1979), knowledge is inferred from the data. For example, if the child recalls story information in a pattern consistent with some hypothesized schema, then that schema is assumed to have guided recall. If the recall pattern is not in accord with the hypothesized pattern, then it is assumed that the individual may not have acquired that knowledge. Or, depending upon the pattern of recall, the individual may have used an alternative schema to guide recall. In a sense then, knowledge is "measured" by performance within the experiment itself. Of course, the power of the interpretation for such research would be greater if there were an independent test to determine the extent of one's knowledge of hypothesized text structures.

CONTRASTIVE RESEARCH

Contrastive research refers to studies in which the investigator (a) establishes that individuals have high or low ability with respect to some skill(s) (and/or high and low knowledge within a particular subject matter domain) and (b) determines how performance on some task varies in relation to the ability or knowledge differences. An important criticism of contrastive research is, of course, that it is basically correlational. This fact implies the usual dictum that performance differences of high- and low-ability (or knowledge) individuals may be attributed to a third factor related both to ability or knowledge and task performance. However, an even more important point is that knowledge and ability differences often involve differences in age, training, and experience, such as those found, for example, between experts who are physicists and novices who are undergraduate physics majors. When such differences are apparent, the investigator must exercise caution concerning what other factors may be contributing to observed performance differences.

One way that the confounding of knowledge or ability and other potentially important attributes can be handled, at least to some degree, is to equate high- and low-knowledge individuals as much as possible on skills, experience, or other factors that distinguish the populations. For example, if the study is on text processing, one way to carry this out is to equate the individuals on some general skill such as reading comprehension. Another way is to include individuals who share similar backgrounds and training with the experts of a particular domain, but whose field of specialization is different (see for example, Voss, Tyler, & Yengo, 1981).

Two other facets of contrastive research that are of importance pertain to (a) the explanations given for any performance differences obtained and (b) the need to identify similarities in performance. It is not difficult to obtain performance differences between groups of individuals who vary in some ability or knowledge. The more difficult task is to develop plausible explanations of what has produced the differences; to attribute such differences to "knowledge" really begs the question. Performance differences should be explained in terms of how knowledge functions. To say that schemata are activated or instantiated in the more knowledgeable individual really does nothing more than to restate results unless the components of schemata are made more specific and experiments test specific components of these models of knowledge. In addition, because performance differences related to knowledge or ability are so readily obtained, it is quite important to develop a rationale for when differences *should not occur*. After all, if one looks at previous research in a Bayesian-like manner, the ''prior'' is that there is a strong possibility of obtaining performance differences. Thus, a pattern of similarities and differences in performance becomes a powerful means of testing a particular model.

ISSUES OF SCORING

As anyone knows who has scored recall protocols, there are problems that confront any investigator (for a detailed discussion see Voss, Tyler, & Bisanz, 1982). We mention one issue that relates to knowledge. A typical scoring procedure is to take a text and develop a template for its contents based on some system of passage representation (see Voss et al., 1982). Recall is then scored in relation to the template. Of course the text is never recalled just as it is presented. By this we mean not only that the order may vary, but the same words or phrases are not used. The problem for the investigator is to decide when to give credit for recall. Where knowledge becomes a factor is that the means of expression is often different for low- and high-knowledge individuals. For example, the latter group may use more general or abstract statements, and may also add more inferences and details. Low-knowledge individuals tend to simplify the text contents or recall it in shorter sentences, a pattern that likely depicts the lack of coherence in the information that the low-knowledge person has remembered. It is of interest to note that similar problems exist in developmental research when scoring the recall protocols of younger and older children. An investigator has the option of handling this either at the point of developing a template for the passage (by making passage units and relations fine-grained enough to capture such differences), or when devising the criteria to be used by scorers. The former approach is certainly preferable as it is more likely to lead to reliability in the findings obtained from different laboratories.

THE INTERACTION OF THE TEXT CONTENTS AND KNOWLEDGE

Although we have indicated that it is relatively easy to obtain performance differences in text processing between high- and low-knowledge individuals, it is not inherently the case that knowledge differences produce performance differences. Instead, texts must be chosen that have characteristics that can be sensitive to such performance differences. However, if the question is raised regarding what these characteristics are, then we are getting to the crux of a major problem that is at once both conceptual and methodological. For example, in the Voss et al. (1980) paper, it was shown that high-knowledge individuals performed better than low-knowledge individuals when the texts presented were generated by high-knowledge individuals. However, there was little difference in performance between high-knowledge and low-knowledge individuals when the texts were generated by low-knowledge individuals. The texts generated by the high-knowledge and low-knowledge individuals were examined for differences, and the results of this examination were discussed in Part 1 of this volume. However, the text characteristics that resulted in these performance differences were not self-evident, except in the simplest and most extreme cases. To determine the characteristics, one should have some theory about the nature of the knowledge and how it interacts with text structure. However, such a framework does not currently exist. A theoretical marriage of the concerns reflected in expository research focused on the role of text structure and narrative research on the role of knowledge is clearly in order.

CONCLUDING REMARKS

We have discussed some problems that are of significance in current research on the effects of knowledge and text processing. However, as our discussion suggests, research in this area is at a point where certain methodological issues can only be addressed by advances in our theoretical conceptions.

ACKNOWLEDGMENTS

Research reported in this paper was supported by the Centre for the Study of Mental Retardation, University of Alberta, Edmonton, Alberta, Canada, and the Learning Research and Development Center (LRDC) at the University of Pittsburgh, Pittsburgh, Pennsylvania. The LRDC is supported, in part, as a research and development center by funds from the National Institute of Education, United States Department of Education.

REFERENCES

Bisanz, G. L. Knowledge of persuasion and story comprehension: Developmental changes in expectations. *Discourse Processes,* in press.
Bisanz, G. L., & Voss, J. F. Sources of knowledge in reading comprehension: Cognitive development and expertise in a content domain. In A. M. Lesgold & C. A. Perfetti (Eds.), *Interactive processes in reading.* Hillsdale, N.J.: Lawrence Erlbaum Associates, 1981.

Bisanz, G. L., & Voss, J. F. *Developmental changes in understanding story themes: Scaling and process analyses.* Manuscript in preparation.

Bower, G. H., Black. J. B., & Turner, T. J. Scripts in memory for text. *Cognitive Psychology,* 1979, *11,* 177–220.

Graesser, A. C., Gordon, S. E., & Sawyer, J. D. Recognition memory for typical and atypical actions in scripted activities: Tests of a script pointer and tag hypothesis. *Journal of Verbal Learning and Verbal Behavior,* 1979, *18,* 319–332.

Mandler, J. M., & Johnson, N. S. Remembrance of things parsed: Story structure and recall. *Cognitive Psychology,* 1977, *9,* 111–151.

Means, M., & Voss, J. F. *Knowledge and development in the processing of an expanded narrative text.* Unpublished manuscript, 1981.

Spilich, G. J., Vesonder, G. T., Chiesi, H. L., & Voss, J. F. Text processing of domain-related information for individuals with high and low domain knowledge. *Journal of Verbal Learning and Verbal Behavior,* 1979, *18,* 275–290.

Stein, N. L., & Glenn, C. G. An analysis of story comprehension in elementary school children. In R. O. Freedle (Ed.), *New directions in discourse processing* (Vol. 2). Norwood, N.J.: Ablex, 1979.

Voss, J. F., Tyler, S. W., & Bisanz, G. L. Prose comprehension and memory. In C. R. Puff (Ed.), *Handbook of research methods in human memory and cognition.* New York: Academic Press, 1982.

Voss, J. F., Tyler, S. W., & Yengo, L. A. *Problem solving in a social science domain by experts and novices.* Unpublished manuscript, 1981.

Voss, J. F., Vesonder, G. T., & Spilich, G. J. Text generation and recall by high knowledge and low knowledge individuals. *Journal of Verbal Learning and Verbal Behavior,* 1980, *19,* 651–667.

15 A Knowledge-Based Model of Prose Comprehension: An Annotated Trace

James R. Miller

Texas Instruments

AN ANNOTATED TRACE OF THE MODEL'S PROCESSING: SAINT

Table 15.1 contains an example of the model's processing of part of the SAINT text (Fig. 7.1 in the chapter in Part 1) studied earlier (Miller & Kintsch, 1980)[1]; the line numbers annotating this example are used in the discussion below. The model processes a text by allowing its knowledge sources to observe and operate upon the contents of its hypothesis structure; Table 15.1 then contains "reports" from the knowledge sources that describe the additions or modifications they have made to the hypothesis structure. This section is meant to illustrate the model's processing; the model is described in detail in the preceding chapter.

Text Element 1: (REQUEST OBJECT CANONIZE (REQUEST SUBJECT-POSITION))

The processing of the "Saint" text begins (line 1) with the model receiving the text's first element:

(REQUEST OBJECT CANONIZE (REQUEST SUBJECT-POSITION))

Two nodes in the hypothesis structure are built from this element: the BUILD-PROPOSITION knowledge source constructs a node at the PROPOSITION level

---

[1]One modification has been made in the text for this analysis: the phrase, "bishop of Philadelphia in the 19th century" has been deleted.

TABLE 15.1
Sample Execution Trace of the Macroprocessing Model*

1   Element 1: (REQUEST OBJECT CANONIZE
                    (REQUEST SUBJECT-POSITION)
     There is no macroproposition.
     No frame is currently active.
     Working memory is currently empty.
2   Build-propositions/1: build Prop1 around REQUEST.
3   Fill-propositions/1: add an argument to Prop1:
                (REQUEST (OBJECT CANONIZE)
4   Instantiate-frame/3: load REQUEST from the knowledge base as the propositional frame.
5   Match-propositions/5: (REQUEST (OBJECT CANONIZE)) matches
                (REQUEST (OBJECT (A ACTION))).

6   Element 2: (CANONIZE RECIP JOHN-NEUMANN)
     There is no macroproposition.
     The REQUEST frame is currently active.
     Working memory is currently:
                Prop1: (REQUEST (OBJECT CANONIZE))
7   Build-propositions/1: build Prop2 around CANONIZE.
8   Fill-propositions/1: add an argument to Prop2:
                (CANONIZE (RECIP JOHN-NEUMANN))
9   Link-propositions/1: substitute Prop2 for CANONIZE in Prop1:
                (REQUEST (OBJECT PROP2)).
10 Link-propositions/3: build a link from Prop1 to Prop2.
11 Instantiate-frame/3: load CANONIZE from the knowledge base as the propositional frame.
12 Match-propositions/4: assume that (CANONIZE
                (RECIP JOHN-NEUMANN)) will match (CANONIZE
                (RECIP (a RELIGIOUS)).

13 Element 3: (JOHN-NEUMANN PROPERTY PRIEST)
     There is no macroproposition.
     The CANONIZE frame is currently active.
     Working memory is currently:
                Prop1: (REQUEST (OBJECT PROP2))
                Prop2: (CANONIZE (RECIP JOHN-NEUMANN))
14 Build-propositions/1: build Prop3 around JOHN-NEUMANN.
15 Fill-propositions/1: add an argument to Prop3:
                (JOHN-NEUMANN (PROPERTY PRIEST))
16 Link-propositions/5: build a link from Prop3 to Prop2.
17 Instantiate-frame/3: Load JOHN-NEUMANN from the knowledge base as the propositional
                frame.
18 Match-propositions/7: (JOHN-NEUMANN (PROPERTY PRIEST))
                matches (JOHN-NEUMANN (OCCUPATION
                (a OCCUPATION))).
19 Confirmed assumption: (RECIP JOHN-NEUMANN) matches
                (RECIP (a RELIGIOUS)).
20 Element 4: (PRIEST PROPERTY FRONTIER)
     There is no macroproposition.
     The JOHN-NEUMANN frame is currently active.

(continued)

TABLE 15.1   (*Continued*)

Working memory is currently:
Prop1: (REQUEST (OBJECT CANONIZE))
Prop2: (CANONIZE (RECIP JOHN-NEUMANN))
Prop3: (JOHN-NEUMANN (PROPERTY PRIEST))

21 Build-propositions/1: build Prop4 around PRIEST.
22 Fill-propositions/1: add an argument to Prop4:
(PRIEST (PROPERTY FRONTIER))
23 Link-propositions/5: build a link from Prop4 to Prop3.
24 Instantiate-frame/3: load PRIEST from the knowledge base as the propositional frame.
25 Match-propositions/7: (PRIEST (LOCATION FRONTIER)) matches
(PRIEST (LOCATION (a LOCATION))).
26 Build-macroprops/1: the next element is unrelated to working memory: build a macroproposition around CANONIZE.
27 Fill-macroprops/1: add arguments to CANONIZE's macroproposition: (CANONIZE (RECIP
JOHN-NEUMANN)).
28 Instantiate-macroframe/3: load CANONIZE from the knowledge base as the macropropositional frame.
29 Match-macroprops/5: (CANONIZE (RECIP JOHN-NEUMANN)) matches
(CANONIZE (RECIP (a RELIGIOUS))).
30 Manage-memory/1: restructure working memory around Prop2:
(CANONIZE (RECIP JOHN-NEUMANN)).
31 Instantiate-frame/2: reinstate CANONIZE as the propositional frame.
32 Match-propositions/5: (CANONIZE (RECIP JOHN-NEUMANN)) matches
(CANONIZE (RECIP (a RELIGIOUS))).

*a*The numbers following the knowledge source name [e.g., "Build-propositions/*1*"] identify the specific production rule within the knowledge source that produced this action.

for the predicate REQUEST (line 2), and the FILL-PROPOSITION knowledge source constructs an ARGUMENT node for (OBJECT CANONIZE) (line 3). The ARGUMENT and PROPOSITION nodes are then linked. The "(REQUEST SUBJECT-POSITION)" component of the element is stored with this proposition's node; its function is discussed later.

Once this propositional structure has been built in working memory, control shifts to the interpretation component, which searches for a knowledge structure that can provide a meaningful interpretation of this proposition. The question asked by this interpretation step is whether CANONIZE can be the OBJECT of REQUEST—whether canonization is something that can be requested. The IN-STANTIATE-FRAME knowledge source then fires (line 4), bringing the RE-QUEST knowledge structure (Fig. 7.3) into working memory: REQUEST is specified as the topic of the frame, and each of REQUEST'S slots is instantiated as a separate node at the SLOT hypothesis level. The (OBJECT CANONIZE) argument is then compared to the restriction found in the OBJECT slot of the REQUEST knowledge structure, which states that the object of REQUEST must be either an ACTION or an EVENT. Since CANONIZE is an ACTION, as determined by the hierarchical location of CANONIZE in the knowledge base, this proposition has been successfully interpreted (line 5), and links are built between the proposition and knowledge structure nodes to represent this interpretation. This completes the processing of this first text element.

Text Element 2: (CANONIZE RECIP JOHN-NEUMANN)

Processing continues with the second text element, (CANONIZE RECIP JOHN-NEUMANN), in line 6. Proposition and argument nodes, as before, are built to represent the content of this element (lines 7 and 8), links are built between this and the REQUEST proposition (lines 9 and 10), and a search is undertaken for an interpretive knowledge structure. As before, the concept corresponding to this proposition's predicate—CANONIZE—is selected as an initial candidate (line 11); however, the interpretation of this proposition differs from that of the previous cycle in two ways.

First, the capacity limitations of working memory are observed: at the knowledge structure level, the schematic description of REQUEST and the information characterizing the particular REQUEST described in this text are moved from working memory to the long-term component of the hypothesis structure, and the CANONIZE knowledge structure is brought into working memory (line 11) for matching against the newly constructed CANONIZE proposition.

Second, the verification of the RECIPient relation between CANONIZE and JOHN-NEUMANN cannot be verified in the same straightforward way as was the OBJECT relation between REQUEST and CANONIZE. There is, of necessity, a unit representing John Neumann in the model's knowledge base, but this unit has been constructed under the assumption that most people would not know anything about Neumann before reading this article. The model then assumes that, in the absence of information that would allow this interpretation to be rejected, JOHN-NEUMANN is a reasonable recipient of canonization (line 12), and begins to watch for information that will confirm or disconfirm this assumption.

Text Element 3: (JOHN-NEUMANN PROPERTY PRIEST)

Element 3 (line 13) specifies a property to be assigned to Neumann—that Neumann is a priest. The corresponding proposition is built (lines 14 and 15) and linked into the existing set of propositions (line 16). Its interpretation begins by instantiating the JOHN-NEUMANN frame in working memory (line 17) to determine whether the assignment of this property is permissible—whether Neumann can be assigned the occupation of "priest."

This assignment is a two-stage process. First, the nature of the PROPERTY relation specified in the text element is deduced by comparing the slots in the

JOHN-NEUMANN knowledge structure to the units hierarchically above PRIEST in the knowledge base; the model's strategy is to associate PRIEST with the first slot of JOHN-NEUMANN that is encountered in the upward search from PRIEST toward the ROOT node. JOHN-NEUMANN, like any instance of PEO-PLE, has an OCCUPATION slot, which coincides with the OCCUPATION unit immediately superior to PRIEST (see Fig. 7.2 of the chapter in Part 1). The model will therefore try to assign PRIEST to JOHN-NEUMANN's OCCUPA-TION slot. Since nothing is known about Neumann's occupation, any occupa-tion can fill this slot: The match succeeds, and JOHN-NEUMANN is assigned the occupation PRIEST (line 18).

One final event takes place during the processing of this element. Now that it is known that Neumann is a priest, his assumed fitness as a recipient of canoniza-tion can be confirmed: This occupation satisfies the "a RELIGIOUS" restriction of the CANONIZE knowledge structure. The part of the model watching for the addition of such information to the JOHN-NEUMANN knowledge structure thus reports that the previously made assumption can now be confirmed (line 19).

Text Element 4: (PRIEST PROPERTY FRONTIER)

At line 20, the fourth text element is processed. The model builds from this element a proposition that qualifies the PRIEST occupation of Neumann: This particular priest is a "frontier priest." Once this proposition is built and linked into the other propositions in working memory (lines 21–23), the PRIEST knowledge structure is instantiated (line 24). The nature of the FRONTIER qualifier is then determined to be specifying the LOCATION of the priest, through the same general procedure used to determine that PRIEST specified Neumann's occupation: In the knowledge base, the parent node of FRONTIER is LOCATION, which coincides with the LOCATION slot possessed by all ob-jects, including PRIEST (line 25). Since there are no restrictions specified for a priest's location, FRONTIER is accepted.

At this point in the model's processing, macroprocesses fire for the first time. These processes fire because a break in the text is observed: The next text element to be processed—(MIRACLE PROPERTY TWO) (see Table 7.6) has no concepts in common with the propositions currently in working memory. The model will now try to build a macroproposition that will meaningfully summa-rize the four propositions that currently reside in working memory.

These propositions are evaluated with respect to four criteria, with points assigned to each proposition according to the presence of the features described earlier:

—*Propositional connections:* Propositions 2 and 3 are each connected to two other propositions, while Propositions 1 and 4 are connected only to one other proposition. Two points and one point are then awarded to these propositions, respectively.

—*A priori importance:* Proposition 2 receives one point, because the knowledge structure for its predicate, CANONIZE, refers to miracles, which were defined as intrinsically interesting.

—*Action propositions:* Propositions 1 and 2 describe actions, and so receive one point each.

—*Syntactic markers:* the text element that led to the creation of Proposition 1 contained the syntax note (REQUEST SUBJECT-POSITION): in this sentence, REQUEST is the subject of the sentence. Proposition 1 therefore receives one point for this syntax note.

The scores for these propositions are then:

Proposition 1: 3 points
Proposition 2: 4 points
Proposition 3: 2 points
Proposition 4: 1 point

As a result, Proposition 2 is selected for instantiation as a macroproposition; this macroproposition is constructed by the BUILD-MACROPROPS and FILL-MACROPROPS knowledge sources (lines 26 and 27).

The remainder of the knowledge sources that fire in this cycle are responsible for the actions that reconfigure working memory around this macroproposition. First, the CANONIZE knowledge source is instantiated in the macropropositional level of the hypothesis structure (line 28), and interpretational procedures similar to those at the text propositional level match the macroproposition against this knowledge source (line 29). Second, the propositional level of the model is also reorganized to correspond to the macropropositional level, by retaining Proposition 2, (CANONIZE (RECIP JOHN-NEUMANN)) in working memory (line 30). Following this restructuring, the model's propositional FRAME level is reset to provide an interpretation of this remaining proposition: the CANONIZE knowledge structure is reinstated into working memory (line 31), and the connection between this knowledge structure and the proposition is reestablished (line 32). This example stops at this point, with the model set to move on to the processing of the next text element.

Author Index

Numbers in *italics* denote pages with bibliographic information.

Subject Index

U,V,W